PHP 5 in Practice

Elliott White III and
Jonathan Eisenhamer

**DEVELOPER'S
LIBRARY**

Sams Publishing, 800 East 96th Street, Indianapolis, Indiana 46240 USA

PHP 5 in Practice

International Standard Book Number: 0-672-32888-7

Library of Congress Catalog Card Number: 2005909640

Printed in the United States of America

First Printing: July 2006

09   08   07   06   4   3   2   1

Trademarks

All terms mentioned in this book that are known to be trademarks or service marks have been appropriately capitalized. Sams Publishing cannot attest to the accuracy of this information. Use of a term in this book should not be regarded as affecting the validity of any trademark or service mark.

Warning and Disclaimer

Every effort has been made to make this book as complete and as accurate as possible, but no warranty or fitness is implied. The information provided is on an "as is" basis. The authors and the publisher shall have neither liability nor responsibility to any person or entity with respect to any loss or damages arising from the information contained in this book.

Bulk Sales

Sams Publishing offers excellent discounts on this book when ordered in quantity for bulk purchases or special sales. For more information, please contact

U.S. Corporate and Government Sales
1-800-382-3419
corpsales@pearsontechgroup.com

For sales outside of the U.S., please contact

International Sales
international@pearsoned.com

Acquisitions Editors
Shelley Johnson
Betsy Brown

Development Editor
Damon Jordan

Managing Editor
Patrick Kanouse

Senior Project Editor
Matthew Purcell

Copy Editor
Geneil Breeze

Indexer
Larry Sweazy

Proofreader
Elizabeth Scott

Technical Editor
Timothy Boronczyk

Publishing Coordinator
Vanessa Evans

Book Designer
Gary Adair

Contents At a Glance

Table of Contents

About the Authors

Elliott White III (who prefers to be called Eli) is a Senior Web Programmer for digg.com with more than 11 years of experience developing web applications. He has presented at various PHP conferences around the world and has been involved with a number of books. He can be reached at php@eliw.com.

Jonathan Eisenhamer has been programming professionally for more than 20 years, predominantly in support of the astronomical community. Over this time period, he earned an M.S. in Computer Science and has been coauthor on papers in the fields of astronomy, astronomical computing, and computing technology in the classroom. Mr. Eisenhamer is currently supervisor and lead programmer for the web and print services group within the Office of Public Outreach at the Space Telescope Science Institute, dedicated to providing the public with the latest results from the Hubble Space Telescope.

Acknowledgments

First of all I must sing the praises of my wife, Heather, for allowing me to undertake this project and supporting me throughout it. It would not have been possible to write this book while still working a full-time job without her love and support. Also to my son, Ramsey, your father apologizes for all the times he has had to walk away from playing with you to go work on this book. You weren't even born when I started talking about writing a book, were eight months old when I started writing, and are over a year old as I finish. Hopefully I will be able to make up the lost time to you soon.

I must also give thanks to George Schlossnagle who at a conference first got me on the track to writing a book. If not for your initial advice this wouldn't have happened. To Shelley Johnston, my first Acquisitions Editor at Sams Publishing, thank you for believing in me and sticking with me for that year of preliminary work. I cannot forget to thank my coauthor Jonathan. Without him this book would not have been finished on time, nor at the quality within it. His vision and concepts were the driving forces that made this book into what it is.

Finally, I want to thank all my friends in the SCA (Society for Creative Anachronism) for providing me with fun, excitement, companionship, and much needed breaks from the realm of technology that my mundane life encompasses. Without the SCA's influence over the last 15 years I would not be half the person I am today.

— Eli

First and foremost, heartfelt thanks go to my family—my wife, Bonnie, and my son, Jonathan—for putting up with me with yet another undertaking. Your support has been unwavering; your humor and thoughtfulness are the greatest joys in my life. Also, thank you Eli for your companionship while we were co-workers and having me as partner in this endeavor; your technical prowess is always enlightening and your wit refreshing.

I must also thank the two individuals who unwittingly helped me choose my path, oh, so long ago: John Hill and Alan Koski. To John, for giving me the opportunity of a lifetime and showing me the real meaning of discovery. To Alan, for his patience in listening to a novice programmer and providing me with a deeper understanding of computation than I would have ever received in the classroom.

— Jonathan

We Want to Hear from You!

As the reader of this book, *you* are our most important critic and commentator. We value your opinion and want to know what we're doing right, what we could do better, what areas you'd like to see us publish in, and any other words of wisdom you're willing to pass our way.

You can email or write me directly to let me know what you did or didn't like about this book—as well as what we can do to make our books stronger.

Please note that I cannot help you with technical problems related to the topic of this book, and that due to the high volume of mail I receive, I might not be able to reply to every message.

When you write, please be sure to include this book's title and author as well as your name and phone or email address. I will carefully review your comments and share them with the author and editors who worked on the book.

E-mail: opensource@samspublishing.com

Mail: Mark Taber
          Associate Publisher
          Sams Publishing
          800 East 96th Street
          Indianapolis, IN 46240 USA

Reader Services

Visit our website and register this book at www.samspublishing.com/register for convenient access to any updates, downloads, or errata that might be available for this book.

Introduction

Some books are to be tasted, others to be swallowed, and some few to be chewed and digested: that is, some books are to be read only in parts, others to be read, but not curiously, and some few to be read wholly, and with diligence and attention.

− Sir Francis Bacon (1561-1626)

Purpose, Scope, and Target of This Book

This book is designed with a certain programmer in mind. It is not really meant to be an introductory book to PHP. Instead, it is written with the intermediate to advanced PHP programmer in mind. Given this, however, it should be useful to any level of programmer, and the base knowledge level assumed could be picked up in an evening spent on the online PHP documentation at http://php.net.

To that point, the online PHP documentation is an excellent resource and should certainly not be overlooked. In this book we will refer to it often to get more detailed information on various topics. What the PHP documentation lacks, however, is what this book attempts to cover.

This book is full of solutions to problems. It has actual situations that you will need to solve during a career as a PHP programmer and has a solution for you, completely written out and working. This allows you to see one approach to solving your problem. Do you need to calculate mortgage interest? Validate credit card numbers? Localize a web page into different languages? Work with a database? Even create your own web server?

All these problems are presented in this book and many more, with code listings and verbose explanations of what exactly the code is doing. It presents the problems and gives you a solution.

Its role in your programming library can be seen as one of two things. You may choose to use this book literally as stock solutions. In the middle of writing some code you realize you need a function to handle some specific data for you, so you look it up in this book, find the answer, and use it in its entirety. Others may choose to use the book as a guide down a certain path, to look at the solution presented and use the knowledge within as a guide to writing similar code.

The book is not designed to be read from front to back; instead you can pick it up at any point without hindrance. Those who are newer to PHP, though, may still find it useful to read through certain chapters on topics that they are less acquainted with. Reading through a certain chapter and examining the contents held within will be sure to expand your understanding of that particular topic.

Because this book is intended as a reference, each chapter begins with a section called "Quick Hits." This section lists functions applicable to the subject being covered in that chapter but that do not warrant their own section. The intent is to provide a convenient location to find functions that you don't quite remember the name of or the arguments for, but you know relates to a particular subject. These lists are not intended to be exhaustive; functions are included based on their relevancy to the topic and on how common the problem is that they solve. The listed functions also are not fully documented. Only the basic arguments and common results are described. However, with each function, a URL that points directly to the full documentation is provided. The Quick Hits can be seen as a mini-reference to the most useful functions on a topic.

Web Support

This book is well supported online. The Sams Publishing website at http://www.samspublishing.com/ hosts all the code listings in this text as well as a list of errata. Also by visiting http://eliw.com/books/ you will be able to find additional information, errata, and electronic versions of all the code included in this text. Therefore if you want to use a particular example directly, you can download it without having to transcribe it into the computer yourself.

Coding Standards Used

Throughout this book, all examples have been written to a certain set coding standard that the authors consider the best coding practice for PHP at this time. For the most part, it follows the PEAR coding standard (http://pear.php.net/) but has some additions and modifications.

These standards are explained in the following sections, both so that you can understand why the code was written in certain ways and also so that you may hopefully choose to adopt these standards yourself.

Runs Against E_STRICT and E_ALL Without Error

All code in this book has been designed to run under E_STRICT and E_ALL without causing any PHP errors. This means that prodigious care is placed on making sure that all variables are initialized before use and other such concerns.

Varying Use of Quotation Marks

Throughout this book you will find some strings specified with single quotes (') and some with double quotes ("). This practice has been done on purpose. PHP parses strings surrounded by double quotes for slash (\) commands and embedded variables. This is convenient when needed. However, it also uses some (slight) additional computer resources to do this. Therefore, if you surround any strings that are just pure strings with single quotes instead, it saves the PHP engine just a little bit of time because it knows up front that it doesn't need to parse it.

More importantly is that this judicial use of quotes helps future programmers who are looking at your code. If they see a string delimited by single quotes, they know that they can safely skip over it, not having to scan it themselves for imbedded variables.

Comments and Whitespace

One of the most important things that you can do as a programmer is make liberal use of whitespace and write many comments. Without these not only will other programmers have problems viewing your code and understanding it later, but you yourself will when you need to look on code that you wrote years ago.

Also, this book relies completely on the double slash (//) as a comment marker. Optionally, you may use the C standard /* to start and */ to end a comment as well. The authors do not prefer this method because it is more difficult to distinguish comments if you use an editor that does not do color coding for you. It also is easy to make a mistake and accidentally comment out a large block of code.

Although the Perl style of comments using a pound sign (#) is still supported in PHP, its use has been discouraged by the PEAR standards.

Indentation and Braces

This book uses the PEAR standard, which happens to be the C standard for the use of braces (squiggly brackets as they are sometimes called). Essentially, the { should come on the same line of the command that needs it. The } should be indented to the same level as the command but on a line by itself if it is the last closing brace. This is best demonstrated by an example:

```
if ($test) {
    while ($num < 5) {
        $num++;
    }
} elseif ($test2) {
    echo 'here';
} else {
    echo 'there';
}
```

The authors consider it acceptable to insert comments about the details of a line such as the elseif line above by either placing them on the line underneath or inserting them on a new line between the } and the elseif.

All the code in this book is indented four spaces per level of code nesting. According to the PEAR standard these should be actual spaces inserted into the file; however, the authors feel that tabs, with your tab spacing set to 4, are an acceptable alternative.

Parentheses

It is the authors' firm belief that you can never have enough parentheses around statements. Though the rules of precedence are generally intuitive, relying on them not only increases the opportunities for creating bugs but also promotes code obfuscation, making it all that more difficult to understand the intent of the code. Therefore although the following line works:

```
if (isset($bob) && $bob != 9) { echo 'Yes'; }
```

it is not nearly as clear as instead writing:

```
if (isset($bob) && ($bob != 9)) { echo 'Yes'; }
```

For a more visible example of why this is needed, take a look at the following line of code:

```
if ($x + $y / $z < 9 or $a && $n ? $m : $o == $b || $c and $d) { echo 'Y'; }
```

By looking at that, can you figure out exactly what it means? Chances are that it isn't doing what you would guess it might do because some operator precedence rules cause certain operations to happen before others. However, if liberal use of parentheses had occurred, it would be clear what the author was trying to do (and to know whether it was wrong). Therefore that test could be rewritten as the following, which does something different than the preceding example:

```
(((($x + $y) / $z < 9) or (($a && (($n ? $m : $o) == $b)) || $c)) and $d)
```

Although the line has been cluttered up with many parentheses, it is possible via carefully tracing them to see exactly what comparisons are happening. Without this, it becomes a nightmare to debug the code when it isn't working.

PHP Short Tags

PHP has a configuration option that allows for something known as *short tags*. When this is turned on (and it is by default), it allows you to use two shorthand techniques to start a PHP code block. Instead of saying `<?php ?>` you can use `<? ?>` as a shorter version. Similarly, you gain the ability to say `<?= ?>` as a shortcut for a short line of PHP that would have otherwise looked like `<?php echo 'something'; ?>`.

It is generally accepted at this point in time that the `<?` notation is a bad concept because it can interfere with XML documents or other languages that also try to use that format. Therefore using that style of code blocks should be avoided.

Unfortunately, you cannot turn off short tags and still have access to the `<?=` construct. The authors find `<?=` a useful shortcut and use it regularly because it greatly simplifies the code when inserting a few PHP values into a large block of HTML. Therefore, the code in this book currently will run only on servers with short tags turned on.

If you need to run the code in this book on a server that does not support this construct, simply replace all instances of `<?=` with `<?php echo`, and the code will run fine.

Jumping In and Out of PHP Mode

One of the great benefits of PHP is the ability to embed PHP code in to an HTML page, and to jump into and of out PHP mode at will. However, this needs to be done with care to the appearance of the resulting code. You should not be constantly opening and closing PHP code blocks to just insert a couple lines of text. In these cases it often makes for clearer code to use `echo` statements to write the code to the screen. If needed this could even be done via multiline strings or by using the heredoc syntax. More on these options can be found at http://php.net/string.

In general use your common sense. Try to make code as legible as possible.

Use of {} Within Strings

PHP allows any variable reference within a string to be surrounded by curly braces ({}) to ensure that they are parsed correctly. This leads to a string that might look like the following:

```
$str = "{$name} said that {$pronoun}{$action['extra']}";
```

This syntax is required when using associate array elements or other situations where the code may be ambiguous as to what is a variable reference and what isn't.

However, this book always uses {} notation because it is simply good practice to do so. Not only does it help programmers recognize that a string contains a variable, but side effects that can happen when a string is parsed incorrectly can be the most difficult to debug. Both authors of this book have lost more time to debugging situations where a string was parsed incorrectly than we would care to admit. If you always wrap variables in {}, this is something you will never have to worry about.

Language Constructs (`echo`, `include`, `return`)

Many "functions" in PHP are not actually functions at all but constructs of the language, such as `echo`, `include`, and `return`. Therefore, although these allow you to wrap their parameters in parentheses like a function, it is not required and is actually discouraged because it causes PHP to do some extra work when you do.

`include` Versus `require` Versus the "Once" Options

Four different language constructs are available for importing one PHP file into another. All four exist because all four have conceptually different purposes. Therefore they should be used specifically and with conscious effort when they are needed. If the file must be included in the web page for it to function properly, `require` should be used because it will cause the page to fail if the included document is not found or able to be opened. `include`, therefore, should be used only in cases where it is optional for the file to exist. If the file didn't exist, the page would still function.

Similarly, `require_once` and `include_once` should be favored if the file in question should only ever be loaded once. This is the case with most library and support files.

Using the "once" options ensures that the file will not be loaded a second time and cause errors in the process.

echo **Versus** print

Both of these language constructs do essentially the same thing but with a slight variation. print returns a value of 1 and has precedence so that it can be used in the middle of a longer expression. However, the need for this is rare, and the fact that it returns a value makes it ever so slightly slower than echo.

More importantly, echo allows for a comma-separated list of many different values to echo to the screen. Because of both of these points, this book uses echo exclusively.

Naming of Functions, Methods, and Classes

A few naming schemes are generally good common practice, and this book attempts to stick to them. These are

- Function names—Should be all lowercase with words separated by underscores, for example: my_function_name()
- Method names—Should be in StudlyCaps format with the first character lowercase. This means that all separate words in a method name will be capitalized to distinguish them, for example: myMethodName()
- Class names—Should be in StudlyCaps format but with the first character uppercase, for example: MyClassName
- Private properties and methods within a class—Should start with a single underscore to denote that they are internal only, for example: _myPrivateMethod()
- Variable and property names—Should be all lowercase, optionally using underscores as desired
- Constant names—Should be all uppercase

I

PHP Internals

Strings

BY FAR, MOST PROBLEMS A DEVELOPER ENCOUNTERS involve the manipulation of strings. Especially when used in a web environment, nearly all input and output to a PHP script are simply strings. It is no surprise then to find that the number of string functions comprises, by far, the most of any of the standard extensions. In fact, string functions are actually found in a number of different extensions, such as the regular expression extensions.

Due to the wide variety of tasks that involve string manipulations, this chapter focuses on the most general string functions. More specialized issues, such as HTML character encoding, are handled in their respective chapters.

Quick Hits

▶ **Find the length of a string:**

```
$length = strlen($string);
```

This function returns the number of characters in a string.

Full documentation: http://php.net/strlen

▶ **Split a string using a string as a separator:**

```
$array_of_strings = explode($separator, $string);
```

This function returns the array of substrings created by splitting a string at every point the separator string appears.

Full documentation: http://php.net/explode

▶ **Create a string from an array of strings, with a separator:**

```
$string = implode($separator, $array_of_strings);
```

The returned string will be a concatenation of all the strings in the array, with the separator string between them.

Full documentation: http://php.net/implode

▶ Remove extra space from the beginning and end of a string:

```
$trimmed_string = trim($string);
```

The returned string will have any whitespace characters removed from the beginning and end of the string. The functions `rtrim()` and `ltrim()` remove whitespace from only the right or left end of the string, respectively.

Full documentation: http://php.net/trim, http://php.net/rtrim, and http://php.net/ltrim

▶ Replace all occurrences of one string with another string:

```
$result_string = str_replace($old, $new, $full);
```

All occurrences of the old string within the full string are replaced with the new string. A case-insensitive version is also available as the function `str_ireplace()`.

Full documentation: http://php.net/str_replace and http://php.net/str_ireplace

▶ Pad a string to a specified length:

```
$padded = str_pad($string, $length);
```

The returned string is at least `$length` characters long. Spaces are added to the right of the string to achieve this. With optional arguments, any string can be used as padding along with whether the padding will occur at the beginning or end of string.

Full documentation: http://php.net/str_pad

▶ Create a larger string via repetition:

```
$repeat = str_repeat($string, $nrepeats);
```

The input string is replicated the specified number of times to create the result.

Full documentation: http://php.net/str_repeat:

▶ Split a string into an array of characters

```
$array = str_split($string);
```

This function returns an array comprising the characters that make up the string.

Full documentation: http://php.net/str_split

▶ Return a portion of a string:

```
$substring = substr($string, $n, $length);
```

The portion of the string starting at the nth character for `$length` number of characters is returned. If `$n` is negative, the substring will start that many characters from the end of the string. If `$length` is negative, that many characters will be omitted from the end of the string.

Full documentation: http://php.net/substr

▶ **Make a string all uppercase or lowercase letters:**

```
$lower = strtolower($string);

$upper = strtoupper($string);
```

These functions simply return, respectively, the lowercase or uppercase versions of the string.

Full documentation: http://php.net/strtolower and http://php.net/strtoupper

▶ **Parse a string based on a format:**

```
$array = sscanf($string, $format);
```

The returned array contains each extracted value from the string according to the specified format.

Full documentation: http://php.net/sscanf

▶ **Output values using well-defined formats:**

```
printf($format, $var1, $var2,…);
```

Using a simple syntax, the format argument defines how the subsequent arguments are printed. This function is part of a family of formatting functions.

Full documentation: http://php.net/printf, http://php.net/sprintf, http://php.net/fprintf

▶ **Compare two strings:**

```
$result = strcmp($string1, $string2);
```

This function returns a number less than, equal to, or greater than 0 depending on how the strings compare alphabetically. 0 is returned if the strings are equivalent. A case-insensitive version is also available as strcasecmp().

Full documentation: http://php.net/strcmp and http://php.net/strcasecmp

▶ **Compare two strings as a human would do so:**

```
$result = strnatcmp($string1, $string2);

$result = strnatcasecmp($string1, $string2);
```

The comparison is based on how people order strings—that is, strings with numbers in them are ordered based on value, not just characters. The comparison is case-sensitive for the former call while being case-insensitve for the latter.

Full documentation: http://php.net/strnatcmp

▶ **Determine where the first occurrence of a string is within another string:**

```
$pos = strpos($bigstring, $search);
```

This function returns the position of the search string in $bigstring. If not found, false is returned. A case-insensitive version is also available as stripos().

Full documentation: http://php.net/strpos and http://php.net/stripos

▶ Determine where the last occurrence of a string is within another string:

```
$lastpos = strrpos($bigstring, $search);
```

This function returns the position of the last occurrence of the search string in `$bigstring`. If not found, false is returned. A case-insensitive version is also available as `strripos()`.

Full documentation: http://php.net/strrpos and http://php.net/strripos

▶ Search for any of a set of characters within a string:

```
$found = strpbrk($string, $characters);
```

The string is scanned for any of the characters in the `$characters` string. If a match is found, it returns a string starting from the character it just matched to the end of the string.

Full documentation: http://php.net/strpbrk

1.1 Matching Patterns (Regular Expressions)

Any discussion of string manipulation must include the use of regular expression pattern-matching functions (often referred to as *regex*). Regular expressions are a powerful minilanguage used to find complicated patterns in strings.

PHP includes a couple of different sets of regex functions that you can use. The one we will use exclusively in this book is the PCRE extension. The PCRE functions (all prefaced by `preg_`) is the preferred library to use. It tends to be faster than the other option, and it uses the same regex syntax as Perl, another popular programming language that many programmers are already familiar with.

To best demonstrate the usefulness of regular expressions, let's examine a relatively simple problem: searching for a United States ZIP Code. Such numbers are either a five-digit number, or are known as a ZIP+4 and look like "12345-6789." Attempting this search with the standard PHP string functions would require a multiline algorithm. However, with regular expressions, a single function, `preg_match()`, is all that is required, as shown in Listing 1.1.1.

Listing 1.1.1 **Detecting ZIP Codes in Strings**

```php
<?php
// A function to detect zipcodes in a string.
function detect_zipcode($string) {
    // Use regex to look for zipcodes, return true or false
    return preg_match('/\b\d{5}(-\d{4})?\b/', $string);
}

// Try a few examples:
echo '<pre>';

// A true example:
if (detect_zipcode('Frederick, MD  21701-3883')) {
```

Listing 1.1.1 **Continued**

```
    echo "Test 1: true\n";
}
// Another true example:
if (detect_zipcode('The zipcode 26623 is the area in which I grew up.')) {
    echo "Test 2: true\n";
}
// A False example:
if (detect_zipcode('The Phone Number is 301-555-1212')) {
    echo "Test 3: true\n";
}
// Another false example:
if (detect_zipcode('426969-313109')) {
    echo "Test 4: true\n";
}

echo '</pre>';
?>
```

The first argument of `preg_match()` is the regular expression pattern. Patterns always start and end with some delimiter character, traditionally a /. The next item, \b, is the syntax used to match a word-boundary character. This means it will find any whitespace, punctuation, or the beginning or end of the string. The next item, \d, indicates that the next character must be a digit. The {5} after it, indicates that it must find five of the previous items, in this case, five digits. We then have a parenthesis. These are used for grouping items together. The next item, -, simply represents the dash character. We then have \d{4} meaning four more digits. The parenthesis then closes, and we have a ?. The question mark is a modifier meaning that the previous item (in this case the group specified by the parenthesis), is optional.

Therefore, we have created a regex that matches a five-digit string, surrounded by word boundaries, optionally having a dash and four more digits after it.

As a quick reference, here are some of the most common syntax characters for use in PCRE regular expressions:

Pattern matches:

\d = Digit	. = Any character (except \n)
\D = Not a digit	^ = Start of string
\s = Whitespace	$ = End of string
\S = Not whitespace	\b = Word boundary

Pattern match extenders:

? = Previous item is match 0 or 1 times.

* = Previous item is matched 0 or more times.

+ = Previous item is matched 1 or more times.

{n} = Previous item is matched exactly n times.

{n,} = Previous item is matched at least n times.

{n,m} = Previous item is matched at least n and at most m times.

? (after any of above) = Match as few as possible times.

Option patterns:

(pattern) = Groups the pattern to act as one item and captures it

(x|y) = Matches either pattern x, or pattern y

[abc] = Matches either the character a, b, or c

[^abc] = Matches any character except a, b, or c

[a-f] = Matches characters a through f

Note

Regular expressions are powerful, and a full discussion of them is beyond the scope of this book. You may want to study them more by reading the PHP documentation at http://php.net/pcre.

1.2 Cleaning Up Whitespace

Often when dealing with data coming from a user, or perhaps from a database, you can have extra spaces (or tabs, carriage returns, and so on) in your strings. This often causes problems later when you want to compare strings. It also can waste storage space if you save those extra useless characters.

If you want to just remove space from the beginning or end of a string, you can use the built-in function trim() to do that for you. However, often you want to completely clean up the data. You will want to remove leading/trailing spaces, collapse multiple spaces into a single one, and even replace all other types of whitespace with a regular space.

To accomplish this, you can use the regular expression functions of PHP, as shown in Listing 1.2.1.

Listing 1.2.1 **Removing Extra Whitespace**

```php
<?php
$str = " This line  contains\tliberal \r\n use of   whitespace.\n\n";

// First remove the leading/trailing whitespace
$str = trim($str);

// Now remove any doubled-up whitespace
$str = preg_replace('/\s(?=\s)/', '', $str);
```

Listing 1.2.1 **Continued**

```
// Finally, replace any non-space whitespace, with a space
$str = preg_replace('/[\n\r\t]/', ' ', $str);

// Echo out: 'This line contains liberal use of whitespace.'
echo "<pre>{$str}</pre>";
?>
```

Listing 1.2.1 removes all whitespace step-by-step. First we use `trim()` to clean the beginning and end of the string. Second, we use `preg_replace()` to remove duplicates. The `\s` stands in regex for "any whitespace." The `(?=)` notation is a forward lookup. It means to only match the previous character if the character within the parenthesis follows it. Therefore this regex means: "Any whitespace character that is followed by a whitespace character." We tell it to replace this with a blank string and therefore remove them. This removes all duplicates, leaving only single whitespace characters.

Finally, we use another regex—`[\n\r\t]`—to find any remaining newlines (\n), carriage returns (\r), or tabs (\t). We then replace these with a single space.

1.3 Expanding and Compressing Tabs

It is a common practice for tabs to be used when writing text files. The problem is that different editors, and different computers, may show a tab as a different amount of space. This can cause no end of problems when a different user opens the file, and the formatting is thrown off.

To fix this, you may choose to expand the tabs out into a set number of spaces, or compress a certain number of spaces back into tabs. By doing this, you can ensure that the visual look of the string will remain no matter how it is viewed. Let's start by looking at expanding the tabs into spaces. In Listing 1.3.1, by simple application of `str_replace()`, we will turn all tabs, into four spaces.

Listing 1.3.1 **Replacing Tabs with Spaces**

```
<?php
$str = "
\tWHILE (NOT FINISHED) {
\t\tIF (PSUEDOCODE IS PRESENT) {
\t\t\tTHEN REMOVE TABS
\t\t}
\t}
";

// Do the replacement
$replaced = str_replace("\t", '    ', $str);
```

Listing 1.3.1 **Continued**

```
// Echo out the string with spaces.
echo "<pre>{$replaced}</pre>";
?>
```

Similarly, when you are finished viewing a string (and perhaps editing it), you may want to collapse them back into tabs before saving. To accomplish this, just repeat the process in reverse, as shown by Listing 1.3.2.

Listing 1.3.2 **Replacing Extra Spaces with Tabs**

```
<?php
$str = "
    WHILE (NOT FINISHED) {
        IF (PSUEDOCODE IS PRESENT) {
            THEN REMOVE TABS
        }
    }
";

// Do the replacement
$replaced = str_replace('    ', "\t", $str);

// Echo out the string with tabs.
echo "<pre>{$replaced}</pre>";
?>
```

1.4 Converting Text Between Macintosh, UNIX, and PC Format

Unfortunately in this world of multiple operating systems that we live in, sometimes slight differences end up causing major problems. Such is the case of line breaks in the various operating systems.

UNIX denotes a line break in a text file with a single newline character (\n). Microsoft PCs use two characters together, a newline and a carriage return (\n\r) (which might be in either order). Finally to add to the confusion, classic Macintosh uses just a carriage return (\r). The current Mac OS X uses the UNIX notation.

This can end up causing problems when transferring files across systems, especially if you have multiple people editing a single file, each using a different OS. The simple way to fix this is to create some functions that convert the line breaks into the format you choose (see Listing 1.4.1).

Listing 1.4.1   **Converting Line Breaks**

```php
<?php
// Declare our generic function that will fix all these problems.
// $subject will be the string to fix, and $type will be the
// format that you wish in the end, either 'unix', 'mac', or 'pc'
function line_break_set($subject, $type) {
    // Determine our replacement
    switch ($type) {
        case 'mac':
            $ending = '\r';
            break;
        case 'pc':
            $ending = '\r\n';
            break;
        default:
            $ending = '\n';
    }

    // Now perform the replacement
    return preg_replace('/\r\n|\n\r|\n|\r/', $ending, $subject);
}

$str = "Multiple\rtypes of\n\rline breaks\r\nhave been placed
within this string\n\nSee?";

// Convert this three times now
$mac = line_break_set($str, 'mac');
$unix = line_break_set($str, 'unix');
$pc = line_break_set($str, 'pc');

// Echo out the strings, using addcslashes to make the line breaks visible.
echo '<pre>mac = ', addcslashes($mac, "\n\r"), "\npc = ",
    addcslashes($pc, "\n\r"), "\nunix = ",
    addcslashes($unix, "\n\r"), '</pre>';
?>
```

In this case, we have taken the $type parameter that was passed in and use it to determine the appropriate ending. Then using a regular expression, all potential line endings arc located and replaced with the chosen ending. This does end up doing a little bit of extra work, as it finds already proper line endings to replace them with an exact copy. However, it makes for a single, simple function that performs all three tasks.

1.5 Parsing CSV (Comma-Separated Values)

Comma-separated value (CSV) is a common format for data to be in—usually as an export/import option to get data from one system to another. PHP provides an excellent function, `fgetcsv()`, if you want to read in the CSV data from a text file. However, no such function is provided if you have the data in a string and need to break it apart.

You could choose to just use `explode()` to break up the string by commas. However, that only works for simple CSV data. Often CSV data allows for quoted text (with either " or ' as the delimiter), and potentially it might actually use something other than a comma to break apart different values. Therefore if you want to have a robust CSV parser, it takes a little bit more work. We need to allow for a comma within a quoted string as well as allow for the use of a double quote ("") to mean that a single quote should appear, as shown in Listing 1.5.1.

Listing 1.5.1 **Parsing CSV Strings**

```php
<?php
// Generate a function to parse CSV strings,
//  with configurable delimiters and quote characters
function parse_csv($string, $delim = ',', $quote='"') {
    // First clean up any double-quotes, our algorithm doesn't need them:
    $new = str_replace("{$quote}{$quote}", $quote, $string);

    // Grab all matches
    $matches = array();
    preg_match_all("/\s*({$quote}?)(.*?)\\1\s*(?:{$delim}|$)/",
        $new, $matches);

    // matches[2] holds our answers but will always grab one too many
    // matches with the final match being blank.  Remove it then return:
    // with the final match being blank.  Remove it then return:
    array_pop($matches[2]);
    return $matches[2];
}

$str = 'comma, "separated ""values"""', are    , "shown, here", "for\nyou " ';

// Parse the string into values:
$values = parse_csv($str);

// Echo out the array, displays the following:
// Array
// (
//     [0] => comma
//     [1] => separated "values"
//     [2] => are
//     [3] => provided, here
//     [4] => for\nyou
// )
echo '<pre>';
```

Listing 1.5.1 **Continued**

```
print_r($values);
echo '</pre>';
?>
```

The bulk of the work in this function is a regular expression that separates out a single entry and a call to `preg_match_all()`, which finds all matches in the string for that regex. This regular expression is as follows:

```
/\s*({$quote}?)(.*?)\\1\s*(?:{$delim}|$)/
```

Looking at this from left to right, you can read it as follows: First it looks for any amount of whitespace: `\s*`. Then it optionally detects the quote character: `({$quote}?)`. The `(.*?)` tells it to capture the actual value. However, the `?` tells it not to be greedy and to grab only as many characters as it can before the next section of code matches. The next section of the code: `\\1` is a little bit of magic. It says that it will now match the exact same character as the first pattern marked with a parenthesis did. This was the optional search for our quote character. What does this mean?

It means that if we found a quote, we need to match another quote, but if we didn't, ignore it. Finally, it then allows optionally for any more whitespace—`\s*`—and finishes by stating that it needs to find either our delimiter, or the end of the line: `(?:{$delim}|$)`. The vertical bar means or, and the `$` matches the end of the string. The `?:` notation tells the parser that the parentheses here are only being used to create the or statement and do not need to have their values captured, as parentheses normally would. This is not needed for the code to work; this is an optimization and good programming practice.

1.6 Truncating Text to Fit Within a Specific Space

When programming, you may often find yourself with a large block of text and yet a small area that it must fit in. A common tactic in these situations is to only display a certain number of the characters of the text followed by an ellipsis (…) or something similar. On the Web, this is often a linked word, such as "(more)", that will take you to the full text.

Simply truncating the string cannot solve this problem. Doing so invariably ends the string in the middle of a word, producing ugly results. The solution is to find the largest substring that ends with a whole word, as shown in Listing 1.6.1.

Listing 1.6.1 **Truncating Text on Word Boundaries**

```
<?php
// A function to truncate text to a length and indicate more is available.
function truncate_text_nicely($string, $max, $moretext) {
    // Only begin to manipulate if the string is longer than max
```

Listing 1.6.1 **Continued**

```
    if (strlen($string) > $max) {
        // Modify $max by removing the length of moretext to allow room
        $max -= strlen($moretext);

        // Snag only the appropriate part of the string.
        $string = strrev(strstr(strrev(substr($string, 0, $max)), ' '));

        // Add the moretext onto it:
        $string .= $moretext;
    }

    // Return the string, whether it was modified or not.
    return $string;
}

$str = 'It was a dark and stormy night when the Baron prepared his plane.';

// Parse the string into values:
$values = truncate_text_nicely($str, 35, '...');

// Echo out the result, will display:  It was a dark and stormy night ...
echo "<pre>{$values}</pre>";
?>
```

This function is straightforward. After determining that the string is longer than the available space, it removes the length of $moretext to ensure that there will be room to insert the $moretext without breaking the character limit. Then, the various transformations are done.

To understand these, you need to start from the inside of this chain of function calls and work your way out. First, a call to substr() ensures that the string has been cut down to the appropriate maximum length. We then use strrev() to reverse the order of the string so that strstr() works properly. The function strstr() returns all characters in a string following the first occurrence of a given character. In this case, we pass it space, and it gives us the first space it finds and all remaining text. After passing this one last time through strrev(), we end up with all the text, up to and including the last space.

We then only have to add the given text to the end of the string and return it. It should be trivial to modify this code to, instead of just inserting a text string, create an HTML link to the full text.

1.7 Padding Arrays of Data to Display as Columns

Often when programming for the Web you may find yourself needing to display an array of data as an HTML table. However, what can you do when you need to display this table of data as pure text? This might be needed for writing a command–line PHP program, or perhaps when making a text only version of a web page to help those with accessibility problems or basic web browsers.

The approach you need is to pad the values with an appropriate amount of spaces to make them, when displayed in a monospaced font (such as with a `<pre>` tag), to appear to be in columns (see Listing 1.7.1).

Listing 1.7.1 **Displaying Multidimensional Arrays**

```php
<?php
// A function to display a multidimensional array as text columns.
// $spacing should be set to the number of spaces you wish between columns
function display_array($arr, $spacing) {
    // We need to determine the maximum width of each column in the array
    $widths = array();

    // Loop through all rows
    foreach ($arr as $row) {
        // Examine each column
        foreach ($row as $key => $col) {
        // If this entry is wider than others in the column, store it
            if (!isset($widths[$key]) || (strlen($col) > $widths[$key])) {
                $widths[$key] = strlen($col);
            }
        }
    }

    // Now that we have the maximum widths, we can loop through the
    //  array, printing out each row
    echo '<pre>';
    foreach ($arr as $row) {
        $count = 0;
        foreach ($row as $key => $col) {
            // If this is not the first one, add the spacing:
            if ($count++) {
                echo str_repeat(' ', $spacing);
            }

            // Echo out the column, padded appropriately
            echo str_pad($col, $widths[$key]);
        }
```

Listing 1.7.1 **Continued**

```
        echo "\n";
    }
}

$test_array = array(
    array('NAME', 'CITY', 'STATE', 'PHONE', 'EMAIL'),
    array('Bob Smith', 'Baltimore', 'MD', '410-555-1212', 'bs@nomail.com'),
    array('Jane Doe', 'Gary', 'IN', '999-555-7136', 'jane@tarzan.com'),
    array('William Fences', 'Redmond', 'WA',
            '123-555-4567', 'opening@fencesinc.com'),
    array('Steven Works', 'Cupertino', 'CA',
            '023-555-4991', 'works@orange.com')
    );

// Display the array, echos:
// NAME            CITY          STATE  PHONE         EMAIL
// Bob Smith       Baltimore     MD     410-555-1212  bsmith@nomail.com
// Jane Doe        Indianapolis  IN     999-555-7136  jane@tarzan.com
// William Fences  Redmond       WA     123-555-4567  opening@fencesinc.com
// Steven Works    Cupertino     CA     023-555-4991  works@orange.com
display_array($test_array, 3);
?>
```

We begin our function by looping through the array, row by row, and column by column, to determine the maximum length entry in any column. At each step, we first use `isset()` to see whether we have already stored any number, and if so, we store this new length if it is longer than any previous value.

After that, we can loop through the array again in the same manner. This time we use `str_repeat()` to create our spacing between columns, and use `str_pad()` to make each column always as wide as its longest entry.

1.8 Checking the Spelling of a Word

It is handy to be able to check the spelling of a word entered by a user. In fact, any application that requires input of large amounts of text, such as a blog or email client, is expected to have some type of spell-checking functionality. PHP performs spell checks via the pspell library.

In Listing 1.8.1, a function is created that takes a block of text and replaces any potentially misspelled words with a drop-down giving possible replacements (see Listing 1.8.1).

Caution

Default installations of PHP may not have the pspell library enabled because it must be separately compiled into the language. Visit http://php.net/pspell for details on how to enable it.

Listing 1.8.1   **Spell Checker with Suggestions**

```php
<?php
// A function to check a string for bad spelling, and offer replacements.
function spellcheck_string($str) {
    // First we must initialize pspell and tell it to use English
    $dict = pspell_new('en');

    // Now grab every word in this string, referenced by its position
    $words = str_word_count($str, 2);

    // Reverse the words, so that we can loop backward, from end to start.
    $rwords = array_reverse($words, true);
    foreach ($rwords as $pos => $word) {
        // If it is NOT spelled correctly
        if (!(pspell_check($dict, $word))) {
            // Determine a list of suggestions:
            $suggestions = pspell_suggest($dict, $word);

            // Generate a droplist with current word and all suggestions:
            $list = '<select name=\"position[{$pos}]\">';
            $list .= "<option value=\"{$word}\">{$word}</option>";
            foreach ($suggestions as $s) {
                $list .= "<option value=\"{$s}\">{$s}</option>";
            }
            $list .= '</select>';

            // Now, insert this into the original string in place
            //  of the original word.
            $str = substr_replace($str, $list, $pos, strlen($word));
        }
    }

    // Return the string surround by a form so that the form will display
    echo "<form>{$str}</form>";
}

$test_string = "My speling is not the bset.  I oftan end up with
rong characters in my sentenences.";

// Spellcheck the text, output is similar to:
// My [speling] is not the [bset].  I [oftan] end up with
// [rong] characters in my [sentenences].
spellcheck_string($test_string);
?>
```

Though the extension has many functions, only three functions are needed for basic usage: `pspell_new()` initializes the environment for use with a specific language dictionary, `pspell_check()` returns a false if a word may be misspelled, and `pspell_suggest()` returns a list of suggested words to correct the potential misspelling.

In this example, we use `str_word_count()`, which when passed a 2 as its second parameter, returns a list of all words referenced by their position in the string. We could have just tried to split the string with `explode()` or `preg_split()`. However, we would have had to deal with punctuation rules, whereas `str_word_count()` takes care of that for us.

Having this list of words, we then proceed to loop over them backward from end to beginning. This is so that whenever we find a misspelled word, we can use `substr_replace()` to insert our replacement drop list based on the string position. If it started at the beginning of the string, after the first insert, the position of all following matches would have changed, and it would be difficult to keep track of them. It's easier to work backward so that you never destroy the position of any word you haven't looked at yet.

1.9 Matching Similar Strings

When a user performs a search through data for a term that he typed in, it is easy to misspell the term and end up getting no results. A technique sometimes called *fuzzy matching* can be used to prevent this. The idea is to retrieve all words that are close to the word that was given.

This could be accomplished using the pspell spelling checker as used in the previous example. However, that only works for actual dictionary words. What if you are searching through people's names, acronyms, or technical jargon? Fortunately, PHP comes with a built-in function that allows you to do this easily: `similar_text()`. Passed two strings, it calculates a value denoting how similar they are. Most conveniently, if you pass a variable as a third parameter, it will be filled with a percentage value for the similarity. Using percentages, you can use logic such as "If any two words are at least 80% similar, display them." Listing 1.9.1 demonstrates how you use `similar_text()`.

Listing 1.9.1   **Checking for Similar Names**

```php
<?php
// Create an array of names we wish to test against
$names = array('Robert Smith', 'Bobby Smythe',
                'Roberto Thithe', 'Robin Smith');

// Loop over them checking them against the name 'Roberto Smyth'
$output = '';
foreach ($names as $name) {
    similar_text($name, 'Roberto Smyth', $percent);
    $output .= "{$name} = {$percent}%\n";
}
```

Listing 1.9.1   **Continued**

```
// Now display the output with each name and its percentage similarity.
// Outputs the following:
// Robert Smith = 88%
// Bobby Smythe = 64%
// Roberto Thithe = 74.074074074074%
// Robin Smith = 66.666666666667%
echo "<pre>{$output}</pre>";
?>
```

As demonstrated, `similar_text()` is straightforward to use. The trick is deciding what percentage of similar is similar enough for your application. As seen here, "Robert Smith" and "Roberto Smyth", each off by only two letters, are still only considered 88% similar. Therefore you may have to set your thresholds lower than you might assume.

> **Note**
>
> Another function `levenshtein()` also exists, which does a similar function but is slightly more complicated. You may read more about it at http://php.net/levenshtein.

1.10 Performing Proper Capitalization on Titles

You will sometimes find yourself in a situation where you need to print out a title—be it the title of a book, of a report, or of a web page. The rules for capitalization in English are varied, depending on what manual of style you refer to.

In Listing 1.10.1, we implement a simpler set of rules: All words should be capitalized except for a, an, the, but, as, if, and, or, nor, of, by. However, if these exceptions appear at the beginning or end of the title, they are still capitalized.

Listing 1.10.1   **Uppercase Titles**

```
<?php
// A function to properly uppercase a title
function title_upcase($str) {
    // First of all, uppercase all these words using ucwords
    $str = ucwords($str);

    // Retrieve all the words referenced by their position in the string:
    $wordlist = str_word_count($str, 2);

    // Remove the first and last word, since they are to remain capitalized
    $wordlist = array_slice($wordlist, 1, -1, true);

    // Loop over all the remaining words.
    foreach ($wordlist as $position => $word) {
```

Listing 1.10.1 **Continued**

```
            // If this word is one of those that should be lowercased
            switch ($word) {
                case 'A':
                case 'An':
                case 'The':
                case 'But':
                case 'As':
                case 'If':
                case 'And':
                case 'Or':
                case 'Nor':
                case 'Of':
                case 'By':
                    // Replace the first letter with a lowercase version:
                    $lower = strtolower($word);
                    $str{$position} = $lower{0};
            }
        }

    // Return the formatted string
    return $str;
}

$sample = "a study of intersteller galaxies as presented by scientists";

// Uppercase a title and echo out the results.  It will output:
// A Study of Intersteller Galaxies as Presented by Scientists
$upcased = title_upcase($sample);
echo "<pre>{$upcased}</pre>";
?>
```

The format of this solution is straightforward and uses as many of the built-in functions as possible. The function starts by using `ucwords()` to capitalize every word in the string. That's half of the solution; now we just need to lowercase the special cases. To find the words in the string, `str_word_count()` is used. When passed a format parameter of 2, this built-in function returns an array of all words in the string, referenced by their position in the string.

We then need to remove the first and last elements of the array so that we don't ever lowercase them, which is easily accomplished with `array_slice()`; passing it the final parameter of true makes it keep the array indices intact. It is then possible to loop through each word, checking whether it is one of the special words that need lowercased.

If one of the special words is found, we can use the position indicator that `str_word_count()` gave us, in conjunction with the ability to directly reference any character in a string via string{position}, to set the character to its lowercase equivalent.

This function can be modified to include other words that you might need to be forced to lowercase, and via a slight modification, could even be made aware of certain words that always need to be completely uppercase, such as NASA, FBI, or GNU.

1.11 Generating Unique Identifiers

Often to solve a problem, you need to generate a unique identifier for something. This could be for a piece of data in a database, or perhaps to identify a user through the use of cookies.

In any case, the problem is the same: You need a way to generate a (hopefully) unique string to be used as this identifier. There are a number of techniques to do this, but one of them is to take a set of information that you have that should be unique about the data, add to it some randomness, and then call sha1() on it to generate a unique 40-character string. The US Secure Hash Algorithm 1, which is implemented by sha1(), gives you a unique 40-character string based on the data passed to it.

By going through these hoops, you will have created a string that should be unique to the specific data you passed in (see Listing 1.11.1).

Listing 1.11.1 **Generating a Unique Identifier**

```php
<?php
// A function to return a unique identifier for the user's browser
function create_unique() {
    // Read the user agent, IP address, current time, and a random number:

    $data = $_SERVER['HTTP_USER_AGENT'] . $_SERVER['REMOTE_ADDR'] .
            time() . rand();

    // Return this value hashed via sha1
    return sha1($data);
}

// Echo out the hashed data - This will be different every time.
$newhash = create_unique();
echo "<pre>{$newhash}</pre>";
?>
```

This technique can be used for any data. Just substitute the unique data that you have instead of the browser data used in Listing 1.11.1. Keys will be generated that will almost always be unique. Any key-generation algorithm has a small chance of generating the same key twice. If that absolutely cannot happen in your situation, you need to keep track of the keys that have been generated and check to make sure that the one you just made has never been generated before.

That same concept can be used if you must generate the ID before you have any data. In that case, all you can really use is the time and a random number. There is then a greater chance (though still slight) that you might generate two keys that are the same.

1.12 Counting the Number of Times Certain Words Appear

When dealing with a lot of text, you may find yourself needing to know how many times a certain word appears, or even how many times every word appears. Though there is no single built-in function for this task, you only need a few existing ones to create a simple solution, as demonstrated in Listing 1.12.1.

Listing 1.12.1 **Counting All Words in a String**

```php
<?php
// A function to return a count of all words used in the string
function full_count_words($str) {
    // Use str_word_count passing it a '1' so it breaks words out for us
    $words = str_word_count($str, 1);

    // Loop over all elements of this array forming a new array that uses
    // the word as a key and counts how many times each one is found
    $results = array();
    foreach ($words as $w) {
        // Convert the entire word to lowercase,
        //  so that 'The' and 'the' will still match
        $lw = strtolower($w);
        // If it's the first time we have seen this word,
        //  add it to the array, else increment it
        if (!(isset($results[$lw]))) {
            $results[$lw] = 1;
        } else {
            $results[$lw]++;
        }
    }

    // We now have the count we wanted, return it
    return $results;
}

$test_string = "There are many top secret chemical compounds that we are
trying to keep a secret from the director of the institute.  Perhaps the
secret society could hold a meeting and ask all the members to attend and
discuss this issue.";
```

Listing 1.12.1 **Continued**

```
// Determine the word count:
$wordcount = full_count_words($test_string);

// First echo out the number of times the word 'secret' is used:
// prints: The word secret was used 3 times.
echo '<pre>';
echo "The word secret was used {$wordcount['secret']} times.\n\n";

// Now go ahead and echo out the entire array:
print_r($wordcount);
echo '</pre>';
?>
```

There are a few subtleties to this code that allow it to work. First, by passing a second parameter of 1 to str_word_count(), instead of returning a number, it returns a full array of every word in the string. We then loop over this, creating a new array as we go, keeping a separate count for each word. Because case is not important when counting words, all words are made lowercase.

You might find it odd that we check to see whether it is the first time that we have run into this string before. If so, we set the value to 1, and increment otherwise. It would work if you just incremented all the time; however, that isn't as clean code because it assumes that the uninitialized value will be the equivalent of zero. Also, if you do that you will generate PHP Notice level warnings about using an uninitialized value. Writing it this way is safer, cleaner, and allows you to run PHP in strict mode and still not see any errors.

2

Numbers

BEING A GENERAL-PURPOSE LANGUAGE, PHP has the basic set of mathematical operators and a basic set of mathematical functions. A full list can be found at http://php.net/math. Though it is beyond of the scope of this book, PHP also comes with an extension, BCMath, http://php.net/bc, to handle arbitrary precision operations.

As with strings, nearly all types of applications require some use of the math functions. Hence, this chapter focuses on those examples that demonstrate "math-centric" issues only, leaving examples based on other topics to those chapters so devoted.

Quick Hits

▶ Find the absolute value of a number:

```
$absvalue = abs($number);
```

If the number is negative, the value returned is positive. If the number is positive, this function simply returns the number.

Full documentation: http://php.net/abs

▶ Find the integer remainder of a division:

```
$remainder = $dividend % $divisor;
```

Called the *modulus operator*, the integer remainder resulting from dividing the $dividend by the $divisor is returned.

Full documentation: http://php.net/language.operators.arithmetic

▶ Raise a number to a power:

```
$result = pow($number, $power);
```

Unlike other languages, PHP does not have a power operator. This function must be used instead.

Full documentation: http://php.net/pow

▶ Find the square root of a number:

```
$root = sqrt($number);
```

As true with the mathematical operation, one cannot take a square root of a negative value.

Full documentation: http://php.net/sqrt

▶ Round a fractional number up to the next highest whole number:

```
$ceilinged = ceil($number);
```

This function, if necessary, rounds a fractional number up to the next integer. The rounding occurs for any fractional value.

Full documentation: http://php.net/ceil

▶ Round a fractional number down to the next lowest whole number:

```
$floored = floor($number);
```

This function performs essentially the same operation as casting a float value as type integer, removing the decimal portion of the number. However, the value returned is still type float.

Full documentation: http://php.net/floor

▶ Round a number to the nearest whole number:

```
$rounded = round($number);
```

This function rounds to the nearest whole number. If the fractional part is less than 0.5, the result is the next lowest whole number. If greater than or equal to 0.5, the result returned is the next highest whole number.

Full documentation: http://php.net/round

▶ Find the largest or smallest value in an array:

```
$maximum = max($array);
$minimum = min($array);
```

Return, respectively, the maximum and minimum value of an array of numbers.

Full documentation: http://php.net/max and http://php.net/min

▶ Convert a number in one base system to another:

```
$newnumber = base_convert($number, $oldbase, $newbase);
```

This function converts a number in any base, up to base 36, to a number in any other base, again up to base 36.

Full documentation: http://php.net/base_convert

▶ Generate a random integer:

```
$result = rand($min, $max);
```

This function returns an integer between $min and $max, inclusive.

Full documentation: http://php.net/rand

▶ **Calculate an exponent:**

```
$result = exp($power);
```

This function returns the natural base "e" raised to the specified power.

Full documentation: http://php.net/exp

▶ **Calculate a logarithm:**

```
$result = log($number, $base);
```

This function returns the logarithm of the specified number to the base provided. If the base is left off, it performs a natural logarithm.

Full documentation: http://php.net/log

2.1 Retrieving a Number from a String

When a user enters a number into a form field online, it comes to PHP as a text string. When you want to get the actual number back out as an integer or float, you may have to do some work. Now typically in PHP it doesn't really matter if you have a string representation of a number, or the number itself; you can use the value in math operations, and PHP will automatically translates the number for you.

In many cases; however, PHP can let you down because it doesn't handle extra spaces, commas, dollar signs, or other characters when it automatically translates a number. This leaves you with a zero, when you wanted instead the number that was contained. Listing 2.1.1 makes sure that you always get a number out of a string.

Listing 2.1.1 **Converting a String to a Number**

```php
<?php
// A function to retrieve the number from a string no matter what.
function retrieve_number($str) {
    // We need to do some cleanup of the string
    //  so remove anything that is not a digit, a period, or a -
    $str = preg_replace('/[^0-9.-]/', '', $str);

    // We can safely call floatval to convert this to a float and return
    return floatval($str);
}

// Setup our test cases:
$test1 = '$123,432.55';
$test2 = '  a  -57.2';

// Echo out these if just directly used as a float ...
// Displays the following:
```

Listing 2.1.1   **Continued**

```
// test1 = 0
// test2 = 0
echo '<pre>';
echo "\ntest1 = " . ($test1 * 1.0);
echo "\ntest2 = " . ($test2 * 1.0);

// Now use our new function:
// Displays the following:
// test1 = 123432.55
// test2 = -57.2
echo "\ntest1 = " . retrieve_number($test1);
echo "\ntest2 = " . retrieve_number($test2);
echo '</pre>';
?>
```

2.2 Printing Proper Plural Text

If you want to output proper English (or other languages), you need to take into account that, when making a statement involving numbers, the plurality of the text may change. For example, an application may need to print the following: "I have 0 buttons"; "I have 1 button"; and then back to "I have 2 buttons".

You could attempt to write a function that automatically handles this for you; however, at least in English, the rules for plurality are complex. Any attempt at automatically handling it would either fail regularly or become complicated. Just think of the odd cases such as 1 goose, 2 geese; 1 datum, 2 data; or 1 index, 2 indices. Therefore in most cases it is usually easier to just write custom code for each word that you need, as demonstrated in Listing 2.2.1

Listing 2.2.1   **Handling Plurality**

```
<?php
echo '<pre>';

// Echo out the statements with a count of 1, prints:
//   I have 1 book
//   I have 1 index
$count = 1;
echo "\n I have {$count} book", ($count == 1) ? '' : 's';
echo "\n I have {$count} ind", ($count == 1) ? 'ex' : 'ices';

// Now the same statements with a count of 2, prints:
//   I have 2 books
//   I have 2 indices
$count = 2;
```

Listing 2.2.1 **Continued**

```
echo "\n I have {$count} book", ($count == 1) ? '' : 's';
echo "\n I have {$count} ind", ($count == 1) ? 'ex' : 'ices';

echo '</pre>';
?>
```

The use of the '?:' (ternary operator) makes this job easy. We can always echo out just the part of the word that doesn't change and then choose the proper ending, based on whether the count is 1 or otherwise.

2.3 Converting Numbers into Roman Numerals

Roman numerals are a great way to add a bit of class to a web page. They are often used in official titles, such as the XXXIV Pennsic War (34th). The rules for Roman numerals are straightforward and therefore lend themselves to being scripted. The basic rules of Roman numerals are

M = 1,000	C = 100	X = 10	I = 1
D = 500	L = 50	V = 5	

Simply add up the letters to equal the number you want. Always list the higher numbers first. The only exception to this rule is that you can place any lower letter in front of a higher letter to mean minus—for example, IV = 4, IX = 9, XL = 40, XC = 90, CD = 400, and CM = 900.

It should be noted that although other prefix combinations could theoretically be possible (such as IC to equal 99), these are not normally used and therefore can be ignored. A function to return the Roman numeral representation of a number is given in Listing 2.3.1.

Listing 2.3.1 **Returning the Roman Numeral Representation of a Number**

```
<?php
// A function to return the Roman Numeral, given an integer
function romanize($num) {
    // Make sure that we only use the integer portion of the value

    $n = intval($num);
    $result = '';

    // Declare a lookup array that we will use to traverse the number:
    $lookup = array('M' => 1000, 'CM' => 900, 'D' => 500, 'CD' => 400,
                    'C' => 100, 'XC' => 90, 'L' => 50, 'XL' => 40,
                    'X' => 10, 'IX' => 9, 'V' => 5, 'IV' => 4, 'I' => 1);
```

Listing 2.3.1 **Continued**

```php
    // Now, let's work our way through the values, building the string
    //  as we go:  At each step, divide out the maximum matches at this
    //  level, echo out that many characters and then drop the number
    //  down to the remainder and repeat:
    foreach ($lookup as $roman => $value) {
        // Determine the number of matches:
        $matches = intval($n / $value);

        // Store that many characters:
        $result .= str_repeat($roman, $matches);

        // Substract that from the number
        $n = $n % $value;
    }

    // The Roman numeral should be built, return it
    return $result;
}

// Convert various numbers to Roman Numerals and echo them. Should display:
// 2005 = MMV
// 1999 = MCMXCIX
// 42 = XLII
echo '<pre>';
echo "\n 2005 = ", romanize(2005);
echo "\n 1999 = ", romanize(1999);
echo "\n 42 = ", romanize(42);
echo '</pre>';
?>
```

We could have used a brute force technique to accomplish this, handling each case one at a time; however, a more elegant solution presents itself. Instead an array is created and filled with all the possible legal combinations in order. Starting with the highest value possible, and working our way down, we see how many times that value will go evenly into the number.

We then insert the value that many times. Next we subtract the value just created from the number and loop again. Of course, some cases such as "IV" should only appear once, but by the virtue of this algorithm, that is the case. If, for example, a number ended in 8, it would first be divided by 5, producing "V", and then reduced to 3, which would produce "III", creating the correct notation. The special cases will never get the chance to be printed multiple times.

2.4 Calculating Interest

A common mathematical problem is calculating the interest on a loan, credit card, or a savings/checking account. Though the basic formula is straightforward, there are many slight variations making it difficult to keep straight. This is where the computer comes to the rescue. So let's look into a few different types of interest.

Listing 2.4.1 implements the most basic interest calculation: Simple interest. This is the type of interest used in most consumer loans, such as car or home loans. It follows a simple formula:

Interest = Principal Balance × Annual Rate of Interest × Years

Listing 2.4.1 **Simple Interest**

```php
<?php
// Calculating Simple Interest:
function calc_simple_interest($principal, $annualrate, $years) {
    return $principal * $annualrate * $years;
}

// Calculate the interest on a 6 year car loan for $22,000,
// with 5.39% interest.  Answer: 7114.8
echo calc_simple_interest(22000, .0539, 6), '<br />';

// Calculate the interest on a 6 month for $1000, at 8.5% interest.
// Answer: 42.5
echo calc_simple_interest(1000, .085, .5);
?>
```

Compound interest is more complicated. In simple interest, as the preceding formula shows, you are calculating the interest once at the start of the loan. Compound interest gets recalculated at regular intervals, and therefore each time it is calculated, it includes the interest that was applied from the last calculation.

This is how credit cards work against the consumer, as well as how money market accounts work for the consumer. It also can vary by the number of times per year that this recalculation is done. Interest can be compounded annually, quarterly, monthly, or even daily. This can be calculated via the use of repeated applications of the simple interest calculator, though there is a formula to calculate it all at once:

Value = $A \times (1 + (R / F))^{(F \times Y)}$

Where A is the original amount, R is the annual percentage rate, F is the number of times a year that you are compounding the interest, and Y is the number of years that you are calculating this for. Listing 2.4.2 implements a compound interest calculator.

Listing 2.4.2   **Compound Interest**

```php
<?php
// Calculating Compound Interest:
// a = the initial amount you are calculating from
// r = the annual percentage rate
// f = the frequency (per year) of compounding
// y = the number of years you wish to calculate this for:
function calc_compound_interest($a, $r, $f, $y) {
    return $a * pow((1 + ($r / $f)), ($f * $y));
}

// Calculate the value of $5000, at 3.25% interest,
//   compounded daily, for 3 years.   Answer: 5512.0332828079
echo calc_compound_interest(5000, .0325, 365, 3), '<br />';

// Calculate the value of $1000, at 8.5% interest,
//   compounded monthly, for 6 months.   Answer: 1043.2597499629
echo calc_compound_interest(1000, .085, 12, .5);
?>
```

Now let's take this one step further. Perhaps you don't want to know the final value. Instead you want to know a monthly breakout. Let's use a credit card statement as an example. You may want to know, if you are making a set payment each month, how long it will take to pay off the current value. This is easily doable by going back to our original example and using that function repeatedly, as shown in Listing 2.4.3.

Listing 2.4.3   **Calculating a Monthly Payment Schedule**

```php
<?php
// Let's calculate and output a table of values showing a monthly balance
//   of a credit card assuming we start with a $5000 debt, have a 9.2% rate,
//   it is compounded monthly, and we make $200 payments a month
$value = 5000;
$rate = .092;
$payment = 200;

// Begin our output:
echo "<style>td { border: 1px solid black; }</style>
<table><tr><th>Month</th><th>Initial Value</th><th>Interest</th>
<th>Payment</th><th>End of Month Balance</th>
<th>Cumulative Payments Made</th></tr>\n";
// Until the value is 0 or less, loop:
$month = 1;
$cumulative = 0;
while ($value > 0) {
```

Listing 2.4.3   **Continued**

```php
    // Calculate the interest that would be applied this month:
    $interest = calc_simple_interest($value, $rate, 1/12);

    // Calculate the new principal
    $newvalue = $value + $interest;

    // Determine if the payment would be too much, and adjust accordingly:
    $payment = ($payment > $newvalue) ? $newvalue : $payment;

    // Add up the cumulative payments made:
    $cumulative += $payment;

    // Now determine the final value:
    $finalvalue = $newvalue - $payment;

    // Echo out the values:
    echo '<tr><td>', $month++, "</td><td>{$value}</td><td>{$interest}</td>
<td>{$payment}</td><td>{$finalvalue}</td><td>{$cumulative}</td></tr>\n";

    // Now reset the value to this month's end, and repeat:
    $value = $finalvalue;
}

// Finish up our display, and exit ... This will end up displaying a table
//  showing that it will take 28 months to pay this debt off, and that you
//  will end up paying $5572.15 in total.
echo '</table>';
?>
```

There is one other variation on compound interest—a concept called *compounded continuously*. The basic concept is just an extension of regular compound interest. The more frequently you compound interest, the higher it gets. Some companies might choose to compound daily, or perhaps even every hour, every minute, or every second. Compounding continuously is the extreme end of this, using higher math to calculate what the interest would be if the compounding frequency was infinity.

The side effect of this, is that the formula ends up becoming simpler, in essence coming down to this:

Value = $A \times e^{(R \times Y)}$

Where *A* is the original amount, *R* is the annual interest rate, *Y* is the number of years you want to calculate, and *e* is the exponential number (approximately 2.71828). This formula is implemented in Listing 2.4.4.

Listing 2.4.4 **Continuously Compounded Interest Calculator**

```php
<?php
// Calculating Continuous Compound Interest:
// a = the initial amount you are calculating from
// r = the annual percentage rate
// y = the number of years you wish to calculate this for:
function calc_continuous_compound_interest($a, $r, $y) {
    return $a * pow(M_E, $r * $y);
}

// Calculate the value of $5000, at 3.25% interest, compounded daily,
//   for 3 years.   Answer: 5512.0572078166
echo calc_continuous_compound_interest(5000, .0325, 3), '<br />';

// Calculate the value of $1000, at 8.5% interest, compounded monthly,
//   for 6 months.   Answer: 1043.4160563737
echo calc_continuous_compound_interest(1000, .085, .5);
?>
```

Finally, there is one other interest-related calculation that we should look at. This is the calculation for how much interest you will receive back if a loan is paid off early. One would assume that as you are making each payment on a car loan or mortgage, that each payment has an equal amount of principal balance and interest. For most lenders, this is not the case.

Lenders decided that they want you to be paying off more of the interest in the beginning of the loan and more principal near the end of the loan. This way, if you pay off your loan early, you get back less money. Also it encourages borrowers to stay with the same loan and not refinance because that will reset their payment schedules.

The formula used is known sometimes as the Rule of 78, and it works like this: For as many months as you will be making payments, add up the numbers of the months. So for a 12-month loan, you get: 1+2+3+4+5+6+7+8+9+10+11+12 = 78 (hence the name of the rule). Now, for each month that you make a payment, you use those numbers in reverse as a fraction. So your first payment, you pay 12/78 of the interest, the next payment includes 11/78, and so on. The rest of your payment is the principal. Listing 2.4.5 creates a function that generates a table of these for a simple compounded mortgage.

Listing 2.4.5 **Generating a Payment Schedule Using the "Rule of 78"**

```php
<?php
// A function to make a table of payments using the Rule of 78 for interest
// a = the initial amount you are calculating from
// r = the annual percentage rate
// y = the number of years of the loan
function create_payment_table($a, $r, $y) {
```

Listing 2.4.5 **Continued**

```
    // First of all calculate the total interest & total Payment
    $interest = calc_simple_interest($a, $r, $y);
    $payment = $a + $interest;

    // Also calculate what the monthly payment will be:
    $monthly = $payment / ($y * 12);

    // Echo these out:
    echo "
Total Payment = {$payment}<br />
Total Interest = {$interest}<br />
Monthly Payments = {$monthly}<br />
";

    // Now calculate what the rule of 78 number will be:
    $rule78 = array_sum(range(1, ($y * 12)));

    // Begin our output:
    echo '<style>td { border: 1px solid black; }</style>';
    echo "<style>td { border: 1px solid black; }</style>
<table><tr><th>Month</th><th>Interest</th><th>Principal</th>
<th>Equity</th></tr>\n";

    // Now loop through all months, backwards
    $equity = 0;
    for ($m = ($y * 12); $m > 0; $m--) {
        // Calculate the actual month number:
        $num = abs($m - ($y * 12) - 1);

        // Calculate the interest, principal & equity:
        $int = $interest * ($m/$rule78);
        $prin = $monthly - $int;
        $equity += $prin;

        // Now echo all that out
        echo "<tr><td>{$num}</td><td>{$int}</td><td>{$prin}</td>
<td>{$equity}</td></tr>\n";
    }

    // Close off our table and exit
    echo '</table>';
}

// Now make the table for a $250,000, 15 year mortgage at 5.5% interest
// Will begin with:
// Total Payment = 456250
```

Listing 2.4.5 **Continued**

```
// Total Interest = 206250
// Monthly Payments = 2534.7222222222
// Month      Interest         Principal        Equity
// 1          2279.0055248619  255.71669736034  255.71669736034
// 2          2266.3443830571  268.37783916513  524.09453652548
create_payment_table(250000, .055, 15);
?>
```

There are a few interesting things to point out about this code. To calculate the Rule of 78 number, instead of creating a `for` loop to add up all the numbers, we used `range()` to create an array with all the numbers in it. Then `array_sum()` nicely gives us the total that we were looking for.

The other interesting use of math is in the `for` loop. We need to count in both directions at the same time. We need to count down from the maximum number, to calculate the interest, but we also want to count up, to give the months their numbers from 1 to maximum. You could have the loop count down, as it currently does, but then keep a counter that also goes upward. But instead we use math to our advantage. If we take the current number in reverse order, subtract from it the maximum minus one more, and then take the absolute value of that, we have the number we originally wanted.

So if we have a 15-year loan, and therefore the numbers start at 180, if the number is 179, you subtract 180 getting -1, subtract one more, getting -2, and then remove the negative, letting you know that you are on month 2.

2.5 Simulating Dice

Random number generation is a useful tool that programmers find themselves using regularly. One potential use is to simulate the rolling of dice. The function shown in Listing 2.5.1 allows you to simulate rolling any number of dice with any number of sides.

Listing 2.5.1 **Dice Rolling Simulator**

```
<?php
// Dice Simulator
function roll_dice($number, $sides, $values = false) {
    // Loop as much as needed filling an array with the random die rolls.
    $dice = array();
    for ($i = 0; $i < $number; $i++) {
        $dice[] = rand(1, $sides);
    }

    // If the optional 3rd parameter is set to true, return the dice array:
    if ($values) {
```

Listing 2.5.1   **Continued**

```
        return $dice;
    } else {
        // Otherwise, return the sum of the dice:
        return array_sum($dice);
    }
}

// Roll 3 six sided dice and echo their result (between 3 & 18)
$roll_3d6 = roll_dice(3, 6);
echo "<pre>Dice roll = {$roll_3d6}\n";

// Roll a 100 sided die, 10 times, and echo all the values:
$rm_stats = roll_dice(10, 100, true);
print_r($rm_stats);
echo '</pre>';
?>
```

This function has two purposes. If you call it just passing it two parameters—the number of times to roll the die and how many sides it has—it will roll them all, add up a total, and just return that total. However, if you provide an optional third parameter of "true", instead after rolling the dice it returns an array full of values.

A more versatile function is created this way; however, at a slight performance hit if all you ever want to do is get the sum of the dice. In that case, the creation of the array is not needed because the sum could just be added as the loop progresses.

2.6 Latitude/Longitude Calculations

Due to the recent popularity of consumer GPS systems, it is likely that you will need to deal with latitude and longitude at some point. Latitude and longitude are a coordinate system for the entire Earth. Latitude refers to your position north or south of the equator. Longitude is your position east or west of the Prime Meridian, the line of longitude that passes through Greenwich, England. Any math used in calculations therefore has to be based on spherical geometry.

Of course, some amount of error is inevitable because the Earth is not a perfect sphere. However, the basic formulas are accurate enough. More complicated formulas exist that take the slightly "squashed" shape of the Earth into account.

It should also be noted that for most calculations involving Lat/Lon there are two different versions. The first is *great circle calculations*. These involve finding the shortest route between two points, which due to the spherical nature of the Earth, is actually an arc across its surface. The other is known as *rhumb lines*. These are paths that end up being slightly longer; however, they follow a constant bearing, making them much easier to navigate.

The functions shown in Listing 2.6.1 create a library to make handling these calculations much easier. Unless noted otherwise in the code, all these calculations assume that you are passing in a decimal degree version of the Lat/Lon, that north and east are positive numbers, and that south and west are negative. So, for example, if you were dealing with the coordinates in the standard format that most GPSs display them, such as 39° 25.773 N, 077° 06.272 W., the functions would expect to see them as 39.42955 and -77.10453.

Listing 2.6.1 **Longitude/Latitude Library**

```php
<?php
// A Library of Latitude/Longitude functions for various calculations:


// A number of functions need to know the mean radius of the Earth for its
//  calculations. You need to set this constant to that value, in whatever
//  unit you wish the calculations to be carried out in.  For reference, it
//  is 6371m; however we will use its value in miles.
define('EARTH_R', 3956.09);


// Function: _deg2rad_multi
// Desc: A quick helper function.  Many of these functions have to convert
//   a value from degrees to radians in order to perform math on them.
function _deg2rad_multi() {
    // Grab all the arguments as an array & apply deg2rad to each element
    $arguments = func_get_args();
    return array_map('deg2rad', $arguments);
}


// Function: latlon_convert
// Function: latlon_convert
// Desc:  This is a conversion function to help transform more standard
//   notation coordinates into the form needed by these functions.  This
//   allows entry as separate Degree, Minute and Second.  It also accepts
//   a 'N', 'S', 'E', or 'W'  All parameters (except for degree) are
//   optional and can be floats.
//   You might enter 77 34 45.5, or 75 54.45644
function latlon_convert($degrees, $minutes = 0, $seconds = 0, $dir = '') {
    // Prepare the final value and keep adding to it:
    $final = $degrees;

    // Add in the minutes & seconds, properly converted to decimal values:
    // Uses the fact that there are 60 minutes in a degree,
    //   and 3600 seconds in a degree.
    $final += $minutes / 60.0;
    $final += $seconds / 3600.0;
```

Listing 2.6.1 **Continued**

```
    // If the direction is West or South, make sure this is negative
    //  in case someone forgot and put a -degree and said South:
    if (($dir == 'W') || ($dir == 'S')) {
        $final = abs($final) * -1.0;
    }

    return $final;
}


// Function: latlon_distance_great_circle
// Desc:  Calculate the shortest distance between two pairs of coordinates.
//   This calculates a great arc around the Earth, assuming that the Earth
//   is a sphere.  There is some error in this, as the earth is not
//   perfectly a sphere, but it is fairly accurate.
function latlon_distance_great_circle($lat_a, $lon_a, $lat_b, $lon_b) {
    // Convert our degrees to radians:
    list($lat1, $lon1, $lat2, $lon2) =
        _deg2rad_multi($lat_a, $lon_a, $lat_b, $lon_b);

    // Perform the formula and return the value
    return acos(
            ( sin($lat1) * sin($lat2) ) +
            ( cos($lat1) * cos($lat2) * cos($lon2 - $lon1) )
            ) * EARTH_R;
}


// Function: latlon_bearing_great_circle
// Desc:  This function calculates the initial bearing you need to travel
//   from Point A to Point B, along a great arc.  Repeated calls to this
//   could calculate the bearing at each step of the way.
function latlon_bearing_great_circle($lat_a, $lon_a, $lat_b, $lon_b) {
    // Convert our degrees to radians:
    list($lat1, $lon1, $lat2, $lon2) =
        _deg2rad_multi($lat_a, $lon_a, $lat_b, $lon_b);

    // Run the formula and store the answer (in radians)
    $rads = atan2(
            sin($lon2 - $lon1) * cos($lat2),
            (cos($lat1) * sin($lat2)) -
                (sin($lat1) * cos($lat2) * cos($lon2 - $lon1)) );

    // Convert this back to degrees to use with a compass
    $degrees = rad2deg($rads);
```

Listing 2.6.1 **Continued**

```
    // If negative subtract it from 360 to get the bearing we are used to.
    $degrees = ($degrees < 0) ? 360 + $degrees : $degrees;

    return $degrees;
}


// Function: latlon_distance_rhumb
// Desc:  Calculates the distance between two points along a Rhumb line.
//   Rhumb lines are a line between two points that uses a constant
//   bearing.  They are slightly longer than a great circle path; however,
//   much easier to navigate.
function latlon_distance_rhumb($lat_a, $lon_a, $lat_b, $lon_b) {
    // Convert our degrees to radians:
    list($lat1, $lon1, $lat2, $lon2) =
        _deg2rad_multi($lat_a, $lon_a, $lat_b, $lon_b);

    // First of all if this a true East/West line there is a special case:
    if ($lat1 == $lat2) {
        $mid = cos($lat1);
    } else {
        $delta = log( tan(($lat2 / 2) + (M_PI / 4))
            / tan(($lat1 / 2) + (M_PI / 4)) );
        $mid = ($lat2 - $lat1) / $delta;
    }

    // Calculate difference in longitudes, and if over 180, go the other
    //   direction around the Earth as it will be a shorter distance:
    $dlon = abs($lon2 - $lon1);
    $dlon = ($dlon > M_PI) ? (2 * M_PI - $dlon) : $dlon;
    $distance = sqrt( pow($lat2 - $lat1,2) +
                      (pow($mid, 2) * pow($dlon, 2)) ) * EARTH_R;

    return $distance;
}


// Function: latlon_bearing_rhumb
// Desc:  Calculates the bearing for the Rhumb line between two points.
function latlon_bearing_rhumb($lat_a, $lon_a, $lat_b, $lon_b) {
    // Convert our degrees to radians:
    list($lat1, $lon1, $lat2, $lon2) =
        _deg2rad_multi($lat_a, $lon_a, $lat_b, $lon_b);

    // Perform the math & store the values in radians.
    $delta = log( tan(($lat2 / 2) + (M_PI / 4))
```

Listing 2.6.1 **Continued**

```
                / tan(($lat1 / 2) + (M_PI / 4)) );
   $rads = atan2( ($lon2 - $lon1), $delta);

   // Convert this back to degrees to use with a compass
   $degrees = rad2deg($rads);

   // If negative subtract it from 360 to get the bearing we are used to.
   $degrees = ($degrees < 0) ? 360 + $degrees : $degrees;

   return $degrees;
}


// Prepare for output
echo '<pre>';

// Use the conversion function to make two values decimal degree format.
$home_lat = latlon_convert(30, 25.773, 0, 'N');
$home_lon = latlon_convert(77, 06.272, 0, 'W');

// Echo them out, they should be:  Lat = 30.42955, Lon = -77.104533333333
echo "Converted Coordinates:  Lat = {$home_lat}, Lon = {$home_lon}\n\n";

// Prepare another set of coordinates.
$z_lat = 37.318776;
$z_lon = -122.008452;

// Calculate the great arc distance between these: 2540.3642964141 miles
$distance = latlon_distance_great_circle(
               $home_lat, $home_lon, $z_lat, $z_lon);
echo "Great Circle distance between 'home' and 'z': {$distance} miles\n\n";

// Calculate the initial bearing for the great arc: 292.92619009409 degrees
$bearing = latlon_bearing_great_circle(
               $home_lat, $home_lon, $z_lat, $z_lon);
echo "Great Circle bearing from 'home' to 'z': {$bearing} degrees\n\n";

// Calculate the distance if following a Rhumb line: 2561.6194141687 miles
$rdistance = latlon_distance_rhumb($home_lat, $home_lon, $z_lat, $z_lon);
echo "Rhumb Line distance between 'home' and 'z': {$rdistance} miles\n\n";

// Now calculate the bearing for this Rhumb line: 280.48113814226 degrees
$rbearing = latlon_bearing_rhumb($home_lat, $home_lon, $z_lat, $z_lon);
echo "Rhumb Line bearing from 'home' to 'z': {$rbearing} degrees\n\n";
?>
```

Although the formulas are complex enough that a full discussion of them would take too much room; one thing should be pointed out. All math functions in PHP that deal with angles (`sin()`, `cos()`, `tan()`, and so on) expect radians instead of degrees. Therefore if you want to deal in degrees, you need to convert to radians, make your math function calls, and then convert them back to degrees in the end.

> **Note**
>
> Not only does the PHP math library provide many functions, it also provides a basic set of mathematical constants. In the previous example, the constant `M_PI` is used. A complete listing of these constants can be found in the overview of the PHP math library at http://php.net/math.

2.7 Metric/English Conversion

For people living in the United States, or those who have to deal with the United States, handling different units of measure is a regular problem.

At the same time, it is useful to be able to convert between any two units of measure, Metric to Metric, English to English, Metric to English. One set of functions can be made generic enough to handle any of these situations. The basic concept behind this is to always do two conversions. You see, it would be time consuming to make a conversion table with the factor needed to convert any unit to every other possible unit.

However, it isn't nearly as difficult to simply record the factor needed to convert any unit at all to a certain base unit. Then, with two steps, you can convert any value to any other. First convert the original value into the base unit by multiplying by the conversion factor. Then, reversing the process, divide the value by the conversion factor of the desired result. You have now converted between the two units. This algorithm is implemented in Listing 2.7.1.

Listing 2.7.1 **Measurement Unit Conversion**

```php
<?php
// A Library to provide the conversion between different units of measure

// Declare an array of metric prefixes.  Each value is the power of 10
// each prefix stands for over the base unit.
$metric_prefixes = array( 'Y' => 24, 'Z' => 21, 'E' => 18, 'P' => 15,
    'T' => 12, 'G' => 9, 'M' => 6, 'k' => 3, 'h' => 2, 'da' => 1, '' => 0,
    'd' => -1, 'c' => -2, 'm' => -3, 'µ' => -6, 'n' => -9, 'p' => -12,
    'f' => -15, 'a' => -18, 'z' => -21, 'y' => -24 );

// Table with conversion factors for other length units in relation to 'm'
$length_equiv = array( 'pc' => 3.085678E+16, 'ly' => 9.46073E+15,
```

Listing 2.7.1   **Continued**

```php
    'AU' => 1.495979E+11, 'mi' => 1609.344, 'ch' => 20.11684,
    'rd' => 5.029210, 'yd' => .9144, 'ft' => .3048, 'in' => .0254 );

// A table with conversion factors for units of mass in relation to 'g'
$mass_equiv = array( 'ton' => 907184.7, 'lb' => .00045359237,
    'oz' => 20.834952, 'gr' => .06479891 );

// A table with conversion factors for volume, in relation to 'L'
$volume_equiv = array( 'bu' => 35.23907, 'pk' => 8.809768,
    'gal' => 3.785412, 'qt' => .9463529, 'pt' => .4731765,
    'cup' => .2365882, 'oz' => .02957353, 'tbsp' => .01478676,
    'tsp' => .004928922 );

// Base Units for these lookups
$base_units = array( 'length' => 'm', 'mass' => 'g', 'volume' => 'L' );

// The following function is an internal function to convert_any()
//   It does the heart of the work, determining from the unit passed in what
//   conversion factor it will take to convert that unit to the base unit.
function _determine_factor($unit, $type) {
    global $metric_prefixes, $length_equiv;
    global $mass_equiv, $volume_equiv, $base_units;

    // Determine details about the base unit
    //  - including the length (as a negative)
    $base = $base_units[$type];
    $l = -1 * strlen($base);

    // If we find the unit in the specific unit reference table:
    if (isset(${"{$type}_equiv"}[$unit])) {
        // Simply read the factor from there
        $factor = ${"{$type}_equiv"}[$unit];
    // Else if we can determine this to be Metric and recognize the prefix
    } elseif (((substr($unit, $l)) == $base)
            && (isset($metric_prefixes[substr($unit, 0, $l)]))) {
        // Calculate the full factor from the power of 10
        $factor = pow(10, $metric_prefixes[substr($unit, 0, $l)]);
    } else {
        // Otherwise we did not understand the unit, and return false.
        $factor = false;
    }

    return $factor;
}
```

Listing 2.7.1 **Continued**

```php
// Convert_any is a function that will handle conversions of any possible
//  value it needs given the value to convert, the units to convert from,
//  and to.  Also a type string of either 'length', 'mass', or 'volume'.
function convert_any($value, $from, $to, $type) {
    // Determine the conversation factors for the two units provided.
    $from_factor = _determine_factor($from, $type);
    $to_factor = _determine_factor($to, $type);

    // If either result is false, one unit is undecipherable, return false
    if (($from_factor === false) || ($to_factor === false)) {
        return false;
    } else {
        // Otherwise, divide the from factor by the to factor to get the
        //  conversion ratio for this specific case.  Multiply that by the
        //  base value, and return
        return $value * ($from_factor / $to_factor);
    }
}

// The following three functions are just for convenience.  It is nicer
// to have separate functions, instead of passing a configuration variable.
function convert_length($value, $from, $to) {
    return convert_any($value, $from, $to, 'length');
}

function convert_mass($value, $from, $to) {
    return convert_any($value, $from, $to, 'mass');
}

function convert_volume($value, $from, $to) {
    return convert_any($value, $from, $to, 'volume');
}

// Perform a few conversions:
echo "<pre>\n";

// Convert 42 inches, into meters: 42 in = 1.0668 m
echo '42 in = ', convert_length(42, 'in', 'm'), " m\n";

// Convert 1.5 Gigagrams, into Tons: 1.5 Gg = 1653.467039292 tons
echo '1.5 Gg = ', convert_mass(1.5, 'Gg', 'ton'), " tons\n";

// Convert 723 nanoliters, into milliliters: 723 nL = 0.000723 mL
echo '723 nL = ', convert_volume(723, 'nL', 'mL'), " mL\n";

echo '</pre>';
?>
```

Notice that although we directly store the conversion factors for each English unit, we only store the powers for the metric prefixes. We could have stored the full value; however, there was no need, and 9 can be more legible than 1000000000, or even 1E9.

One programming trick was used in the creation of this library, which is known as *variable variables*. This is a method by which you use the value of a variable to be seen as the name of another variable. In this case, we have a parameter passed into the conversion function as a string, such as `'length'`. Instead of having an `if` statement to decide what array to look in for the conversion factors based on this string, we simply use the string as part of the name. We conveniently named our array `$length_equiv`; therefore, having a variable called `$type` holding the string `'length'` for us, we can access this array via `${"{$type}_equiv"}`. PHP expands the string and then references a variable by that name. For situations where arrays are not involved or there are not other ambiguities, you may use the shortcut syntax `$$variablename` to also create variable variables.

2.8 Temperature Conversion

Another difference between the United States and most of the world is the reliance on the Fahrenheit temperature scale. Celsius is the most common scale in use elsewhere, and Kelvin and Rankine are used primarily for scientific purposes.

A similar method to Listing 2.7.1 can be used to solve this conversion issue—with one difference. The conversion between these values requires a formula, not just a conversion factor. (This is caused by the fact that the differences include different definitions of zero, whereas in linear measurements, a zero of any unit is always equal to any other zero.)

Therefore in this case, instead of just storing conversion factors, we actually store entire functions. Beyond that, we use the same logic, converting everything to one base (in this case, Kelvin), and then from Kelvin, to the desired result.

As an example, Listing 2.8.1 uses this to create a visual reference table in our web browser between Celsius and Fahrenheit.

Listing 2.8.1   **Temperature Conversion**

```php
<?php
// An array of conversion functions to convert any unit to Kelvin
$to_K = array(
    'K' => create_function('$x', 'return $x;'),
    'C' => create_function('$x', 'return $x + 273.15;'),
    'F' => create_function('$x', 'return ($x + 459.67) / 1.8;'),
    'R' => create_function('$x', 'return $x / 1.8;') );

// And an array of conversion functions to convert Kelvin, to any unit
$from_K = array(
    'K' => create_function('$x', 'return $x;'),
```

Listing 2.8.1 **Continued**

```php
    'C' => create_function('$x', 'return $x - 273.15;'),
    'F' => create_function('$x', 'return ($x * 1.8) - 459.67;'),
    'R' => create_function('$x', 'return $x * 1.8;') );

// The conversion function.  Pass it the value, the unit to convert from
// and the unit to convert to.
function convert_temp($value, $from, $to) {
    global $to_K, $from_K;

    // First check that we can understand the units passed to us else bail.
    if (!(isset($to_K[$from]) && isset($from_K[$to]))) {
        return false;
    } else {
        // Since we found the units all we need to do now is to convert the
        //  value to Kelvin using the provided function, then convert it
        //  again to the desired unit.  Two function calls and we are done.
        return $from_K[$to]($to_K[$from]($value));
    }
}

// Output a Celsius <-> Fahrenheit comparison table with formatting:
?>
<style>
td, th { text-align: center; font-size: 20px; }
.extreme { border: 2px solid red; }
.hot { border: 2px solid orange; }
.comfort { border: 2px solid green; }
.cold { border: 2px solid blue; }
.freeze { border: 2px solid navy; }
</style>
<table>
 <tr><th>C</th><th>F</th></tr>
<?php
// Loop from 50 C down to -10 C, by 5's
foreach (range(50, -10, 5) as $c) {
    // Convert the temp
    $f = convert_temp($c, 'C', 'F');

    // Based upon known Farhenheit values, determine the range of heat:
    if ($f > 100) { $heat = 'extreme'; }
    elseif ($f > 80) { $heat = 'hot'; }
    elseif ($f > 55) { $heat = 'comfort'; }
    elseif ($f > 32) { $heat = 'cold'; }
    else { $heat = 'freeze'; }
```

Listing 2.8.1 **Continued**

```
    // Echo out the row of information, including formatting
    echo "<tr><td class=\"{$heat}\">{$c}</td>
<td class=\"{$heat}\">{$f}</td></tr>";
}
?>
</table>
```

The function `create_function()` is at the heart of this example. It allows for a function to be created dynamically and stored in a variable (often called a *lambda function*). The function can then be called by referencing the variable.

This capability of PHP can be useful in situations where you need to call a different function based on different input.

2.9 Statistics Package Creation

PHP's math functions (and array functions) are missing a significant set of statistics-based functionality. The common tasks of calculating mean, mode, median, and range of a set of numbers have been left to programmers to do.

Although most of these are trivial to perform, it is useful to have these features in a library that can be reused regularly. Some formulas also have slight variations on them that can be missed when quickly implemented.

Range is the simplest of the calculations, consisting of the difference between the largest and the smallest value in the set. *Mean* (commonly called *average*) is the sum of all the values, divided by the number of values. The *median* of a set of numbers is the one that appears in the middle when they are sorted. However, this is only the case if the number of values is odd. If even, there is no exact middle; therefore, the median is defined as the mean (average) of the two middle values.

Finally we have *mode*. Mode is the value that appears the most times within a set. There can be more than one mode if certain numbers appear the same number of times. Because of this, the implementation in Listing 2.9.1 always returns an array of values, to allow for 1, 2, or any number of modes. Also, if the set of values contains only single entries, where no value is ever duplicated, there is no mode of the set. Listing 2.9.1 implements a library of these basic functions.

Listing 2.9.1 **Statistics Library**

```
<?php
// Various statistical functions that operate on arrays.

// The range of a list, is the maximum value minus the lowest value.
function array_range($values) {
    // Use PHP builtin functions max, and min, to make this easy.
```

Listing 2.9.1 **Continued**

```php
    return max($values) - min($values);
}

// The mean is the average of all values in the list
function array_mean($values) {
    // Simply sum all the values, and divide it by the number of values.
    return array_sum($values) / count($values);
}

// The median is the value in the middle of the list.  Or the average
// of the two middle values if there is an even number of values.
function array_median($values) {
    // First sort the array
    sort($values);

    // Now, if even, average the middle two values
    $length = count($values);
    if ($length % 2) {
        // It's odd, just return the middle value
        return $values[$length / 2];
    } else {
        // Else even, divide by 2 for the upper middle number and
        // then subtract 1 to get the lower middle.
        return ($values[$length / 2] + $values[($length / 2) - 1]) / 2;
    }
}

// The mode is the value (or values) that occur the most times.
// A value must occur more than once to be a mode, else there is none.
function array_mode($values) {
    // Array count values will return us an array with only unique values
    // and a count of how many times each occurred.
    $unique_count = array_count_values($values);

    // Now sort these, keeping keys intact, in descending order
    arsort($unique_count);

    // Now loop down through these keys and count values:
    $mode = array();
    $stored_count = 0;
    foreach ($unique_count as $value => $count) {
        // First of all, if the count is 1, then exit, we are done
        if ($count == 1) { break; }

        // Now if we don't have a mode yet, or this one is equal to the
        // stored modes, then keep this one.
```

Listing 2.9.1   **Continued**

```php
            if ( (count($mode) == 0) || ($count == $stored_count) ) {
                $mode[] = $value;
                $stored_count = $count;
            } else {
                // Otherwise we have found a lesser count meaning we are done.
                break;
            }
    }

    // Return the mode, this might be an empty array if there was none.
    return $mode;
}

// Declare a set of numbers, and run the various procedures on them:
$set = array(1, 4, 12, 4, 6, 4, 7, 8, 1, 3, 1, 7, 0, 15);

// Output the values:
echo '<pre>';
echo 'The mean is: ', array_mean($set), "\n";
echo 'The range is: ', array_range($set), "\n";
echo 'The median is: ', array_median($set), "\n";
echo "The mode is: \n";
print_r(array_mode($set));
echo '</pre>';
?>
```

3

Time and Date

APPLICATIONS THAT DEAL WITH TIME ARE forever present, especially in web-based applications: times of form submittals, user input such as date of birth, and the updating and removal of pages when out of date are just a few examples. Though potentially complicated, the date extensions in PHP are relatively simple and straightforward.

This chapter deals mainly with the core date and time functions. These functions provide all the basics for time manipulation: retrieving, formatting, and converting. One other extension, the Calendar functions, is devoted to conversion between different calendar systems, such as converting dates between the Gregorian and Jewish calendars. See the functions `cal_to_jd()` and `cal_from_jd()` in the "Quick Hits" section.

A subject beyond the scope of this chapter is that of schedule or calendar management, such as meeting and event scheduling. An extension is available, called MCAL, which does provide such functionality. For more information, see http://php.net/mcal.

To fully utilize the time functionality of PHP, you must understand how PHP measures time. For PHP, time is measured as the number of seconds since January 1, 1970, the *UNIX epoch*. Hence any moment in time is stored as a simple integer. Time, when stored this way, is often referred to as a *time stamp*. As you will see, many functions either return a time stamp or use a time stamp as a parameter. You must be careful however, when reading documentation or code comments. Depending on context, the term *time stamp* can also be used in its more generic sense: a time at which something occurs. For example, when referring to web server log files, the time at which an event is logged is referred to as a time stamp.

Quick Hits

▶ **Get the time stamp for the current time:**

```
$timestamp = time();
```

Taking no parameters, this function returns the time stamp of the current time—that is, when `time()` is called.

Full documentation: http://php.net/time

▶ Get the current time stamp to the microsecond resolution:

```
$result = microtime($format);
```

Returns the UNIX time stamp but resolved to microseconds in accuracy. If $format is false, the default, the time is returned as the string "seconds microseconds" with the seconds portion the same as that returned by time(), and microseconds as a fraction of a second. If $format is true, the time is returned as a floating point number.

Full documentation: http://php.net/microtime

▶ Create a time stamp for a specified date and time:

```
$timestamp = mktime($hour, $minute, $second, $month, $day, $year);
```

Returns a time stamp that corresponds to the specified time and date.

Full documentation: http://php.net/mktime

▶ Format the specified time:

```
$string = date($format, $timestamp);
```

Returns a string representing the given time stamp based on the specified format. If $timestamp is not specified, the current time is used.

Full documentation: http://php.net/date

▶ Format a date and time, adjusting the result to be Greenwich Mean Time (GMT):

```
$string = gmdate($format, $timestamp);
```

This function is equivalent to date(). However, the time is adjusted to be relative to GMT representation of the given time.

Full documentation: http://php.net/gmdate

▶ Get various information about a specified time:

```
$time_array = getdate($timestamp);
```

Returns an array of various values based on the given time stamp. The keys to the array are seconds, minutes, hours, mday, wday, mon, year, yday, weekday, month.

Full documentation: http://php.net/getdate

▶ Get and set the time zone used by the time functions:

```
$string = date_default_timezone_get();
date_default_timezone_set($string);
```

This pair of functions gets or sets the timezone identifier.

Full documentation: http://php.net/date_default_timezone_set and http://php.net/date_default_timezone_get

▶ Parse any English string representation of time and produce a time stamp:

```
$timestamp = strtotime($english_time);
```

This function can take nearly any string containing a textual description of a date and time, in English, and produce the corresponding time stamp.

Full documentation: http://php.net/strtotime

▶ **Validate a date against the Gregorian calendar:**

```
$isvalid = checkdate($month, $day, $year);
```

Returns true if the specified date can be found on the Gregorian calendar. Useful to make sure that user input or calculated time is valid.

Full documentation: http://php.net/checkdate

▶ **Find sunrise and sunset times for a given position:**

```
$time_rise = date_sunrise($day_ts, SUNFUNCS_RET_TIMESTAMP, $latitude, $longitude);
$time_set  = date_sunset($day_ts, SUNFUNCS_RET_TIMESTAMP, $latitude, $longitude);
```

This pair of functions returns the time of sunrise and sunset at the specified location. The constant, SUNFUNCS_RET_TIMESTAMP, tells the function to return the time as a time stamp.

Full documentation: http://php.net/date_sunrise and http://php.net/date_sunset

▶ **Convert a date between different calendars and Julian Day Count:**

```
$jday_count = cal_to_jd($calendar, $month, $day, $year);
$date_array = cal_from_jd($jday_count, $calendar);
```

This pair of functions converts a date, in a specified calendar system, to and from a Julian Day Count. These are useful for converting dates from one calendar to another. The supported calendar systems are CAL_GREGORIAN, CAL_JULIAN, CAL_JEWISH, and CAL_FRENCH.

Full documentation: http://php.net/cal_to_jd and http://php.net/cal_from_jd

3.1 Calculating the Difference Between Two Dates

Finding the number of weeks, days, or even seconds between two dates is something that programs regularly need to do. Often a database will have powerful built-in procedures for comparing dates and doing date arithmetic. In PHP, though, you need to handle this yourself.

As discussed in the introduction, PHP deals with dates in UNIX epoch format. This means that all dates are stored as the number of seconds since midnight, January 1, 1970. This makes it easy if you just need to know the number of seconds that have passed between two points in time. All you need to do is subtract the two values. However, doing the more common "days between" type arithmetic takes some extra care.

While doing date math, you need to keep leap years, months with different numbers of days, months with a fifth week, years with a 53rd week, daylight savings time, and all other such variations in mind. Otherwise, you may find yourself with an algorithm that only works most of the time.

Let's begin with a look at the common problem of finding the number of days between two dates. In Listing 3.1.1, note that we will use the powerful function strtotime() to make the PHP date stamps for ourselves. This function takes many different forms of text representations of dates and converts them into a time stamp for you.

> **Note**
>
> Since PHP 5.1 you must make a call to date_default_timezone_set() to specify what time zone you want calculations to take place in before calling any date functions. Otherwise, STRICT mode errors are generated as it tries to guess the appropriate time zone. More information about time zones is presented in section 3.4, "Handling Time Zones," later in this chapter. If your code needs to run on both PHP 5.0 and PHP 5.1 systems, you will have a little bit of a problem because these functions don't exist in PHP 5.0. Therefore, you can use the function function_exists() to check whether date_default_timezone_set() exists, and if so, call it. Alternatively, the default time zone can be set in your PHP configuration file in the PHP 5.1 server and then you don't need to worry about it.

Listing 3.1.1   **Number of Days Between Two Dates**

```php
<?php
// Set the default timezone to US/Eastern
date_default_timezone_set('US/Eastern');

// Will return the number of days between the two dates passed in
function count_days($a, $b) {
    // First we need to break these dates into their constituent parts:
    $a_parts = getdate($a);
    $b_parts = getdate($b);

    // Now recreate these timestamps, based upon noon on each day
    // The specific time doesn't matter but it must be the same each day
    $a_new = mktime(12, 0, 0, $a_dt['mon'], $a_dt['mday'], $a_dt['year']);
    $b_new = mktime(12, 0, 0, $b_dt['mon'], $b_dt['mday'], $b_dt['year']);

    // Subtract these two numbers and divide by the number of seconds in a
    //  day.  Round the result since crossing over a daylight savings time
    //  barrier will cause this time to be off by an hour or two.
    return round(abs($a_new - $b_new) / 86400);
}

// Prepare a few dates
$date1 = strtotime('12/3/1973 8:13am');
$date2 = strtotime('1/15/1974 10:15pm');
$date3 = strtotime('2/14/2005 1:32pm');

// Calculate the differences, they should be 43 & 11353
echo "<p>There are ", count_days($date1, $date2), " days.</p>";
echo "<p>There are ", count_days($date2, $date3), " days.</p>";
?>
```

You might think that this would be a simple problem. Subtract the two numbers and divide by the number of seconds in a day. This is true and would work, if you were interested in a pure mathematical definition of a day. However, think about having two dates, such as November 11 at 11:00 p.m. and November 12 at 1:00 a.m. To the way we think about dates, there is one day between these dates. However, if you just divided as discussed previously, you would end up with only a two-hour difference.

The solution is to recalculate the dates you are given to a set time of day, say noon. Now we can subtract them, take the absolute value so that the order of dates does not matter, and divide by the number of seconds in a day. This is almost a perfect solution, except for daylight savings time. If the span of dates you are looking at happens to pass over a daylight savings boundary, the difference can be off by up to a few hours. Rounding the answer to the nearest whole number, thus removing any small error caused by daylight savings, easily solves this.

Similar tactics can be used to calculate the number of weeks, months, or years between any two dates as well. There are two different points of view toward these larger increments, though. For example, sometimes when people refer to the phrase "it happened one week ago" they mean seven days. In that case, it is easy to just use the `count_days()` function just created and divide the result by 7. However, other times, it just means during that previous week. In this case, you need to use a similar scheme as mentioned previously, where we bring all days to noon to calculate a week difference. You can recalculate all weeks to Sunday and then do the math. An example of this can be seen in section 3.6, "Determining Number of Business Days," later in this chapter.

3.2 Determining Last Day of a Given Month

It is often useful to determine what the last day of a given month is. Although a lookup table could tell you what the actual day is (although you would have to still calculate February based on leap years), it is often useful to have an actual time stamp for that day.

Fortunately, through the use of `mktime()` this is not difficult. This function accepts the following variables in order: hour, minute, second, month, day, and year. The powerful part is that `mktime()` automatically determines zero or negative numbers for you correctly.

Therefore, whereas entering a month of 3 (March) and a day of 1 returns a stamp for March 1, entering a day of 0 returns one day prior to that, therefore, the last day of February. Listing 3.2.1 demonstrates how to take advantage of `mktime()` in calculating last-day-of-month time stamps.

Listing 3.2.1 **Find Last-Day-of-Month Time Stamp**

```
<?php
// Set the default timezone to US/Eastern
date_default_timezone_set('US/Eastern');

// Will return a timestamp of the last day in a month for a specified year
function last_day($month, $year) {
```

Listing 3.2.1 **Continued**

```php
    // Use mktime to create a timestamp one month into the future, but one
    //  day less.  Also make the time for almost midnight, so it can be
    //  used as an 'end of month' boundary
    return mktime(23, 59, 59, $month + 1, 0, $year);
}

// Determine the last day for February, 2006
$stamp = last_day(2, 2006);

// Output the result, it will be: 28
echo '<p>The last day for February in 2006 is: ', date('d', $stamp) ,'</p>';
?>
```

3.3 Leap Year Calculation

A common task for which PHP does not have a built-in function is determining whether a certain year is a leap year. Although a simple formula determines this, many people forget parts of it. A year is only a leap year if it is divisible by 4, but not divisible by 100, unless it is divisible by 400. Listing 3.3.1 implements this functionality.

Listing 3.3.1 **Leap Year Determination**

```php
<?php
// Let's you know if a certain year is a leap year or not:
function is_leap_year($year) {
    // If the year is divisible by 4 but not by 100 unless by 400
    return ((($y % 4) == 0) && ((($y % 100) != 0) || (($y % 400) == 0)));
}

// Determine for a few years if they are leap years or not:
foreach (range(1999, 2009) as $year) {
    // Output the result:
    echo "<p>{$year} = ", is_leap_year($year) ? 'Leap Year' : 'not', '</p>';
}
?>
```

3.4 Handling Time Zones

Handling time zones can be cumbersome. Fortunately, PHP provides many different solutions. Many of these rely on PHP 5.1's feature of using `date_default_timezone_get()` to specify the time zone you want calculations to take place in. Let's explore a few of these different methods because they each have their best uses.

For all these examples, we will assume that your home time zone is U.S./Eastern (-5:00 from GMT) and that the different time zone you want to know about is Asia/Tokyo (+9:00 from GMT).

If you simply want to know how a certain time in one zone translates to another, use a combination of resetting the default time zone and mktime() to generate the time in another time zone; then print it back out in your own (see Listing 3.4.1).

Listing 3.4.1   **Calculating Time in Different Time Zones**

```php
<?php
// Discover what 8am in Tokyo relates to on the East Coast of the US

// Set the default timezone to Tokyo time:
date_default_timezone_set('Asia/Tokyo');

// Now generate the timestamp for that particular timezone, on Jan 1st, 2000
$stamp = mktime(8, 0, 0, 1, 1, 2000);

// Now set the timezone back to US/Eastern
date_default_timezone_set('US/Eastern');

// Output the date in a standard format (RFC1123), this will print:
// Fri, 31 Dec 1999 18:00:00 EST
echo '<p>', date(DATE_RFC1123, $stamp) ,'</p>';
?>
```

The powerful function strtotime() also has a number of ways to help you convert between time zones. Into any string can be inserted a number of time zone modifiers. strtotime() attempts to parse statements such as EST (Eastern Standard Time); however, use of these is discouraged because they can be ambiguous in different languages. It also accepts the actual offset amount from UTC time, such as "-0500" for the U.S. East coast or "+0900" for Tokyo. Therefore we can generate the code in Listing 3.4.2.

Listing 3.4.2   **Determining Time in Different Time Zones with** strtotime()

```php
<?php
// Set the default timezone to US/Eastern time:
date_default_timezone_set('US/Eastern');

// Generate a timestamp for Jan 1st, 2000 at 8am in Tokyo
// First using the 'JST' notation (Japan Standard Time)
$stamp1 = strtotime('1/1/2000 8am JST');
// Then with the actual time variation: 9 hours ahead of UTC
$stamp2 = strtotime('Jan 1 2000 08:00 +0900');

// Output these dates in a standard format (RFC1123), they will print:
// Fri, 31 Dec 1999 18:00:00 EST
```

Listing 3.4.2 **Continued**

```
echo '<p>', date(DATE_RFC1123, $stamp1) ,'</p>';
echo '<p>', date(DATE_RFC1123, $stamp2) ,'</p>';
?>
```

Of course, it may become burdensome to do conversions in this manner. Perhaps you store your data in local time and just want to be able to display it in various time zones. This can often be accomplished by simply keeping your own conversion table to modify the hours. However, this will not take into account any odd situations such as daylight savings time differing from place to place. Listing 3.4.3 uses this table lookup method changing time zones.

Listing 3.4.3 **Determining Time in Different Time Zones with Table Lookup**

```
<?php
// Set the default timezone to US/Eastern time:
date_default_timezone_set('US/Eastern');

// Create our own lookup table relative to US/Eastern
$locals = array('Seattle' => -3, 'London' => 5, 'Tokyo' => 14);

// Produce the day and time in these locals, based upon localtime:
$now = time();
foreach ($locals as $place => $offset) {
    // Output the day and time only, after converting
    echo "<p>The time in {$place} is ", date('m/d/Y H:i',
        $now + 3600 * $offset) ,'</p>';
}
?>
```

3.5 Handling Time Stamps Within Databases or in Files

Often you will be handed date markers within a data file. The format of these is beyond your control; however, you need to read them into PHP to handle as a date. You can parse the date into its constituent parts using regex, but if you are lucky, the format that they arrive in happens to be one that strtotime() handles. This is usually the case because it is difficult to find a format that strtotime() doesn't handle. Listing 3.5.1 is an example of using strtotime() to parse the date out of an Apache log file line:

```
127.0.0.1 - - [02/Nov/2005:22:04:41 -0500] "GET / HTTP/1.1" 200 41228
```

Listing 3.5.1 **Parsing Apache Log Lines with** `strtotime()`

```php
<?php
// Set the default timezone to US/Eastern time:
date_default_timezone_set('US/Eastern');

// Simulate reading an Apache log file, with the following line:
$logline =
    '127.0.0.1 - - [02/Nov/2005:22:04:41 -0500] "GET / HTTP/1.1" 200 41228';

// Since we only want the date section, use regex to obtain it:
$matches = array();
preg_match('/\[(.*?)\]/', $logline, $matches);

// Take the date, and convert it:
$timestamp = strtotime($matches[1]);

// Now echo it out again to ensure that we read it correctly:
echo date(DATE_RFC1123, $timestamp);
?>
```

A similar but common problem that programmers face is getting dates into and out of databases. Each database has its own methods that it prefers to accept and present dates back to you.

Fortunately, again, the dates usually all come back out in a format that `strtotime()` can process. (Plus they have their own formatting directions to simply return the data in the format that you want.) The details for each database differ, and it is recommended that you read the documentation for the particular database you are dealing with.

However, the real trick is in getting PHP date data into a database. Each database has a certain format that it will accept dates in. A warning, though: In almost all databases this default date format can be changed on the server. It can therefore be safer to use the database's own string-to-date conversion functions to make sure that you are always inserting the proper value. With that said, the following are a few `date()` commands in PHP that format strings to a default understandable format in various databases:

- Oracle—`date('d-M-Y H:i', $timestamp)`
- MySQL—`date('Y-m-d H:i', $timestamp)`
- Sybase and SQL Server—`date('m/d/Y H:i', $timestamp)`

3.6 Determining Number of Business Days

Although section 3.1, "Calculating the Difference Between Two Dates," showed how to determine the number of days between any two dates, that isn't helpful in the business world, which lives by business days—defined as Monday through Friday in most places of the world. Business days may, or may not include holidays, and if holidays are not included, the specifics vary from business to business. Therefore, we will focus on the primary definition.

One method to calculate the number of business days between any two given dates is to just loop over every date in between, counting whether that day is a weekend. This is inefficient, though, and a better solution exists, as implemented in Listing 3.6.1. We know that there are five days in a business week. Therefore, we just need to count the number of full weeks between the two dates provided and multiply by 5. We then just need to add on the number of days that existed in the first and last weeks provided.

Listing 3.6.1   **Calculating the Number of Business Days Between Dates**

```php
<?php
// Set the default timezone to US/Eastern time:
date_default_timezone_set('US/Eastern');

// This function will count the number of business days between two dates
function count_business_days($a, $b) {
    // First, sort these.  We need to know which one comes first
    if ($a < $b) {
        $first = $a;
        $second = $b;
    } else {
        $first = $b;
        $second = $a;
    }

    // Break these timestamps up into their constituent parts:
    $f = getdate($first);
    $s = getdate($second);

    // Calculate the number of business days in the first week left.
    // Do this by subtracting the number of the day of the week from Friday
    $f_days = 5 - $f['wday'];
    // If it was Saturday or Sunday you will get a -1 or 5 but we want 0
    if (($f_days == 5) || ($f_days < 0)) { $f_days = 0; }

    // Do the same for the second week except count to the beginning of
    // the week.  However, make sure that Saturday only counts as 5
    $s_days = ($s['wday'] > 5) ? 5 : $s['wday'];

    // Calculate the timestamp of midday, the Sunday after the first date:
    $f_sunday = mktime(12, 0, 0, $f['mon'],
                        $f['mday'] + ((7 - $f['wday']) % 7), $f['year']);
```

Listing 3.6.1   **Continued**

```
    // And the timestamp of midday, the Sunday before the second date:
    $s_sunday = mktime(12, 0, 0, $s['mon'],
                    $s['mday'] - $s['wday'], $s['year']);

    // Calculate the full weeks between these two dates by subtracting
    //  them, then dividing by the seconds in a week.  You need to round
    //  this afterwards to always ensure an even number.  Otherwise
    //  daylight savings time can offset the calculation.
    $weeks = round(($s_sunday - $f_sunday) / (3600*24*7));

    // Return the number of days by multiplying weeks by 5 and adding
    //  the extra days:
    return ($weeks * 5) + $f_days + $s_days;
}

// Try a couple of examples:
$date1 = strtotime('12/3/1973 8:13am');
$date2 = strtotime('1/15/1974 10:15pm');
$date3 = strtotime('2/14/2005 1:32pm');

// Calculate the business days between, They are: 31 & 8109
echo "<p>There are ", count_business_days($date1, $date2), " days.</p>";
echo "<p>There are ", count_business_days($date2, $date3), " days.</p>";
?>
```

You see that we determine the days of the Sunday after the first date and before the last date. From that we can calculate the number of full weeks between them. This is accomplished by dividing the seconds between the two Sundays by the number of seconds in a week. The result is then rounded to the nearest whole number. This is required in case the dates crossed a daylight savings time boundary. If so, an hour or two of error could have appeared, and rounding removes that.

Finally, we simply add in the days of the first and last week, and the value is found. This formula even works when the days are in the same week. On one hand it counts the days down to the end of the week and the days up to the start of the week, counting certain days multiple times, in fact, always incrementing the value by 5 days. However, the full week calculation returns -1 in that case, meaning that we end up subtracting those 5 days back off again.

One further modification you may want to make is to include holidays in the calculation. Using some method of determining applicable holidays, the algorithm would simply count the number of holiday days within the time period and subtract those from the final result.

3.7 Generating a Calendar for a Given Month

Dates are a common part of life, and calendars are part of that. People like to be able to visually look at a calendar to get a feeling for how one date relates to another. Because of this many applications on the Web may display a calendar. The function in Listing 3.7.1 takes a month and year as parameters and outputs a basic HTML table for that month.

This can be easily modified to meet your specific needs. One configuration directive has already been added to it in that you can tell it what day of the week to start on. It defaults to 0 (Sunday).

Listing 3.7.1 **Producing an HTML Calendar**

```php
<?php
// This function will print an HTML Calendar, given a month and year
function print_calendar($month, $year, $weekdaytostart = 0) {
    // There are things we need to know about this month such as the last day:
    $last = idate('d', last_day($month, $year));

    // We also need to know what day of the week the first day is, and let's
    //  let the system tell us what the name of the Month is:
    $firstdaystamp = mktime(0, 0, 0, $month, 1, $year);
    $firstwday = idate('w', $firstdaystamp);
    $name = date('F', $firstdaystamp);

    // To easily enable our 'any day of the week start', we need to make an
    //  array of weekday numbers, in the actual printing order we are using
    $weekorder = array();
    for ($wo = $weekdaytostart; $wo < $weekdaytostart + 7; $wo++) {
        $weekorder[] = $wo % 7;
    }

    // Now, begin our HTML table
    echo "<table><tr><th colspan=\"7\">{$name} {$year}</th></tr>\n";

    // Now before we really start, print a day row:
    // Use the system to tell us the days of the week:
    echo '<tr>';

    // Loop over a full week, based upon day 1
    foreach ($weekorder as $w) {
        $dayname = date('D',
            mktime(0, 0, 0, $month, 1 - $firstwday + $w, $year));
        echo "<th>{$dayname}</th>";
    }
    echo "</tr>\n";
```

Listing 3.7.1   **Continued**

```
// Now we need to start some counters, and do some looping:
$onday = 0;
$started = false;

// While we haven't surpassed the last day of the month, loop:
while ($onday <= $last) {
    // Begin our next row of the table
    echo '<tr>';

    // Now loop 0 through 6, for the days of the week, but in the order
    //   we are actually going, use mod to make this work
    foreach ($weekorder as $d) {
        // If we haven't started yet:
        if (!($started)) {
            // Does today equal the first weekday we should start on?
            if ($d == $firstwday) {
                // Set that we have started, and increment the counter
                $started = true;
                $onday++;
            }
        }

        // Now if the day is zero or greater than the last day make a
        //   blank table cell.
        if (($onday == 0) || ($onday > $last)) {
            echo '<td> </td>';
        } else {
            // Otherwise, echo out a day & Increment the counter
            echo "<td>{$onday}</td>";
            $onday++;
        }
    }

    // End this table row:
    echo "</tr>\n";
}

    // Now end the table:
    echo '</table>';
}

// Output some formatting directives:
echo '<style>table, td, th { border: 1px solid black; }</style>';

// Now make a couple sample tables:
// November 2005, with the default (Sunday) as the first day:
```

Listing 3.7.1   **Continued**

```php
print_calendar(11, 2005);
echo '<br />';

// Create an entire year calendar for 2006 with Monday as the first day:
foreach(range(1, 12) as $m) {
    print_calendar($m, 2006, 1);
    echo '<br />';
}
?>
```

This starts by collecting various pieces of information that it needs. It uses the `last_day()` function created in Listing 3.2.1 to determine the last day of the month. It also needs to know the weekday of the first day of the month.

Because the function is going to need to loop over the weekdays regularly, it needs an easy way to handle this. If it were only ever handling the weeks from Sunday through Saturday (0 through 6), there wouldn't be a problem. However, because it allows starting on any day, the function needs to know what order to loop in. For example, if the starting day was Wednesday, the weekdays need to be handled in the following order: 3, 4, 5, 6, 0, 1, 2.

To do this, an array is created with these numbers by starting with the day of the week it was told to start with, incrementing it 7 times, and each time doing a modulus 7 on it.

It uses the built-in functions to read in the month name and weekday names. This way the function always prints a language-proper version of the calendar. All that is left is to loop, week by week, printing out the days.

The function has to take care not to print out the first day until its proper position, outputting blanks instead. Also, it needs to fill the last row with an appropriate number of blanks as well.

4

Variables

PHP PROVIDES THE BASIC VARIABLE TYPES: Boolean, integer, floating point, and strings. Strings and the number types were covered in Chapter 1, "Strings," and Chapter 2, "Numbers." In addition to these basic types, PHP also provides an object type, used by PHP's implementation of classes, which is discussed in Chapter 7, "Classes and Objects." And, of course, PHP supports arrays of any type, which are discussed in Chapter 5, "Arrays."

PHP also provides for two special types. The first is the NULL type, which, not surprisingly, has only one value: NULL. When assigned NULL, a variable is considered uninitialized; it has no value. For example, the function isset() would return false if passed a variable set to NULL (see the "Quick Hits" section). The other special type is the resource type. Essentially, a resource is a reference to some external resource, such as opened files or database connections. Resources are managed by the functions for a particular resource, such as the file handling functions discussed in Chapter 8, "Files and Directories."

PHP allows the use of variables before any value has been assigned. In these situations, the default value of the required type is used: 0 for numbers, the empty string for strings, FALSE for booleans, and an empty array for arrays. However, an E_NOTICE error is generated every time an uninitialized variable is used. It is strongly recommended that variables explicitly be given some initial value before referring to them. Not only is it good programming practice, it also prevents possible security issues when running in a web server environment.

Quick Hits

▶ Check whether a variable has bee. given a value:

```
$bool = isset($variable);
```

This function returns true if the variable exists and is not NULL.

Full documentation: http://php.net/isset

▶ Check whether a variable is empty:

```
$bool = empty($variable);
```

This function defines the broad concept of an "empty" variable: a variable that may be set but has a null or zero value. Specifically, this function returns true if the variable has any of the following values or properties: `""`, `0`, `"0"`, `NULL`, false, or `array()`.

Full documentation: http://php.net/empty

▶ Remove any variable and its value:

```
unset($variable);
```

The variable is destroyed, and its value is gone.

Full documentation: http://php.net/unset

▶ Force a variable to be of a specific type:

```
$success = settype($variable, $type);
```

This function forces `$variable` to be of type specified by `$type`. TRUE is returned if the conversion is successful.

Full documentation: http://php.net/settype

▶ Cast a value to be of a specific type:

```
$newvar = (TYPE) $oldvar;
```

The value of `$oldvar` is cast into the type specified by the word TYPE and assigned to the new variable. The word TYPE can be any of the allowed types in PHP.

Full documentation: http://php.net/manual/language.types.type-juggling.php

4.1 Determining Whether a Variable Is Equal to Another

PHP is normally a programmer-friendly language. One of PHP's key features is that you almost never have to worry about what type your data is. It automatically converts data between data types for you, so a "0" can be the string 0, the integer 0, the Boolean false, or the float 0.0, whichever is needed at the time.

This is usually convenient, until you start trying to do comparison tests. PHP follows the C standard of considering 0 to mean false, and any other number to be true. It also supports the Boolean type, and therefore has a true/false relationship as well.

For example, what happens when you use a function, such as `strpos()`, that returns false if it cannot find the value within the string? Yet at the same time it might return 0, validly meaning that it found a match at position 0 in the string. If you try to do comparisons, it becomes difficult to tell the difference between 0 and false.

Because of this ambiguity, PHP introduced the concept of the *triple-equals*. By using "===" or "!==" instead of "==" and "!=", you do not test just for equality but that the two values are of exactly the same type as well.

This is useful, but it can still be confusing as to exactly what comparison, with what values, returns a true or false. Listing 4.1.1 attempts to help figure this out by creating a visual lookup table. You can modify it with additional examples as you want.

Listing 4.1.1   **Create a Table of Comparison Operators**

```php
<style type="text/css">
table { border-collapse: collapse; }
td, th {
    border: 1px solid #333333;
    width: 25px;
    text-align: center;
}
</style>
<?php
// Create an array of values. The key is a printable version of it:
$values = array("'0'" => '0', 0 => 0, "'1'" => '1', 1 => 1, "'-1'" => '-1',
    -1 => -1, "'2'" => '2', 2 => 2, '0.0' => 0.0, '0.1' => 0.1,
    '-0.1' => -0.1, '1.0' => 1.0, "'0.0'" => '0.0', "'0.1'" => '0.1',
    "'.1'" => '.1', "'-0.1'" => '-0.1', "'-.1'" => '-.1', "'1.0'" => '1.0',
    "'00'" => '00', "'01'" => '01', 'false' => false, 'true' => true,
    "''" => '', "'a'" => 'a', "'b'" => 'b', "'A'" => 'A', 'NULL' => NULL,
    'array()' => array(), "array('a')" => array('a') );

// Create an array of comparison functions, The Key is the printable version
$cmp = array (
    '==' => create_function('$a,$b', 'return $a == $b ? "<b>1</b>" : 0;'),
    '===' => create_function('$a,$b', 'return $a === $b ? "<b>1</b>" : 0;'),
    '!=' => create_function('$a,$b', 'return $a != $b ? "<b>1</b>" : 0;'),
    '!==' => create_function('$a,$b', 'return $a !== $b ? "<b>1</b>" : 0;'),
    '<' => create_function('$a,$b', 'return $a < $b ? "<b>1</b>" : 0;'),
    '>' => create_function('$a,$b', 'return $a > $b ? "<b>1</b>" : 0;'),
    '<=' => create_function('$a,$b', 'return $a <= $b ? "<b>1</b>" : 0;'),
    '>=' => create_function('$a,$b', 'return $a >= $b ? "<b>1</b>" : 0;'),
    'strcmp()' => create_function('$a,$b', 'return @strcmp($a,$b);'),
    'strcasecmp()' => create_function('$a,$b', 'return @strcasecmp($a,$b);'),
    );

// Now, for every comparison function, create a reference table.
foreach ($cmp as $name => $function) {
    create_reference_table($values, $name, $function);
}

// The function that creates the reference tables for us
function create_reference_table($array, $name, $func) {
    // Start off the table
    echo '<br /><table>';
    echo "<caption>PHP comparisons with operator: {$name}</caption>";
```

Listing 4.1.1 **Continued**

```php
    // Now create the first header row
    echo '<tr><th></th>';
    foreach ($array as $x => $v) { echo "<th>{$x}</th>"; }
    echo "</tr>\n";

    // Now for each item, compare it to every other item:
    foreach ($array as $nm => $y) {
        echo "<tr><th>{$nm}</th>";
        foreach ($array as $x) {
            echo '<td>', $func($x, $y), '</td>';
        }
        echo "</tr>\n";
    }

    // Wrap up and we are done.
    echo "</table>\n";
}
?>
```

4.2 Accessing a Variable Outside a Function, from Within it (Global Variables)

When inside a function, you cannot, by default, access any variables from outside that function. This behavior can be changed, however, for specific variables by using the global language construct on it inside the function, as demonstrated in Listing 4.2.1.

Listing 4.2.1 **Accessing Global Variables**

```php
<?php
$name = 'Ramsey';

function print_and_change_name() {
    // Declare the variable $name to be accessible within this function
    global $name;

    // Output this name, and then change the name.
    echo "<p>{$name}</p>";
    $name = 'Heather';
}

// Call the function once and it prints: 'Ramsey'
print_and_change_name();
// Call the function again, and it prints: 'Heather'
print_and_change_name();
?>
```

There is also another way to access global variables. Instead of using `global` to declare the variable as accessible, you can just use the array `$GLOBALS` to immediately access the variable. `$GLOBALS` is one of the superglobal arrays discussed in Chapter 5. Listing 4.2.1 rewritten with `$GLOBALS` would be as shown in Listing 4.2.2.

Listing 4.2.2   **Using the** `$GLOBALS` **Array**

```php
<?php
$name = 'Ramsey';

function print_and_change_name() {
    // Output this name, and then change the name.
    echo "<p>{$GLOBALS['name']}</p>";
    $GLOBALS['name'] = 'Heather';
}

// Call the function once and it prints: 'Ramsey'
print_and_change_name();
// Call the function again, and it prints: 'Heather'
print_and_change_name();
?>
```

4.3 Keeping a Persistent Value Within a Function (Static Variables)

Normally, after a function runs and exits, any variables created within the function is thrown away. At times, however, it can be useful to have a variable whose value persists between each invocation of the function. In PHP, a variable is made persistent via the `static` language construct. For example, this might be useful when creating a function that needs to keep count of how many times it has been called, as in Listing 4.3.1.

Listing 4.3.1   **Using Static Variables**

```php
<?php
function print_alias($alias) {
    static $number_of_aliases = 1;

    // Output this alias and increment the counter
    echo "{$number_of_aliases}. {$alias}\n";
    $number_of_aliases++;
}

// Call the function multiple times.
// Each time it increments the count and the output will be:
// 1. Eli
```

Listing 4.3.1 **Continued**

```
// 2. HyPeR aCtIvE
// 3. THL Siegfried Sebastian Faust
echo '<pre>';
print_alias('Eli');
print_alias('HyPeR aCtIvE');
print_alias('THL Siegfried Sebastian Faust');
echo '</pre>';
?>
```

4.4 Having One Variable Refer to Another (References)

Another useful task is having a variable that just points to another variable. This way it acts like an alias for that first variable. This is called a *reference* in PHP. The most common use of references is in function parameters and is discussed in Listing 6.5.1 in Chapter 6, "Functions." However, it is still useful just to be able to create variables that reference another variable.

The syntax to accomplish this is to put an "&" in front of the variable you are referencing. The reference can then be used as if it was the original variable itself, and any changes made to it are reflected in the original variable. Listing 4.4.1 demonstrates the effects of using references.

Listing 4.4.1 **Using References**

```
<?php
// Create a variable
$pet = 'Wiley';

// Now create a reference to it:
$petref = &$pet;

// Echo out the value of $pet : 'Wiley'
echo "<p>{$pet}</p>";

// Now change the value via the reference
$petref = 'Mimi-ow';

// And echo it out again : 'Mimi-ow'
echo "<p>{$pet}</p>";
?>
```

Note that references are not the same as C-style pointers. You cannot retrieve a pointer to a variable nor do pointer arithmetic on variables. References are simply a way of giving another name to a variable.

4.5 Using a Variable to Hold the Name of Another Variable

An interesting programmer trick to keep up your sleeve is storing a variable name as a string in another variable and then referencing the original variable. PHP calls this *variable variables*.

The syntax for this is `${$string}`, where `$string` holds the name of the variable. Note that if your case is as simple as this example, the syntax can be shorted to just `$$string`. Listing 4.5.1 demonstrates how to create variable variables.

Listing 4.5.1   **Variable Variables**

```php
<?php
// Create a couple variables
$color = 'blue';
$weapon = 'crossbow';
$drink = 'bourbon';

// Make an array of these variable names
$favorite_things = array('color', 'weapon', 'drink');

// Now access all these variables programmatically via variable variables
// This will output:
// color = blue
// weapon = crossbow
// drink = bourbon
foreach ($favorite_things as $thing) {
    echo '<p>', $thing, ' = ', $$thing, '</p>';
}
?>
```

An often useful variation on this is not directly including the variable name but using the string to help build up the variable name—so perhaps storing `'bob'` in a variable called `$name` and using it to access a variable called `$bob_smith`. The syntax for this would be `${"{$name}_smith"}`. This can be useful. Listing 4.5.2 shows Listing 4.5.1 rewritten to use this.

Listing 4.5.2   **Using Variable Variables to Create Associations**

```php
<?php
// Create a couple variables
$favorite_color = 'blue';
$favorite_weapon = 'crossbow';
$favorite_drink = 'bourbon';

// Make an array of these variable names
$favorite_things = array('color', 'weapon', 'drink');
```

Listing 4.5.2 **Continued**

```
// Now access all these variables programmatically via variable variables
// This will output:
// color = blue
// weapon = crossbow
// drink = bourbon
foreach ($favorite_things as $thing) {
    echo '<p>', $thing, ' = ', ${"favorite_{$thing}"}, '</p>';
}
?>
```

A more advanced use of this technique can be seen in the Metric conversion example—Listing 2.7.1 in Chapter 2.

4.6 Declaring a Constant Instead of a Variable

Like variables, a *constant* is simply a way of assigning a symbolic, meaningful name to a value. A constant can be used in nearly every situation that a variable can be used in; however, there the similarity ends. The most important difference is the basic concept of a constant. Whereas a value of a variable is meant to change, once defined, the value of a constant cannot be changed. Constants are meant to be reference values. Another good point is that constants can be referenced from anywhere in your code (essentially they have automatic global scope).

These are the same as some of the already defined ones such as those in the Math extension (M_PI for π). It is a common coding convention to always use capital letters for your constants. This makes it easy to see what is a constant when reading code.

The syntax for declaring constants is similar to a function call, where the first parameter is your constant name, and the second parameter is the value:

```
define('COLOR', 'blue');
```

Listing 4.6.1 provides an example of using constants: defining the title of a simple web page and referencing it in various places—in the HTML page title, as a title block at the top of the page, and in a footer at the bottom of the page.

Listing 4.6.1 **Using Constants**

```
<?php
define('TITLE', "An Excellent Page");
?>
<html>
<head><title><?= TITLE ?></title></head>
<body>
<h1><?= TITLE ?></h1>
<!-- Page content here -->
<p>This has been the page: "<?= TITLE ?>"</p>
</body>
</html>
```

4.7 Coalescing a List of Values to Determine the First Non-False Value

Sometimes you have many values, and you simply want the first one of them that isn't false/empty/null/and so on. Most databases provide this functionality through a function called `coalesce` that takes any number of arguments and returns the first one of them that isn't false.

PHP doesn't supply this functionality, but luckily we can create it as shown in Listing 4.7.1.

> **Note**
>
> This function implementation uses variable length argument lists that are explained in full detail in Listing 6.6.1 in Chapter 6.

Listing 4.7.1   **Coalesce: Find First Non-False Value in a List of Arrays**

```php
<?php
// A function that will take any number of arguments, and
// return the first one that isn't equal to false
function coalesce() {
    // Loop through all arguments given
    foreach (func_get_args() as $value) {
        // If this argument doesn't equal false, return it
        if ($value) { return $value; }
    }
}

// Try this on a list of arguments.  Should return 42
echo coalesce('', 0, NULL, false, 1-1, 42, 'triccare', '0.0');
?>
```

The function is simple, just looping over all the values until one of them is non-false. If it was needed, it would be simple to modify this for other purposes by changing the `if` statement, such as to check for exactly not false—`$value !== false`—or even something completely different, such as the first value not equal to `'red'`—`$value != 'red'`.

5

Arrays

ARRAYS ARE A NECESSARY PART OF ANY computer language. However, in PHP, arrays
are especially versatile. In most languages, arrays are implemented simply as many-dimen-
sional tables; each element is accessed by a set of numbers. Each value in a traditional
array has a numeric address.

PHP on the other hand uses a more generalized concept to implement arrays called
ordered maps (also sometimes known as *associative arrays*). Each value in a PHP array is
indexed by or mapped to a *key*. The keys of an array can be the traditional numeric
index keys such as `$a[0]`, `$a[1]`, and so on. However, the real power of PHP arrays lies
in the fact that keys do not have to be integers; keys can also be strings, such as
`$hexcolor['red']` or `$info['address']`. As you will see not only in the following
examples but also in the rest of this book, this mapping of keys to values provides great
flexibility in solving problems.

As previously mentioned, PHP is not terribly concerned about variable types, converting variables as necessary to the required type. Arrays are no different; an array does
not need to contain values of a single type. Each value can be of a completely different
type. Listing 5.0.1 creates an array of every possible type in PHP.

Listing 5.0.1 **An Array Containing Values of All Possible Types**

```php
<?php
// Create an array of all possible PHP types
$alltypes = array(
  'integer' => 1,
  'float' => -12.353,
  'string' => 'string value here',
  'array' => array('elements', 'of', 'another', 'array'),
  'resource' => fopen('file.txt', 'w'),
  'object' => dir('.'),
  'function' => create_function('', 'echo "Hello, world!\n";')
);
```

Listing 5.0.1 **Continued**

```
// Echo this out:
echo '<pre>';
print_r($alltypes);
echo '</pre>';
?>
```

These two capabilities, mixing types and using key/value pairing, provide PHP with a powerful data structure that is both versatile and easy to use.

Quick Hits

▶ Create a new, empty array:

```
$array = array();
```

Very simply, this function initializes an empty array. If given arguments, the array is initialized with those values.

Full documentation: http://php.net/manual/function.array.php

▶ Find the number of elements in an array:

```
$size = count($array, $count_recursive);
```

This function returns the number of elements in the array. If $count_recursive is specified and true, all elements of any arrays that are elements of the main array are also counted.

Full documentation: http://php.net/count

▶ Create an array filled with a value:

```
$array = array_fill($start, $number, $value);
```

An array is returned filled with elements equal to $value, starting from the $start numeric index, for $number times. Note that this does not overwrite an existing array but creates a new one.

Full documentation: http://php.net/array_fill

▶ Create an array with a range of values:

```
$array = range($start, $end, $step);
```

The array will contain the values starting at $start and continuing to $end, either incrementing or decrementing as necessary, by $step.

Full documentation: http://php.net/range

▶ Merge two arrays:

```
$big_array = array_merge($array1, $array2);
```

The result contains all of the key=>value pairs of the input arrays. If there are duplicate, non-numeric, keys, the key->value pair of the last array is used. For purely numerically indexed arrays, every element will be in the result, with the result array reindexed.

Full documentation: http://php.net/array_merge

▶ **Convert a one-dimensional array into two dimensions:**

```
$two_d_array = array_chunk($one_d_array, $size);
```

The one-dimensional array is broken into arrays of $size number of elements. These are returned in an array. Note that the last array has whatever elements are left from the split.

Full documentation: http://php.net/array_chunk

▶ **Create a key-based array from two different arrays:**

```
$key_based_array = array_combine($keys, $values);
```

This function uses the values from the first array as keys and associates them with the values from the second array, returning an associative array of the key=>value pairs.

Full documentation: http://php.net/array_combine

▶ **Extract a subarray from an array:**

```
$subarray = array_slice($array, $start, $length);
```

The subarray consists of the elements beginning with the $start index and going on for the next $length elements.

Full documentation: http://php.net/array_slice

▶ **Replace a section of an array with another array:**

```
$extracted = array_splice($array, $start, $length, $replace);
```

The subarray starting at the $start index for the next $length elements is replaced by the values in the $replace array. The extracted subarray is returned.

Full documentation: http://php.net/array_splice

▶ **Sort arrays:**
```
$sorted = asort($array);
$reverse = arsort($array);
```

Sort arrays, either in ascending (asort) or descending (arsort) order. Key associations are preserved.

Full documentation: http://php.net/asort and http://php.net/arsort

▶ **Sort arrays based on keys:**
```
$sorted = ksort($array);
$reverse = krsort($array);
```

Unlike the previous functions that operate on values, these functions sort arrays based on the keys.

Full documentation: http://php.net/ksort and http://php.net/krsort

▶ **Find out how many times elements appear in an array:**

```
$counts = array_count_values($array);
```

This function returns an array containing how many times each value appears in the input array. The values of the input array are used as the keys.

Full documentation: http://php.net/array_count_values

▶ **Determine whether a given key or index exists in an array:**

`$exists = array_key_exists($key, $array);`

This returns TRUE if the specified key exists in the array.

Full documentation: http://php.net/array_key_exists

▶ **Returns all the keys of an array:**

`$key_array = array_keys($array);`

The values in the returned array are all the keys of the input array.

Full documentation: http://php.net/array_keys

▶ **Return just the values of an array:**

`$value_array = array_values($array);`

This function returns a numerically indexed array of just the values from the input array.

Full documentation: http://php.net/array_values

▶ **Find an element in an array:**

`$key = array_search($value, $array);`

The key with the corresponding value is returned. If no such value exists, FALSE is returned.

Full documentation: http://php.net/array_search

▶ **Remove duplicate values from an array:**

`$result = array_unique($array);`

A new array is created with all duplicate values removed.

Full documentation: http://php.net/array_unique

▶ **Filter an array based on a user-specified criteria:**

`$filtered = array_filter($array, $compare_function);`

The returned array contains only the values from the input array for which the user-defined compare function evaluates to be true. The keys are preserved.

Full documentation: http://php.net/array_filter

▶ **Find which values are common between two arrays:**

`$common = array_intersect($first, $second);`

The returned array contains the values found in the first array that are also found in the second array.

Full documentation: http://php.net/array_intersect

▶ **Find the difference between arrays:**

```
$diff = array_diff($first, $second);
```

This function returns an array of all the values from the first array that are not found in the second array.

Full documentation: http://php.net/array_diff

▶ **Pick random elements from an array:**

```
$key_array = array_rand($array, $number);
```

An array is returned with $number of randomly chosen keys from the original array.

Full documentation: http://php.net/array_rand

▶ **Reverse an array:**

```
$reversed = array_reverse($array, $preserve_key);
```

This function returns the array with all the elements in reverse order. If $preserve_key is TRUE, the key=>value association remains.

Full documentation: http://php.net/array_reverse

▶ **Exchange all the keys in a array with their values:**

```
$flipped = array_flip($array);
```

The keys from the input array become the values of the output array using their corresponding values from the input array as the new key. If the original value cannot be a valid key, such as an array, a warning is generated, and the key=>value pair is ignored.

Full documentation: http://php.net/array_flip

▶ **Apply a function to each value of an array:**

```
$result = array_map($function, $array);
```

The function is called once for each value of array as its argument. The results of this are returned in an array.

Full documentation: http://php.net/array_map

5.1 Superglobal Arrays and Their Usage

The role of global variables in PHP was explained in Listing 4.2.1 in Chapter 4, "Variables"; however, PHP also has a set of variables known as *superglobals*. These all happen to be arrays and have two common characteristics: They are accessible from anywhere in your code, and they are all automatically filled in for you with various values. These are:

- $_ENV—Contains any environment variables present in the operating system for your PHP process.

- $_SERVER—Contains variables set by, and specific to, your web server. Commonly used ones are $_SERVER['HTTP_HOST'], which has your hostname in it; $_SERVER['PHP_SELF'], which has the operating system path to your PHP script; and $_SERVER['REMOTE_ADDR'], which contains the IP address of the browser connecting to you.

- $_COOKIE—Holds any cookies that the browser has returned to your script.

- $_GET, $_POST, and $_REQUEST—The most commonly used superglobals. $_GET and $_POST contain all the values of any submitted forms (via the GET and POST methods, respectively), as well as any manually created GET items. This makes web programming easy because these are readily available without having to worry about them. $_REQUEST is a convenience version that contains all the values from $_GET, $_POST, and $_COOKIE together. If two values have the same name, only one appears, the order of which is determined by a configuration setting.

- $_FILES—Anytime you have a file upload, information about the uploaded file is in this array.

- $_SESSION—Holds any information saved into a PHP session. PHP sessions are discussed in Chapter 12, "Sessions and User Tracking."

- $GLOBALS—The one superglobal that doesn't start with an underscore, this holds the values of any global variables that you create. It is discussed in more detail in Chapter 4.

Listing 5.1.1 shows the usefulness of superglobals, creating a web page with a link that increments a count each time you click on it. Superglobals are used regularly throughout Part II, "Applications," of this book.

Listing 5.1.1   **Accessing Web Page Parameters Through the Superglobal** $GET

```php
<?php
// A function that returns a value one greater than the GET variable 'count'
function increment_count() {
    if (isset($_GET['count'])) {
        return $_GET['count'] + 1;
    } else {
        return 1;
    }
}

// Save the value of the GET variable 'count', otherwise default to 0
$counter = 0;
if (isset($_GET['count'])) {
    $counter = $_GET['count'];
}
```

Listing 5.1.1 **Continued**

```
// Prepare a statement about the number of clicks:
echo "<p>You have clicked on this page {$counter} times.</p>\n";

// Now offer to let them click again, using PHP_SELF to automatically link
// back to this script, and incrementing the count:
echo '<p>Do you want to <a href="', $_SERVER['PHP_SELF'],
        '?count=', increment_count(), '">click again</a>?</p>';
?>
```

5.2 Stack Implementation

A *stack* is a programming data structure that follows the rules of *LIFO* (Last In First Out). This is similar to a stack of plates. The last one placed on top of the stack, is the first one that is going to be taken back off the stack. This logic is used in an RPN calculator, event handling, state machines such as compilers and interpreters, inventory systems and many other uses.

PHP provides the basic building blocks of handling stacks via arrays with its array_push() and array_pop() functions. However, it still takes a little bit of work to truly treat an array like a stack. Listing 5.2.1 shows an implementation of a library that provides all common stack operations.

Listing 5.2.1 **Stack Handling Library**

```
<?php
// A library to implement stacks in PHP via arrays

// The Initialize function creates a new stack:
function &stack_initialize() {
    // In this case, just return a new array
    $new = array();
    return $new;
}

// The destory function will get rid of a stack
function stack_destroy(&$stack) {
    // Since PHP is nice to us, we can just use unset
    unset($stack);
}

// The push operation on a stack adds a new value onto the top of the stack
function stack_push(&$stack, $value) {
    // We are just adding a value to the end of the array, so we can use the
    // [] PHP Shortcut for this.  It's faster than using array_push
```

Listing 5.2.1 **Continued**

```php
    $stack[] = $value;
}

// Pop removes the top value from the stack and returns it to you
function stack_pop(&$stack) {
    // Just use array pop:
    return array_pop($stack);
}

// Peek returns a copy of the top value from the stack, leaving it in place
function stack_peek(&$stack) {
    // Return a copy of the value on top of the stack (the end of the array)
    return $stack[count($stack)-1];
}

// Size returns the number of elements in the stack
function stack_size(&$stack) {
    // Just using count will give the proper number:
    return count($stack);
}

// Swap takes the top two values of the stack and switches them
function stack_swap(&$stack) {
    // Calculate the count:
    $n = count($stack);

    // Only do anything if count is greater than 1
    if ($n > 1) {
        // Now save a copy of the second to last value
        $second = $stack[$n-2];
        // Place the last value in second to last place:
        $stack[$n-2] = $stack[$n-1];
        // And put the second to last, now in the last place:
        $stack[$n-1] = $second;
    }
}

// Dup takes the top value from the stack, duplicates it,
//   and adds it back onto the stack
function stack_dup(&$stack) {
    // Actually rather simple, just reinsert the last value:
    $stack[] = $stack[count($stack)-1];
}

// Let's use these to create a small stack of data and manipulate it.
//  Start by adding a few numbers onto it, making it: 73 74 5
```

Listing 5.2.1   **Continued**

```
$mystack =& stack_initialize();
stack_push($mystack, 73);
stack_push($mystack, 74);
stack_push($mystack, 5);

// Now duplicate the top, giving us:  73 74 5 5
stack_dup($mystack);

// Check the size now, it should be 4
echo '<p>Stack size is: ', stack_size($mystack), '</p>';

// Now pop the top, giving us: 5
echo '<p>Popped off the value: ', stack_pop($mystack), '</p>';

// Next swap the top two values, leaving us with: 73 5 74
stack_swap($mystack);

// Peek at the top element to ensure it is 74
echo '<p>Current top element is: ', stack_peek($mystack), '</p>';

// Now destroy it, we are done.
stack_destroy($mystack);
?>
```

Note that throughout this library we are always passing the stack around as a reference. This is so that we are actually performing all actions on one, single, stack, and not constantly making duplicate copies of it. In some cases this is crucial, such as the push, swap, initialize, destroy, and dup implementations where the function needs to be able to modify the original stack. The other functions do not have to have it passed by reference; however, it makes it more efficient, especially if the stack gets large.

The implementation of each of these functions has been done in an efficient manner, though there are other solutions. For example the stack_dup() function could have been implemented by performing a pop and then pushing that value twice. Similarly the stack_swap() could have been created via popping twice and then pushing the values back on in reverse order. Although those other implementations are straight forward, they are inefficient and so were discarded. Instead all implementations used the nature of the underlying arrays to their fullest.

5.3 Queue Implementation

The opposite of a stack, a *queue* is a data structure that follows a *FIFO* (First In First Out) rule. This means that it works like a line at a movie theater. The person who gets in line first, gets served first.

Similar to the stack implementation, PHP provides most of the needed functionality within its array functions to handle an array like a queue, but lacks the final touches of a full library to treat them as such. Listing 5.3.1 provides just such a library.

Listing 5.3.1 **Queue Handling Library**

```php
<?php
// A library to implement queues in PHP via arrays

// The Initialize function creates a new queue:
function &queue_initialize() {
    // In this case, just return a new array
    $new = array();
    return $new;
}

// The destroy function will get rid of a queue
function queue_destroy(&$queue) {
    // Since PHP is nice to us, we can just use unset
    unset($queue);
}

// The enqueue operation adds a new value onto the back of the queue
function queue_enqueue(&$queue, $value) {
    // We are just adding a value to the end of the array, so we can use the
    //   [] PHP Shortcut for this.  It's faster than using array_push
    $queue[] = $value;
}

// Dequeue removes the front of the queue and returns it to you
function queue_dequeue(&$queue) {
    // Just use array unshift
    return array_shift($queue);
}

// Peek returns a copy of the front of the queue, leaving it in place
function queue_peek(&$queue) {
    // Return a copy of the value found in front of queue
    //   (at the beginning of the array)
    return $queue[0];
}

// Size returns the number of elements in the queue
function queue_size(&$queue) {
    // Just using count will give the proper number:
    return count($queue);
}
```

Listing 5.3.1   **Continued**

```
// Rotate takes the item on the front and sends it to the back of the queue.func-
tion queue_rotate(&$queue) {
    // Remove the first item and insert it at the rear.
    $queue[] = array_shift($queue);
}

// Let's use these to create a small queue of data and manipulate it.
// Start by adding a few words to it:
$myqueue =& queue_initialize();
queue_enqueue($myqueue, 'Opal');
queue_enqueue($myqueue, 'Dolphin');
queue_enqueue($myqueue, 'Pelican');

// The queue is: Opal Dolphin Pelican

// Check the size, it should be 3
echo '<p>Queue size is: ', queue_size($myqueue), '</p>';

// Peek at the front of the queue, it should be: Opal
echo '<p>Front of the queue is: ', queue_peek($myqueue), '</p>';

// Now rotate the queue, giving us: Dolphin Pelican Opal
queue_rotate($myqueue);

// Remove the front element, returning: Dolphin
echo '<p>Removed the element at the front of the queue: ',
    queue_dequeue($myqueue), '</p>';

// Now destroy it, we are done.
queue_destroy($myqueue);
?>
```

Similar to the stack implementation in Listing 5.2.1, we use array functions to implement the queue. We again pass everything by reference so that we can directly edit the base array, and we implement all code in the most efficient manner knowing the underlying structure. For example, using true queue logic, a rotate would have been implemented by performing a dequeue and then an enqueue; however, taking advantage of knowing how the queue has been implemented, array functions are used instead.

5.4 Sorting with User-Defined Comparisons

The built-in sort functions can handle almost every basic sort you can think of: forward, backward, numeric, alphabetic, natural language, by key, by value. In fact, using `array_multisort()` you can even do this sorting across multiple arrays, or recursively down into a multidimensional array. However, none of this helps you if your sorting criteria are more complicated.

More often than you might think, you end up needing to sort by some custom criteria where standard comparison operators fail you. In this case you can sort using your own comparison function. Three functions in PHP allow you to do this. The first is usort(), which is the basic one. The two variations are uasort(), which keeps associative indexes intact whereas usort() renumbers the array, and uksort(), which sorts by the keys instead of by the values.

For all these functions, you need to pass them your array and the name of your user-defined sort procedure. This function you create must take two parameters and return a negative or positive value from its comparison indicating the direction of the sort. It should return a zero if the two values are identical.

For example, let's assume that we have an array of arrays, and we want to sort these arrays by the number of elements that they each have. This normally would not be possible because it relies on the output of another function: count(); however, using user-defined comparisons, we can do that. Another situation would be to sort by the maximum value in one of the subarrays. Listing 5.4.1 sorts arrays based on the length of their subarrays.

Listing 5.4.1 **Sorting Arrays with User-Defined Functions**

```php
<?php
// Create a nested array structure
$scores = array (
    'Siegfried' => array(117, 72, 53.3),
    'Francesca' => array(84.7),
    'Jonathas' => array(96.7, 37),
    'Mika' => array(113, 100, 81),
    'Timothy' => array(80.7, 80.3),
    );

// Create a function that will sort based upon the length of the subarray
function compare_length($a, $b) {
    // For each look at the length of the subarray
    $a_length = count($a);
    $b_length = count($b);

    // If they are the same, return 0
    if ($a_length == $b_length) {
        return 0;
    } else {
        // See which one is bigger
        return ($a_length > $b_length) ? -1 : 1;
    }
}
```

Listing 5.4.1 **Continued**

```php
// Using that formula, sort the array, keeping the key associations intact:
uasort($scores, 'compare_length');

// Echo out the keys in their new order ... Will be in order:
// Mika, Siegfried, Timothy, Jonathas, Francesca
echo '<pre>';
echo "Sorted by array length: \n";
print_r(array_keys($scores));
echo "\n\n";

// Create a function to sort them by the maximum value in the subarray
function compare_max($a, $b) {
    // Take a look a the maximum values:
    $a_max = max($a);
    $b_max = max($b);

    // If they are the same, return 0
    if ($a_max == $b_max) {
        return 0;
    } else {
        // See which one is bigger
        return ($a_max > $b_max) ? -1 : 1;
    }
}

// Resort the array by maximum value:
uasort($scores, 'compare_max');

// Echo out the keys now sorted by max ... Will be in order:
// Siegfried, Mika, Jonathas, Francesca, Timothy
echo "Sorted by array maximum value: \n";
print_r(array_keys($scores));
echo '</pre>';
?>
```

One major point to note is that within our user functions, we cannot rely on comparison operators alone. Most of them return `true` or `false` (or 1 and 0). This doesn't work for these comparison functions because we need to return –1, 0, or 1, respectively. Therefore, we have to make each comparison and manually return the proper value to ensure it works.

5.5 Sorting with Alternative Algorithms

The sort functions of PHP all use the Quicksort algorithm. They do this with good reason because this is the most generically useful sorting algorithm. Most of the time, it sorts in decent (if not the best) amount of time. However, there are cases when another algorithm can actually work more quickly. Usually this is because you know the form of the data you are sorting and can tell that a different algorithm may be faster. Or sometimes it is to meet other requirements, such as a sorting algorithm that doesn't need all the data loaded into memory at the same time. There are many different reasons to use another algorithm; however, in all these you will be left to implement the algorithm yourself.

One special situation might be if you have a web server log file. Web server log files are almost completely in order; however, the nature of them tends to mean that various lines can be slightly out of order. But in the whole, the list is already sorted. In this case a traditional sorting algorithm that looks over the whole array of data is inefficient. An efficient algorithm in this case is a variation of the bubble sort.

The *bubble sort* is normally a slow sort only used as a teaching tool in beginning computer programming classes. It loops over the array, at each step comparing the current element with the one after it. It swaps them if they are out of order. When it finishes its pass through the array, it starts over again and continues this process until it has made a loop where it didn't have to change anything.

One slight variation on this algorithm can make it viable when sorting lists, such as web server log files, that are just slightly out of order. All that must be done is to let the sorting move up or down. So at each step, if the value is bigger, it moves it down and continues, just like a normal bubble sort. If the value is smaller, however, it swaps the two values and takes a step backward. This way, it toggles back and forth through the data as it goes. For that reason, let's refer to this as a *toggle sort*, shown in Listing 5.5.1.

Listing 5.5.1 **Bubble Sort Variation: Toggle Sort**

```php
<?php
// Implement the Toggle Sort
function toggle_sort(&$a) {
    // Prepare some starting values.
    $i = 0;
    $lastindex = count($a) - 1;

    // Continue looping until we reach the last element.
    while ($i < $lastindex) {
        // Compare this value to the next one
        if ($a[$i] <= $a[$i+1]) {
            // It is less than or equal to the next one, therefore
            //  this is the proper order, move on
            $i++;
        } else {
            // It is greater than the next one, swap it
            $tmp = $a[$i];
            $a[$i] = $a[$i+1];
            $a[$i+1] = $tmp;
```

Listing 5.5.1 **Continued**

```php
            // Step back one in our loop in case the value needs to rise
            // again. Don't do this at the beginning of the array.:
            if ($i) { $i--; }
        }
    }
}

// Prepare an array of values:
$values = array(73, 3, 42, 6, 14, 23, 15, 9, 74, 1, 234, 45, 23, 76, 12, 3);

// Sort them:
toggle_sort($values);

// Echo them out in order:
//   1 3 3 6 9 12 14 15 23 23 42 45 73 74 76 234
foreach ($values as $v) { echo "{$v} "; }
?>
```

A simple but useful sort for small arrays (especially small arrays that are already almost sorted), is the *insertion sort*. The insertion sort divides an array into two sections: the part that is already sorted and the part that is not. It walks down the part that is not sorted, removing one value at a time. It then loops through the sorted section, finds the right place to insert this value, and does so, shifting all the other values down by one. It continues until all values have been moved to the sorted section.

This sort is rarely used by itself but is the basis of other better algorithms, as you will see. Listing 5.5.2 implements the insertion sort algorithm.

Listing 5.5.2 **Insertion Sort**

```php
<?php
// Implement the Insertion Sort
function insertion_sort(&$a) {
    // Loop through all entries in the array
    $count = count($a);
    for ($i = 0; $i < $count; $i++) {
        // Save the current value which we are going to compare:
        $value = $a[$i];

        // Now loop backwards from the current value until we reach the
        // beginning of the array or a value less than our current one
        for ($x = $i - 1; ( ($x >= 0) && ($a[$x] > $value) ); $x--) {
            // Swap this value down one place:
            $a[$x + 1] = $a[$x];
        }
```

Listing 5.5.2 **Continued**

```
        // Now assign our value to its proper sorted position:
        $a[$x + 1] = $value;
    }
}

// Prepare an array of values:
$values = array(73, 3, 42, 6, 14, 23, 15, 9, 74, 1, 234, 45, 23, 76, 12, 3);

// Sort them:
insertion_sort($values);

// Echo them out in order:
//   1 3 3 6 9 12 14 15 23 23 42 45 73 74 76 234
foreach ($values as $v) { echo "{$v} "; }
?>
```

The insertion sort can be slow for use on large arrays that are out of order because it would need to be swapping values constantly. However, it is good at short arrays, especially when they are mostly in order. This concept inspired the invention of the *shell sort*.

The shell sort uses the insertion sort but decides to make bigger movements. Although it still moves only one element at a time, it can move them over much greater distances. It does this by looking at cross-sections of the data. Conceptually, it breaks the data into a two-dimensional array and then sorts the columns of the array. The array is reassembled and sorted again, breaking it into fewer columns. This process is repeated until only one column exists. At this point, a regular insertion sort is performed.

To look at it another way, let's say that it breaks the data into seven columns to start. Then it does an insertion sort on data elements 0, 7, 14, and 21; then on 1, 8, 15, and 22; and so on. After finishing that, it may switch to sorting on three columns, making the elements to sort 0, 3, 6, and 9; then 1, 4, 7, and 10; and so on.

This way allows a value to jump further up the chain, slowly making narrower and narrower passes through the data. A good choice is necessary on the number of columns to split the data into. The steps need to grow rapidly. In our case, we will use a series of numbers following the formula: $2x + 1$, where x is equal to the previous value in the series.

This gives a list of columns of: 1, 3, 7, 15, 31, and so on. Other methods for determining a set of numbers could be used. In general the shell sort, shown in Listing 5.5.3, is one of the fastest sorts when dealing with a small set of numbers.

Listing 5.5.3 **Shell Sort**

```
<?php
// Implement the Shell Sort
function shell_sort(&$a) {
    $count = count($a);
```

Listing 5.5.3 **Continued**

```php
    // Determine in our sequence of 2x + 1, what the highest value that is
    //   less than the count of the array is:
    $columns = 1;
    while ($columns < $count) {
        $columns = $columns * 2 + 1;
    }

    // Ok, Columns went one too far that way, so step back one
    $columns = ($columns - 1) / 2;
    // Now, as long as our number of columns to sort by is at LEAST 1
    while ($columns > 0) {
        // Loop for as many columns as we have:
        for ($c = 0; $c < $columns; $c++) {
            // Loop through all members of this column:
            for ($i = $columns; $i < $count; $i += $columns) {
                // Save the current value which we are going to compare:
                $value = $a[$i];

                // Loop backwards from the current value until we reach the
                //   start of the array or a value less than our current one
                for ($x = $i - $columns;
                        ( ($x >= 0) && ($a[$x] > $value) );
                        $x -= $columns) {
                    // Swap this value down one place:
                    $a[$x + $columns] = $a[$x];
                }

                // Now assign our value to its proper sorted position:
                $a[$x + $columns] = $value;
            }
        }

        // Now that we have finished with one set of columns
        //   reduce the number of columns:
        $columns = ($columns - 1) / 2;
    }
}

// Prepare an array of values:
$values = array(73, 3, 42, 6, 14, 23, 15, 9, 74, 1, 234, 45, 23, 76, 12, 3);

// Sort them:
shell_sort($values);
```

Listing 5.5.3 **Continued**

```
// Echo them out in order:
//  1 3  3  6  9  12  14  15  23  23  42  45  73  74  76  234
foreach ($values as $v) { echo "{$v} "; }
?>
```

We would be remiss if we did not discuss the *heap sort*. This method of sorting typically rivals the speed of the traditional quick sort; however, the implementation to get this speed often requires system-level coding. It relies on the concept of a data structure known as a *heap*, which allows for a fast maximum command (the top of the heap), and for quick rediscovery of the maximum value again afterward. Attempting to do this in PHP is not really worth the effort. This algorithm would be inefficient because of the need to simulate this heap structure with higher-level language.

Beyond that, the algorithm is straightforward. Grab the maximum from the heap, add it to the end of a new array, and grab the maximum from the heap again. Repeat until the heap is empty, and your sorted array is finished.

5.6 Recursive Handling of Multidimensional Arrays

You may at times find yourself with a multidimensional array and needing to perform some task across all values in it. It would be cumbersome (and in some cases impossible) to actually perform the task manually on all the elements. This is where recursion can help you. By using a recursive function, as shown in Listing 5.6.1, you can craft a simple function that performs the final task for you. Note that recursive functions are discussed in more detail in Listing 6.1.1 in Chapter 6, "Functions."

Listing 5.6.1 **Find the Maximum Value in a Multidimensional Array**

```
<?php
// A function to find the maximum value from a multidimensional array:
function recursive_array_max($a) {
    // Loop through all entries comparing them to each other
    foreach ($a as $value) {
        // If this is an array find its maximum.

        if (is_array($value)) {
            $value = recursive_array_max($value);
        }

        // Now if this is our first value:
        if (!(isset($max))) {
            // Store this and move on:
            $max = $value;
```

Listing 5.6.1   **Continued**

```
        } else {
            // Compare this value to the max, and pick the highest:
            $max = $value > $max ? $value : $max;
        }
    }

    // Return the final maximum value:
    return $max;
}

// Prepare a multidimensional array of numbers:
$dimensional = array(
    57,
    array(3, 35),
    array(235, 534, 73, array(3, 4, 956), 6),
    14,
    2,
    array(5, 74, 73)
    );

// Find the maximum value within this:
$max = recursive_array_max($dimensional);

// Print out the result: It will be 956
echo "<p>The maximum value was: {$max}</p>";
?>
```

In this case a function is created that finds the maximum value within the array. Like the built-in function max(), however, this recursive function dives deep into the array. Note the use of is_array() to detect whether each entry happens to be an array itself. If so, the function is called recursively on that array to find its maximum value. Eventually every element has been individually compared, or each array has been collapsed to its single highest value. Then the final answer is known.

5.7 Performing Set Operations on Arrays

Set theory describes a number of operations that you can perform on sets of values (in this case, arrays). PHP provides the capability to handle these, but it is worthwhile to explore them fully because they may come in handy.

The first is the concept of a *union*. A union is the combination of two sets of values, usually involving the removal of any duplicate values. PHP provides an array union operator by simply using "+" between two arrays. This, however, does not work like a set union. The PHP version takes all values from the first array and adds in any values of the second array, only where the second array has a key that does not exist in the first array. It might be seen as a union of the keys of the array, as opposed to a union of the values of the array.

The better solution is to use a combination of `array_merge()`, which combines the two arrays together, and `array_unique()`, which removes any duplicates. Listing 5.7.1 demonstrates the difference between the array '+' operator and a true union operation.

Listing 5.7.1   **Demonstrate the Difference Between the Array '+' Operator and a True Array Union**

```php
<?php
// Declare two arrays:
$first = array('e', 'h', 'r', 'j', 'b');
$last = array('w', 'e', 'c');

// Combine them using PHPs + operator
$plus_union = $last + $first;

// Echo this out:  w e c j b
echo '<p>';
foreach ($plus_union as $v) { echo "{$v} "; }
echo "</p>\n";

// Combine them using merge & unique, getting a true union
$union = array_unique(array_merge($first, $last));

// Echo this out:  e h r j b w c
echo '<p>';
foreach ($union as $v) { echo "{$v} "; }
echo "</p>\n";
?>
```

The next concept is that of *intersection*. The intersection of two sets is simply defined as only those elements that appear in both sets. PHP provides for this with its `array_intersect()` function, as demonstrated in Listing 5.7.2.

Listing 5.7.2   **Array Intersection**

```php
<?php
// Declare two arrays:
$first = array('e', 'h', 'r', 'j', 'b');
$last = array('w', 'e', 'c');

// Determine the intersection of these sets
$intersection = array_intersect($last, $first);
```

Listing 5.7.2 **Continued**

```
// Echo this out:  e
echo '<p>';
foreach ($intersection as $v) { echo "{$v} "; }
echo "</p>\n";
?>
```

The final concept to explore is a *set complement*. A complement is a difference. So if you take the complement of sets A and B (referred to as the *relative complement of A in B*), it is the elements that only exist in B and not in A. PHP implements this via the `array_diff()` function, as shown in Listing 5.7.3. You need to make the first array the one you want to know the different values from, in this case B.

Listing 5.7.3 **Array Complement**

```
<?php
// Declare two arrays:
$first = array('e', 'h', 'r', 'j', 'b');
$last = array('w', 'e', 'c');

// Determine the different (complement) of these sets
$diff = array_diff($last, $first);

// Echo this out:  w c
echo '<p>';
foreach ($diff as $v) { echo "{$v} "; }
echo "</p>\n";
?>
```

5.8 Matrix Math Execution Using Arrays

An area in mathematics that lends itself to the use of arrays is *matrix math*. In oversimplified terms, matrix math is taking two different tables of numbers, performing some mathematical operation between them, and producing a result that is another table of numbers.

In practice, matrix math is often used in situations where coordinate systems are being employed and coordinates must be transformed between one system and another. This is commonly found in computer-generated graphics, where three-dimensional objects must be mapped onto a two-dimensional computer screen. Such topics are beyond the scope of this book. However, we can create a basic but complete matrix library that can be used for any application that requires matrix manipulation.

Matrix operations come in three general definitions. The first, and simplest, is multiplying a single matrix by a number, called *scalar multiplication*. Essentially, scalar multiplica-

$$\begin{bmatrix} a & b \\ c & d \end{bmatrix} \times s = \begin{bmatrix} a \cdot s & b \cdot s \\ c \cdot s & d \cdot s \end{bmatrix}$$

tion scales the matrix by the specified value by multiplying every element by that value, as shown in Figure 5.8.1.

Figure 5.8.1   Scalar multiplication.

The next set of operations can generally be called *matrix element* operations. Standard matrix addition and subtraction are matrix element operations. For such operations, the

$$\begin{bmatrix} a & b \\ c & d \end{bmatrix} + \begin{bmatrix} e & f \\ g & h \end{bmatrix} = \begin{bmatrix} a + e & b + f \\ c + g & d + h \end{bmatrix}$$

matrices involved must have the same number of rows and columns, as shown in Figure 5.8.2.

Figure 5.8.2   Matrix element operations.

The final set of operations is referred to as *full matrix* operations. Standard matrix multiplication and division are full matrix operations. Unlike addition and subtraction, only one dimension of first matrix must be the same size as the opposite dimension of the

$$\begin{bmatrix} a & b & c \\ d & e & f \end{bmatrix} \times \begin{bmatrix} g & h \\ i & j \\ k & l \end{bmatrix} = \begin{bmatrix} a \cdot g + b \cdot i + c \cdot k & a \cdot h + b \cdot j + c \cdot l \\ d \cdot g + e \cdot i + f \cdot k & d \cdot h + e \cdot j + f \cdot l \end{bmatrix}$$

second matrix. For example, the number of rows of the first matrix must equal the number of columns of the second matrix, as shown in Figure 5.8.3.

Figure 5.8.3   Full matrix operations.

Listing 5.8.1 creates a library that allows all these calculations (and more) to be performed.

Listing 5.8.1   **Matrix Math Library**

```php
<?php
// A Library of Matrix Math functions.
// All assume a Matrix defined by a 2 dimensional array, where the first
//  index (array[x]) are the rows and the second index (array[x][y])
//  are the columns

// First create a few helper functions
```

Listing 5.8.1   **Continued**

```php
// A function to determine if a matrix is well formed.  That is to say that
//   it is perfectly rectangular with no missing values:
function _matrix_well_formed($matrix) {
    // If this is not an array, it is badly formed, return false.
    if (!(is_array($matrix))) {
        return false;
    } else {
        // Count the number of rows.
        $rows = count($matrix);

        // Now loop through each row:
        for ($r = 0; $r < $rows; $r++) {
            // Make sure that this row is set, and an array.  Checking to
            //   see if it is set is ensuring that this is a 0 based
            //   numerically indexed array.
            if (!(isset($matrix[$r]) && is_array($matrix[$r]))) {
                return false;
            } else {
                // If this is row 0, calculate the columns in it:
                if ($r == 0) {
                    $cols = count($matrix[$r]);
                // Ensure that the number of columns is identical else exit
                } elseif (count($matrix[$r]) != $cols) {
                    return false;
                }

                // Now, loop through all the columns for this row
                for ($c = 0; $c < $cols; $c++) {
                    // Ensure this entry is set, and a number
                    if (!(isset($matrix[$r][$c]) &&
                            is_numeric($matrix[$r][$c]))) {
                        return false;
                    }
                }
            }
        }
    }

    // Ok, if we actually made it this far, then we have not found
    //   anything wrong with the matrix.
    return true;
}

// A function to return the rows in a matrix -
```

Listing 5.8.1   **Continued**

```php
//   Does not check for validity, it assumes the matrix is well formed.
function _matrix_rows($matrix) {
    return count($matrix);
}


// A function to return the columns in a matrix -
//   Does not check for validity, it assumes the matrix is well formed.
function _matrix_columns($matrix) {
    return count($matrix[0]);
}


// This function performs operations on matrix elements, such as addition
//   or subtraction. To use it, pass it 2 matrices, and the operation you
//   wish to perform, as a string: '+', '-'
function matrix_element_operation($a, $b, $operation) {
    // Verify both matrices are well formed
    $valid = false;
    if (_matrix_well_formed($a) && _matrix_well_formed($b)) {
        // Make sure they have the same number of columns & rows
        $rows = _matrix_rows($a);
        $columns = _matrix_columns($a);

        if (($rows == _matrix_rows($b)) &&
                ($columns == _matrix_columns($b))) {
            // We have a valid setup for continuing with element math
            $valid = true;
        }
    }

    // If invalid, return false
    if (!($valid)) { return false; }

    // For each element in the matrices perform the operation on the
    //   corresponding element in the other array to it:
    for ($r = 0; $r < $rows; $r++) {
        for ($c = 0; $c < $columns; $c++) {
            eval('$a[$r][$c] '.$operation.'= $b[$r][$c];');
        }
    }

    // Return the finished matrix:
    return $a;
}


// This function performs full matrix operations, such as matrix addition
```

Listing 5.8.1 **Continued**

```
//  or matrix multiplication.  As above, pass it to matrices and the
//  operation: '*', '-', '+'
function matrix_operation($a, $b, $operation) {
    // Verify both matrices are well formed
    $valid = false;
    if (_matrix_well_formed($a) && _matrix_well_formed($b)) {
        // Make sure they have complementary numbers of rows and columns.
        // The number of rows in A should be the number of columns in B
        $rows = _matrix_rows($a);
        $columns = _matrix_columns($a);

        if (($columns == _matrix_rows($b)) &&
               ($rows == _matrix_columns($b))) {
            // We have a valid setup for continuing
            $valid = true;
        }
    }

    // If invalid, return false
    if (!($valid)) { return false; }

    // Create a blank matrix the appropriate size, initialized to 0
    $new = array_fill(0, $rows, array_fill(0, $rows, 0));

    // For each row in a ...
    for ($r = 0; $r < $rows; $r++) {
        // For each column in b ...
        for ($c = 0; $c < $rows; $c++) {
            // Take each member of column b, with each member of row a
            // and add the results, storing this in the new table:
            // Loop over each column in A ...
            for ($ac = 0; $ac < $columns; $ac++) {
                // Evaluate the operation
                eval('$new[$r][$c] += $a[$r][$ac] '.
                    $operation.' $b[$ac][$c];');
            }
        }
    }

    // Return the finished matrix:
    return $new;
}

// A function to perform scalar operations.  This means that you take the,
//  scalar value and the operation provided, and apply it to every element.
```

Listing 5.8.1   **Continued**

```php
function matrix_scalar_operation($matrix, $scalar, $operation) {
    // Verify it is well formed
    if (_matrix_well_formed($matrix)) {
        $rows = _matrix_rows($matrix);
        $columns = _matrix_columns($matrix);

        // For each element in the matrix, multiply by the scalar
        for ($r = 0; $r < $rows; $r++) {
            for ($c = 0; $c < $columns; $c++) {
                eval('$matrix[$r][$c] '.$operation.'= $scalar;');
            }
        }

        // Return the finished matrix:
        return $matrix;
    } else {
        // It wasn't well formed:
        return false;
    }
}

// A handy function for printing matrices (As an HTML table)
function matrix_print($matrix) {
    // Verify it is well formed
    if (_matrix_well_formed($matrix)) {
        $rows = _matrix_rows($matrix);
        $columns = _matrix_columns($matrix);

        // Start the table
        echo '<table>';

        // For each row in the matrix:
        for ($r = 0; $r < $rows; $r++) {
            // Begin the row:
            echo '<tr>';

            // For each column in this row
            for ($c = 0; $c < $columns; $c++) {
                // Echo the element:
                echo "<td>{$matrix[$r][$c]}</td>";
            }

            // End the row.
            echo '</tr>';
        }
```

Listing 5.8.1   **Continued**

```
        // End the table.
        echo "</table>\n";
    } else {
        // It wasn't well formed:
        return false;
    }
}

// Let's do some testing.  First prepare some formatting:
echo "<style>table { border: 1px solid black; margin: 20px; }
td { text-align: center; }</style>\n";

// Now let's test element operations.  We need identical sized matrices:
$m1 = array(
    array(5, 3, 2),
    array(3, 0, 4),
    array(1, 5, 2),
    );
$m2 = array(
    array(4, 9, 5),
    array(7, 5, 0),
    array(2, 2, 8),
    );

// Element addition should give us:  9   12    7
//                                  10    5    4
//                                   3    7   10
matrix_print(matrix_element_operation($m1, $m2, '+'));

// Element subtraction should give us:  1   -6   -3
//                                      -4   -5    4
//                                      -1    3   -6
matrix_print(matrix_element_operation($m1, $m2, '-'));

// Do a scalar multiplication on the 2nd matrix: 8   18   10
//                                              14   10    0
//                                               4    4   16
matrix_print(matrix_scalar_operation($m2, 2, '*'));

// Define some matrices for full matrix operations.
// Need to be complements of each other:
$m3 = array(
    array(1, 3, 5),
    array(-2, 5, 1),
    );
```

Listing 5.8.1 **Continued**

```
$m4 = array(
    array(1, 2),
    array(-2, 8),
    array(1, 1),
    );

// Matrix multiplication gives:  0   31
//                              -11  37
matrix_print(matrix_operation($m3, $m4, '*'));

// Matrix addition gives:  9   20
//                         4   15
matrix_print(matrix_operation($m3, $m4, '+'));
?>
```

First, the one routine to point out that is crucial to the functioning of the library is `_matrix_well_formed()`. Matrix math requires that all the input matrices be rectangular and that all cells have a value. This function checks that this is the case by using `count()`, `isset()`, and `is_numeric()` to ensure all the arrays are of the right length and have numeric values.

The operation functions are implemented in only three routines, `matrix_operation()` for full matrix operations, `matrix_element_operation()` for the element operations, and `matrix_scalar_operation()` for the scalar operations. Note that the actual math operation to be performed—addition, multiplication, and so on—is passed as a parameter to these functions.

How do you use a string representation of an operation to actually get the operation to be performed? An obvious way would be to use an `if` or `switch` statement to compare the string and then perform the operation. However, we use a much more general method—the `eval()` function. `eval()` takes a string and executes that string as PHP code. All our functions create the necessary PHP-valid statement, using the string containing the operation to be performed, and then execute the desired operation. The PHP statement uses `return` to pass the result of the evaluated statement back to our script, storing the result in the resulting matrix.

6

Functions

Functions in PHP are generally like functions in most other programming languages: They identify blocks of code that can be referenced over and over again. Hence, PHP functions have many of the same characteristics as other languages. Arguments can be given to a function, and values can be returned from them. All arguments and return values can be passed by value or by reference (see Listing 6.6.1, "Passing Arguments and Returning Values by Reference," later in this chapter). Functions can call themselves (see section 6.2, "Creating Recursive Functions," later in this chapter).

However, there are a few key differences, most of which stem from the fact that PHP can easily create and execute PHP code dynamically while it is running. Section 6.4, "Dynamically Creating a Function (Lambda-Style)," later in this chapter answers this in more detail. References to functions can be placed in variables, allowing functions to be passed as arguments to other functions or even stored in arrays, as shown in Section 6.3, "Calling Functions Using a Function Name Stored in a Variable." These capabilities allow PHP to be self-modifying; an application can change its behavior depending on input. This can enable the programmer to write concise yet versatile code.

Quick Hits

▶ **Dynamically define a function:**

```
$function = create_function($args, $code);
```

Returns a reference to the created function. The arguments are defined by a comma-delimited list of variable names, and the code is simply a string containing valid PHP code. See Section 6.4,"Dynamically Creating a Function (Lambda-Style)" later in this chapter for a full discussion.

Full documentation: http://php.net/create_function

▶ **Call a user-defined or variable function:**

```
$result = call_user_func($function, $arg1, $arg2);
$result = call_user_func_array($function, $arg_array);
```

Execute the specified function using the given arguments. The first function explicitly lists the arguments, whereas the second passes the arguments as an array.

Full documentation: http://php.net/call_user_func and http://php.net/call_user_func_array

▶ **Check whether a variable references a function:**

```
$result = is_callable($some_variable);
```

Returns true if the variable contains a name of an existing function or object.

Full documentation: http://php.net/is_callable

▶ **Check to see whether a function or method exists:**

```
$result = function_exists($name);
$result = method_exists($object, $name);
```

Checks whether a function or method of the specified name has been defined. This specifies that the function exists; however, it does not guarantee that the function is usable.

Full documentation: http://php.net/function_exists and http://php.net/method_exists

▶ **Get a list of all currently defined functions:**

```
$array = get_defined_functions();
```

Returns a multidimensional array with the key internal holding an array of all internally defined functions, and the key user holding all user-defined functions.

Full documentation: http://php.net/get_defined_functions

6.1 Setting Optional Parameters

When declaring a function, you may have a parameter that you almost always assign to the same value. You occasionally need to use a different value, though, so you cannot just hard-code the value. PHP provides a solution for just this situation: default values for parameters. If you declare a default for a certain parameter, if it is not provided, it will be automatically set to the default for you.

An example might be a security script that checks against a list to see whether a user is authorized. However, certain pages may only allow administrators to have access. Therefore, having an optional parameter to make it check for administrative access instead of regular access could be useful ,as shown in Listing 6.1.1.

Listing 6.1.1   **Using Optional Parameters**

```php
<?php
// Generate access list:
$access = array('aramsey', 'cdennison', 'hcline', 'rcook', 'rwhite');
$admin = array('ewhite', 'eisenhamer');
```

Listing 6.1.1 **Continued**

```php
// The function to check access.  Pass it a username, and optionally if
//  you want administrative access only:
function check_access($username, $adminonly = false) {
    global $access, $admin;

    // First of all, if they are an admin, always return true:
    if (in_array($username, $admin)) {
        return true;
    }

    // If we are allowing non-admins and they are in the list return true
    if (!($adminonly) && in_array($username, $access)) {
        return true;
    }

    // Otherwise, they should not have access:
    return false;
}

// Try a couple of test cases, regular access - both are true
echo "<p>'rwhite' ",
    check_access('rwhite') ? 'is' : 'is NOT' ," allowed.</p>";
echo "<p>'eisenhamer' ",
    check_access('eisenhamer') ? 'is' : 'is NOT' ," allowed.</p>";

// Now for administrative, eisenhamer does, but rwhite does not.
echo "<p>'rwhite' ",
    check_access('rwhite', true) ? 'is' : 'is NOT' ," an admin.</p>";
echo "<p>'eisenhamer' ",
    check_access('eisenhamer', true) ? 'is' : 'is NOT' ," an admin.</p>";
?>
```

Placing the equals sign and a value after the parameter creates the default for us. In this case, it was used like a flag, telling the function whether to perform some extra code. It could just as easily hold a string, float, array, or other data type.

A few rules must be followed with default arguments. The defaults cannot be a variable, class member, or function call. All default parameters must appear together on the right side of the parameter list, and you cannot make a default value for a parameter that is passed by reference.

6.2 Creating Recursive Functions

A *recursive function* is defined simply as a function that calls itself. (Also falling under the definition would be any group of functions that loop among themselves, such as function A calling function B, which in turn calls A.) PHP supports recursive functions, and they are often an elegant solution instead of a lengthy, deep, set of static instructions. Let's look at a simple comparison of two functions that do the same thing, one written recursively, and the other not (see Listing 6.2.1).

Listing 6.2.1   **Recursive Function Example**

```php
<?php
// A function to add all the numbers from 1 to the number given.
// Excuted in this case, with a for loop
function sum_up_to($number) {
    $result = 0;
    for ($i = 1; $i <= $number; $i++) {
        $result += $i;
    }
    return $result;
}

// And now the same function, written as a recursive function
function sum_up_recursive($number) {
    return ($number) ? ($number + sum_up_recursive($number - 1)) : 0;
}

// Try this in both cases, with the number 42, which should return: 903
echo '<p>Regular version = ', sum_up_to(42), "</p>\n";
echo '<p>Recursive version = ', sum_up_recursive(42), "</p>\n";
?>
```

Notice how even in this simple example of adding numbers, the code for the recursive version is much shorter and simpler. The only extra effort that must always go into recursive functions is ensuring that they exit. It is easy to write a function that will run forever. In this case, we are using the recursive function to count down, so we need to detect when we are at zero and return zero, ending the recursion.

When writing recursive functions, keep in mind two issues. The first issue is execution time. By default, PHP restricts the execution time of any script. This helps ensure that a script does not lock up a web server. Hence, you should make sure that any recursion will complete within the allotted time or modify the limit using set_time_limit().

The second issue is resources. With each call to a function, memory is allocated for all arguments passed by value and for all local variables created in a function. This memory is released on exit of that function call. Normally, this is not an issue because a function is called, does its job, and then exits. However, when a function is called recursively, this normal pattern is interrupted. When a function is called recursively, each call consumes whatever memory is needed until the recursion finally ends, when each recursive call starts returning. Normally this is not an issue. However, it is good practice to ensure that recursive functions do not create large arrays or use other "consumable" resources, such as opening files.

Finding how to end your recursion properly is the most important skill to learn in this regard. For another good example of recursion, see section 5.6, "Recursive Handling of Multidimensional Arrays" in Chapter 5, "Arrays."

6.3 Calling Functions Using a Function Name Stored in a Variable

It is possible to store the name of a function as a string and then to call the function from this. Why would you ever want to use this? Well it allows for the function name to be passed in as a string to another function (such as how usort() takes the name of your user-defined sort function). It also allows for an array of these strings to be stored. Another use is actually storing the function names in a database with other data and therefore being able to pull out not just the data but also the function that should operate on it.

One of the more unique uses of this is having the ability to generate a function name. This can be accomplished through the combination of multiple strings, by including an automatically incrementing number, or other methods. Calling a function in this manner is accomplished by simply adding the function call characters () to the end of your variable name. Listing 6.3.1 demonstrates a simple use of variable function names.

Listing 6.3.1   **Variable Function Names**

```php
<?php
// Define a few functions that echo different strings, based upon whether
//  the number is divisible by a certain other number.
function is_divisible_by_1($num) {
    echo "<p>Of course $num is divisible by 1, everything is!</p>";
}

function is_divisible_by_2($num) {
    if ($num % 2 == 0) {
        echo "<p>$num is divisible by 2.  That means it is even.</p>";
    }
}

function is_divisible_by_3($num) {
    if ($num % 3 == 0) {
        echo "<p>$num is divisible by 3.</p>";
    }
}

function is_divisible_by_4($num) {
    if ($num % 4 == 0) {
```

Listing 6.3.1 **Continued**

```php
        echo "<p>$num is divisible by 4.  It is double-even!</p>";
    }
}

function is_divisible_by_5($num) {
    if ($num % 5 == 0) {
        echo "<p>$num is divisible by 5.  It ends in a 0 or a 5.</p>";
    }
}

// Now, using a loop, going from 5 to 1, see what a given number (2000) is
//   divisible by.  This will be true for all cases except for '3'
for ($i = 5; $i > 0; $i--) {
    // Check for divisibility by calling the appropriate function:
    $var = 'is_divisible_by_' . $i;
    $var(2000);
}
?>
```

In this case we used it as a way to loop through calling different functions. Of course, a similar way to do this would be via an array of functions, which is discussed in section 6.5, "Using an Array of Functions for Processing," later in this chapter.

6.4 Dynamically Creating a Function (Lambda-Style)

It is possible in PHP to dynamically create a function and store it in a variable. These functions are often referred to as *anonymous functions* or *Lambda-style functions*. (This naming scheme comes from the older programming languages Lisp and Scheme.) The format to do this is straightforward, with a call to the PHP function create_function(). The first parameter of this function call is a string representing the function's arguments, and the second parameter is the body of the function.

Having the ability to create functions on-the-fly allows for some interesting constructs to be created. For example, you can have a certain function do a completely different task, based on certain conditions. Listing 6.4.1 demonstrates dynamically created functions for handling form input.

Listing 6.4.1 **Dynamically Creating Functions**

```php
<?php
// If input came via _POST then it was a form submission, trim the
//   data and return it:
if (count($_POST) > 0) {
    $prepped = create_function('$a', 'return trim($_POST[$a]);');
}
```

Listing 6.4.1   **Continued**

```php
// If this is a GET, then assume these are configuration parameters,
//  and that we need to not trim, but ensure they are upper case:
elseif (count($_GET) > 0) {
    $prepped = create_function('$a', 'return strtoupper($_GET[$a]);');
}
// Else, we had no input, create a function that just always returns false.
else {
    $prepped = create_function('$a', 'return false;');
}

// Now call this function to retrieve a certain value:
echo $prepped('file');
?>
```

Notice in this example that the same functionality could have been built into a single function that checks for POST or GET variables and returns the appropriate string. This setup is more efficient in this case, though, because the existence of POST or GET variables do not change at each call of the function. By writing it this way, that logic is only performed once, and then the function is written optimally for the situation.

Another inventive use of dynamically created functions is literally to change the definition of the function based on input, such as taking the input from a form and using it directly in your own function. Listing 6.4.2 provides a simple example based on numeric input.

Listing 6.4.2   **Create a Function Based on Input**

```php
<?php
// A function that will multiply numbers by a number passed in via a form:
$refactor = create_function('$i', 'return $i * '.$_REQUEST['factor'].';');

// Now call this on a number - If factor was 2.2, it would return 11
echo $refactor(5);
?>
```

It should not be taken for granted that this was a very simple example. In this case, it would have been easier to just multiply the number 5 by the request value directly. However, suppose that you were doing a large loop of such operations and the function was not just a simple adding of a number but performed much more complex calculations, making the use of a function all the more necessary.

Note that creating functions based on input, especially through form input, can be a dangerous thing to directly do, and you should be cautious in actual implementation. As with any form input handling, always validate any input before acting on that input. If not, a malicious user may find a way to execute arbitrary commands using your script, leading to system disruption to the theft of personal data. For more information, see to Chapter 11, "Data Validation and Standardization."

Between the uses of Lambda functions, variable functions, and variable variables, the possibilities for advanced PHP code are almost endless.

6.5 Using an Array of Functions for Processing

The creation of one Lambda function can add great versatility to a script. Now imagine creating a whole array of Lambda functions. Such an array allows for easy, programmatic access to a function. As an example, let's rewrite Listing 6.3.1 as an array of Lambda functions (see Listing 6.5.1).

Listing 6.5.1   **Using Arrays of Lambda Functions**

```php
<?php
// Define a few functions that echo different strings, based upon whether
//  the number is divisible by a certain other number.
$divisible = array(
    1 => create_function('$n',
        'echo "<p>Of course $n is divisible by 1, everything is!</p>";'),
    2 => create_function('$n',
        'if ($n % 2 == 0) {
            echo "<p>$n is divisible by 2.  It is even.</p>"; }'),
    3 => create_function('$n',
        'if ($n % 3 == 0) {
            echo "<p>$n is divisible by 3.</p>"; }'),
    4 => create_function('$n',
        'if ($n % 4 == 0) {
            echo "<p>$n is divisible by 4.  It is double-even!</p>"; }'),
    5 => create_function('$n',
        'if ($n % 5 == 0) { echo "<p>$n is divisible by 5.
            It therefore ends in a 0 or a 5.</p>"; }'),
    );

// Now loop through these functions, calling them all on the number 2000
//  They will be true for all cases except for '3'
foreach($divisible as $func) {
    $func(2000);
}
?>
```

Another good example demonstrating the use of arrays of functions can be found in Listing 2.8.1 in Chapter 2, "Numbers." In that example, arrays of functions are created that store the various formulas for converting between temperature scales. These functions are then called as needed.

6.6 Passing or Returning a Value by Reference

Normally in PHP all arguments are passed by value. This means that when you pass a variable in as one of the functions parameters, you get a copy of that variable's value. This way, if you change the variable, you are only updating a copy, and the original value never changes. This is the "safe" method of passing parameters.

However, at times you want to take the variable in and change it directly. This is referred to as *passing by reference*. To do this, you need to declare the function's parameter with an & in front of it, such as this:

```php
function myfunc($value, &$reference) {};
```

With this, the parameter named $value is a copy, but the variable $reference actually refers to the original variable. Similarly, you can specify that the value you return is a reference, by placing an & in front of the function name itself. Listing 6.6.1 demonstrates the use of passing arguments by reference.

Listing 6.6.1   **Passing Arguments and Returning Values by Reference**

```php
<?php
// Define a function that will increment a variable by 2, and returns a
//   copy of the new value.  Similar to the ++ operator, but going by 2
//   at a time.
function add2(&$number) {
    $number += 2;
    return $number;
}


// Use this to add 2 to a number, storing the output.
$mynum = 5;
$output = add2($mynum);

// Now add one to the $output variable and echo out the values:
//   output = 8, mynum = 7
$output++;
echo "<p>output = {$output}, mynum = {$mynum}</p>\n";

// Define a function that will initialize a 10 by 10 array, and
//   return a reference to it:
function &initialize() {
    $new = array_fill(0, 10, array_fill(0, 10, 0));
    return $new;
}

// Initialize a new array with this, and echo it out:
$newarray =& initialize();
echo '<pre>', print_r($newarray, true), '</pre>';
?>
```

If you are used to programming in other languages, you may have the concept that passing by reference would be a performance increase. That way PHP doesn't have to make a copy of the value, just use the one copy. Most of the time this is not true in PHP, though, because it uses internal optimizations to speed this up.

In PHP, when you pass a variable by value, it doesn't actually make a copy of the value until, and if, you actually change the value. So if all you are doing is passing in a value to be read, it isn't a concern. One case where it does matter is objects. Objects cannot be optimized this way; however, PHP 5 fixed the performance aspects by the fact that all objects are automatically passed by reference. You cannot pass an object by value in PHP 5, which is fine because that concept is contrary to how objects work.

With all that said, there are some cases where passing by reference can be faster—for example, if you had a function that took the value, changed it, returned it, and was only ever used to save it back into the same variable. In this case it does have to make a copy of the new value while the old one exists just to return it. Here a reference and direct access to the data would be faster, although, this is a very specialized case.

6.7 Using an Arbitrary Number of Parameters

Default parameters can give you an almost arbitrary list of parameters, although there will always be a limit imposed on how many you declare. There are times when it is useful to allow for any number of arguments to your function.

This is possible via a few functions that PHP provides. `func_num_args()` lets you know how many arguments were passed to a function. `func_get_arg(n)` returns the nth parameter that was passed (starting from 0), and `func_get_args()` returns the entire argument list as an array.

Having an unlimited list of arguments can be used in different ways. A common use is simply to perform some task on any number of values passed into it. A good example of this can be seen in Listing 4.7.1 in Chapter 4, "Variables," where a function is created that looks through all values passed to it to find the first one that is not null.

Another use is to actually have different functionality based on different numbers of arguments. For example, in Listing 6.7.1, we create a function that accepts numbers and, if it receives one argument, squares it; two arguments, multiplies them; and three or more arguments, sums them all together.

Listing 6.7.1   **Using Varying Argument Lists**

```php
<?php
// Define an 'interesting' function that does different math based
//   on the number of arguments
function interesting() {
    // Read in the number of arguments:
    $args = func_num_args();

    // If one argument, square it and return it
    if ($args == 1) {
```

Listing 6.7.1   **Continued**

```
        $num = func_get_arg(0);
        return $num * $num;
    }
    // If two arguments, multiply them and return it:
    elseif ($args == 2) {
        return func_get_arg(0) * func_get_arg(1);
    }
    // Otherwise, sum up all the values and return them
    else {
        $nums = func_get_args();
        return array_sum($nums);
    }
}

// Try the function in all 3 forms:

// Pass it a 2, and it should return 4
echo '<p>', interesting(2), '</p>';

// Pass it a 2 and a 4, and it should return 8
echo '<p>', interesting(2, 4), '</p>';

// Pass it a 2, 4, 1, and 8, and it will add them to get 15
echo '<p>', interesting(2,4,1,8), '</p>';
?>
```

6.8 Requiring a Parameter to Be a Certain Type

PHP 5 has implemented *type hinting*. Type hinting requires the parameter of your function (or an object's method) to be of a specific type. As of the writing of this book, PHP 5.1 only allows this to be an object type or an array. You cannot require a basic type (such as int or string).

To perform type hinting, simply insert the object name or array in front of the function parameter shown. After that, if the function is called without the proper type of argument, a fatal error is triggered. Type hinting is demonstrated in Listing 6.8.1.

Listing 6.8.1   **Type Hinting**

```
<?php
// A function that multiplies together all members of the array its given
function array_multiply(array $a) {
    return array_reduce($a, create_function('$x,$y', 'return $x * $y;'), 1);
}
```

Listing 6.8.1 **Continued**

```php
// First try this, passing an array with a few values:
//  This will return: 1288
$test_array = array(2, 7, 23, 4);
echo '<p>', array_multiply($test_array), '</p>';

// Now try it again, just passing it a scalar value: 2
//  A fatal error will be generated by PHP because of the type mismatch.
echo '<p>', array_multiply(2), '</p>';
?>
```

Just because PHP does not directly provide a way to do type hinting for basic types, it does not mean that it cannot be done. You can check the type of a variable either by a call to gettype(), which returns a string representation of the type ('boolean', 'integer', 'string', and so on), or by calls to the various specific functions that check for a certain type, such as is_integer(), is_boolean(), is_string(), and so on.

Using these functions, and custom calls to trigger_error(), you can simulate type hinting for whatever types you want as demonstrated in Listing 6.8.2.

Listing 6.8.2 **Implementing Custom Type Hinting**

```php
<?php
<?php
// Define a function that does lots of type checking
function many_hints($int, $flt, $str) {
    // Ensure that $int is an integer
    if (!(is_integer($int))) {
        trigger_error('$int is not of type integer', E_USER_ERROR);
    }
    // Ensure that $flt is a float
    if (!(is_float($flt))) {
        trigger_error('$flt is not of type float', E_USER_ERROR);
    }
    // Ensure that $str is a string
    if (!(is_string($str))) {
        trigger_error('$str is not of type integer', E_USER_ERROR);
    }

    // Now that we know we have proper variables, multiply the integer &
    //  float together and return that with the string
    return ($int * $flt) . ' ' . $str;
}

// Use this first giving it valid parameters
//  This will print: '83.664 dollars owed'
echo '<p>', many_hints(1992, .042, 'dollars owed'), '</p>';
```

Listing 6.8.2   **Continued**

```
// Now try it again, Passing it incorrect data types.
//  An error will be generated because of the type mismatch.
echo '<p>', many_hints('bob', 3, true), '</p>';
?>
```

Using this in your own custom code where you know the proper values to pass just ends up wasting processor power. It will be constantly checking that the values are of proper types.

PHP automatic type conversion does an excellent job of handling type mismatches, so normally you do not need to worry about forcing specific type checking. Doing so unnecessarily can end up wasting needed processing resources, such as when serving pages on a high-volume web server. This can be useful, however, when writing libraries that other people will use because it gives them a much more stable environment by letting them know when they have made a mistake.

7

Classes and Objects

BEFORE DELVING INTO OBJECT-ORIENTED PROGRAMMING in PHP, you must first note that PHP 5 has seen a complete rewrite of its object-oriented capabilities. Because a full discussion of object-oriented programming (OOP) is well beyond this text, the basics, as they pertain to PHP, can be found at http://www.php.net/oop5. This chapter gives a cursory introduction to the concept followed by numerous in-depth examples.

OOP is a programming paradigm. OOP is a particular approach to solving problems that is not necessarily tied to any specific language or hardware architecture. Nevertheless, language syntax and the software environment can make it much easier to implement OOP solutions. This is exactly the case with PHP. PHP is inherently a procedural language that has added the syntax necessary to support solutions using OOP techniques.

As implied by the name, the central concept of OOP is the object. At a practical level, an *object* is simply a data structure comprised of functions and variables local to each object. The class from which the object is created defines what an object can do. A *class* is the code that defines the functions and variables an object created from the class will have. The class definitions can be thought of as templates from which objects are created. An application can create many objects based on a single class definition. In OOP jargon, an object is an *instance* of a class, and the act of creating an object from a class is called *instantiation*.

To illustrate the relationship between the class definition and its object, and to show the basic syntax used in PHP, Listing 7.0.1 defines a simple class, instantiates an object based on that class, and uses the object.

Listing 7.0.1 **Implementing a Simple Class**

```php
<?php
// Define a simple class that simply echoes the value given it.
class SimpleClass {
    public $data;
    public function echoMyData() {
```

Listing 7.0.1 **Continued**

```php
        echo $this->data;
    }
}

// Create an object based on SimpleClass
$sc_object = new SimpleClass();

// Set a value for the data of the object
$sc_object->data = "Hello, world! ";

// Now let us create another object and give it a different value.
$another_object = new SimpleClass();
$another_object->data = "Goodbye, world! ";

// Use the class method to print out the value of our two objects.
$sc_object->echoMyData();
$another_object->echoMyData();

// The output from this script will be:
//    Hello, world! Goodbye, world!
?>
```

In words, the class `SimpleClass` is defined to have two members: a variable named `$data` and a function named `echoMyData()`. The PHP statement `new` uses the class definition to create two objects, each of which references its own copies of the class members. Here a note on terminology is in order. In OOP, functions of a class are referred to as *class methods*. Variables associated with a class are referred to as *variables*, *parameters*, or, as in the PHP manual, *members*.

Quick Hits

▶ Create a new object:

```php
$object = new ClassName;
```

The PHP statement `new` creates a new object of the specified class.

Full documentation: http://php.net/new

▶ Destroy an object:

```php
unset($object);
```

Unsetting an object causes the resources associated with that object to be removed. If a `__destruct()` method is defined for the class, it will be called.

Full documentation: http://php.net/unset and http://php.net/destruct

▶ **Create a copy of an object:**

```
$object_copy = clone $object;
```

In PHP 5, simple assignment only creates a reference to an object. The clone statement must therefore be used to create a whole copy of an object. If a __clone() method is defined for the class, it will be called.

Full documentation: http://php.net/clone

▶ **Compare two separate objects:**

```
$isequal = ($obj1 == $obj2);
```

The comparison operator, ==, checks whether the two objects are of the same class and whether all class variables have the same value.

Full documentation: http://php.net/manual/language.oop5.object-comparison.php

▶ **Compare whether two object variables are referencing the same instance of an object:**

```
$issameinstance = ($obj1 === $obj2);
```

The identity operator, ===, returns true if both object variables refer to the same instance of an object.

Full documentation: http://php.net/manual/language.oop5.object-comparison.php

7.1 Automatically Loading Class Source Files

It is a common OOP practice to place each of your class definitions into separate files. Even if this is not done, it is a good practice to group various class definitions into multiple files based on their usage. This makes it so that you don't need to include one large library file in every page, even if it is not all needed. You only need to include the files containing the specific classes that page needs.

Although a good programming practice because it keeps things organized, separating definitions into individual files can lead to complications. The biggest annoyance is the need for a large block of require_once statements in the top of every PHP file to include all these different files. This tends to lead to sloppy programming over time, as programmers not wanting to make these multiple includes will end up making a single include file that then includes all the other files. Although this is simple for the programmer, it defeats the original purpose of breaking all the classes into separate files in the first place: reducing the number of included files per page.

The programmers of PHP realized this and in PHP 5 added a feature that makes all this much easier. It is a magic function called __autoload() (note the two underscores in that name). You can define this function, and it will automatically be called anytime a new object attempts to be instantiated, and yet the appropriate class file has not been loaded yet. This allows you, inside that function, to determine the appropriate filename and perform a require_once on it. An example is useful at this point. Assume that you name all your class files in the following scheme: class-{CLASSNAME}.php. Listing 7.1.1 shows you how to make those files automatically load.

> **Note**
>
> PHP reserves for itself any functions with a double-underscore prefix (__) as "magic functions" that provide various automatic features. Do not make any of your own functions have a double-underscore, unless you specifically want to invoke one of these magic functions.

Listing 7.1.1   **Creating an __autoload() Function**

```php
<?php
// Declare the autoload function to automatically find our files for us.
function __autoload($classname) {
    require_once "class-{$classname}.php";
}

// Instantiate an object of class 'cd'.
//   This will make it try to load the file: class-cd.php
$mydisk = new cd();
?>
```

As you can see, this is simple, and yet you could easily have complex logic in the __autoload() function to determine how to load the file. There is a limitation to this, however. You can define only one __autoload() function because any subsequent definition will cause a fatal error for attempting to redefine a function.

Normally this would not be a problem because you only need to create one __autoload() that contains all your class loading logic. However, this can be a problem for people writing third-party libraries. If a library uses __autoload(), anyone using that library will not be able to use __autoload() in his own code, or use any other library that also needs to use __autoload().

Expecting this problem, PHP 5.1 developers added a new way to do autoloading into the SPL (Standard PHP Library). (The SPL is covered in detail in Appendix B, "SPL.") A set of functions is provided that allow you to register multiple autoloading functions at once. The primary function that you use when doing this is spl_autoload_register(). You just pass this function the name (as a string) of another function that you have created, and it uses that function for autoloading. Call it multiple times to register more functions. For example, imagine that you always write your code to use the class- prefix shown in Listing 7.1.1, but someone else contributing to your project uses obj-. Listing 7.1.2 registers two functions to handle these.

Listing 7.1.2   **Using SPL to Create __autoload() Functions**

```php
<?php
// Declare an autoload function and register it using SPL
function my_class_autoload($classname) {
```

Listing 7.1.2 **Continued**

```
    @require_once "class-{$classname}.php";
}

spl_autoload_register('my_class_autoload');

// Now create another one and register it:
function another_class_autoload($classname) {
    @require_once "obj-{$classname}.php";
}

spl_autoload_register('another_class_autoload');

// Instantiate an object of class 'cd'.
//   This will make it try to load the file: class-cd.php or obj-cd.php
$mydisk = new cd();
?>
```

Granted, this is a contrived example because one function could have looked for both files. However, imagine those two calls being in different library files and that when each was written, they didn't know about each other. In this case, it still works fine.

You may notice that @'s were added in front of the require_once calls. This is so that errors do not get thrown when one function tries to load the file but fails. Because the other function still has a chance, we shouldn't exit.

One problem still can happen. If an __autoload() has been declared and then spl_autoload_register() is used to register a function, the original __autoload() will be destroyed.

This is fairly simple to work around however. If you want to make a library that always works, just check to see whether an __autoload() has been declared before ever calling spl_autoload_register(). If it exists, first register it with spl_autoload_register(), as shown in Listing 7.1.3.

Listing 7.1.3 **Using Both** __autoload() **and SPL**

```
<?php
// Declare an autoload function and register it using SPL
function __autoload($classname) {
    @require_once "class-{$classname}.php";
}

// Now create another one.
function another_class_autoload($classname) {
    @require_once "obj-{$classname}.php";
}
```

Listing 7.1.3 **Continued**

```
// Check __autoload() has been declared before registering our function
if (function_exists('__autoload')) {
    spl_autoload_register('__autoload');
}


// Now register our own function.
spl_autoload_register('another_class_autoload');


// Instantiate an object of class 'cd'.
//   This will make it try to load the file: class-cd.php or obj-cd.php
$mydisk = new cd();
?>
```

7.2 Protecting Object Data (`public`/`private`/ `protected`)

PHP 5 includes a full object model that, like other object-oriented languages, allows for visibility permissions to be set on variables and methods. The keywords for doing this and their definitions are

- `public`—This declares that the variable or method is fully accessible at all times.
- `private`—The opposite of `public`, this means that the variable or method can only be seen from inside the object itself.
- `protected`—A middle ground between the other two options. A variable or method declared as such can be accessed from within the object itself, or from within any other class that extends this one. It cannot be accessed externally.

All variable declarations within the class must be prefaced by one of these terms. Methods should also be prefaced by one of these; however, if not specified, the default permission for methods is `public`. It should be noted that these visibility permissions apply only to the class variables and functions. They cannot be applied to variables used within the functions. Listing 7.2.1 demonstrates the effects of the visibility permissions.

Listing 7.2.1 **Using Class Visibility Operators**

```
<?php
class cd {
    public $artist;
    public $title;
    protected $tracks;
    private $disk_id;
}
```

Listing 7.2.1   **Continued**

```
// Instantiate an object of class 'cd'.
$mydisk = new cd();

// Now update the artist's name
$mydisk->artist = 'The Child Song Singers';

// Now try to update the protected or private values.
// This will cause a fatal error:
$mydisk->tracks = array('Wheels on the Bus', 'Mary had a Little Lamb');
?>
```

7.3 Automatically Running Code On Creation or Destruction of an Object

There are times when you want to automatically have certain code run when a new instantiation of an object is created. This might be used to automatically fill data elements, to open a database connection, or any other of a number of tasks. Similarly, you may want to have something done when the object is destroyed, either via unset() or by the script ending. This could be closing a database connection, saving data to disk, and so on.

You can perform these tasks by declaring __construct() or __destruct() methods, respectively. These methods will automatically be run for you at the appropriate times. Listing 7.3.1 uses them to generate a random disk identifier upon creation.

Listing 7.3.1   **Declaring and Using Object Constructors and Destructors**

```
<?php
// Define our class for Compact disks
class cd {
    // Declare variables (properties)
    public $artist;
    public $title;
    protected $tracks;
    private $disk_id;

    // Declare the constructor
    public function __construct() {
        // Generate a random disk_id
        $this->disk_id = sha1('cd' . time() . rand());
    }

    // Create a method to return the disk_id, it can't be accessed directly
    // since it is declared as private.
```

Listing 7.3.1 **Continued**

```
    public function get_disk_id() {
        return $this->disk_id;
    }
}

// Instantiate an object of class 'cd'.
$mydisk = new cd();

// Now use the provided function to retrieve, and display, the id
echo '<p>The compact disk ID is: ', $mydisk->get_disk_id(), '</p>';
?>
```

Note that the __construct() function must be declared as public; otherwise, it won't work because when it is called on object creation, it is assumed to be an outside call. You may also note that to generate the ID, a tactic similar to that described in Chapter 1, "Strings," section 1.11, "Generating Unique Identifiers," was used.

7.4 Accessing a Class's Members Without Instantiation

Sometimes you may want to create a class but have its methods or variables accessible without creating a new instantiation of the class. To allow for this, you need to declare any variable you want accessible as a const or static. (Methods can only be declared static.)

The difference between const and static is simple. A const is a constant value. It cannot be the result of a function call, and it must just be a set value that is being stored and cannot ever be changed. In this sense, it is similar to using define() to make a global constant value, just that this one exists only within the class namespace. Something defined as static just means that it will be accessible at a class level. If you define a method as static you cannot make any references to $this within that method because that refers to an instantiated object. If a variable is defined as static, just like with const, it must be a set value to begin; however, it can be updated later.

To reference a static or const class member, instead of the regular -> operator, you need to use the scope resolution operator ::. This is known in PHP as the *Paamayim Nekudotayim* (which means double-colon in Hebrew). As an example, Listing 7.4.1 creates a math class that defines some extra constants and methods that the math package of PHP does not.

Listing 7.4.1 **Extending Classes: Creating a Statistics Class**

```
<?php
// Define a Math class that provides static and const members for use
class Math_Extended {
```

Listing 7.4.1   **Continued**

```
    // Declare some constant variables for reference:
    // Speed of light (meters per second) (exact)
    const C = 299792458;

    // Temperature of the Sun (Kelvin) (approximate)
    const T_SUN = 5780;

    // Radius of the Earth (meters) (approximate)
    const R_EARTH = 6378000;

    // Now let's declare some static methods - Start with a cube root one:
    public static function curt($num) {
        return pow($num, 1/3);
    }

    // A method that will generate the length of a side of a right-angle
    // triangle, given the length of one side, and of the hypotenuse
    public static function triSide($hypot, $side) {
        return sqrt(pow($hypot, 2) - pow($side, 2));
    }
}

// See how long it takes for light to traverse the diameter of the Earth
$seconds = (Math_Extended::R_EARTH * 2) / Math_Extended::C;
echo "<p>The light would take {$seconds} seconds</p>\n";

// Calculate the side of a right triangle.  Use a 1,2,sqrt(3) triangle
$side = Math_Extended::triSide(2, sqrt(3));
echo "<p>The other side of the triangle is {$side}</p>\n";

// Calculate the cube root of 27
$root = Math_Extended::curt(27);
echo "<p>The cube root of 27 is {$root}</p>\n";
?>
```

By using const and static this way, you can create a library that has all its methods and variables encapsulated into a protected name area. This is similar to namespaces and packages of other languages. This keeps you from worrying about reusing a variable or function name that someone else might have.

7.5 Extending a Class Definition

Inheritance, a core concept of object-oriented design, is the idea that one class may be the child, or extension, of another class. In this case the child inherits all properties of the parent, and yet at the same time can extend the capabilities. The child class can declare new variables and new methods if it wants, but all those from the parent will also be available. It can also even overwrite the parent's methods with its own. It is possible for the parent to stop this from happening. By declaring a variable or a method as `final`, it can be inherited but is not changeable.

Inheritance is accomplished via the `extends` keyword. It essentially tells PHP to copy the definition of the original class and to then let you modify it. If you override a method of the original class, it can still be accessed via prefacing your call to it with `parent::`.

Listing 7.5.1 takes the CD example that we used previously and defines a `cd_album` that takes the concept of multidisk CD collections into account.

Listing 7.5.1 **Example of Inheritance**

```php
<?php
// Define our class for Compact disks
class cd {
    // Declare variables (properties)
    public $artist;
    public $title;
    protected $tracks;
    private $disk_id;

    // Declare the constructor
    public function __construct() {
        // Generate a random disk_id
        $this->disk_id = sha1('cd' . time() . rand());
    }

    // Create a method to return the disk_id, it can't be accessed directly
    // since it is declared as private.
    public function get_disk_id() {
        return $this->disk_id;
    }
}

// Now extend this and add multi-disk support
class cd_album extends cd {
    // Add a count for the number of disks:
    protected $num_disks;

    // A constructor that allows for the number of disks to be provided
    public function __construct($disks = 1) {
        $this->num_disks = $disks;

        // Now force the parent's constructor to still run as well
        //  to create the disk id
```

Listing 7.5.1   **Continued**

```
        parent::__construct();
    }

    // Create a function that returns a true or false for whether this
    //  is a multicd set or not?
    public function is_multi_cd() {
        return ($this->num_disks > 1) ? true : false;
    }
}

// Instantiate an object of class 'cd_album'.  Make it a 3 disk set.
$mydisk = new cd_album(3);

// Now use the provided function to retrieve, and display, the id
echo '<p>The compact disk ID is: ', $mydisk->get_disk_id(), '</p>';

// Use the provided function to check if this is a a multi-cd set.
echo '<p>Is this a multi cd? ',
    ($mydisk->is_multi_cd()) ? 'Yes' : 'No',
    '</p>';
?>
```

Note that when we instantiate an object, it accepts a parameter as to the number of disks but defaults to 1. It then calls the parent class's __construct() function to create the random disk id for us. Also while testing the new extended class, methods are called from both the original class and the new one.

7.6 Creating an Abstract Class

As the previous section demonstrated, extending classes can be a powerful tool. However, there may be times you want to create a class that must be extended to use it. Abstract classes are just this. In declaring a class to be abstract, you can also declare functions, where you give the name and what parameters they take; however, leave the implementation up to classes that will extend this one.

In doing this, you can define a template of how the child class must look. The child must implement all of the abstract class's abstract methods to extend it, as shown in Listing 7.6.1.

Listing 7.6.1   **Example of an Abstract Class**

```
<?php
// Define an abstract class for animals.
abstract class animal {
    // Declare variables (properties)
    public $name;
```

Listing 7.6.1 **Continued**

```php
    // Make a constructor to be shared that requires a name.
    public function __construct($namesake) {
        $this->name = $namesake;
    }

    // Declare abstract methods that each animal must implement.
    abstract public function makeSound();
    abstract public function eat($what);
}

// Define a cat class
class cat extends animal {
    public function makeSound() {
        echo "Meow\n";
    }

    public function eat($what) {
        switch ($what) {
            case 'kibble':
            case 'cat food':
            case 'mouse':
            case 'bird':
                echo "The cat says yum!\n";
                break;
            case 'grass':
            case 'tinsel':
            case 'hair':
                echo "The cat purrs contentedly.\n";
                break;
            default:
                echo "The cat raises its head haughtily and walks off.\n";
        }
    }
}

// Define a cow class
class cow extends animal {
    public function makeSound() {
        echo "Mooooooooo!\n";
    }

    public function eat($what) {
        switch ($what) {
            case 'grass':
            case 'hay':
```

Listing 7.6.1   **Continued**

```
            case 'salt':
                echo "The cow chews its cud.\n";
                break;
            default:
                echo "The cow walks off ignoring it.\n";
        }
    }
}

// Declare a cat & a cow.
$my_cat = new cat('Mimi-ow');
$my_cow = new cow('Gertrude');

echo '<pre>';

// The cat says: Meow
$my_cat->makeSound();

// The cow says: Moo
$my_cow->makeSound();

// What do they each do when they eat grass?
$my_cat->eat('grass');
$my_cow->eat('grass');

echo '</pre>';
?>
```

In this way you can define a set of objects that must all follow the same format, and therefore be interoperable. Any number of classes can extend the original. The only requirements are that each child class must declare all abstract functions, and that they must be declared at the same (or a less restrictive) visibility level. Beyond that, the new class may define as many other methods and properties as you want.

7.7 Using Object Interfaces

Abstract classes as just described are powerful ways to define how new classes are constructed. Sometimes, however, you don't want to fully define a class. Instead you need to specify that classes must implement a certain set of methods. This way you can have vastly different classes created, but all define these methods and therefore can operate the same.

This can be done by defining an interface. Interfaces are made by using the interface keyword instead of class and specifying public methods, just as you would have for an abstract class. Other classes can now use the `implements` keyword instead of `extends` and state that they are going to implement all methods that the interface specified.

This can be used to create common access methods, data manipulations, or conversions. Listing 7.7.1 defines an interface that requires methods that will return a text or HTML representation of the object. The objects can be different, and yet still implement these methods.

Listing 7.7.1   **Object Interfaces**

```php
<?php
// Define an interface that will allow conversion of objects to strings
interface conversionOptions {
    public function asString();
    public function asHTML();
}

// Define a 'cat' class that implements the interface
class cat implements conversionOptions {
    // Properties of a cat
    public $name;
    public $color;

    // Constructor that requires a name
    public function __construct($namesake) {
        $this->name = $namesake;
    }

    // Implement the string function of the interface
    public function asString() {
        return "Cat - Name: {$this->name}, Color: {$this->color}";
    }

    // Implement the HTML function of the interface
    public function asHTML() {
        return "<ul><li>Cat</li><ul><li>Name: {$this->name}</li>
<li>Color: {$this->color}</li></ul></ul>";
    }
}

// Define class that implements the interface, for acronym definitions
class acronym implements conversionOptions {
    // Properties of an acronym
    private $name;
    private $definition;
```

Listing 7.7.1 **Continued**

```
    // Constructor that requires the term entry and definition
    public function __construct($entry, $def) {
        $this->name = $entry;
        $this->definition = $def;
    }

    // Implement the string function of the interface
    public function asString() {
        return "{$this->name}: {$this->definition}";
    }

    // Implement the HTML function of the interface
    public function asHTML() {
        return "<dl><dt>{$this->name}</dt>
<dd>{$this->definition}</dd></dl>";
    }
}

// Instantiate a cat & give it data
$my_cat = new cat('Wiley');
$my_cat->color = 'grey tabby';

// Now return the cat as a string & echo it:
$catstring = $my_cat->asString();
echo "<pre>{$catstring}</pre>\n";

// And do the same as HTML
echo $my_cat->asHTML();

// Now construct an acronym definition
$my_anac = new acronym('SCA', 'Society for Creative Anacronism');

// Covert it into string form:
$anac = $my_anac->asString();
echo "<pre>{$anac}</pre>\n";

// Now output as HTML
echo $my_anac->asHTML();
?>
```

7.8 Dynamic and Overloaded Variable Names

PHP 5 allows you to dynamically accept any variable name accessed within an object.
By defining the __set() and __get() methods, you can tell the object how to handle

any variable names that it did not originally have. The __set() method is automatically called when any variable is set that did not directly exist. It is passed the name of the variable and the value.

Similarly the __get() is called and passed the name of the variable desired whenever variable access is attempted. To round out these, you can also define a __isset() and __unset(), which again are automatically called when the regular PHP isset() or unset() are called on one of these variable values.

By combining the definitions of all these functions, you can create powerful class definitions. For example, Listing 7.8.1 creates a class used simply for data storage, essentially acting as a separate namespace, by holding any data value passed into it. It accomplishes this through a private array that it fills with values.

Listing 7.8.1 **Object Overloading**

```php
<?php
// Define a class that will store values for any property it is given.
class Data_Holder {
    // The data storage array
    private $data = array();

    // A method to set any variable passed to this object.
    // Store it in the array
    public function __set($name, $value) {
        $this->data[$name] = $value;
    }

    // A method to return any values that are set:
    public function __get($name) {
        if (isset($this->data[$name])) { return $this->data[$name]; }
    }

    // A method that will allow 'isset' to work on these variables
    public function __isset($name) {
        return isset($this->data[$name]);
    }

    // Finally a method to allow 'unset' calls to work on these variables
    public function __unset($name) {
        unset($this->data[$name]);
    }
}

// Create a data holding object & store some data in it:
$data = new Data_Holder();
$data->name = 'Francesca';
```

Listing 7.8.1 **Continued**

```php
// Now echo the value out to see that the __get method is working:
echo "<p>The data value of 'name' is {$data->name}</p>";

// Now unset the value, and then use isset to ensure that it happened.
unset($data->name);
echo '<p>The value is ', isset($data->name) ? '' : 'not ', 'set.</p>';
?>
```

Using these same tools, you can also overload variable names. This means that you can have the same name actually store different values based on some custom logic. Because the __set() method is called for each data storage attempt, you can place code in here that figures out how to actually store the data. For example, Listing 7.8.2 creates a class that actually stores text and numeric data passed to the same variable name as separate data. Note that it would be difficult to create a __get() method that would actually know which version you want. Therefore we create a different data access routine that returns our values.

Listing 7.8.2 **Variable Overloading**

```php
<?php
// Define a class that overloads a variable name by allowing the same
//  name to hold a number, and text.
class Multi_Data_Holder {
    // variables to hold various versions of the same named property
    private $number = array();
    private $text = array();

    // Define __set, which stores data based upon the type of value.
    public function __set($name, $value) {
        // Check if it is one of the types we are allowing, and store
        //  appropriately. If it is an int or float, store it as a number:
        if (is_int($value) || is_float($value)) {
            $this->number[$name] = $value;
        } elseif (is_string($value)) {
            $this->text[$name] = $value;
        }
    }

    // Defining isset to understand the 'multi' nature of values here.
    public function __isset($name) {
        // If it exists in either case, claim it exists.
        return isset($this->number[$name]) || isset($this->text[$name]);
    }

    // Define a method such that unset will unset all values.
    public function __unset($name) {
```

Listing 7.8.2 **Continued**

```php
            unset($this->number[$name]);
            unset($this->text[$name]);
        }

        // It won't be possible to define a get that knows which one to return,
        //  so let's define a function instead that takes a second parameter of
        //  either 'number' or 'text' to determine which one to read:
        public function value($name, $type) {
            // Use the $type as a variable variable to return the right value:
            return $this->{$type}[$name];
        }
    }

// Create a data holding object
$data = new Multi_Data_Holder();

// Store a number, and the English representation of the number
$data->x = 173;
$data->x = 'One Hundred Seventy Three';

// Now echo the number and it's text:
echo '<p>The number ', $data->value('x', 'number'), ' is written: ',
    $data->value('x', 'text'), '</p>';

// Now unset the value, and then use isset to ensure that it happened.
unset($data->x);
echo '<p>The value is ', isset($data->x) ? '' : 'not ', 'set.</p>';
?>
```

So far, we have just concentrated on the data storage aspect of the __set() method and its friends. However, because it is a method, and it can hold any code, much more than just data storage can be done. The data can be manipulated, or any other number of actions can be set off. It could even automatically open a database connection and immediately store the data upon setting and, when the data was asked for, read it back in from the database. To demonstrate this capability, Listing 7.8.3 creates a class similar to the data storage class created in Listing 7.8.1, which automatically formats the data based on what type of data it is.

Listing 7.8.3 **Overloading with Execution**

```php
<?php
// Define a class that will store values for any property it is given,
//  and format them nicely
class Data_Formatter {
```

Listing 7.8.3   **Continued**

```php
    // The data storage array
    private $data = array();

    // Method to set any variable passed to this object.
    public function __set($name, $value) {
        if (is_int($value)) {
            // It is an integer, format it with commas, but no decimal
            $new_value = number_format($value, 0);
        } elseif (is_float($value)) {
            // It is a float value, format it with commas, and 2 decimals:
            $new_value = number_format($value, 2);
        } elseif (is_bool($value)) {
            // A boolean value, turn it into the string 'true' or 'false'
            $new_value = $value ? 'true' : 'false';
        } else {
            // Otherwise just store the data as is:
            $new_value = $value;
        }

        // Now store the data in our array
        $this->data[$name] = $new_value;
    }

    // A method to return any values that are set:
    public function __get($name) {
        if (isset($this->data[$name])) { return $this->data[$name]; }
    }

    // A method that will allow 'isset' to work on these variables
    public function __isset($name) {
        return isset($this->data[$name]);
    }

    // Finally a method to allow 'unset' calls to work on these variables
    public function __unset($name) {
        unset($this->data[$name]);
    }
}

// Create a data holding object & store some data in it:
$data = new Data_Formatter();
$data->number = 1200;
$data->money = 189000.452;
$data->lies = false;
$data->place = 'Mount Airy';
```

Listing 7.8.3 **Continued**

```
// Now echo these values out to see their formatted values:
//    1,200      189,000.45     false      Mount Airy
echo "<p>The value of 'number' is {$data->number}</p>";
echo "<p>The value of 'money' is {$data->money}</p>";
echo "<p>The value of 'lies' is {$data->lies}</p>";
echo "<p>The value of 'place' is {$data->place}</p>";
?>
```

7.9 Overloading Methods

PHP, like most object-oriented languages, supports the idea of overloading methods. Overloading is simply the ability to define multiple functions that have the same name but differ in the type or number of parameters that they are expecting. Therefore, the appropriate method is called based on the parameters given in.

PHP's implementation is not quite this straightforward, though. Instead, similar to the special methods for handling overloading of variable names, there is a single special function __call() that is used anytime a method is called that does not really exist. Similarly then, you can use logic to determine what actual method to call, or what else to do. The first parameter is the name of the method that was called, and the second parameter is an array of arguments.

One tactic of doing this is actually to just define all the logic for your method within the __call() method itself, as shown in Listing 7.9.1.

Listing 7.9.1 **Object Method Overloading**

```
<?php
// Define a class that will overload a method definition
class Overloaded_Math {
    // Define an addition function that handles many different variations:
    public function __call($name, $args) {
        // If the function name was 'add' then:
        if ($name == 'add') {
            // If the first argument is a string:
            if (is_string($args[0])) {
                // Concatenate all the strings together:
                return implode('', $args);
            } elseif ((count($args) == 1) && is_array($args[0])) {
                // Ok we have exactly one argument, and it's an array
                // so sum up the values of the array:
                return array_sum($args[0]);
            } elseif ((count($args) > 1) && is_numeric($args[0])) {
                // if there are more than 1 arguments, and the
                // first one at least is numeric, then add them all:
```

Listing 7.9.1 **Continued**

```
                return array_sum($args);
            }
        }

        // In any other case, we didn't have a proper method call, exit
        trigger_error('Invalid Method Access', E_USER_ERROR);
    }
}

// Create a new object
$mobj = new Overloaded_Math();

// Examine the output of calling this method in multiple ways:
// As strings: 'RedWhiteBlue'
echo '<p>Accessed as strings: ', $mobj->add('Red', 'White', 'Blue'), '</p>';
// As an array of numbers: 16
echo '<p>Accessed as array: ', $mobj->add(array(7, 6, 3)), '</p>';
// And as a bunch of numbers: 42
echo '<p>Accessed as individual numbers: ',
    $mobj->add(37.83, 3.17, 1), '</p>';
?>
```

This works; however, in a large class definition with many overloaded functions this could be unwieldy. It is often advisable instead to do the smallest amount of work possible in the __call() method. Define all your own other functions that do the work and just use __call() to determine which one needs to be run, as shown in Listing 7.9.2.

Listing 7.9.2 **Object Method Overloading: Alternate Solution**

```
<?php
// Define a class that will overload a method definition
class Money {
    // Define an addition function that handles many different variations:
    public function __call($name, $args) {
        // If the function name was 'format' then:
        if (($name == 'format') && (count($args) == 1)) {
            // If the first argument is a string:
            if (is_string($args[0])) {
                // Call the string version of the formatter:
                return $this->_format_string($args[0]);
            } elseif (is_numeric($args[0])) {
                // If numeric, call the number version
                return $this->_format_number($args[0]);
            } elseif (is_array($args[0])) {
                // Use the array version now.
```

Listing 7.9.2 **Continued**

```
                    return $this->_format_array($args[0]);
        }
    }

    // In any other case, we didn't have a proper method call, exit
    trigger_error('Invalid Method Access', E_USER_ERROR);
}

// Define the private/internal function for formatting a number as money
private function _format_number($number) {
    // First round it to 2 decimal places:
    $number = round($number, 2);

    // Now output it, with formatting:
    return '$' . number_format($number, 2);
}

// Define the private/internal function for formatting a string as money
private function _format_string($str) {
    // Clean up the string by removing all chars that are not digits:
    $str = preg_replace('/[^0-9.]/', '', $str);

    // Ensure that only one decimal separator exists:
    $str = preg_replace('/\.([^.]*)(?=\.)/', '$1', $str);

    // Now that it is clean, call format number on it:
    return $this->_format_number($str);
}

// Define the private/internal function for formatting an array as money
private function _format_array($arr) {
    // Loop through the entire array
    $new = array();
    foreach ($arr as $a) {
        // Depending on whether this is a string, call the appropriate
        // function to format it, and save it in a new array:
        if (is_string($a)) {
            $new[] = $this->_format_string($a);
        } else {
            $new[] = $this->_format_number($a);
        }
    }

    // Now return the new array back:
```

Listing 7.9.2   **Continued**

```
        return $new;
    }
}

// Create a new object
$my_money = new Money();

// Examine the output of calling this method in multiple ways:
// As a number: $1,234.57
echo '<p>Accessed as number: ', $my_money->format(1234.567), '</p>';
// As a string with some garbage in it: $7,561.20
echo '<p>Accessed as array: ', $my_money->format('big7,56.1.2'), '</p>';
// And as an array of these mixed values:
//   Array ( [0] => $2.22 [1] => $2,345.64 [2] => $42.00 )
echo '<p>Accessed as individual numbers: ';
print_r($my_money->format(array(2.217, '2-345.64', 42)));
echo '</p>';
?>
```

7.10 Linked List Implementation

Linked lists are one of the basic data structures found in computer programming and are often the basis of more complicated data structures. The features of a linked list are that new elements can be added and removed from anywhere in the list, there is no preset size to the list, and the relative order of elements is simple to maintain.

This last characteristic distinguishes linked lists from arrays. Arrays are useful for situations where data is expected to be at a particular location—for example, a person's first name is found in the array location 'firstname'. However, for information where the relative order of the data is important—as with alphabetical lists or time-ordered events such as web server logs—storage in arrays is less than optimal. Linked lists, on the other hand, are good for storing information, as we will now demonstrate.

So, what exactly does a linked list look like? A linked list consists of a set of nodes. Each node consists of two values: The data element stored at that node and a reference to the next node (see Figure 7.10.1).

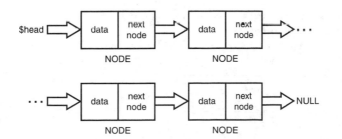

Figure 7.10.1   Structure of a linked list.

Every linked list has at least, one "special" node, the last node of the list. Traditionally, the last node has a reference value of NULL, indicating that there is no following node. The one other special case is the empty list. In Listing 7.10.1, an empty list is indicated when the first node has both a NULL reference and a NULL data element.

The basic operations on a linked list are simple. They include setting the value of a node, inserting a new node after the current node, removing a node after the current node, and printing out the list.

Let's now implement linked lists using objects. Because the basic component of linked lists is the node, all that is needed is to define the node as a class.

Listing 7.10.1 **Linked List** Node **Class**

```php
<?php
// Define a class to implement linked lists, a linked list node.
class Linked_List_Node {
    // Define the variable to hold our data:
    public $data;
    // And a variable to hold the next object in the chain:
    public $next;

    // A constructor method that allows for data to be passed in
    public function __construct($d = NULL) {
        $this->data = $d;
    }

    // Now create some methods that will make handling lists more automatic:

    // First of all a method that will insert a Node after this one
    public function insertAfter(Linked_List_Node $insert) {
        // This assumes a single node will be passed in not an entire list.
        // If you pass a node from a list the rest of the list will be lost.

        // Set the new node's next, to be this node's next.
        $insert->next = $this->next;

        // Now set this node's next, to the new node:
        $this->next = $insert;
    }

    // Now a method that will remove the node after this one:
    public function removeAfter() {
        // Store a reference to the node in question:
        $ref = $this->next;
```

Listing 7.10.1   **Continued**

```php
        // Now jump over this node, linking to its child (if it existed)
        if (isset($this->next->next)) {
            $this->next = $this->next->next;
        } else {
            // Otherwise just make it null
            $this->next = NULL;
        }

        // Now, destroy the original object:
        unset($ref);
    }

    // Now also define a method that will output an entire linked
    //   list, starting from this node.
    public function asString() {
        // If another child exists, then retrieve its value:
        $children = '';
        if ($this->next) {
            $children = ', ' . $this->next->asString();
        }

        // Return this data, concatenated with that of all its children:
        return $this->data . $children;
    }
}

// Create a new linked list:
$list = new Linked_List_Node('PHP');

// Now add an element after that one:
$list->insertAfter(new Linked_List_Node('Perl'));

// And then insert one in between the two:
$list->insertAfter(new Linked_List_Node('Javascript'));

// Echo this out as a string:  PHP, Javascript, Perl
echo '<p>', $list->asString(), '</p>';

// Now remove the last element:
$list->next->removeAfter();

// And output the string again: PHP, Javascript
echo '<p>', $list->asString(), '</p>';
?>
```

The particular type of linked list implemented in Listing 7.10.1 is called a *singly linked list*. This is the most basic type of linked list. One obvious modification to this is to add a reference in each node to the preceding node. This creates a list type known as a *doubly linked list* and allows the list to be traversed in either direction. Other data structures that can be built directly from linked lists are stacks and queues. In short, linked lists are excellent structures for data that is linearly ordered.

7.11 Binary Tree Implementation

The binary tree and its many variants are the mainstays of the data structure family. A variation of the linked list, binary trees excel in situations where data must be quickly organized and quickly retrieved in a particular order. As shown in Figure 7.11.1, a binary tree consists of nodes with pointers to up to two other nodes. The nodes pointed to are generally referred to as the *children nodes*, generically called *left* and *right*, and the current node is the *parent node* of the children.

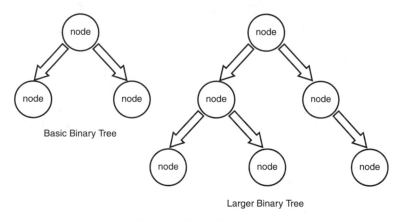

Figure 7.11.1   Binary tree.

Let's construct a class that implements the basic binary tree node. The class consists of three variables: the data value associated with the current node and the two children nodes. Because this class simply deals with the node concept, the only methods a node can have are to read out the values of the node and all its children. Listing 7.11.1 demonstrates the standard practice of traversing a tree: Get all the left children before all the right children. The one option remaining is where to put the value of the current node: before all its children, after all its children, or between the left and right children. These three options are called, respectively, preorder, post-order, and in-order traversal. To illustrate, Figure 7.11.2 shows a simple tree.

Using a preorder traversal, the values from this tree are retrieved as "a", "b", "c". For post-order traversal, the order of retrieval is "b", "c", "a". Finally, in-order traversal produces the list "b", "a", "c".

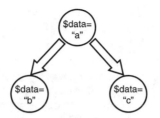

Figure 7.11.2 Binary tree example.

Listing 7.11.1 **Binary Tree Implementation**

```php
<?php
// Define a class to implement a binary tree
class Binary_Tree_Node {
    // Define the variable to hold our data:
    public $data;
    // And a variable to hold the left and right objects:
    public $left;
    public $right;

    // A constructor method that allows for data to be passed in
    public function __construct($d = NULL) {
        $this->data = $d;
    }

    // Traverse the tree, left to right, in pre-order, returning an array
    // Preorder means that each node's value preceeds its children.
    public function traversePreorder() {
        // Prep some variables.
        $l = array();
        $r = array();

        // Read in the left and right children appropriately traversed:
        if ($this->left) { $l = $this->left->traversePreorder(); }
        if ($this->right) { $r = $this->right->traversePreorder(); }

        // Return a merged array of the current value, left, and right:
        return array_merge(array($this->data), $l, $r);
    }

    // Traverse the tree, left to right, in postorder, returning an array
    // Postorder means that each node's value follows its children.
    public function traversePostorder() {
        // Prep some variables.
```

Listing 7.11.1 **Continued**

```php
        $l = array();
        $r = array();

        // Read in the left and right children appropriately traversed:
        if ($this->left) { $l = $this->left->traversePostorder(); }
        if ($this->right) { $r = $this->right->traversePostorder(); }

        // Return a merged array of the current value, left, and right:
        return array_merge($l, $r, array($this->data));
    }

    // Traverse the tree, left to right, in-order, returning an array.
    // In-order means that values are ordered as left children, then the
    //  node value, then the right children.
    public function traverseInorder() {
        // Prep some variables.
        $l = array();
        $r = array();

        // Read in the left and right children appropriately traversed:
        if ($this->left) { $l = $this->left->traverseInorder(); }
        if ($this->right) { $r = $this->right->traverseInorder(); }

        // Return a merged array of the current value, left, and right:
        return array_merge($l, array($this->data), $r);
    }
}

// Let's create a binary tree that will equal the following:     3
//                                                              / \
//                                                             h   9
//                                                                / \
// Create the tree:                                              6   a
$tree = new Binary_Tree_Node(3);
$tree->left = new Binary_Tree_Node('h');
$tree->right = new Binary_Tree_Node(9);
$tree->right->left = new Binary_Tree_Node(6);
$tree->right->right = new Binary_Tree_Node('a');

// Now traverse this tree in all possible orders and display the results:

// Pre-order: 3, h, 9, 6, a
echo '<p>', implode(', ', $tree->traversePreorder()), '</p>';
```

Listing 7.11.1   **Continued**

```
// Post-order: h, 6, a, 9, 3
echo '<p>', implode(', ', $tree->traversePostorder()), '</p>';

// In-order: h, 3, 6, 9, a
echo '<p>', implode(', ', $tree->traverseInorder()), '</p>';
?>
```

When used in conjunction with ordering logic between nodes, this structure provides a wonderful organization method. At any node, all the elements that satisfy a certain condition are located at the left node and its children, and all the elements that satisfy the converse of the condition are located at the right node and its children. When inserting a new element, all you need to do is start at the first, or "root" node, of the tree, discover which side the element belongs on, and then descend that side until its proper location is found. Similarly, to read back out the information, it is a simple matter of traversing the tree using the in-order traversal method.

To demonstrate, Listing 7.11.2 takes the simplest case of ordering: less than, greater than, and equal to. For each node, any values that are less than or equal to the value of the current node are placed in the left child and its children; any value greater than the value of the current node are placed in the right child and its children. This concept is encapsulated in the class `Sorting_Tree`. The one member, `$tree`, contains the root `Binary_Tree_Node` of the tree. There are two methods: one to insert a new value and one to return an array of the ordered values.

Listing 7.11.2   **Self-Sorting Binary Tree**

```
// Define a class to implement self sorting binary tree
class Sorting_Tree {
    // Define the variable to hold our tree:
    public $tree;

    // We need a method that will allow for inserts that automatically place
    // themselves in the proper order in the tree
    public function insert($val) {
        // Handle the first case:
        if (!(isset($this->tree))) {
            $this->tree = new Binary_Tree_Node($val);
        } else {
            // In all other cases:
            // Start a pointer that looks at the current tree top:
            $pointer = $this->tree;
            // Iteratively search the tree for the right place:
            for(;;) {
                // If this value is less than, or equal to the current data:
                if ($val <= $pointer->data) {
```

Listing 7.11.2 **Continued**

```php
                    // We are looking to the left ... If the child exists:
                    if ($pointer->left) {
                        // Traverse deeper:
                        $pointer = $pointer->left;
                    } else {
                        // Found the new spot: insert the new element here:
                        $pointer->left = new Binary_Tree_Node($val);
                        break;
                    }
                } else {
                    // We are looking to the right ... If the child exists:
                    if ($pointer->right) {
                        // Traverse deeper:
                        $pointer = $pointer->right;
                    } else {
                        // Found the new spot: insert the new element here:
                        $pointer->right = new Binary_Tree_Node($val);
                        break;
                    }
                }
            }
        }
    }

    // Now create a method to return the sorted values of this tree.
    // All it entails is using the in-order traversal, which will now
    // give us the proper sorted order.
    public function returnSorted() {
        return $this->tree->traverseInorder();
    }
}

// Declare a new sorting tree:
$sort_as_you_go = new Sorting_Tree();

// Let's randomly create 20 numbers, inserting them as we go:
for ($i = 0; $i < 20; $i++) {
    $sort_as_you_go->insert(rand(1,100));
}

// Now echo the tree out, using in-order traversal, and it will be sorted:
// Example: 1, 2, 11, 18, 22, 26, 32, 32, 34, 43, 46, 47, 47, 53, 60, 71,
//    75, 84, 86, 90
echo '<p>', implode(', ', $sort_as_you_go->returnSorted()), '</p>';
?>
```

The value of using a binary tree should now be apparent. The structure orders itself in a highly efficient manner; while inserting a new value, at every existing node, you get halfway closer to the value's final location. This method is as efficient as the QuickSort algorithm already mentioned for arrays. Though there are more efficient methods for specific applications, a sorted binary tree works much better than arrays for most problems. Also, at any point during processing, the data already stored will be sorted and ready for whatever the next step is. No post-processing, cleanup, or re-sorting when new data is added is required.

Two aspects about the code itself should be pointed out. First, two distinct classes are used to implement the concept of the binary tree. For this example, you could easily have defined a single class that contains both the node concept and the tree concept. Another approach would be to create the `Sorting_Tree` class as an extension of the `Binary_Tree_Node` class. In general, any of these approaches is perfectly valid. The choice used here is simply a convenience to create self-contained examples that can easily be used independently. Many different guidelines and philosophies exist that can assist you in defining classes and their relationships. The common rule of most any approach; however, is to keep it simple.

The second aspect is the choice to use an iterative algorithm to traverse the tree to insert new values. Both from a logical and code-conciseness viewpoint, a recursive solution would have been more appropriate. The iterative approach was chosen because the potential exists that the tree will be large. Using a recursive solution, memory resources would be consumed for each level of recursion that takes places, ultimately leading to an exhaustion of resources. The iterative solution takes no more resources than that used by the tree already.

The general topic of trees themselves can take many chapters of a data structure book. The next obvious extension is to allow a node to have more than two children, called an *n-ary tree*. Using such concepts, structures such as Self-Balancing (Btree) trees, which attempt to keep the number of levels deep a tree becomes to a minimum, can be developed that greatly enhance search efficiency and data storage. Also, n-ary trees allow for complicated hierarchical data to be organized and stored. N-ary trees form the basis upon which the XHTML Document Object Model (DOM) and XML itself are built.

Finally, Listing 7.11.2 demonstrates the power of object-oriented design. All the trees mentioned share common characteristics, such as inserting new elements and retrieving them. Because the actual details of such functions are encapsulated into the individual classes, a larger application using such objects does not need to know exactly whether the object is a binary tree, n-ary tree, or some other type of tree. It only needs to know that the object has the methods needed to get the task completed. An application will simply have a statement such as `$anobject->insert($data);`. Whether the object is of any particular instance is inconsequential to the application. The application code will be more concise; focusing on solving the bigger problem while the details of the data structures themselves can be optimized separately without affecting the larger application.

8

Files and Directories

A S IS NECESSARY FOR ANY LANGUAGE, PHP has a complete set of file and directory support functions. However, one feature that makes these functions particularly useful in a web environment is the capability to operate on URLs and other network-specific resources as well as local files. If the filename begins with 'http://', 'https://', or 'ftp://', the specified URL will be opened as if it were a local file. The sections "Reading a File Via HTTP or FTP" and "Caching Remote Files Locally" later in this chapter give examples using this functionality.

Quick Hits

▶ **Open a file:**

```
$handle = fopen($filename, $mode);
```

This function opens the specified file or URL, returning a file resource to be used in other file functions. $mode is a string consisting of various single-character flags, which specify how the file will be opened. Common modes are 'r' to open the file read-only, 'w' to open for writing with completely new content, and 'a' to append data to an already existing file

Full documentation: http://php.net/fopen

▶ **Close a file:**

```
fclose($handle);
```

Close a previously opened file.

Full documentation: http://php.net/fclose

▶ **Read a line from an opened file:**

```
$string = fgets($handle, $maxlen);
```

This function returns the next line from a file, ending at the next end-of-line, end-of-file, or $maxlen minus 1 characters.

Full documentation: http://php.net/fgets

▶ Read the next group of bytes from a file:

```
$string = fread($handle, $nbytes);
```

The next `$nbytes` are read from the file or up to the end-of-file.

Full documentation: http://php.net/fread

▶ Write to a file:

```
$nwritten = fwrite($handle, $string);
```

Write the string to the file, returning how many bytes have been written, or FALSE if there is an error.

Full documentation: http://php.net/fwrite

▶ Read the contents of a file into a string:

```
$string = file_get_contents($filename);
```

The entire specified file or URL is returned.

Full documentation: http://php.net/file_get_contents

▶ Read the contents of a file into an array:

```
$array = file($path);
```

The entire contents of the file or URL are returned in an array with each line of the file as an array element (with the end-of-line character included).

Full documentation: http://php.net/file

▶ Echo a file directly to output:

```
$nwritten = readfile($filename);
```

The contents of the specified file are written directly to the output, returning the number of bytes written.

Full documentation: http://php.net/readfile

▶ Write a string to a file:

```
$nwritten = file_put_contents($filename, $string);
```

This is a convenience function that writes the specified string into the `$path` file or URL, reinitializing an already existing file.

Full documentation: http://php.net/file_put_contents

▶ Change the current position in a file:

```
$success = fseek($handle, $offset);
$success = rewind($handle);
$position = ftell($handle);
```

`fseek()` sets the current position at `$offset` bytes from the beginning of the file. `rewind()` sets the current position back at the beginning of file, and `ftell()` returns the current position.

Full documentation: http://php.net/fseek, http://php.net/rewind, and http://php.net/ftell

▶ **Delete a file:**

```
$success = unlink($filename);
```

Deletes the specified file, returning true on success.

Full documentation: http://php.net/unlink

▶ **Rename a file:**

```
$success = rename($old, $new);
```

Changes the name of a file from $old to $new, returning true on success.

Full documentation: http://php.net/rename

▶ **Copy a file:**

```
$success = copy($original, $copy);
```

Copies the original file to the copy, returning true on success.

Full documentation: http://php.net/copy

▶ **Retrieve various statistics about a file:**

```
$array = stat($filename);
```

This function returns an array containing various pieces of information about the specified file. Some various useful keys are: 'size', which contains the size of the file in bytes, 'ctime', containing the time stamp of when the file was created, and 'mtime', containing the time stamp of when the file was last modified.

Full documentation: http://php.net/stat

▶ **Create or delete a folder:**

```
$success = mkdir($foldername);
$success = rmdir($foldername);
```

Creates or deletes folder, both functions returning true on success. The system permissions must allow such actions.

Full documentation: http://php.net/mkdir and http://php.net/rmdir

▶ **Open a stream to a system command:**

```
$handle = popen($command, $mode);
pclose($handle);
```

Starts a system process with the given command. Note that the stream can only be read or write stream and must be closed with pclose().

Full documentation: http://php.net/popen and http://php.net/pclose

▶ **Execute a system command:**

```
$output = `commandstring`;
$output = shell_exec($command);
```

Both statements do the same thing: execute the given string as a system command. Note that, in the first form, the characters are not quotes, but backticks.

Full documentation: http://php.net/shell_exec

8.1 Generating a Full Directory Listing

Most web servers display a list of all files in a directory for you, allowing users to select any one of their choosing. However, this is usually turned off for security reasons. You don't want users stumbling around your web server and finding access to files that they shouldn't.

Nevertheless, there are times when you want to give users access to a particular directory. Via custom PHP, you can easily choose which files to display and which to remain hidden. Also you can format the data in whatever style you want, making it have a completely custom look that matches your website. For all these reasons a custom directory listing program is handy, as shown in Listing 8.1.1.

Listing 8.1.1 **Custom index.php File**

```php
<?php
// This program works well as an index.php file in a directory you wish to
//  display all files for.  It automatically excludes itself from the list,
//  and is easy to modify to make it ignore others as well:

// Define an array to hold the files
$files = array();

// Open the current directory
$d = dir('.');

// Loop through all of the files:
while (false !== ($file = $d->read())) {
    // If the file is not this file, and does not start with a '.' or '~'
    // and does not end in LCK, then store it for later display:
    if ( ($file{0} != '.') &&
         ($file{0} != '~') &&
         (substr($file, -3) != 'LCK') &&
         ($file != basename($_SERVER['PHP_SELF']))    ) {
        // Store the filename, and full data from a stat() call:
        $files[$file] = stat($file);
    }
}

// Close the directory
$d->close();

// Now let's output a basic table with this information
echo '<style>td { padding-right: 10px; }</style>';
echo '<table><caption>The contents of this directory:</caption>';

// Sort the files so that they are alphabetical
ksort($files);
```

Listing 8.1.1 **Continued**

```
// Prepare for using date functions:
date_default_timezone_set('America/New_York');

// Now loop through them, echoing out a new table row for each one:
foreach ($files as $name => $stats) {
    // Start the row, and output a link via the filename:
    echo "<tr><td><a href=\"{$name}\">{$name}</a></td>\n";
    // Now a table cell with the filesize in bytes:
    echo "<td align='right'>{$stats['size']}</td>\n";
    // Finally a column for the date:
    echo '<td>', date('m-d-Y h:ia', $stats['mtime']), "</td></tr>\n";
}

echo '</table>';
?>
```

Listing 8.1.1 uses a call to `stat()` to retrieve vital statistics about the file. This function returns many attributes of the file, including its current access restrictions, owner, size, various timestamps, and more. It is a powerful function, and it is recommended that you read the full documentation at http://php.net/stat.

8.2 Natural Display of File Sizes

Listing 8.1.1 gave a way to visibly display a directory listing. There was one odd part to it though. When displaying the file sizes, they were shown in bytes because this is what the size of a file is returned to you as from the operating system.

Such a display isn't the most useful method though for most people. Instead of being presented with 2202009 bytes, they feel more comfortable with seeing 2.10MB (Megabytes). To accomplish this, a simple function transforms any number of bytes passed to it, into a nicely formatted version.

There is still a slight problem, though, which is that the world does not 100% agree on whether a kilobyte is 1000 bytes (by the SI metric standard), or 1024 bytes (the typical computer meaning of the term). This begins to get more confusing as different parts of the computer industry have begun to use different meanings. Hard drives are often 1000 based, but system memory is 1024 based. Depending on the context, in networking it can mean either case.

There isn't a good answer to this currently, and you will need to choose specifically what solution you want to use. We will present three different variations. Listing 8.2.1 illustrates a 1000-based solution.

Listing 8.2.1 **Formatting File Sizes in a Natural Format**

```php
<?php
// A function to format the bytes of a file, as a natural looking string.
// This version handles it via 1000 based logic:
function format_bytes($bytes) {
    // Define an array of the different display forms:
    $display = array('B', 'kB', 'MB', 'GB', 'TB', 'PB', 'EB', 'ZB', 'YB');

    // Now, constantly divide the value by 1000 until it is less than 1000
    $level = 0;
    while ($bytes > 1000) {
        $bytes /= 1000;
        $level++;
    }

    // Now we have our final value, format it to just 1 decimal place
    // and append on to the appropriate level moniker.
    return round($bytes, 1) . ' ' . $display[$level];
}

// Echo out a few examples to test the function:
echo '<p>4200 bytes = ', format_bytes(4200), "<p>\n"; // 4.2 kB
echo '<p>420000 bytes = ', format_bytes(420000), "<p>\n"; // 420 kB
echo '<p>42000000 bytes = ', format_bytes(42000000), "<p>\n"; // 42 MB
?>
```

Listing 8.2.2 modifies this function slightly to instead work on 1024-based arithmetic.

Listing 8.2.2 **Formatting Files Sizes Using 1024-Based Kilobytes**

```php
<?php
// A function to format the bytes of a file, as a natural looking string.
// This version handles it via 1024 based logic:
function format_bytes($bytes) {
    // Define an array of the different display forms:
    $display = array('B', 'kB', 'MB', 'GB', 'TB', 'PB', 'EB', 'ZB', 'YB');

    // Now, constantly divide the value by 1024 until it is less than 1024
    $level = 0;
    while ($bytes > 1024) {
        $bytes /= 1024;
        $level++;
    }

    // Now we have our final value, format it to just 1 decimal place
    // and append on to the the appropriate level moniker.
```

Listing 8.2.2 **Continued**

```
    return round($bytes, 1) . ' ' . $display[$level];
}

// Echo out a few examples to test the function:
echo '<p>4200 bytes = ', format_bytes(4200), "<p>\n"; // 4.1 kB
echo '<p>420000 bytes = ', format_bytes(420000), "<p>\n"; // 410.2 kB
echo '<p>42000000 bytes = ', format_bytes(42000000), "<p>\n"; // 40.1 MB
?>
```

Now, we would be done at this point; however, there is one other variation that we must contend with. Because of the confusion between the two definitions of a kilobyte, the IEC (International Electrotechnical Commission) released a standard in 1998 to help the world differentiate between these two uses. The standard was that anytime one refers to a 1024-based measurement, the prefix should be modified, keeping the first two letters, and then inserting "bi" for the rest (standing for *binary*). Therefore you end up with *kibibytes* and *mebibytes*, instead of kilobytes and megabytes.

The symbols for these change as well, making the first letter always capitalized and inserting an "i" in between the two letters. Therefore a kilobyte is "kB"; however, a kibibyte is "KiB." Unfortunately, these new classifications have not caught on in the international community. You may find yourself needing, or wanting, to use them, and therefore one final modification of our code will accomplish that, as shown in Listing 8.2.3.

Listing 8.2.3 **Format File Sizes: International-Standard Compliant**

```
<?php
// A function to format the bytes of a file, as a natural looking string.
// This version handles it via 1024 based logic:
function format_bytes($bytes) {
    // Define an array of the different display forms:
    // These are the SI approved binary variations:
    $display = array('B', 'KiB', 'MiB', 'GiB', 'TiB', 'PiB', 'EiB',
        'ZiB', 'YiB');

    // Now, constantly divide the value by 1024 until it is less than 1024
    $level = 0;
    while ($bytes > 1024) {
        $bytes /= 1024;
        $level++;
    }

    // Now we have our final value, format it to just 1 decimal place
    // and append on to the the appropriate level moniker.
```

Listing 8.2.3   **Continued**

```
    return round($bytes, 1) . ' ' . $display[$level];
}

// Echo out a few examples to test the function:
echo '<p>4200 bytes = ', format_bytes(4200), "<p>\n"; // 4.1 KiB
echo '<p>420000 bytes = ', format_bytes(420000), "<p>\n"; // 410.2 KiB
echo '<p>42000000 bytes = ', format_bytes(42000000), "<p>\n"; // 40.1 MiB
?>
```

8.3 Renaming All Files Within a Directory

PHP is well known as a web programming language; however, it is also useful as a command-line scripting language. Most distributions of PHP now come with the command-line version by default. As an example of using command-line PHP, let's use it to solve a common problem with filenames. Many times a user may end up with a number of files, all of which have something incorrect in their filename. Perhaps their extension is wrong, or there is a dash in the filename that shouldn't be. Listing 8.3.1 can be used to rename these files for you.

Listing 8.3.1   **Renaming Files**

```
<?php
// Read in all passed parameters and ensure they are correct:
if (!(isset($argc))) {
    // Someone tried to run this through the web.
    echo "This script is for command line use only!";
    exit();
}

// Now check that we have at least 2, and at most 3, parameters:
// Remember that the filename appears as $argv[0] and counts as one.
if (($argc < 3) || ($argc > 4)) {
    // Improper usage, give an error and exit:
    echo "
Improper Usage!  Please use the following:
 {$argv[0]} <regex_to_match> <replacement> [directory]
";
    exit();
}

// Now, if we've made it here, we have a valid number of parameters,
// so store the data into appropriately named variables:
$old = $argv[1];
```

Listing 8.3.1 **Continued**

```php
$new = $argv[2];
// Grab the directory name, default to the current directory if none given
$dir = isset($argv[3]) ? $argv[3] : '.';

// Ensure at this point that the directory exists, otherwise exit
if (!(is_dir($dir))) {
    echo "Error: Directory {$dir} does not exist!\n";
    exit();
}

// Before we get any farther, if the directory string ends in a
// '/' or '\' then remove it for later use:
$dir_noslash = preg_replace('|([/\\])$|', '', $dir);

// Now we can begin our filename transformations.  Open the directory:
$d = dir($dir);

// Loop through all the files:
while (false !== ($file = $d->read())) {
    // Skip . and .., we don't want to try to rename them:
    if (($file == '.') || ($file == '..')) { continue; }

    // Perform the requested translation of the filename:
    $newname = preg_replace($old, $new, $file);

    // Guard against someone passing in regex that breaks:
    if (!(isset($newname))) {
        echo "Error: There has been a problem with the regex provided\n";
        exit();
    }

    // Now if this name is now different, then rename the file:
    if ($newname != $file) {
        rename("{$dir_noslash}/{$file}", "{$dir_noslash}/{$newname}");
    }
}
?>
```

This script is straightforward, if you ignore all the error checking that it does. In its simplest form, it takes two parameters: first some regex code to perform a search and, second, a replacement string for what the regex found. It loops over all filenames within the current directory and makes the appropriate replacements. The optional last parameter specifies a different directory to operate on instead of the current one.

Therefore, to give some usage examples let's assume that you saved this code into a file named rename.php in a root /scripts/ directory. You could do the following transformations:

- Rename a directory full of PHP files to have a .phpc extension:

  On Windows:

  ```
  php /scripts/rename.php /\.php$/ .phpc
  ```

  On UNIX:

  ```
  php /scripts/rename.php '/\.php$/' .phpc
  ```

- What if you had a directory full of mp3 files, and they were all named in the format of `'artist - song.mp3'`. You want them instead to be named `'(artist) song.mp3'`:

  On Windows:

  ```
  php /scripts/rename.php "/^([^-]+) - (.+)$/" "($1) $2" /mp3
  ```

  On UNIX:

  ```
  php /scripts/rename.php '/^([^-]+) - (.+)$/' '($1) $2' /mp3
  ```

Note that the differences between Windows and UNIX usage are because of how each one handles special characters. On UNIX, if you want to include spaces and dollar signs in a string, you need to surround it by single quotes ('). Whereas in Windows, you can only use a double quote to accomplish this ("), and you do not need to worry about dollar signs because they are not special to Windows. Normally you might also think you need to worry about UNIX's slash (/) versus Windows use of backslash (\) for directories. However, all modern versions of Windows are fine with using either one, therefore allowing UNIX-style notation to be used in both cases.

8.4 Search for Filenames Within a Directory Tree

Another common task using the file system is the need to find a file of a certain name. This can be useful either in command-line programming to replace similar tools that the operating system provides, or via the Web for various automated tasks.

The concept is straightforward; simply start with a given directory, and keep looking for a match. Dive deeper into subdirectories as you go, and build a list of matches (see Listing 8.4.1).

Listing 8.4.1 **Searching for Files in a Directory Tree**

```php
<?php
// A function that will traverse a directory tree, looking for files
// that match a given regular expression, and returns all files:
function find($regex, $dir) {
    $matches = array();
```

Listing 8.4.1 **Continued**

```php
    // Ok, open up the directory and prepare to start looping:
    $d = dir($dir);

    // Loop through all the files:
    while (false !== ($file = $d->read())) {
        // Skip . and .., we don't want to deal with them.
        if (($file == '.') || ($file == '..')) { continue; }

        // If this is a directory, then:
        if (is_dir("{$dir}/{$file}")) {
            // Call this function recursively to look in that subdirectory:
            $submatches = find($regex,    "{$dir}/{$file}");
            // Add them to the current match list:
            $matches = array_merge($matches, $submatches);
        } else {
            // It's a file, so check to see if it is a match:
            if (preg_match($regex, $file)) {
                // Add it to our array:
                $matches[] = "{$dir}/{$file}";
            }
        }
    }

    // Ok, that's it, return the array now:
    return $matches;
}

// Look for all PHP files on your website, starting with the document root:
$found = find('/\.php$/', $_SERVER['DOCUMENT_ROOT']);

// Sort, then Display them:
sort($found);
echo '<pre>', print_r($found, true), '</pre>';
?>
```

8.5 Handling Relative and Absolute File Paths

When working on the Web, or just with your local file system, you have to deal with the difference between a relative and an absolute file path. An absolute path contains the directory structure within it starting from the root of the hard drive (or of the web server). It looks something like this:

/docs/book/php5/01.php

A relative path, on the other hand, contains only the part of the path needed to get from your current directory to the file in question. It can include just directories/files deeper in the structure, or, by using "." or "..", it can refer to the current directory and the parent directory, respectively. Therefore, if you are in the context of the "book" directory in the preceding example, you might have one of the following three relative paths to the same file:

```
php5/01.php
```

```
./php5/01.php
```

```
../book/php5/01.php
```

The one additional variation of this theme is when you are talking about absolute URLs. This can be seen as one step further toward giving a full description of the file location. An absolute URL does not just give the path starting from the document root but also specifies the server as well, such as in the following form:

```
http://eliw.com/docs/book/php5/01.php
```

If you find yourself taking paths from input, or perhaps parsing a web page to redisplay it in a different manner, you may find the need to detect what type of path any given one is, or even to convert them to different types. The functions provided in Listing 8.5.1 make it easy to detect the different types of file paths and to convert them all to absolute paths so that they will always work.

Listing 8.5.1   **Convert All File or URL Specifications to Absolute Paths**

```php
<?php
// A function to detect absolute paths:
function is_absolute($path) {
    // Check if it begins with a '/', if so, it is an absolute path
    if ($path{0} == '/') {
        return true;
    } else {
        return false;
    }
}


// A function to detect full/absolute URLs
function is_absoluteurl($path) {
    // Check if it begins with a protocol specification:
    if (preg_match('|^[a-zA-Z]+://|', $path)) {
        return true;
    } else {
        return false;
    }
}
```

Listing 8.5.1 **Continued**

```php
// A function to detect relative paths:
function is_relative($path) {
    // In this case, if it is neither of the absolute options, then
    // it is relative:
    if ( !(is_absolute($path)) && !(is_absoluteurl($path)) ) {
        return true;
    } else {
        return false;
    }
}


// Now, a function that given any path, will turn it into an
// absolute url and return it:
function ensure_absoluteurl($path) {
    // If this already is an absolute URL, just return it:
    if (is_absoluteurl($path)) {
        return $path;
    }
    // Else if it is an absolute path, add the http & host to it:
    elseif (is_absolute($path)) {
        return "http://{$_SERVER['HTTP_HOST']}{$path}";
    }
    // Finally it is relative, so we need to build the entire string:
    else {
        return 'http://' . $_SERVER['HTTP_HOST'] .
            dirname($_SERVER['PHP_SELF']) . '/' . $path;
    }
}


// Create some test cases:
$tests = array('http://eliw.com/docs/book/php5/01.php',
    '/docs/book/php5/01.php', 'php5/01.php', '../book/php5/01.php');

// For each case, run all the functions on it:
foreach ($tests as $tc) {
    echo "<p>\n";
    echo "Is {$tc} relative? ", is_relative($tc) ? 'Yes' : 'No', "<br>\n";
    echo "Is {$tc} absolute? ", is_absolute($tc) ? 'Yes' : 'No', "<br>\n";
    echo "Is {$tc} an absolute URL? ",
        is_absoluteurl($tc) ? 'Yes' : 'No', "<br>\n";
    echo "Converted to an absolute URL we get: ", ensure_absoluteurl($tc);
    echo "</p>\n";
}
?>
```

8.6 Reading a File Via HTTP or FTP

Built into the core of the PHP file-handling system is support for accessing files across a network. All that you need to do to use this is use a full URL instead of a filename when using any file access function. Combined with `readfile()` or `file_get_contents()` it becomes a powerful tool allowing you to do many things—the simplest of which, is just to read in and display another web page, such as in Listing 8.6.1: Google.

Listing 8.6.1 **Simple Example of Reading from a URL**

```php
<?php
readfile('http://www.google.com/');
?>
```

In this situation it retrieves and displays the HTML; however, all the links to graphics, CSS, and other pages are broken because they will still be written as if the web page was viewed on Google's server. To fix this, you need to use tactics discussed in Section 8.5, "Handling Relative and Absolute File Paths," to scan for all links in the document and update them to work as absolute URLs.

A useful purpose of this is retrieving data from another server, such as an XML file that you then intend to parse. Another way to use this functionality is to actually read in PHP libraries, or CSS files, from one server to another. This way if you have multiple websites that could benefit from sharing libraries, this is easily accomplished. This would end up making an HTML page that could look something like Listing 8.6.2.

Listing 8.6.2 **Creating an HTML Page Based on Components from Other Websites**

```php
<?php
<!DOCTYPE html PUBLIC "-//W3C//DTD XHTML 1.0 Strict//EN"
 "http://www.w3.org/TR/xhtml1/DTD/xhtml1-strict.dtd">
<html xmlns="http://www.w3.org/1999/xhtml">
<head>
<title>Test File</title>
<meta http-equiv="Content-Type" content="text/html; charset=iso-8859-1" />
<style type="text/css">
<?php
// Read in our CSS file
readfile('http://scadian.info/personal.css');
?>
</style>
<?php
// Read in a php library
require_once 'http://scadian.info/lib/library.php.lib';
?>
</head>
<body>
```

Listing 8.6.2   **Continued**

```
<p>Testing our CSS and library include.</p>
<p>Calling a function from the library: <?php lib_func(); ?></p>
</body>
</html>
?>
```

If you look closely you will notice that the library we are requiring ends in .lib. There is a reason for this. For `require` to work and pull in a PHP library file, the server hosting the file needs to serve it as plain text. If the server instead sees the file as PHP and parses it, your script will only get the output, not the PHP code that it wants. An easy way around this is to name your file with a different extension (such as .lib or .phpc) so that the server sends it as plain text.

Doing this does not inherently open up a security risk because no code is being run on the server presenting the file. It is just serving some text. However, you should still be careful as to what files you allow to be seen this way. If you open up scripts that contained database usernames and passwords or other specific details of the implementation of your system, people could access these and break into your system. This technique is therefore more useful for providing some basic safe PHP functionality to multiple servers.

8.7 Watching the Contents of a File As It Grows (Simulating UNIX `tail -f`)

UNIX has a program called `tail` that is useful for watching the contents of a file. Normally it simply shows the last lines of a file; however, when invoked as `tail -f` it keeps running, showing you new lines as they appear. It can be useful to replicate this on a web server via PHP to watch various files. Perhaps you want to be able to see your web server's error log through a web page. Or you may have some output file generated by a script that you want to keep an eye on. Either way, Listing 8.7.1, once modified with the filename that it should be reading in your case, will serve you well.

Listing 8.7.1   **Watching the End of a File**

```
<?php
// Don't allow this page to be cached, since it should always be fresh.
header("Cache-Control: no-cache, must-revalidate"); // HTTP/1.1
header("Expires: Mon, 26 Jul 1997 05:00:00 GMT"); // Date in the past
?>
<!DOCTYPE html PUBLIC "-//W3C//DTD XHTML 1.0 Strict//EN"
   "http://www.w3.org/TR/xhtml1/DTD/xhtml1-strict.dtd">
<html xmlns="http://www.w3.org/1999/xhtml">
<head><title>Tail of logfile</title></head>
<body><pre>
<?php
```

Listing 8.7.1   **Continued**

```php
// Open the file we wish to read - In this case the access log of our server
if (!($fp = fopen("/var/log/apache2/access.log", 'r'))) {
    // We couldn't open the file, error!
    echo "ERROR: Could not open file for reading!\n";
    exit();
}

// We don't want to display the entire file, it could be huge, so
//  let's use a quick way to just display some of the file.  Use fseek
//  to head to the end of the file, but back up by 500 bytes.
fseek($fp, -500, SEEK_END);

// Read one line of data to throw away, as it may be an incomplete
//  line due to our seek.
fgets($fp);

// Keep looping forever
for (;;) {
    // We can begin to loop through reading all lines and echoing them:
    while (!feof($fp)) {
        if ($line = fgets($fp)) { echo $line; }
    }

    // Ok, we hit the end of the file, there are a few odds-n-ends we need:
    // First reseek to the end of the file, this is necessary to reset
    //  the filepointer, else it won't read anything else.
    fseek($fp, 0, SEEK_END);

    // Secondly flush the output buffers so that all text appears:
    flush();

    // Also reset the time limit for PHP so that we never time out:
    set_time_limit(15);

    // Now sleep for 1 second, and then we will try to access it again.
    sleep(1);
}
?>
</pre></body>
</html>
```

In this example a few tricks are used to get PHP to create this web page that essentially never ends. First we use some cache control commands to make sure that the web browser never tries to cache this content because it will be always changing and always fresh.

Then, after preparing to use the file, we need to do a couple of steps to properly look at the end of the file. We use the `fseek()` command to jump to almost the end of the file but not quite. We back up by 500 bytes. This is so that we are looking only at the end of the file to begin with. At that point the file pointer may be sitting in the middle of a line of text, and for display purposes we only want to deal with full lines. Therefore the easiest way to solve this is to read one line from the file and just discard it. This brings us up to the beginning of a full line, and ready to truly start.

At that point the program just enters an infinite loop. It reads all that it can from the file echoing it to the screen. We then need to move the file pointer back to the end of the file with another `fseek()`. The reason for this is that because we have read completely up to the end of the file, `feof()` knows that we did that and will continue to always return true even if more data has been inserted into the file. By seeking to the end of the file, `feof()` is reset and won't return true until another read is performed.

The program then uses `flush()` to clear any buffers and to attempt to force a write of this current data to the client. The script then sleeps for one second and starts looking at the file for more data again.

> **Warning**
>
> A number of configuration issues can cause this script not to work. The `flush()` command tries to empty any write buffers that exist but can only do so much. If your web server has any kind of buffering enabled, the script will not work properly. (A common case of this is the use of `mod_gzip` for Apache.) Similarly, if you have output buffering turned on in your php.ini file via the `output_buffering` command, `flush()` cannot clear this, and you will see data only in buffer-sized chunks, not live as the file changes.

8.8 Generating a Difference Report Between Two Files

Finding changes between two versions of a file is a common task—that's why the UNIX program `diff` and other such utilities exist. It can be useful to have a PHP version of this utility, one that can show changes between two files, especially by highlighting them visibly.

The algorithm used in Listing 8.8.1 is an iterative one that walks through each file at the same time, detecting changes as it goes. This method is straightforward to code; however it does have some drawbacks, sometimes grabbing larger "changed areas" than necessary. The results are still accurate, just not optimal. Other algorithms exist to solve this but become multitudes more complicated.

Listing 8.8.1 **File Comparison**

```php
<?php
// A function to compare two revisions of a file
function diff($old_file, $new_file, $type = 'array') {
```

Listing 8.8.1   **Continued**

```
// Read both files completely into memory for comparison:
$old = file($old_file);
$new = file($new_file);

// Initialize the old and new line counters:
$oc = 0;
$nc = 0;

// Store once, to use often, the number of lines in each array
$nold = count($old);
$nnew = count($new);

// Initialize the state engine to state 0
$state = 0;

// Initialize our data arrays to hold removed and added lines:
$removed = array();
$added = array();

// Enter the state engine, and begin processing:
while ($state < 3) {
    switch ($state) {
        case 0: // Mutual comparison, hoping for a match
            // skip over all matches until we mis-match
            while (($oc < $nold) && ($nc < $nnew) &&
                    ($old[$oc] == $new[$nc])) {
                $oc++;
                $nc++;
            }

            // Now figure out why we broke, both are beyond bounds:
            if (($oc == $nold) && ($nc == $nnew)) {
                // We are finished, set state to 3
                $state = 3;
            } elseif ($oc == $nold) {
                // Ok, just the old one was higher, therefore all that
                //  is left in the 'new' array, is in fact added.
                $added = array_merge($added, range($nc, $nnew - 1));
                $state = 3;
            } elseif ($nc == $nnew) {
                // Just the new one was higher, therefore all that is
                // left in the old array, was removed.
                $added = array_merge($added, range($nc, $nnew - 1));
                $state = 3;
            } else {
```

Listing 8.8.1 **Continued**

```
                    // Now we found a mismatch, enter state 1
                    $state = 1;
                }
                break;
        case 1: // Looking for a match to the new file line
                $oc2 = $oc;
                // As long as they don't match or we run out of lines
                while (($oc2 < $nold) && ($old[$oc2] !== $new[$nc])) {
                    $oc2++;
                }

                // Figure out what happened.  If we ran out of lines:
                if ($oc2 == $nold) {
                    // The new line was added -- Store this
                    $added[] = $nc;

                    // Increment the counter, and reset the algorithm
                    $nc++;
                    $state = 0;
                } else {
                    // We actually found a match, that means that all lines
                    // between where we started, and now, were deleted.
                    $removed = array_merge($removed, range($oc, $oc2 - 1));
                    // Reset the counter to the new location
                    $oc = $oc2;
                    // Change the state back to 0 to reset the algorithm
                    $state = 0;
                }
                break;
        }
    }

    // Ok, at this point we should have our entire diff in memory.
    // Based upon the optional 3rd parameter, figure out what
    // format to return it in:

    // If they asked for 'lines' - Return all the lines that were
    //   changed with some data:
    if ($type == 'lines') {
        $retval = '';
        // To get these in approximate order, loop for all possible values
        foreach(range(0, max($nold, $nnew) - 1) as $line) {
            // Output the removed row:
            if (isset($removed[$line])) {
                $retval .= "-{$line}: {$deleted[$line]}\n";
            }
```

Listing 8.8.1 **Continued**

```
                // Output the added row:
                if (isset($removed[$line])) {
                    $retval .= "-{$line}: {$deleted[$line]}\n";
                }
            }
        }
        // Else if they asked for a 'visual' view, create that:
        elseif ($type == 'visual') {
            // We are going to create a table, with Each file in one column/cell
            // and appropriate highlighting for deleted/added lines.

            // First declare some CSS styles
            $retval = '
<style>
.diff td {
    border: 1px solid black;
    padding: 5px;
    font-family: "Courier New", Courier, mono;
    font-size: 10px;
    vertical-align: top;
}
.diff .removed {
    background-color: #FF9999;
}
.diff .added {
    background-color: #00CC00;
}
</style>
';
            // Begin the table, and the first (old) cell
            $retval .= '<table class="diff"><tr><td>Original File:<br /><pre>';

            // Now loop through the entire old file, highlighting as needed
            foreach ($old as $num => $line) {
                // If deleted, highlight as such, else just echo it.
                if (in_array($num, $removed)) {
                    $retval .= $num . '. ' . '<span class="removed">' .
                            htmlspecialchars($line) . '</span>';
                } else {
                    $retval .= $num . '. ' . htmlspecialchars($line);
                }
            }

            // Now close off the cell and start the new one:
            $retval .= '</pre></td><td>Revised File:<br /><pre>';
```

Listing 8.8.1   **Continued**

```
        // And now repeat the exact same process for the new ones.
        foreach ($new as $num => $line) {
            if (in_array($num, $added)) {
                $retval .= $num . '. ' . '<span class="added">' .
                        htmlspecialchars($line) . '</span>';
            } else {
                $retval .= $num . '. ' . htmlspecialchars($line);
            }
        }

        // Ok, close off the table, and we are done
        $retval .= '</pre></td></tr></table>';
    }
    // Else, assume they wanted the arrays
    else {
        $retval = array('removed' => $removed, 'added' => $added);
    }

    // Return, and be finished
    return $retval;
}

// Test this on two files:
echo diff('file-1.1.php', 'file-1.2.php', 'visual');
?>
```

8.9 Locking a File for Exclusive Use

The Web, by its nature, will have multiple people running the same script/web page at the exact same time. This can cause a problem if you have a page that is updating a file. Two scripts can have race conditions and end up both trying to write to the file at the same time. This can cause corrupt data, or worse, complete destruction of the file.

This can get even worse in situations such as a data file, where you need to read in all the data, do some calculations, and then output new. This takes enough time that it makes it more likely that another script will start reading the data after the first one but before the first one has saved its changes to the file.

To solve these problems, you need to enable the script to lock the file for exclusive access and make other scripts wait their turn. PHP provides a flock() function that attempts to gain an exclusive lock and halts your script until it can achieve that lock. However, flock() alone is rarely enough, and it gets a little more complicated. A couple of examples will help you understand the situations fully.

First, take the example of appending data to a file. A web server log file is a good example of this. If you just opened to append the data, there is a situation where data can be corrupted. It occurs if the following order of events happens:

1. Script 1) opens the file to append.
2. Script 2) also opens the file to append.
3. Script 1) writes some data to the file.
4. Script 2) writes some data, destroying what Script 1 did.

The reason that the final write destroys the data is because when the second script opened the file it placed the file pointer at the end of the file as it saw it at that time. After the first script writes, there is more data in the file, and the second script overwrites it. Listing 8.9.1 should keep this situation from happening.

Listing 8.9.1 **File Locking**

```php
<?php
// Open the file to append data to it
if (!($fp = fopen('data.log', 'a'))) {
    die ('ERROR: Could not open file!');
}

// At this point we need to remove the ability for a user to abort
ignore_user_abort(true);

// Now attempt to get an exclusive lock
if (!(flock($fp, LOCK_EX))) {
    die('ERROR: Could not get exclusive lock!');
}

// We now have the lock, To make sure that another file didn't
// write data into this file while we waited for the lock, seek
// to the end of the file:
fseek($fp, 0, SEEK_END);

// Now we can write our data:
fwrite($fp, 'A Random Number: ' . rand() . "\n");

// Close the file - Which also releases the lock
fclose($fp);

// And now allow a user abort again:
ignore_user_abort(false);

// Now echo out our file contents so that we can see what happened:
echo '<pre>';
```

Listing 8.9.1 **Continued**

```
readfile('data.log');
echo '</pre>';
?>
```

Listing 8.9.1 solves the problems with appends, as well as variations such as reading and then appending, and so on. The use of the function `ignore_user_abort()` allows you to ensure that the process presented always goes to completion. Otherwise, a user clicking the stop button in his browser could cause the script to exit prematurely and leave files in a bad state.

The technique just presented works fine when appending to a file, or for other variations such as reading, parsing, and then appending. There is a serious flaw to this, however, when you want to open the file with write access. Because `flock()` requires that a file pointer obtain the lock, and because opening a file with write access erases the current contents of the file, a problem exists. A second process would end up destroying the contents of the file before it could ever realize that the first script had an exclusive lock on the file!

To solve this, you need to use a second, separate file to perform the lock command on, and only open your primary file for writing after you have procured a lock on the second file. This solution can also work if you don't want to use `fopen()` and `fwrite()` to manipulate your file but the various convenience functions such as `file()` and `file_put_contents()`. The code to accomplish all of these machinations would look something like Listing 8.9.2.

Listing 8.9.2 **File Locking Using a Separate Lock File**

```
<?php
// A function to creating a secondary locking file for us
function lock($filename) {
    // Remove the ability for user aborts until we are finished
    ignore_user_abort(true);

    // Attempt to open, and/or create, the lock file:
    if (!($fp = fopen("{$filename}.lock", 'w'))) {
        die ('ERROR: Could not open file!');
    }

    // Now attempt to get an exclusive lock
    if (!(flock($fp, LOCK_EX))) {
        die('ERROR: Could not get exclusive lock!');
    }

    // We now have the lock, return the locked file pointer
    return $fp;
}
```

Listing 8.9.2 **Continued**

```php
// Now create a function that will handle unlocking for us:
function unlock($filepointer) {
    // Unlock the secondary lock file:
    if (!(flock($filepointer, LOCK_UN))) {
        die('ERROR: Could undo exclusive lock!');
    }

    // Remove the restriction on user aborts:
    ignore_user_abort(false);
}

// Now use these functions to do a full read/write loop on a file
// incrementing a number for each time the file is written:

// Obtain the lock:
$lock = lock('data.counter');

// Read in the file:
$filedata = @file('data.counter');

// Determine our new count:
$count = isset($filedata[0]) ? $filedata[0] + 1 : 1;

// Now we can write our data:
file_put_contents('data.counter', $count);

// Release the exclusive lock
unlock($lock);

// Now echo out our file contents so that we can see what happened:
echo '<pre>';
readfile('data.counter');
echo '</pre>';
?>
```

Unfortunately, a few things still need to be pointed out. One is that these techniques are not 100% foolproof. They are almost 100% foolproof, but because of the various implementations of file systems, you cannot with 100% certainty know that two processes could not step on each other. The chances of this happening are extremely small given the techniques described previously, but it is still a good idea for keeping backups of all your data.

The other thing that must be discussed is that flock() does not work on all operating systems and on all file systems. Some, such as Windows 98 and the earlier FAT file system simply do not support it. In other cases, various methods of network-mounted storage, such as the UNIX NFS mount, do not allow it to work.

You can still attempt to do locking with a workaround, though it is not as robust. The solution in these cases, is to use the creation of a secondary file, and its existence alone, to determine whether you have gained an exclusive lock on a file. This is still potentially a problem because a process cannot be 100% sure that it created the file, and therefore you will often see modifications to this that involve the process writing its own process ID into the file, or creating the file with its process ID in the name of the file, and so on, just to ensure that it was the one that created it.

A potentially safer solution, though, is to create directories, instead of files. On almost all file systems the creation of a directory is a single atomic action. Therefore you can simply try to make the lock directory, and, if it fails, you don't have access because it already exists, and try again. This is the best solution to use when flock() is not available to you. Listing 8.9.3 demonstrates how to use directory creation as a locking method.

Listing 8.9.3 **Using Directory Creation As a Locking Method**

```php
<?php
// A function to creating a lock directory for us, getting around
// the need to use flock()
function lock($filename) {
    // Remove the ability for user aborts until we are finished
    ignore_user_abort(true);

    // Start a counter, we only want to try to obtain a lock
    // a certain number of times:
    $counter = 0;

    // Until we get a lock, or die trying, go for it:
    do {
        // Sleep for counter squared seconds, longer each time:
        sleep($counter * $counter);

        // Make the directory:
        $success = @mkdir("{$filename}.dirlock");
    }
    while ( !($success) && ($counter++ < 10) );

    // If counter is 11, then we never got the lock:
    if ($counter == 11) {
        die('ERROR: Could not get exclusive lock!');
    }

    // Otherwise we now have the lock and are done!
}

// Now create a function that will handle unlocking for us:
function unlock($filename) {
```

Listing 8.9.3 **Continued**

```
    // Remove the directory:
    if (!(rmdir("{$filename}.dirlock"))) {
        die('ERROR: Could undo exclusive lock!');
    }

    // Remove the restriction on user aborts:
    ignore_user_abort(false);
}

// Now use these functions to do a full read/write loop on a file
// incrementing a number for each time the file is written:

// Obtain the lock:
$lock = lock('data.counter');

// Read the file, determine our count, and write the data:
$filedata = @file('data.counter');
$count = isset($filedata[0]) ? $filedata[0] + 1 : 1;
file_put_contents('data.counter', $count);

// Release the exclusive lock
unlock('data.counter');

// Now echo out our file contents so that we can see what happened:
echo '<pre>';
readfile('data.counter');
echo '</pre>';
?>
```

8.10 Caching Remote Files Locally

Often a website may include files from another website. These could be graphics, XML data, JavaScript or even some embedded HTML. There are often good reasons for doing this, such as including a banner graphic from a news site that always has information about the top story included in it.

Two problems can happen while doing this, though. First, this can slow down the loading of your web page while a connection is made to the remote server to retrieve data. Second, though, is the lack of good user experience when the other website is down currently. The user may see a broken graphic, or even a completely unusable website. Having the file locally would be more ideal.

Some simple solutions can exist to actually cache the file locally to solve these problems. One method would be to update all your files that reference this remote file to actually just point to a local file instead. Then, using PHP, on a regular basis update that local file with the remote data. This is a good solution when you want to have a current version of the file, but it doesn't have to be instantly up to date. You can run your update program once a day, or even once an hour if you want. Listing 8.10.1 is an example of a simple version of what one of these update scripts could look like. Take this code and set it to run via command-line PHP in an automated fashion (such as cron on UNIX or Scheduled Tasks on Windows), and then point your web pages to the output file of this script. In this case we will simulate this by grabbing a particular graphic.

Listing 8.10.1   Caching Information from a Web Server

```php
<?php
// A script to cache the output of a graphic producing PHP script on
// another server: First try to open a connection to the remote file.
// If it fails then do nothing. That way if the remote server is down,
// we don't lose our local cached version:
if ($remote = fopen('http://hubblesite.org/news/latest_big.php', 'r')) {
    // Since we were able to open it, open our cache version to output to ..
    // again, if this fails, just exit and don't worry about it.
    if ($local = fopen('hubble_news.jpg', 'w')) {
        // We made it, copy all the data from the remote, to the local:
        stream_copy_to_stream($remote, $local);
        // Now close the files up
        fclose($remote);
        fclose($local);
    }
}
?>
```

This method does require that you are okay with not having the most current version of the file. So what if you are in a situation where you do want that, yet fall back on a cached version otherwise. Listing 8.10.2, although highly inefficient due to constantly rewriting the cached file, does accomplish this. To use it in this same example, you would place your image link to point at this PHP file. It would always attempt to access the remote graphic for you, retrieve it for display, and at the same time store a copy of it in case it needs to use it later.

Listing 8.10.2   Remote Web Server Access with Constant Cache Update

```php
<?php
// We are going to be outputting a graphic so start with the proper headers
header('Content-type: image/jpeg');

// Register a shutdown function, so if we fail, the basic file is returned
function shutdown() {
    // If we never managed to read the file:
    if (!(isset($GLOBALS['data'])) || !($GLOBALS['data'])) {
```

Listing 8.10.2   **Continued**

```
            // Output the cached file, ensure a full absolute path:
            readfile(dirname(__FILE__) . '/hubble_news.cache');
    }
}
register_shutdown_function('shutdown');

// Set a quick timeout value so if we don't get it quickly it uses the cache
set_time_limit(5);

// Try to read in the remote file:
if ($data = @file_get_contents(
        'http://hubblesite.org/news/latest_big.php')) {
    // Quickly reset the timer so we don't timeout while writing the cache
    set_time_limit(60);

    // We got the file, so echo out the contents
    echo $data;

    // Now we need to save this to the cache file as well.
    // Give file_put_contents the LOCK_EX flag which makes it
    // attempt to get an exclusive lock before writing to the file.
    ignore_user_abort(true);
    file_put_contents(dirname(__FILE__) . '/hubble_news.cache',
        $data, LOCK_EX);
}
?>
```

Listing 8.10.2 uses a couple of tricks that should be explained. To properly detect a failed connection or one that times out in a timely manner, you normally would need to use the socket functions. With them you can detect various failures and set appropriate time-outs. However, for this example, we wanted to use the much simpler `file_get_contents()` function to retrieve our data. If you just used it and tried to check whether its return value was false, you may be left waiting for minutes before it gives up trying to make the connection.

The workaround is with the `set_time_limit()` function that sets the number of seconds allowed before the script halts execution. Therefore setting it to 5 seconds before trying to read the file ensures that this script ends in a timely manner. To then make sure that we still return the cached version of the file, we register a function to run at script shutdown. The function `register_shutdown_function()` lets you give it a function name and parameters that should be run upon completion of the script. We give it our custom function, which detects whether we ever managed to get the data, and then if so, goes ahead and returns the cached version of the file.

The other thing to notice, is the use of the line `dirname(__FILE__)`. This is because during the shutdown function, it has lost its normal context because the script has already "ended." We therefore need to be able to exactly specify the directory that the file exists in.

Another example of caching files, in this case local files, can be found in Section 9.7, "Localizing a Web Page for Different Languages," and some of the techniques shown there can be applied in these situations as well.

8.11 Compressing and Uncompressing Files

File space and network bandwidth are always at a premium, and therefore compressing data is usually a good thing. PHP provides a set of functions that allow you to deal with compressed files and make them yourself. Note that these functions are immediately available under Windows and some other binary distributions, although you may need to specifically compile PHP with Zlib support to access these functions on other machines.

Before we go further, it should also be noted that there is rarely a need to bother to compress the output of your PHP script to send it to the browser. The reason is that PHP has this capability automatically built in, and you can enable it for all your pages if you want by changing the value of the `zlib.output_compression` setting in your php.ini file. To read more about this, see http://php.net/zlib.

One good use of this is to store various data files that you may want to access in compressed format to save space but to read them into memory when needed. Listing 8.11.1 demonstrates this technique.

Listing 8.11.1 **Accessing Compressed Files**

```php
<?php
// Read a gz-compressed file into a variable
$data = gzfile('compressed-data.gz');
?>
```

Another common use is to store raw files that will be served to the public in gzipped format but use PHP to serve them back up in the end. Listing 8.11.2 shows a script that takes a filename passed in and returns the contents of said file uncompressed. Use it, for example, by calling it in an image source tag like this:

```
<img src="decompress.php?file=image.jpg" alt="A Photo" width="100" height="150" />
```

Listing 8.11.2 **Uncompress Files for Serving**

```php
<?php
// For safety, we need to make sure that the file passed in does not
// start with a '/', nor does it ever contain '..'.  This way we
// can ensure that someone doesn't use this to leave the document tree:
$file = $_GET['file'];
if (($file{0} == '/') || (strstr($file, '..') !== false)) {
    exit("ERROR: Attempt to navigate directory tree detected!");
}
```

Listing 8.11.2   **Continued**

```php
// Now we need to try to detect the file type from the ending provided
// so that we can return the proper Content-Type:
$parts = pathinfo($file);
switch (strtolower($parts['extension'])) {
    case 'gif':
        header('Content-type: image/gif');
        break;
    case 'jpg':
    case 'jpeg':
        header('Content-type: image/jpeg');
        break;
    case 'png':
        header('Content-type: image/png');
        break;
    case 'html':
        header('Content-type: text/html');
        break;
    default:
        exit("ERROR: Unsupported filetype accessed!");
}

// If we made it this far, then go ahead and return the file:
readgzfile("{$file}.gz");
?>
```

Finally you may want to take data that is passed into your script and compress it for storage into a file. This way you can allow for uploaded files on a system but mitigate the amount of disk space used by this feature. Using `gzencode()` prepares data to be written to a gzip file as shown in Listing 8.11.3. (Also of note are `gzdeflate()` and `gzinflate()`, which can be used to compress and restore data for storage in a binary field of a database.)

Listing 8.11.3   **Compressing User Input**

```php
<?php
// Let's capture all data that was passed to this script, and
// serialize it into a text string:
$ized = serialize($_REQUEST);

// Now prepare this to be written to a gzipped file - Highest Compression:
$compressed = gzencode($ized, 9);

// Generate a guaranteed unique file using tempnam, with a GZ- prefix
$filename = tempnam('.', 'GZ-');
```

Listing 8.11.3   **Continued**

```
// Now write the compressed file!
file_put_contents($filename, $compressed);
?>
```

8.12 Automatically Including Certain Files from the Parent Tree

A semicommon templating technique is to have identically named files with variables and functions in them that vary for each subdirectory that they are in. This way you can customize various data for each subdirectory. However, it can become an administrative problem to constantly make sure that each of your PHP files include all appropriate header/library files at all times.

Fortunately, it is possible to script this, making it an automatic process for you. Listing 8.12.1 automatically includes any file named header.php from the current directory, or any directory higher than it but still within the web server's document root. As coded, this includes all header.php files, allowing for an inheritance scheme of sorts, because each subdirectory will have not only its header.php file included but also those from all its parent directories.

It is a small modification to this script to make it instead stop at the first one it finds, or perhaps to work backward, starting at the document root and including them from top to bottom.

Listing 8.12.1   **Including Files Throughout a Directory Tree**

```
<?php
// Store a copy of our current file, making sure it uses forward slashes:
$curdir = str_replace('\\', '/', __FILE__);
// Store a copy of document root, ensuring forward slashes:
$root = str_replace('\\', '/', $_SERVER['DOCUMENT_ROOT']);

// As long as we haven't just done Document Root:
while ($root !== $curdir) {
    // Remove one directory level from the current directory
    $curdir = dirname($curdir);

    // Try to include the file, hide any error:
    @include("{$curdir}/header.php");
}
?>
```

The manipulation of the various directories to ensure forward slashes is just so that we know that our comparison between the root and current directory returns true. This is because on some operating systems, such as Windows, it is common for the __FILE__ constant and $_SERVER['DOCUMENT_ROOT'] to have different types of slashes in them. If you know the server that you are working on has consistent slashes, you can remove that portion of code.

II

Applications

9

Web Page Creation/XHTML/CSS

Tнis сhapteр may seem a bit odd considering that nearly every example in this book uses PHP to create a web page. However, the focus has been on other aspects of the language. This chapter explores techniques that take advantage of PHP's web capabilities, in particular, its use when integrated into a web server. This chapter simply starts with the basics; following chapters expand on concepts such as cookies, user sessions and tracking, and web interaction.

Even for those experienced in web server-side PHP development, it is easy to forget what has set PHP apart from traditional CGI technologies: With CGI, the CGI is executing, producing, as a side effect, output compatible with web browsers. Whereas with PHP, the web page itself is being output, calling on PHP only when it is needed. To illustrate, consider a page that has existed as a static HTML page that now must include some small dynamic element. To implement in CGI, the developer must reimplement the whole page in the CGI language, creating a whole environment to simply support some small feature. With PHP, nothing with the page itself must change; only the one dynamic element need be inserted in the appropriate place. Though fine, this distinction contributes greatly to PHP's ease-of-use and seamless integration into the web environment.

This ease of transition between the web document and PHP is where the power of the language shines. While reading through this chapter's examples, note that few "special web page generating" functions actually exist. PHP by design is weaved into the document, appearing only where it needs to, as opposed to having to create the whole document itself.

Many of the following examples make extensive use of JavaScript, Cascading Style Sheets (CSS), and XHTML, on which there are many other sources of information. If unfamiliar with any of these technologies, a good place to start research is the World Wide Web Consortium's (W3C) website, http://w3.org/.

Quick Hits

▶ **Encode/decode a string for use in a URL:**

```
$urlready = urlencode($normalstring);
$normalstring = urldecode($urlready);
```

These function encode/decode strings to make them usable in a URL, in which all nonalphanumeric characters are encoded using the "%XX" format and "+" for spaces.

Full documentation: http://php.net/urlencode and http://php.net/urldecode

▶ **Encode/decode a string that may contain HTML entities:**

```
$htmlready = htmlentities($normalstring);
$normalstring = html_entity_decode($htmlready);
```

These functions translate any character that may have an HTML entity equivalent into that HTML entity.

Full documentation: http://php.net/htmlentities and http://php.net/html_entity_decode

▶ **Build a URL query string:**

```
$query = http_build_query($array);
```

This function builds a URL-encoded query string from the given array, ready for appending to a URL after the "?".

Full documentation: http://php.net/http_build_query

▶ **Send an HTTP header:**

```
header($headerstring);
```

This function sets an HTTP header to be sent. More than one header may be sent. However, headers must be sent before any output has occurred. Listing 9.8.1 shows a header being sent.

Full documentation: http://php.net/header

▶ **See whether headers have been sent:**

```
$sent = headers_sent();
```

This function returns true if headers have been sent.

Full documentation: http://php.net/headers_sent

▶ **Start/stop output buffering:**

```
$success = ob_start();
ob_flush();
$success = ob_end_flush();
```

These functions help manage output control from the current script. `ob_start()` starts buffering of all output generated by the current script. `ob_flush()` flushes the buffer to the output. `ob_end_flush()` also flushes the output and cancels the buffering.

Full documentation: http://php.net/ob_start, http://php.net/ob_flush, and http://php.net/ob_end_flush

9.1 Creating a Multilayer Drop-Down Menu

When creating a website, navigation is always a problem. On a large complicated website, it can become a burden. Sometimes, having hierarchical drop-down menus can make this easier, allowing for a small amount of space on the screen to be used (the initial menu) to present a complicated menu system.

This can be accomplished through the use of JavaScript, XHTML, and CSS. PHP makes the task easier because it can be configured within PHP, and then PHP can automatically generate the code needed. Listing 9.1.1 ends up creating a function that you can call, passing it a number of configuration parameters, and it creates a menu system for you. It is designed to work in most modern browsers and can be called multiple times on the same web page. Note that it uses both JavaScript and CSS to create the effect; although pure CSS methods exist for creating a menu such as this, they do not work in many browsers as of the creation of this book. Therefore that exercise is left up to the reader.

Listing 9.1.1   **Dynamic Menu System**

```
<!DOCTYPE html PUBLIC "-//W3C//DTD XHTML 1.0 Strict//EN"
    "http://www.w3.org/TR/xhtml1/DTD/xhtml1-strict.dtd">
<html xmlns="http://www.w3.org/1999/xhtml">
<head>
<title>Menu System</title>
<meta http-equiv="Content-Type" content="text/html; charset=iso-8859-1" />
</head>
<body>
<?php
// We need a container function that will create and output all parts to our
//   menuing system.  It accepts an array for the menu, x/y coordinates for
//   where it should appear, a width for each menu (to make them look more
//   uniform), various colors, and a character 'index' for this menu.  It can
//   be left off if you are only making one menu system on a page, give it a
//   different character if you are making a second system.
function create_full_menu_system($menuarray, $x, $y, $width,
                $fgcolor, $bgcolor, $txtcolor, $bordercolor, $idx = 'a') {
    // First use create_menu to create the XHTML, and to give us
    // a list of all menus such created, we need them.
    $xhtml = '';
    $menus = array();
    create_menu($menuarray, $xhtml, $menus, $idx, $idx);

    // Now, before we output the xhtml, prepare the list of menus:
    $menulist = implode(',', $menus);

    // Now, output the CSS that we need custom to this menu system:
    echo "
```

Listing 9.1.1   **Continued**

```
<style type=\"text/css\">
#menu{$idx} {
    visibility: visible;
    padding: 0px;
}
.menu_{$idx} {
    position: absolute;
    top: {$x}px;
    left: {$y}px;
    visibility: hidden;
    border-top: 3px solid {$bordercolor};
    padding: 0px 0px 0px 8px;
}
.menu_{$idx} ul {
    list-style-type: none;
    padding: 0px;
    margin: 0px;
    border-right: 1px solid {$bordercolor};
    border-bottom: 1px solid {$bordercolor};
    border-left: 1px solid {$bordercolor};
}
.menu_{$idx} li {
    border: 1px solid {$bordercolor};
}
.menu_{$idx} a {
    width: {$width}px;
    display: block;
    background-color: {$bgcolor};
    text-align: right;
    text-decoration: none;
    font-family: Geneva, Arial, Helvetica, sans-serif;
    font-size: 12px;
    color: {$txtcolor};
    padding: 2px;
    margin: 0px;
}
.menu_{$idx} a:hover {
    background-color: {$fgcolor};
}
</style>
";

    // Now create the javascript needed to run this menu:
    echo "
<script type=\"text/javascript\">
```

Listing 9.1.1   **Continued**

```
function display_menu_{$idx}(main, submenu, line) {
    // First force all current menus to disappear except parents:
    remove_menus_{$idx}('menu' + main);

    // Make the appropriate submenu appear
    // Find the containing block of the parent:
    var pblock = document.getElementById('menu' + main);

    // Get the Y of the new div
    var y = line.offsetTop + pblock.offsetTop + 12;

    // Figure out the X of the new div:
    var x = pblock.offsetLeft + pblock.offsetWidth;

    // Now display it, and move it into position:
    var newblock = document.getElementById('menu' + main + submenu);
    newblock.style.top = y + 'px';
    newblock.style.left = x + 'px';
    newblock.style.visibility = 'visible';

    // Now also clear the timeout like any other mouseover does:
    on_over_{$idx}();
}

// Create an array holding all submenus:
document.submenus_{$idx} = new Array({$menulist});
// Now a function, that by brute force, makes all submenus invisible
// Has an optional parameter used by submenus, to ensure that their
// parents do not get closed.  Set it to '' to remove ALL.
function remove_menus_{$idx}(except) {
    for (i = 0; i < document.submenus_{$idx}.length; i++) {
        // Only close this submenu if it doesn't match the 'except' menu
        if (document.submenus_{$idx}[i] !=
                except.substr(0,document.submenus_{$idx}[i].length)) {
            document.getElementById(document.submenus_{$idx}[i]
                ).style.visibility = 'hidden';            }
    }
}

function on_out_{$idx}() {
    // Upon leaving a submenu, start a timer to clear it.
    document.menutimer_{$idx} =
        window.setTimeout(\"remove_menus_{$idx}('')\", 1000);
}
```

Listing 9.1.1 **Continued**

```
function on_over_{$idx}() {
    // When on a submenu, make sure the timer is gone.
    window.clearTimeout(document.menutimer_{$idx});
}

function on_over_clear_{$idx}() {
    // When on a primary menu's option without a submenu, clear subs
    remove_menus_{$idx}('');
    on_over_{$idx}();
}
</script>
";

    // Now, finally, we can output the XHTML code:
    echo $xhtml;
}

// Now, we need a function that can be called recursively, that will
// loop through this array, creating the XHTML for it.
function create_menu($m, &$xhtml, &$menus, $subtext = 'a', $top = 'a') {
    // Prep the first character of subtext, we need it for the functions
    $idx = $subtext{0};

    // Determine if this menu should kill itself upon mouseout:
    $mousediv = " onmouseout=\"on_out_{$idx}()\"
onmouseover=\"on_over_{$idx}()\"";
    $mitem = '';
    if ($subtext !== $top) {
        $mitem = " onmouseover=\"on_over_{$idx}()\"";
    } else {
        $mitem = " onmouseover=\"on_over_clear_{$idx}()\"";
    }

    // Start creating a container for this menu:
    $xhtml .= "
<div id=\"menu{$subtext}\" class=\"menu_{$idx}\"{$mousediv}>
<ul id=\"list{$subtext}\">
";

    // Loop through all members of the array, outputting the menu
    $subs = array();
    $counter = 'a';
    foreach ($m as $name => $val) {
        // If this is an array:
        if (is_array($val)) {
```

Listing 9.1.1   **Continued**

```
                // Push the submenu into the subs array with the counter
                $subs[$counter] = $val;

                // Output the line:
                $xhtml .= "
<li><a href=\"javascript:void(0)\"
 onmouseover=\"display_menu_{$idx}('{$subtext}','{$counter}',this)\"
 >{$name} &gt;&gt;</a></li>
";
                // Increment the counter:
                $counter++;
            } else {
                // This is a URL, make a link:
                $xhtml .= "<li><a href=\"{$val}\"{$mitem}>{$name}</a></li>\n";
            }
        }

    // Now finish the division:
    $xhtml .= "</ul></div>\n";

    // Now recursively call this on every submenu:
    foreach ($subs as $stext => $submenu) {
        // First, quickly save a copy of the menuname:
        $menus[] = "'menu{$subtext}{$stext}'";
        // Now call the function:
        create_menu($submenu, $xhtml, $menus, $subtext . $stext, $top);
    }
}

// Declare our menu system as an array with subarrays for submenus:
$menu = array(
    'Useful Sites' => array(
        'Search Engines' => array(
            'Google' => 'http://google.com/',
            'Yahoo' => 'http://yahoo.com/'
            ),
        'Web Browsers' => array(
            'Mozilla' => 'http://mozilla.org/',
            'Opera' => 'http://opera.com/'
            )
        ),
    'News' => array(
        'BBC' => 'http://news.bbc.co.uk/',
        'Washington Post' => 'http://washingtonpost.com/',
        'New York Times' => 'http://nytimes.com/',
```

Listing 9.1.1   **Continued**

```
            'Slashdot' => 'http://slashdot.org/'
            ),
    'Home' => 'http://eliw.com/'
    );

// And create a second menu as well:
$menu2 = array(
    'Not Much' => array(
        'To See' => array(
            'Here' => array(
                'Really!' => 'http://php.net/'
                )
            )
        ),
    'Home' => 'http://eliw.com/'
    );

// Call it:
create_full_menu_system($menu, 5, 5, 120,
    '#00CCFF', '#CCCCCC', 'blue', 'black');
create_full_menu_system($menu2, 150, 250, 80,
    'black', '#CC0000', 'white', '#660000', 'b');
?>
</body>
</html>
```

The heart of this program is the fact that PHP generates the JavaScript and CSS custom to the menu at hand. This allows for a generic function that can be called multiple times on the same web page. All menus, css, and so on are indexed by a series of characters automatically created and updated for each menu. This is a base setup that generates one particular style of menus, a vertical navigation bar meant to be used on the left side of a website. Slight changes could allow this to be manipulated into any form needed.

9.2 Highlighting What Section of a Website the User Is In

Although a site may not always warrant a full multilayer navigation menu, most websites usually have at least a few different sections. Often many pages have links back to the top pages of each section, and therefore it is useful to highlight which section the user is currently in. Listing 9.2.1 looks at the URL of the current web page and, based on that, determines what section of the website it is in and changes the section menu.

Listing 9.2.1   **Navigation Highlighting**

```php
<?php
// Now create a function that will highlight the section you are in:
function create_highlighted_sections($secarray) {
    // Loop over the entire array, making a basic menu:
    echo "<ul>\n";
    foreach ($secarray as $section => $url) {
        // Echo out a link for this section, highlighting if currently in it
        $class = '';
        if (strncmp($url, $_SERVER['PHP_SELF'], strlen($url)) == 0) {
            $class = ' class="current"';
        }
        echo "<li{$class}><a href=\"{$url}\">{$section}</a></li>\n";
    }
    echo "</ul>\n";
}

// An array with all section names and the URL to their top directory:
$sections = array(
    'News' => '/news/',
    'Photos' => '/media/pictures/',
    'Video' => '/media/movies/',
    'Stuff' => '/eliw/'
    );

// Output a little bit of CSS to accomplish the highlighting:
?>
<style>
.current, .current a { color: red }
</style>
<?php
// And call the function to test it:
create_highlighted_sections($sections);
?>
```

As currently coded this just generates a basic UL list and assigns a class to the current section. This can be modified now via CSS to display in whatever manner you want, or the function can be extended to create different XHTML as needed.

The primary trick in this function is that it compares the current value of PHP_SELF to its list of sections. In this manner it can determine what section the current file is within. Of course this relies on the fact that your sections will each be in their own subdirectory. A nice side effect of this setup is that if a file lives at the top level, or within a different subdirectory, no section will be highlighted, because, obviously, you are not in any of those sections.

9.3 Displaying Dynamic Progress Bars

In some situations you might need to display a progress bar—for example, when you are performing many tasks on the back end and they take a while to complete. In these cases it is a good idea to give some indication to the user that you are in fact still performing tasks and that their browser hasn't simply locked up.

There are various methods of doing this, using pure PHP, or including JavaScript, CSS, Ajax, and more. We will explore a couple of simple examples and allow you to develop your own custom solution based on these. First, Listing 9.3.1 illustrates a simple example: You are waiting for a task to end and display a waiting screen during that time using just text.

Listing 9.3.1   **Progress Bar: Simple Text Version**

```php
<?php
// Output a 'waiting message'
echo 'Please wait while this task completes';

// Now while waiting for a certain task to complete, keep outputting .'s
while (true) {
    // Echo an extra dot, and flush the buffers to ensure it gets displayed.
    echo ' .';
    flush();

    // Now sleep for 1 second and check again:
    sleep(1);
}
?>
```

Of course in this example you would need to replace the `while (true)` statement with the actual check you are using to see when the task is done. This could be checking for the creation of a file in the file system, or checking the output of a program or web page. It could even be polling on input from another process—whatever method you have for checking this.

Alternatively, you may just have a lot of PHP code that you are running and want to give periodic updates as to how complete you feel the process is at that time. The benefit in these cases is that you know what percentage of the work is done (or can make a good guess). This allows for a better display, giving a true status until completion for the process.

Let's implement this type of bar in a more visually friendly setup but using PHP, XHTML, and CSS alone, as shown in Listing 9.3.2. It keeps creating new `div` elements that sit on top of the previous ones. This creates a bit of a mess if you view the source afterward but makes for a pretty display.

Listing 9.3.2   **Progress Bar: PHP–Based**

```php
<?php
// A function that will create the initial setup for the progress bar:
// You can modify this to your liking for visual purposes:
function create_progress() {
    // First create our basic CSS that will control the look of this bar:
    echo "
<style>
#text {
    position: absolute;
    top: 100px;
    left: 50%;
    margin: 0px 0px 0px -150px;
    font-size: 18px;
    text-align: center;
    width: 300px;
}
#barbox_a {
    position: absolute;
    top: 130px;
    left: 50%;
    margin: 0px 0px 0px -160px;
    width: 304px;
    height: 24px;
    background-color: black;
}
.per {
    position: absolute;
    top: 130px;
    font-size: 18px;
    left: 50%;
    margin: 1px 0px 0px 150px;
    background-color: #FFFFFF;
}
.bar {
    position: absolute;
    top: 132px;
    left: 50%;
    margin: 0px 0px 0px -158px;
    width: 0px;
    height: 20px;
    background-color: #0099FF;
}
.blank {
    background-color: white;
    width: 300px;
}
```

Listing 9.3.2 **Continued**

```
</style>
";

    // Now output the basic, initial, XHTML that will be overwritten later:
    echo "
<div id='text'>Script Progress</div>
<div id='barbox_a'></div>
<div class='bar blank'></div>
<div class='per'>0%</div>
";

    // Ensure that this gets to the screen immediately:
    flush();
}

// A function that you can pass a percentage as a whole number and it
//  will generate the appropriate new div's to overlay the current ones:
function update_progress($percent) {
    // First let's recreate the percent with the new one:
    echo "<div class='per'>{$percent}%</div>\n";

    // Now, output a new 'bar', forcing its width to 3 times the percent,
    // since we have defined the percent bar to be at 300 pixels wide.
    echo "<div class='bar' style='width: ", $percent * 3, "px'></div>\n";

    // Now, again, force this to be immediately displayed:
    flush();
}

// Ok, now to use this, first create the initial bar info:
create_progress();

// Now, let's simulate doing some various amounts of work, and updating
// the progress bar as we go - The usleep commands will simulate multiple
// lines of code being executed.
usleep(350000);
update_progress(7);
usleep(1550000);
update_progress(28);
usleep(1000000);
update_progress(48);
usleep(1000000);
update_progress(68);
usleep(150000);
update_progress(71);
```

Listing 9.3.2 **Continued**

```
usleep(150000);
update_progress(74);
usleep(150000);
update_progress(77);
usleep(1150000);
update_progress(100);
// Now that you are done, you could also choose to output whatever final
// text that you might wish to, and/or to redirect the user to another page.
?>
```

9.4 Simulating Graphical Charts with XHTML/CSS

When you need to present data in a chart on a web page, it is often worthwhile to generate graphical charts. This method is covered later in Section 18.4, "Creating a Graph/Chart Library"; however, sometimes for a quick chart CSS can suffice. Listing 9.4.1 presents a function that creates a visual chart of data using CSS and XHTML only.

As written it accepts an array of values and plots them each in an area graph 1 pixel wide for each data point. It uses div's, absolute positioning, and CSS heights to create this effect. It allows for the position of the page you want the chart to appear on to be designated and for a maximum height to be defined, which it will scale the values to.

Listing 9.4.1 **XHTML/CSS-Based Graphs**

```
<?php
// Define the chart creation function.
// Have parameters for the data itself and a maximum height for the chart.
// You can also pass in 4 color parameters, for the border,
//   background, bars, and the grid - These are optional.
function create_chart($data, $height,
        $bars = 'red', $bg = 'white', $border = 'black', $grid = '#DDD') {
    // First of all let's ensure that every time we call this we
    // generate a new 'number' for this chart, it's needed to distinguish
    // if we have multiple charts on one page:
    static $idx = 0;
    $idx++;

    // Consider height to be 2 pixels less to take into account the borders:
    $height -= 2;

    // Now let's calculate our scale factor, add in a little because for
    // visual purposes we don't want it to ever hit the top.
    $scale = $height / (max($data) * 1.05);
```

Listing 9.4.1 **Continued**

```
    // Calculate our width:
    $width = count($data);

    // Now we can create some basic CSS that will be used by this:
    echo "
<style>
#chartout{$idx} {
    position: relative;
    height: ", $height + 2, "px;
    width: ", $width + 2, "px;
    background-color: {$border};
}
#chartin{$idx} {
    position: absolute;
    top: 1px;
    left: 1px;
    height: {$height}px;
    width: {$width}px;
    background-color: {$bg};
}
.bar{$idx} {
    position: absolute;
    bottom: 0px;
    background-color: {$bars};
    width: 1px;
    overflow: hidden;
}
.grid{$idx} {
    position: absolute;
    left: 0px;
    height: 1px;
    width: {$width}px;
    background-color: {$grid};
    overflow: hidden;
}
</style>
";

    // Now output the basic parts of the chart:
    echo "
<div id='chartout{$idx}'><div id='chartin{$idx}'>
";

    // Now create a grid pattern, divide the space into 5ths
    foreach(range(1,3) as $line) {
```

Listing 9.4.1   **Continued**

```
        $lh = round($line * ($height / 5));
        echo "<div class='grid{$idx}' style='top: {$lh}px'></div>\n";
    }


    // Now run through all elements of the array, making the actual bars
    foreach ($data as $pos => $val) {
        $barheight = round($val * $scale);
        echo "<div class='bar{$idx}' style='left:{$pos}px;
height:{$barheight}px'></div>\n";
    }


    // Finish off:
    echo "\n</div></div>\n";
}


// Let's generate 200 random points of data in two different arrays
$chartdata = array();
$chartdata2 = array();
for ($i = 0; $i < 200; $i++) {
    $chartdata[$i] = rand(1,1000);
    $chartdata2[$i] = rand(1,1000);
}


// Now generate a chart based upon this, 100 pixels tall:
create_chart($chartdata, 100);


// Generate another one that is only 50 pixels tall, with different colors
create_chart($chartdata2, 50, '#0C0', 'black', 'black', '#666');
?>
```

As currently written, this creates a chart whose width is dictated by the width of the array given it. You could add a width parameter and scale the results; however, if the data would be scaled down, you run into problems of needing to "lose" data to fit everything in. On the other hand, scaling it wider would be easier, because the bars would just stop being 1 pixel wide.

This function only generates the chart itself. It doesn't also display any legends or keys for the chart. The function can be modified to also create these for you, or they could be created otherwise and placed next to the chart within the XHTML and CSS.

Note that each chart is a div, and it is set to be position relative. This outer div must remain being either relative or absolute in its positioning; otherwise, the positioning commands inside it for the bars will not work.

9.5 Pagination of Results on a Web Page

When creating browse or search functionality on a website, you many find that you end up with more data than the page can easily display at once. In these situations it makes for a better user experience to give users only a certain number of results and then present them with options to see the next and/or previous pages.

Listing 9.5.1 is an example of this that assumes that you have all your data in an array in the first place and just want to display parts of it at a time, reloading the page to view another set of options. This example needs customization to work properly for your own situation because all cases where pagination needs to happen end up slightly different.

Listing 9.5.1 **Result Pagination**

```php
<?php
// First of all, handle configuration ... Read in values from a GET
//  and default values that don't exist:
$page = (isset($_GET['page']) && ($_GET['page'] > 0))
    ? intval($_GET['page']) : 1;
$view = (isset($_GET['view']) && ($_GET['view'] > 0))
    ? intval($_GET['view']) : 10;

// Create our fake data to paginate on, just use the alphabet
$data = range('a', 'z');

// Now, chunk the data into equal sized pieces, based upon the view.
$pages = array_chunk($data, $view, true);

// Now output the chunk of data that was asked for:
echo "<p>The results are:</p>\n<p>\n";
foreach($pages[$page - 1] as $num => $datum) {
    echo $num + 1, ". {$datum}<br />\n";
}
echo "</p>\n";

// Now create the options to change what page you are viewing:
echo '<p>Switch to page: |';
$get = $_GET;
foreach(range(1, count($pages)) as $p) {
    // If this is the current page:
    if ($page == $p) {
        echo " {$p} |";
    } else {
        // We need to give them their option - First generate the URL needed
        // We want to duplicate any query string given to us, but replacing
        //  any pagination values with our new page.  Easiest is to take a
        //  current copy of get, update it for our values, then recreate it.
```

Listing 9.5.1   **Continued**

```
        $get['page'] = $p;
        $query = http_build_query($get);
        echo " <a href=\"{$_SERVER['PHP_SELF']}?{$query}\">{$p}</a> |";
    }
}
echo "</p>\n";

// Now let's give some options to change how many results we see per page:
$options = array(3, 5, 10, 50);

// Make a new copy of the $_GET array to play with again
$get = $_GET;

// Always set page to 1 when making a change to the number of results:
unset($get['page']);

// And let's output the options in the same manner as the pages:
echo '<p>Results per page: |';
foreach($options as $o) {
    // If the current option:
    if ($o == $view) {
        echo " {$o} |";
    } else {
        // Give the new option, again by regenerating the GET
        $get['view'] = $o;
        $query = http_build_query($get);
        echo " <a href=\"{$_SERVER['PHP_SELF']}?{$query}\">{$o}</a> |";
    }
}
echo "</p>\n";
?>
```

Two PHP functions make this task straightforward. The first function is http_build_ query(), which takes an array and automatically turns it into a GET query string for you. It takes care of all encoding issues and ensures a valid string. This makes it easy in our example to maintain the current GET parameters and just modify or add a few.

The second is array_chunk(), which breaks an array into equal-sized portions for you. This makes it easy when you have your entire dataset in memory to grab one page's worth of it.

It is usually advantageous to not have all your data stored into memory at once when you are only going to display a subset of it. Not only will this save memory, but it also can speed up the reading of the results as well. How exactly to do this, however, depends on how your data is stored and retrieved, and sometimes is not possible.

9.6 Caching Web Page Output for Server Optimization

Often PHP is used to generate pages that do not change all that often. It isn't that PHP is used to make every page different for every user but that the page is simply built dynamically. In these situations, it is often the case that, the page really doesn't change all that often, perhaps only once a day, if that. In these cases, therefore, it is a waste of CPU time to regenerate the web page for every user.

One solution is to not have your PHP pages accessed directly but to have a separate script that uses your PHP to generate the output and save that to a file. Then have the web server reference that file. This works, but adds an extra step that you must remember to do.

In this situation, instead, we are going to create a dynamic solution. Some code that you can include at the top of every PHP file ensures that the page only gets generated once per hour for each script (see Listing 9.6.1). The function goes one step further and understands that different GET and POST parameters generate different pages and will therefore generate separate cached copies for each different combination of GET and POST parameters that occur.

Listing 9.6.1   **An Output Caching Library—Filename: cache.php**

```php
<?php
// A function to call that will set up & handle the output caching:
// The one optional parameter is to specify how many seconds must pass
//  before the page is recreated (defaults to 1 hour)
function cache_page($refresh = 3600) {
    // First of all generate the filename for this cache file. Base it upon
    //  the filename plus GET and POST variables, and use sha1() to hash it
    //  to a 40 character string so we don't run over filename length limits:
    $hash = sha1($_SERVER['PHP_SELF'] . '|G|' . serialize($_GET) .
        '|P|' . serialize($_POST));

    // Create the actual filename of where to find this.  It will be in a
    //  subdirectory called 'cache' below the location of this library.
    $file = dirname(__FILE__) . '/cache/' . $hash;

    // Now that we've done all that, see if the last modified time is
    // less than the current time plus the refresh time
    if ((time() - @filemtime($file)) < $refresh) {
        // We are done, just return the file and exit
        readfile($file);
        exit();
    } else {
        // Otherwise, we have to actually create the page and save it.
        // To do this, first stop the user from aborting at this point so
```

Listing 9.6.1   **Continued**

```
        // it will definitely complete.
        ignore_user_abort();

        // Now set up a shutdown function, so that we can ensure we actually
        // finish up properly when the script exits (for any reason)
        register_shutdown_function('_cache_page_exit', $file);

        // Now, to finish, we need to start output buffering
        ob_start();
    }
}

// Create the shutdown function that will be called for us when the script
// exits, allowing us to clean up everything.
function _cache_page_exit($file) {
    // We were buffering and are done.  First step is to get the contents
    //  and display it to the user.
    $output = ob_get_flush();

    // Flush all buffers so the user can get the data while we finish up.
    flush();

    // Save this data into the cache file, blowing away current contents
    // if they existed.  Request an exclusive lock for the writing just
    // so that two copies of this don't interfere with each other.
    file_put_contents($file, $output, LOCK_EX);
}
?>
```

This script can be customized to meet your own needs, such as allowing for cookies or even sessions to be considered in whether a page is different. To demonstrate how this is used, Listing 9.6.2 is included that just uses the cache mechanism and outputs the current time. If the cache works, the output will not change for an hour. The test page assumes that you saved the previous code in a file called buffer.php.

Listing 9.6.2   **How To Use Internal Page Caching**

```
<?php
// Include the caching library:
require_once '09c06-1.php';
//require_once 'cache.php';

// Initialize the caching:
cache_page();
```

Listing 9.6.2   **Continued**

```
// Now let's just echo out the date.  If caching works, when you
// reload this page, the date will not change until an hour has passed:
date_default_timezone_set('America/New_York');
echo date(DATE_RSS, time());
?>
```

9.7 Localizing a Web Page for Different Languages

Internationalization and localization of a web page is simply the act of setting it up to be able to handle displaying in multiple languages and adding those different languages in. There are many different ways in which to do this. One of the simplest is to just make sure that all your strings that you ever output are stored as variables or constants in an included file. That way, you can make multiple copies of that file, each with different language versions written into them. Just include the appropriate file for the language that you want to display.

This idea can be extended to images as well because any image with text on it would also need translated. Just define the `imgsrc` of each image in your included file as well.

Listings 9.7.1, 9.7.2, and 9.7.3 are examples of what these included files could look like, given in three different languages.

Listing 9.7.1   **Localization File for English—Filename: en.php**

```php
<?php
// Declare all text strings that we need, in English.
$GLOBALS['text'] = array (
    'welcome' => 'Welcome to our website!',
    'thanks' => 'Thank you for your patronage.',
    'sky' => 'The sky is falling!',
    'game' => 'Would you like to play a game?',
    'switch' => 'Switch the language to:',
    );

// Now, also define alternative imgs for our use
$GLOBALS['imgsrc'] = array (
    'title' => 'graphics/title.en.png',
    'footer' => 'graphics/foot.en.jpg'
    );
?>
```

Listing 9.7.2   **Localization File for French—Filename: fr.php**

```php
<?php
// Declare all text strings that we need, in French.
$GLOBALS['text'] = array (
    'welcome' => 'Bienvenue &agrave; notre site Web!',
    'thanks' => 'Merci de soutenir nos affaires.',
    'sky' => 'Le ciel tombe!',
    'game' => 'Aimez-vous jouer un jeu?',
    'switch' => 'Commutez la langue &agrave;:',
    );

// Now, also define alternative imgs for our use
$GLOBALS['imgsrc'] = array (
    'title' => 'graphics/title.fr.png',
    'footer' => 'graphics/foot.fr.jpg'
    );
?>
```

Listing 9.7.3   **Localization File for German—Filename: de.php**

```php
<?php
// Declare all text strings that we need, in German.
$GLOBALS['text'] = array (
    'welcome' => 'Willkommen zu unserer Web site!',
    'thanks' => 'Danke f&uuml;r Ihr Patronat.',
    'sky' => 'Der Himmel f&auml;llt!',
    'game' => 'Wurden Sie m&ouml;gen ein Spiel spielen?',
    'switch' => 'Schalten Sie die Sprache zu:',
    );

// Now, also define alternative imgs for our use
$GLOBALS['imgsrc'] = array (
    'title' => 'graphics/title.de.png',
    'footer' => 'graphics/foot.de.jpg'
    );
?>
```

Now that we have all the different language versions saved in separate files, we want to make it easy for any page to use these. Therefore, a library should be created to handle this. The library shown in Listing 9.7.4 when included in a web page automatically detects what language should be used based on a GET string or a cookie. It also provides a function for easily creating some XHTML that allows for switching languages.

Listing 9.7.4 **Localization Library—Filename: language.php**

```php
<?php
// This is a library, that by including it, automatically determines
// the proper language to use and includes the language file.

// First define an array of all possible languages:
$languages = array('en' => 'English', 'fr' => 'French', 'de' => 'German');

// Look at the GET string to see if lang is specified:
if (isset($_GET['lang'])) {
    // It's been specified, so set the language
    $lang = $_GET['lang'];
    // While here, send a cookie to remember this selection for 1 year.
    setcookie('lang', $lang, time()+(3600*24*365));
}
// Ok, otherwise look for the cookie itself:
elseif (isset($_COOKIE['lang'])) {
    // Use this
    $lang = $_COOKIE['lang'];
} else {
    // Otherwise, default to English
    $lang = 'en';
}

// Make sure that the language string we have is a valid one:
if (!(in_array($lang, array_keys($languages)))) {
    die("ERROR: Bad Language String Provided!");
}

// Now include the appropriate language file:
require_once "{$lang}.php"


// As one last step, create a function that can be used to output
// language options to the user:
function switch_language_options() {
    // Include a few globals that we will need:
    global $text, $languages, $lang;

    // Start our string with a language specific 'switch' statement:
    $retval = $text['switch'];

    // Loop through all possible languages to create our options.
    $get = $_GET;
    foreach ($languages as $abbrv => $name) {
        // Create the link, ignoring the current one.
```

Listing 9.7.4   **Continued**

```php
        if ($abbrv !== $lang) {
            // Recreate the GET string with this language.
            $get['lang'] = $abbrv;
            $url = $_SERVER['PHP_SELF'] . '?' . http_build_query($get);
            $retval .= " <a href=\"{$url}\">{$name}</a>";
        }
    }

    // Now return this string.
    return $retval;
}
?>
```

With this completed, it can be easy to generate a web page that is language independent, such as Listing 9.7.5.

Listing 9.7.5   **Localization: Complete Example**

```php
<?php
// Include our language library:
require_once 'language.php';
?>
<!DOCTYPE html PUBLIC "-//W3C//DTD XHTML 1.0 Strict//EN"
    "http://www.w3.org/TR/xhtml1/DTD/xhtml1-strict.dtd">
<html xmlns="http://www.w3.org/1999/xhtml">
<head>
<title><?= $text['welcome'] ?></title>
<meta http-equiv="Content-Type" content="text/html; charset=iso-8859-1" />
</head>
<body>
<p><img alt="<?= $text['welcome'] ?>" src="<?= $imgsrc['title'] ?>"
 height="50" width="500" /></p>
<h2><?= $text['thanks'] ?></h2>
<p><?= $text['game'] ?></p>
<p><img alt="<?= $text['sky'] ?>" src="<?= $imgsrc['footer'] ?>"
 height="10" width="220" /></p>
<p><?= switch_language_options(); ?></p>
</body>
</html>
```

> **Note**
>
> PHP also provides an interface to the GNU `gettext` library. This is a generic library created to handle internationalization/localization problems. Using it requires building the support for it into PHP and installing the `gettext` library on your computer. If you want to learn more about this, visit http://php.net/gettext.

9.8 Using Ajax with PHP to Create an Interactive Web Page

Ajax, which stands for Asynchronous JavaScript and XML, is the newest term for a technology that is catching on in popularity. The technology, introduced in 1999, allows a web page, via JavaScript, to make a request back to the server, receive data, and process it without the page ever having to reload.

This technique allows for web pages that have automatically updating parts to them or buttons that automatically save data without ever having to click a submit button or leave the page. A full discussion of Ajax is not within the scope of this book and would be mostly a discussion of JavaScript, not PHP. However, the listings in this section demonstrate one quick example that shows how Ajax can call a PHP script, pass it data, and display the results back to the user.

Ajax in its purest form uses XML as the basis of communication. The requested file on the server will respond as an XML document that the JavaScript can parse. This doesn't have to always be the case, though, as the requested page can return anything it wants as long as the JavaScript knows how to deal with it. Many websites in use today just return text or raw HTML as their Ajax responses because it can be more convenient in some cases. Because the base form of Ajax is using XML, however, to start our example, we will create a service that provides information in XML. Listing 9.8.1 offers a simple PHP script that generates a simple XML result, which is the current time, formatted based on a parameter given to it.

Listing 9.8.1   **XML Time Service—Filename: time.php**

```php
<?php
// Figure out our time format  If none is provided, default
// to RFC 2822 format:
$format = isset($_GET['format']) ? $_GET['format'] : 'r';

// Generate the date:
date_default_timezone_set('America/New_York');
$dstr = date($format);

// Define that we are returning XML content & not to cache:
header('Content-Type: text/xml');
header('Cache-control: no-cache');

// Now output a valid XML file:
echo <<<EOXML
<?xml version="1.0" ?>
<result>{$dstr}</result>
EOXML;
?>
```

Now that this simple PHP file has been created, we can access it via Ajax on a web page. The web page created in Listing 9.8.2 uses JavaScript to update the date on the page when you click a button requesting the update. It also allows you to enter the format that you want the date to be in.

All this is done via the XMLHttpRequest object (or XMLHTTP for Internet Explorer). These allow JavaScript to make the request and read back in the results.

Listing 9.8.2 **Web Page Using Ajax**

```
<!DOCTYPE html PUBLIC "-//W3C//DTD XHTML 1.0 Strict//EN"
    "http://www.w3.org/TR/xhtml1/DTD/xhtml1-strict.dtd">
<html xmlns="http://www.w3.org/1999/xhtml">
<head>
<title>Formatted Time</title>
<meta http-equiv="Content-Type" content="text/html; charset=iso-8859-1" />
<script type="text/javascript">
// Declare our request variable.
var request = false;

// Define a function that will make our request for us:
function retrieveDate() {
    // Clear the curent request
    request = false;

    // Generate the request object and handle different browsers:
    if (window.XMLHttpRequest) { // Mozilla & other compliant browsers
        request = new XMLHttpRequest();
    } else if (window.ActiveXObject) { // Internet Explorer
        request = new ActiveXObject("Microsoft.XMLHTTP");
    }

    // If we don't have a request object, then error out.
    if (!request) {
        alert('Browser does not support AJAX!');
        return false;
    }

    // Ok, now we are ready.  Make the request, and tell it to run the
    // function 'updateDate' when it gets data back.
    request.onreadystatechange = updateDate;

    // Open the connection, sending the current value of the form element:
    request.open('GET',
        'time.php?format=' + escape(document.myform.dformat.value), true);
    request.send(null);
}
```

Listing 9.8.2 **Continued**

```
// The function that will accept the data, and update the page:
function updateDate() {
    // Make sure that the state is '4', which means finished:
    if (request.readyState == 4) {
        // Make sure that the status is 200, or 'ok'
        if (request.status == 200) {
            // If so, read the result back in as XML:
            var xml = request.responseXML;

            // Now, parse the 'result' out of the XML:
            var result = xml.getElementsByTagName('result').item(0);

            // And now, update the text on the page:
            var text = document.getElementById('datetext');
            text.innerHTML = result.firstChild.data;
        } else {
            alert('Error performing request!' + request.status);
        }
    }
}
</script>
</head>
<body>
<p>Click the update button below to receive the current date.  Insert any
 valid PHP date() format string in the field to format it accordingly.</p>
<p id="datetext">--DATE GOES HERE--</p>
<form id="myform" name="myform"><p>
<input type="text" id="dformat" name="dformat" value="r" />
<input type="button" value="Update" onclick="retrieveDate()" />
</p></form>
</body>
</html>
```

Think of the benefits of this technology even in this simple case. What if the original web page was a large dynamically generated web page? Instead of the entire page having to reload to update just one small part of it, a simple request can handle that.

Note

A good source of more information on Ajax can be found online at the Mozilla Developer's Center: http://developer.mozilla.org/en/docs/AJAX

10

Web Form Handling

Aₛ started in Chapter 9, "Web Page Creation/XHTML/CSS," this chapter continues to demonstrate PHP's capabilities when used in the web server-side environment. The first section demonstrates how form data is easily integrated in the PHP environment, including file upload handling. Next, generating forms is discussed, emphasizing how previously submitted data can be verified and sent back to the user. Some techniques to prevent form submission abuse are also presented.

Now is a good time to introduce the issue of security. Website security and form submission go hand-in-hand. Web forms provide the easiest access to a website; forms are an open invitation to the world to upload information to a server. When developing forms, you must always keep in mind how the incoming data is handled. The last sections of this chapter deal with some specific issues. For a general overview of security and PHP, see http://php.net/manual/security.php.

Quick Hits

▶ **Convert certain characters to HTML entities:**

```
$htmlready = htmlspecialchars($string, $quote_style);
```

Certain common characters that have special meaning in HTML are converted to their HTML-entity equivalent, so as not to be interpreted as HTML. The characters converted are the ampersand "&", double quote """, or single quote "'" depending on the value of `$quote_style`, less-than sign "<", and greater-than sign ">".

Full documentation: http://php.net/htmlspecialchars

▶ **Convert all characters to their HTML entities:**

```
$htmlready = htmlentities($string);
```

Any character that has an HTML-entity is converted to that entity.

Full documentation: http://php.net/htmlentities

▶ **Remove HTML tags from a string:**

```
$clean = strip_tags($string, $allow);
```

Anything that looks like an HTML or PHP tag is removed from the string, except for those tags in the optional string $allow.

Full documentation: http://php.net/strip_tags

▶ **Convert new lines to HTML breaks:**

```
$htmlready = nl2br($string);
```

The returned string contains '<br />' before all new lines.

Full documentation: http://php.net/nl2br

10.1 Easily Obtaining Form Data

One of the best features of PHP that many programmers find is how easily it handles form data. PHP automatically populates two superglobal arrays, $_GET and $_POST, with all the values sent as GET or POST data, respectively. Therefore, a form input called 'city' that was sent via POST, would be stored as $_POST['city'].

This makes it remarkably easy to create forms and accept data from them. Listings 10.1.1 and 10.1.2 are small examples showing pages that just have two form elements, a text element and a submit button element. Both listings submit back to themselves, displaying the value typed into them. The first listing uses the GET method, whereas the second uses the POST method.

Listing 10.1.1 **Accessing Form Data Using the** GET **Method**

```php
<?php
// If we had a GET element called 'city', then echo it:
if (isset($_GET['city'])) {
    echo "<p>You said you come from: {$_GET['city']}</p>\n";
}
?>
<form action="<?= $_SERVER['PHP_SELF'] ?>" method="get" name="f1">
<p>What city/town do you hail from? <input name="city" type="text" /></p>
<p><input type="submit" /></p>
</form>
```

Listing 10.1.2 **Accessing Form Data Using the** POST **Method**

```php
<?php
// If we had a POST element called 'city', then echo it:
if (isset($_POST['city'])) {
    echo "<p>You said you come from: {$_POST['city']}</p>\n";
}
?>
```

Listing 10.1.2   **Continued**

```
<form action="<?= $_SERVER['PHP_SELF'] ?>" method="post" name="f1">
<p>What city/town do you hail from? <input name="city" type="text" /></p>
<p><input type="submit" /></p>
</form>
```

One additional superglobal is created in regards to this data. The $_REQUEST variable is created and contains all the data from both the GET and POST. (It also contains cookie data.) This can be a handy shortcut when you don't know which of the two methods are going to provide the data you expect. Unless modified by the variables_order initialization directive, POST data overrides GET data in $_REQUEST.

In normal use, it is usually preferable to state whether you want the GET or POST data specifically. This makes for more robust code, and no unintended side effects can occur because you ended up with a different value for the variable than you expected. Also, you can sometimes do interesting things using both GET and POST data separately, as Section 10.3, "Using GET and POST Form Data Together," discusses later in this chapter.

10.2 Obtaining Multidimensional Arrays of Form Data

What makes the automatic form data handling described in the preceding section, "Easily Obtaining Form Data," even more powerful, is PHP's capability to understand multidimensional data coming from a form. By naming form fields with PHP-styled array constructors, PHP actually creates them as arrays for you.

So having a set of fields all with the same name: 'comment[]', for example, causes an array indexed by the string comment to be created, as shown in Listing 10.2.1.

Listing 10.2.1   **Retrieving Multidimensional Data from a Form**

```
<?php
// If we have a 'cities' from the POST, then loop over and display:
if (isset($_POST['cities'])) {
    echo "<p>You claim to have lived in the following cities:";

    // Loop over each city and output
    foreach ($_POST['cities'] as $num => $val) {
        echo '<br />', ($num + 1), ". {$val}\n";
    }
    echo "</p>\n";
}
?>
<form action="<?= $_SERVER['PHP_SELF'] ?>" method="post" name="f1">
<p>In order, what are the most recent cities you have lived in?</p>
<ol>
<?php
```

Listing 10.2.1 **Continued**

```
// Create a dozen form entries to hold cities:
echo str_repeat('<li><input name="cities[]" type="text" /></li>', 12);
?>
</ol>
<p><input type="submit" /></p>
</form>
```

In this example, there will always be a dozen entries for the cities because any entries that you leave blank still get submitted as a blank string. Therefore, if someone enters data into the seventh position alone, it still comes back in the seventh position.

This is useful for processing large amounts of similar data. It is also possible to specify the array index, instead of just using [] to have it automatically created. This means that you could, for example, use address[state], and it would return to you as such (see Listing 10.2.2).

Listing 10.2.2 **Multidimensional Form Data Using Explicit Indexes**

```
<?php
// If we have a POST, then:
if (count($_POST)) {
    echo "
<p>Your address is:<br />
{$_POST['address']['line1']}<br />
{$_POST['address']['line2']}<br />
{$_POST['address']['line3']}<br />
{$_POST['city']}, {$_POST['state']}  {$_POST['zip']}
</p>
";
}
?>
<form action="<?= $_SERVER['PHP_SELF'] ?>" method="post" name="f1">
<p>Please provide your address:<br />
Line 1: <input name="address[line1]" type="text" /><br />
Line 2: <input name="address[line2]" type="text" /><br />
Line 3: <input name="address[line3]" type="text" /><br />
City: <input name="city" type="text" /><br />
State: <input name="state" type="text" /><br />
Zip: <input name="zip" type="text" />
</p>
<p><input type="submit" /></p>
</form>
```

Finally, one other case allows for you to receive arrays full of data, and that refers to multiple select fields. In XHTML you can create a multiple select field that allows the user to select any number of items from it. To access these in PHP, again give them a name ending in [], and all the selections that are made will arrive as an array (see Listing 10.2.3).

Listing 10.2.3   **Retrieving Multiselect Form Input**

```php
<?php
// If we have a POST, then:
if (isset($_POST['beer'])) {
    // Output all beers that they liked:
    $beers = implode(', ', $_POST['beer']);
    echo "<p>Wow, you like the following beers: {$beers}</p>\n";
}
?>
<form action="<?= $_SERVER['PHP_SELF'] ?>" method="post" name="f1">
<p>What are your favorite types of beer?</p>
<select name="beer[]" multiple="multiple">
  <option value="stout">Stout</option>
  <option value="porter">Porter</option>
  <option value="hefeweizen">Hefeweizen</option>
  <option value="brown ale">Brown Ale</option>
  <option value="lambic">Lambic</option>
  <option value="double bock">Double Bock</option>
</select>
<input type="submit">
</form>
```

As can be seen, with all these variations available, PHP has an amazingly powerful, flexible, and yet simple mechanism to get form data into the script.

10.3 Using GET and POST Form Data Together

Because GET and POST variables are both passed in separately, you can use them both at the same time, even having the same variable names in both cases. The most common practice of this is to pass some configuration variables to your script via GET, while allowing user input to come as a POST.

This can be especially useful in some situations because GET parameters are saved in bookmarks, and POST parameters are not. Therefore you can place a few items in the GET string that will affect whether someone makes a bookmark, giving you the information you need to display the page properly. This is demonstrated in Listing 10.3.1, where we use the GET string to indicate that the page has been posted but send the user's data via a POST. This way if someone bookmarks the "posted" page, the user will be presented a custom error if he returns to the page.

Listing 10.3.1   **Using** GET **and** POST **Data Simultaneously**

```php
<?php
// If we have a 'GET' parameter called state and it is set to 'save'
if (isset($_GET['state']) && ($_GET['state'] == 'save')) {
    // Check if the POST data is blank:
    if (count($_POST) == 0) {
        // Looks like a bookmark, the GET existed but no post:
        die("ERROR:  This page has been improperly accessed.");
    }

    // Otherwise, output some data:
    echo "<p>You claim to live in state: {$_POST['state']}</p>\n";
    echo "<p>The script in is the '{$_GET['state']}' state.</p>\n";
}
?>
<form action="<?= $_SERVER['PHP_SELF'] ?>?state=save"
  method="post" name="f1">
<p>In what state do you live? <input name="state" type="text" /></p>
<p><input type="submit" /></p>
</form>
```

10.4 Accepting Uploaded Files

PHP also provides a straightforward manner in which to handle file uploads as well. Anytime that you have a file upload field on your web page, the $_FILES array is automatically filled in for you with various pieces of data. For example, if you had named your upload field 'attachment', the following data would exist:

- $_FILES['attachment']['name']—The original name of the file from the user's machine.

- $_FILES['attachment']['type']—The mime type of the file (for example: 'text/plain'), but only if the browser provided the type.

- $_FILES['attachment']['size']—The size of the file in bytes.

- $_FILES['attachment']['tmp_name']—The full filename of the uploaded file.

- $_FILES['attachment']['error']—An error code, if there were any problems with the upload.

Using this capability, Listing 10.4.1 accepts an uploaded file and saves it in the same directory as itself, using its original name from the user's machine.

Listing 10.4.1   **File Uploading**

```php
<?php
// If we had any files
if (count($_FILES)) {
    // Doublecheck that we really had a file:
    if (!($_FILES['attachment']['size'])) {
        echo "<p>ERROR:  No actual file uploaded</p>\n";
    } else {
        // Determine the filename to which we want to save this file:
        $newname = dirname(__FILE__) . '/' .
                basename($_FILES['attachment']['name']);

        // Attempt to move the uploaded file to it's new home:
        if (!(move_uploaded_file($_FILES['attachment']['tmp_name'],
                $newname))) {
            echo "<p>ERROR:  A problem occurred during file upload!</p>\n";
        } else {
            // It worked!
            echo "<p>Done!  The file has been saved as: {$newname}</p>\n";
        }
    }
}
?>
<form action="<?= $_SERVER['PHP_SELF'] ?>" method="post"
    enctype="multipart/form-data" name="f1">
<input type="hidden" name="MAX_FILE_SIZE" value="8388608" />
<p>Why don't you upload a file? <input type="file" name="attachment" /></p>
<p><input type="submit" /></p>
</form>
```

The function `move_uploaded_file()` does a lot. Not only does it take care of moving the file to where we really want it to live, but it also performs some sanity checks on the uploaded file to make sure that a hijacking attempt has not occurred. You still need to check that the size of the file is not zero to determine whether a file was really uploaded. If someone submits a filename that doesn't actually exist on her machine, everything will look like a file was uploaded, except that the file size will be zero.

One thing to note is the "special" hidden form field named MAX_FILE_SIZE. This field serves two purposes. First, some web browsers actually pick up on this field and will not allow the user to upload a file bigger than this number (in bytes). This makes for a good user interface because if you are planning on ignoring file uploads that are bigger than a certain size anyway, setting this means that the user doesn't try to sit through a long upload only to find out that it was too big.

Second, PHP itself looks for this value, and it ignores all files bigger than it—setting an error code of UPLOAD_ERR_FORM_SIZE if the file is bigger. Granted, this can be fooled easily by manipulating the form data, so if you really want to make sure that no larger of a file is uploaded, you need to check the file size yourself as well before moving it. At the very least, you should set this value to coincide with the maximum upload size that is set in your PHP's configuration file. It is set with the `upload_max_filesize` directive and the default is 8MB, or 8388608 bytes.

In addition to making sure that the PHP directive `upload_max_filesize` and the form field `MAX_FILE_SIZE` are set appropriately, a number of other parameters need to be set, both on the server and in the HTML form. On the server side, the PHP directive `post_max_size` must be greater than `upload_max_filesize`. Also, the time it takes a file to upload is counted against the script execution time. Hence, the PHP directive `max_execution_time` needs to be set long enough to upload the expected files sizes. This can also be set within your script itself via the function `set_time_limit()`. There is also a directive called `max_input_time`, which is the maximum number of seconds that the script is allowed to parse input data. If the user is on a slow connection, or has a large file to upload, this limit may be exceeded. A small detail often overlooked is to make sure that permissions on the upload directory on the server are set such that the web server can actually write to it.

On the client side, there are two rules to follow: First, make sure that the form uses the `POST` method. Second, the form needs the following attribute: `enctype="multipart/form-data"`. Without all these requirements, your file upload will not work.

10.5 Generating Select Statements

Web applications often need to have a list of options repeated many times on the same web page. These might be a list of countries, states, classes of data, and so on. Even more often, this information may come from a database in the first place, so it is imperative for performance reasons to generate the list of options once and reuse it. Listing 10.5.1 demonstrates a method of creating such repeating options.

Listing 10.5.1 **Dynamically Generating Select Options**

```php
<?php
// If this file was a submission, then output the values
if (count($_POST)) {
    echo "<p>You submitted the following music ID numbers:<br />
1st - {$_POST['1st']}, 2nd - {$_POST['2nd']}, 3rd - {$_POST['3rd']}</p>
";
}

// Array of options in a format that might have come from a database query:
$types = array(
    array('id' => 10, 'desc' => 'Rock'),
    array('id' => 11, 'desc' => 'Alternative'),
    array('id' => 12, 'desc' => 'Metal'),
    array('id' => 20, 'desc' => 'Classical'),
```

Listing 10.5.1 **Continued**

```
    array('id' => 33, 'desc' => 'Jazz'),
    array('id' => 34, 'desc' => 'Blues'),
    array('id' => 42, 'desc' => 'Ska'),
    array('id' => 44, 'desc' => 'Folk'),
    array('id' => 49, 'desc' => 'Blue Grass')
    );

// Now, generate the options portion of a select string, based upon this:
// Start with a blank option:
$options = "<option value=\"\">Select one ...</option>\n";

// Now loop over all possibilities, adding them in:
foreach ($types as $m) {
    $options .= "<option value=\"{$m['id']}\">{$m['desc']}</option>\n";
}

// And now we can output our page, using this multiple times:
?>
<form action="<?= $_SERVER['PHP_SELF'] ?>" method="post" name="f1">
<p>Please choose your favorite types of music:</p>
<p>1st: <select name="1st"><?= $options ?></select></p>
<p>2nd: <select name="2nd"><?= $options ?></select></p>
<p>3rd: <select name="3rd"><?= $options ?></select></p>
<p><input type="submit" /></p>
</form>
```

This technique works fine when you have a list that will always be exactly the same. However, often you will need to have the proper option in the list preselected, based on some saved data. When you have the option list already created, this is not possible (except after the fact with JavaScript) because the HTML will need to change to set a new default value.

This is easily solvable, though. If you already have all the data stored in an array as we have, instead of generating the list once, you can create a function that generates the list of options on-the-fly, but preselecting the proper value based on a parameter. Listing 10.5.2 is a rewrite of Listing 10.5.1 to use this technique to have the select lists show your selection after submission.

Listing 10.5.2 **Dynamic Select Generation with Changing Data**

```
<?php
// If this file was a submission, then output the values
if (count($_POST)) {
    echo "<p>You submitted the following music ID numbers:<br />
1st - {$_POST['1st']}, 2nd - {$_POST['2nd']}, 3rd - {$_POST['3rd']}</p>
```

Listing 10.5.2 **Continued**

```
";
}

// Create a function that will take an ID, and an array of ID's & Desc's as
// parameters, and will output the options of a select list with the
// proper one highlighted.
function create_option_list($id, $data) {
    // The blank option - automatically selected if nothing else is
    $options = "<option value=\"\">Select one ...</option>\n";

    // Now loop over all possibilities, adding them in:
    foreach ($data as $x) {
        // Determine if this one should be selected
        $selected = ($id == $x['id']) ? ' selected' : '';

        // Now add in the option
        $options .=
            "<option value=\"{$x['id']}\"{$sel}>{$x['desc']}</option>\n";
    }

    // Now return the option list
    return $options;
}

// Array of options in a format that might have come from a database query:
$types = array(
    array('id' => 10, 'desc' => 'Rock'),
    array('id' => 11, 'desc' => 'Alternative'),
    array('id' => 12, 'desc' => 'Metal'),
    array('id' => 20, 'desc' => 'Classical'),
    array('id' => 33, 'desc' => 'Jazz'),
    array('id' => 34, 'desc' => 'Blues'),
    array('id' => 42, 'desc' => 'Ska'),
    array('id' => 44, 'desc' => 'Folk'),
    array('id' => 49, 'desc' => 'Blue Grass')
    );

// And now we can output our page, using this multiple times:
// We will use an @ in front of the $_POST references in order to suppress
//  the PHP notice that will occur due to it not being initialized at first.
?>
<form action="<?= $_SERVER['PHP_SELF'] ?>" method="post" name="f1">
<p>Please choose your favorite types of music:</p>
<p>1st: <select name="1st">
<?= create_option_list(@$_POST['1st'], $types) ?>
```

Listing 10.5.2 **Continued**

```
</select></p>
<p>2nd: <select name="2nd">
<?= create_option_list(@$_POST['2nd'], $types) ?>
</select></p>
<p>3rd: <select name="3rd">
<?= create_option_list(@$_POST['3rd'], $types) ?>
</select></p>
<p><input type="submit" /></p>
</form>
```

As one final option to explore, Listing 10.5.3 looks at the common need of generating lists of years and months. When looking at different people's code you may often find hard-coded lists of months or arrays built to hold them. PHP provides the capability to create these on-the-fly through creative use of the date(), mktime(), and range().

Listing 10.5.3 **Generating Date-Based Options**

```
<?php
// Create a function that will return an option list of months:
function month_options() {
    $retval = '';

    // For all twelve months:
    foreach(range(1,12) as $mon) {
        // Make a timestamp for this month:
        $time = mktime(0, 0, 0, $mon);
        // Use date to return the month name as text:
        $name = date('F', $time);
        // Create the select option:
        $retval .= "<option value=\"{$mon}\">{$name}</option>\n";
    }

    return $retval;
}

// Create a function, that will output a list of years
// The first parameter is how many years in the past to start from
// The second parameter is how many years into the future to go:
function year_options($before, $after) {
    $retval = '';

    // From the current year:
    $cyear = date('Y');

    // Loop over the range requested:
    foreach(range($cyear - $before, $cyear + $after) as $y) {
```

Listing 10.5.3   **Continued**

```
        // Store the select option:
        $retval .= "<option value=\"{$y}\">{$y}</option>\n";
    }

    return $retval;
}

// Now we can just output a simple form using these:
?>
<form>
<p>Month:<select name="month"><?= month_options() ?></select></p>
<p>Year:<select name="year"><?= year_options(5, 10) ?></select></p>
</form>
```

10.6 Requiring Certain Fields to Be Filled Out

Often when accepting data from a user, certain fields on a form must be filled out. A common tactic to ensure this is to use JavaScript to check/require that every field is filled before submitting the form. The problem with this approach, however, is that the user might have JavaScript turned off or be using a browser that doesn't support JavaScript.

It is therefore better to use pure PHP and check the result values. You could have the form submit to a separate page, and on that page, if the values are not filled out, display an error. If you do that, the user needs to click the Back button. An interesting solution to remove the need of the back button is to have the page submit the data back to itself. This way, if the required data is not there, the warning can be given, plus any data that the user has already filled out can be repopulated. Using an array of required values makes it easier to do your checking, as shown in Listing 10.6.1.

Listing 10.6.1   **An HTML Page That Submits Back to Itself**

```
<?php
// An array of our required elements, and their real names:
$required = array('phone' => 'Phone Number', 'state' => 'State');

// If we had a POST, then check the data:
if (count($_POST)) {
    $errors = '';
    // Loop over all required fields, and ensure they exist:
    foreach ($required as $field => $desc) {
        // If it is not even set, or is blank after trimming:
        if (!isset($_POST[$field]) || (trim($_POST[$field]) === '')) {
            $errors .= "<br />{$desc} is a required field!\n";
        }
    }
```

Listing 10.6.1   Continued

```
    // If we had any errors, echo them out now:
    if ($errors) {
        echo "<p style=\"color: red\">The following errors were found:
{$errors}</p>\n";
    } else {
        // Here, if this were a real program, you would save your data or
        //  do whatever else you would normally do with it.  Probably
        //  redirecting to a different page afterwards.
    }
}

// Create our form autopopulating the POST variables back into place if
//  they exist.  Using @ to hide errors if they didn't exist.
?>
<form action="<?= $_SERVER['PHP_SELF'] ?>" method="post" name="f1">
<p>Please enter your contact information:</p>
<p>Name:
<input name="name" type="text" value="<?= @$_POST['name'] ?>" /></p>
<p>Phone:
<input name="phone" type="text" value="<?= @$_POST['phone'] ?>" /></p>
<p>Email:
<input name="email" type="text" value="<?= @$_POST['email'] ?>" /></p>
<p>Address:
<input name="address" type="text" value="<?= @$_POST['address'] ?>" /></p>
<p>City:
<input name="city" type="text" value="<?= @$_POST['city'] ?>" /></p>
<p>State:
<input name="state" type="text" value="<?= @$_POST['state'] ?>" /></p>
<p><input type="submit" /></p>
</form>
```

10.7 Manipulating Text for Display on Bulletin Boards (BBCode)

Bulletin board or blog systems often want to strip HTML but allow for special formatting characters to be employed by the users. This is known as *BBCode* (short for *Bulletin Board Code*). Although the exact implementation ends up being different for each situation, some of the basics remain the same. Traditionally, BBCode uses square brackets ([]) to denote formatting and uses terms very close to HTML tags.

This allows for all actual HTML to be cleansed and then just these special commands allowed instead. They are transformed into appropriate formatting when displayed. Listing 10.7.1 handles a few of the most common BBCode markups and can be modified to meet your own needs.

Listing 10.7.1 **Interpreting BBCode in Form Input**

```php
<?php
// A function to format BBCode.  It current translates the following:
//    [b] = <b>,   [i] = <i>,   [code] = <pre>,
//    [quote] = <blockquote><i>,   [img] = <img>
// It also turns double-carraige returns, into appropriate whitespace
function format_bbcode($string) {
    // Define some direct translations:
    $trans = array( 'b' => 'b', 'i' => 'i', 'code' => 'pre' );

    // Using regex to find bbcode, and loop over the string:
    // It is necessary to loop, to handle code within code.
    // This regex looks for [word], followed by anything up to [/word]
    while (preg_match('|\[([a-z]+)\](.*?)\[/\1\]|',
            $string, $r, PREG_OFFSET_CAPTURE)) {
        // So at this point [0][0] contains the full matched string.
        // [0][1] contains the offset position of that string
        // [1][0] is the second match, which is our tag name.
        // [2][0] is the 3rd match, the tag contents

        // So now, based upon the tag, implement the HTML

        // If this is a direct translation tag:
        if (isset($trans[$r[1][0]])) {
            // Simply replace with HTML tag version:
            $replace = "<{$trans[$r[1][0]]}>{$r[2][0]}</{$trans[$r[1][0]]}>";
        }
        // Special case: quote
        elseif ($r[1][0] == 'quote') {
            // Replace with two tags:
            $replace = "<blockquote><i>{$r[2][0]}</i></blockquote>";
        }
        // Special case: img
        elseif ($r[1][0] == 'img') {
            // Create an image tag using the contents.
            $replace = "<img src=\"{$r[2][0]}\" />";
        } else {
            // If we found any other tag, consider it invalid, and strip it:
            $replace = $r[2][0];
        }

        // Now, perform the actual replacement
        $string = substr_replace($string, $replace, $r[0][1],
            strlen($r[0][0]));
```

Listing 10.7.1   **Continued**

```
    }

    // One last step, replace any double-carraige returns, with a
    //  paragraph break, make it work for both Windows servers:
    $string = str_replace("\r\n\r\n", '</p><p>', $string);
    // And unix:
    $string = str_replace("\n\n", '</p><p>', $string);

    // Now return the whole string, surrounded by paragraph tags:
    return "<p>{$string}</p>";
}

// If we had a POST, then output the data for reference:
if (count($_POST)) {
    // Strip the data of special characters, and then BBCode it:
    $bbcode = format_bbcode(htmlspecialchars($_POST['data']));

    // Show as code:
    echo "<p>The BBCode source:</p>\n";
    echo '<p>', htmlspecialchars($bbcode), "</p>\n";

    // Display it:
    echo "<p>The BBCode displayed:</p>\n";
    echo $bbcode;
}
?>
<form action="<?= $_SERVER['PHP_SELF'] ?>" method="post" name="f1">
<p>Enter some data:</p>
<p><textarea name="data" cols="80"
    rows="10"><?= @$_POST['data'] ?></textarea></p>
<p><input type="submit" /></p>
</form>
```

10.8 Accepting and Displaying User Data Giving Warnings for Links

There is one final manipulation of user submitted data that is regularly done. If the script allows users to include URLs in their data, the user could make the link say something completely different from where the URL actually goes. This ends up being a blemish on your website. The common solution is to display beside the actual link, the host name that the link refers to. This gives the browser a visual indication whether the link is going where they think it is.

This can be done whether you are allowing HTML to be entered or BBCode. If BBCode, just call the function defined in Listing 10.8.1 after it has been converted into

HTML. This technique can be useful for other purposes as well, such as scanning HTML data and placing "offsite" links for any external link versus ones to your own website.

Listing 10.8.1   **Check for Links in Form Input**

```php
<?php
// A function to create warnings on any links:
function warn_links($string) {
    // First, find all the links in the string:
    preg_match_all('|<a\s+href\s*=\s*([\'"])(.*?)\1>|i',
        $string, $results, PREG_OFFSET_CAPTURE | PREG_SET_ORDER);

    // Now, loop over all results, BACKWARDS, to make replacements
    // Backwards so that our offsets don't start changing on us:
    foreach (array_reverse($results) as $r) {
        // [0][1] contains the offset position of the link & [2][0]
        //  contains the URL - So parse the URL to get it's host:
        $parsed = parse_url($r[2][0]);

        // Check the host - if it doesn't exist use this server's hostname:
        $host = isset($parsed['host']) ? $parsed['host'] :
            $_SERVER['HTTP_HOST'];

        // Now insert the 'host' warning:
        $string = substr_replace($string, " [{$host}] ", $r[0][1], 0);
    }

    return $string;
}


// If we had a POST, then output the data for reference:
if (count($_POST)) {
    echo "<p>The data, with link warnings:</p>\n";
    echo warn_links($_POST['data']);
}
?>
<form action="<?= $_SERVER['PHP_SELF'] ?>" method="post" name="f1">
<p>Enter some data:</p>
<p><textarea name="data" cols="80"
    rows="10"><?= @$_POST['data'] ?></textarea></p>
<p><input type="submit" /></p>
</form>
```

10.9 Preventing Multiple Form Submissions

For a number of reasons you may need to prevent a form from being submitted multiple times. If you don't, you can end up with duplicate records. This can be caused by a careless user who submits a form once but then clicks reload, causing the data to be submitted a second time. Worse is the case of a spammer attacking your website by rapidly submitting the same form again and again. This not only creates an ugly cleanup problem to solve but also eats precious site resources.

Just redirecting the user to another web page after the form submission is complete can solve the accidental case; however, there is a solution that fulfills both needs. This solution uses sessions, which are explored in depth in Chapter 12, "Sessions and User Tracking." The method is fairly simple. When the user accesses the form page, a session is started in which a variable indicates that the form submission will be valid from this browser. Then on the submission page, the script checks this variable, and if it exists, the submission is allowed and the variable is cleared. If the page is loaded again, an error will be generated, because the variable stating that it was valid is not there. Listing 10.9.1 implements the form page of this pair, and Listing 10.9.2 is the page that accepts the submission.

Listing 10.9.1 **Preventing Multiple Form Submissions, the Basic Form**

```php
<?php
// Begin a session, and save a 'validity' variable to it:
session_start();

// If the validsubmit session variable doesn't exist, create it to be true:
if (!isset($_SESSION['validsubmit'])) {
    $_SESSION['validsubmit'] = true;
}
?>
<!DOCTYPE html PUBLIC "-//W3C//DTD XHTML 1.0 Strict//EN"
    "http://www.w3.org/TR/xhtml1/DTD/xhtml1-strict.dtd">
<html xmlns="http://www.w3.org/1999/xhtml">
<head>
<title>Data Entry Form</title>
<meta http-equiv="Content-Type" content="text/html; charset=iso-8859-1" />
</head>
<body>
<form action="submit.php" method="post" name="f1">
<p>Please enter your name: <input name="name" type="text" /></p>
<p><input type="submit" /></p>
</form>
</body>
</html>
```

Listing 10.9.2 **Preventing Multiple Form Submissions, the Submission Page—Filename: submit.php**

Listing 10.9.2   **Continued**

```php
<?php
// Open the session
session_start();
?>
<!DOCTYPE html PUBLIC "-//W3C//DTD XHTML 1.0 Strict//EN"
    "http://www.w3.org/TR/xhtml1/DTD/xhtml1-strict.dtd">
<html xmlns="http://www.w3.org/1999/xhtml">
<head>
<title>Data Processing Page</title>
<meta http-equiv="Content-Type" content="text/html; charset=iso-8859-1" />
</head>
<body>
<p>
<?php
// If this session is not valid, say so:
if (!isset($_SESSION['validsubmit']) || !$_SESSION['validsubmit']) {
    echo "ERROR:  Invalid form submission, or form already submitted!";
} else {
    // This was valid, so first of all clear the validity:
    $_SESSION['validsubmit'] = false;

    // Now echo out the data:
    echo "Your name is {$_POST['name']}?  That's a nice name.";
}
?>
</p>
</body>
</html>
```

This method can still be circumvented by a user willing to click back, reload the page, re-enter data, and submit again. It can also fall prey to a script that is smart enough to load the form page first, receive the session cookie, and then return that session cookie upon the form submission. It does, however, stop the simple and common forms of abuse. Taking it one step further would be to check against the IP address and only allow so many submissions, per IP address, per a time period. This can backfire, however, because many ISPs place all their users behind dynamic IP systems that make thousands of users look like one IP address.

This concept can be extended to attempt to only allow one submission per user by also storing a cookie on the user's machine that shows that the user already submitted that page. However, because users can edit or delete their cookies, that is not reliable. The only reliable way to make only one submission, per user, ever, is to have users sign up for accounts and restrict posting to one per account.

11

Data Validation and Standardization

WITH ANY TYPE OF GENERAL USER INPUT, such as that retrieved through form submissions, the programmer must always expect the worse, even if you do not consider malicious intent. Hence, you are always faced with the issue of checking whether received input is correct and usable. The listings presented in this chapter demonstrate some algorithms and functions that should prove useful in everyday practice.

When checking input correctness, it is convenient to break the problem into two parts: one of standardizing the input and one of validating the standardized input. *Standardizing* input is the process through which the incoming data is massaged into some unified, or standard, form. For many pieces of information, there may be a number of acceptable ways of representing them. However, for an application, all those forms need to be converted into some standard format. When in a standard format, rules of validation can be applied to make sure that what was input is actually acceptable.

Taking this two-step approach, the process of confirming input is much simpler and more flexible. Having the standardization routine focus solely on format, the application can afford users much more freedom in how they want to supply the requested information, providing a much better user experience. When the input is standardized, the process of validation is much simpler because the input will be in a known form.

Of course, as with any general rule, there are always exceptions, and there are situations where a standardization and validation approach may not be appropriate. For example, situations where the form of the input is an integral part of the validation would preclude this two-step sequence; if the input is in an unexpected form, it is immediately invalid.

All the following examples presume a situation where the user has been asked to provide the requested information through some type of form. No other processing on the user input is expected; the examples are getting the data "raw."

Quick Hits

▶ **Check whether a variable is a number or numeric string:**

```
$success = is_numeric($variable);
```

Returns true if the variable is a number or a string consisting of an optional sign, digits, optional decimal, and optional exponent.

Full documentation: http://php.net/is_numeric

▶ **Check whether a string contains only alphanumeric characters:**

```
$success = ctype_alnum($string);
```

Returns true if only alphabetical or numeric characters exist in the string.

Full documentation: http://php.net/ctype_alnum

▶ **Check whether a string contains simply alphabetic characters:**

```
$success = ctype_alpha($string);
```

Returns true if only the letters "a" through "z" of either case are present in the string.

Full documentation: http://php.net/ctype_alpha

▶ **Check whether a string contains only digits:**

```
$success = ctype_digit($string);
```

Returns true only if the characters "0" through "9" exist in the string. Note, a decimal, ".", is not allowed.

Full documentation: http://php.net/ctype_digit

▶ **Check whether a string contains only hexadecimal digits:**

```
$success = ctype_xdigit($string);
```

The allowed characters are "0" through "9" and "a" through "f", either upper- or lowercase.

Full documentation: http://php.net/ctype_xdigit

▶ **Check whether a string is completely upper- or lowercase:**

```
$success = ctype_upper($string);
```

```
$success = ctype_lower($string);
```

If the string contains the opposite case, false is returned.

Full documentation: http://php.net/ctype_upper and http://php.net/ctype_lower

▶ **Force a variable to be of a specific type:**

```
$success = settype($variable, $type);
```

PHP forces the variable into the specified type, using its internal type-juggling. If no conversion is possible, false is returned.

Full documentation: http://php.net/settype

▶ Interpret a variable as a certain type using type-casting:

```
$result = (typekeyword) $variable;
```

PHP converts the variable's value from whatever type the variable is in to the specified type, typekeyword.

Full documentation: http://php.net/manual/language.types.type-juggling.php

11.1 Phone Numbers

The phone numbers that this example deals with are those in the standard notation used in the United States: A phone number consists of a three-digit area code, followed by a three-digit exchange code, and then a four-digit number. Unfortunately, many standards have developed as how to display (and therefore enter) these numbers. Some examples are (999)555-0100, (999) 555-0100, 9995550100, 999.555.0100, and 999-555-0100 to show a few. Listing 11.1.1 allows numbers to arrive in any of these formats (and more) and standardizes them to the latter one because it is easy to process by a computer later.

As far as validating a phone number, besides making sure that the proper number of digits exist, a few other rules can be applied. For example, if the exchange is 555, then the final four numbers cannot be within the range 0100-0199 because these are reserved for fictitious use. Also, the area code cannot begin with a 0 or 1, and the second digit of it cannot be a 9. With this knowledge, we can create the following functions.

Listing 11.1.1   **Phone Number Library**

```php
<?php
// A function that will accept US phone numbers, in most every format
// and standardize them to xxx-xxx-xxxx format.
function standardize_phone($phone) {
    // First, remove all non-digits from the string
    $p = preg_replace('/[^0-9]/', '', $phone);

    // Now, break it into its appropriate parts and insert dashes.
    return substr($p, 0, 3) . '-' . substr($p, 3, 3) . '-' . substr($p, 6);
}

// A function to check for phone number validity
// It requires a standardized number
function validate_phone($phone) {
    // First split the number into 3 parts:
    $parts = explode('-', $phone);

    // If the middle is '555'
    if ($parts[1] == '555') {
        // Invalid if the final part is between 0100 and 0199
        if (($parts[2] >= 100) && ($parts[2] < 200)) {
            return false;
```

Listing 11.1.1 **Continued**

```
            }
        }

        // Invalid if the first digit of the area code is 0 or 1
        if ($parts[0] < 200) {
            return false;
        }

        // Invalid if the second digit of the area code, is 9
        if ($parts[0]{1} == '9') {
            return false;
        }

        // Check that the last number has 4 characters:
        if (strlen($parts[2]) != 4) {
            return false;
        }

        // Otherwise, we made it, it's valid.
        return true;
}

// Standardize & validate some phone numbers:
$phones = array('(108)355-4688', '354-555-0103', '294.423.8437',
                '301 867-5309', '424-726 739', '829-56628426');
foreach ($phones as $num) {
    $st = standardize_phone($num);
    $valid = validate_phone($st);
    $output = $valid ? 'Valid' : 'Invalid';
    echo "<p>{$st} - {$output}</p>\n";
}
?>
```

Note that these functions as written do not allow a 1 to be placed in front of the number, as sometimes people will do. If you want to allow for these, it would be simple to do so. The easiest method would be to have the standardization function just remove any leading 1 because the area code cannot start with a 1 in the first place.

11.2 ZIP Codes

The format of ZIP Codes in the United States is straightforward and easy to standardize and validate against: five digits followed optionally by a dash and four more digits. Though the format is easily dealt with, the problem of validating whether a correctly formatted ZIP Code actually exists is more difficult; basically you need access to the list of currently active ZIP Codes. These lists must be obtained from the U.S. Postal Service. Therefore, the ZIP Code validation library presented in Listing 11.2.1 deals only with format standardization and validation.

Listing 11.2.1 **ZIP Code Library**

```php
<?php
// A function that will accept US zip codes
// and standardize them to xxxxx-xxxx format.
function standardize_zip($input) {
    // First, remove all non-digits from the string
    $digits = preg_replace('/[^0-9]/', '', $input);

    // Grab the first five digits:
    $ret = substr($digits, 0, 5);

    // If there are more than 5, then include the rest after a dash
    if (strlen($digits) > 5) {
        $ret .= '-' . substr($digits, 5);
    }

    return $ret;
}

// A function to check for zip code validity
// It must have been standardized first.
function validate_zip($input) {
    // First split the number into 2 parts:
    $parts = explode('-', $input);

    // If the first part is not 5 digits - Invalid
    if (strlen($parts[0]) != 5) {
        return false;
    }

    // If the second part exists, and is not 4 digits - Invalid
    if (isset($parts[1]) && (strlen($parts[1]) != 4)) {
        return false;
    }

    // Otherwise, we made it, it's valid.
    return true;
}

// Standardize & validate some zips:
$zips = array('21771', '7177', 'x234 56', '12345-6789', '1313122',
    '14142-77743', '21705-123', '2177-1234', '1-1', '7.42');
```

Listing 11.2.1 **Continued**

```php
foreach ($zips as $num) {
    $st = standardize_zip($num);
    $valid = validate_zip($st);
    $output = $valid ? 'Valid' : 'Invalid';
    echo "<p>{$st} - {$output}</p>\n";
}
?>
```

11.3 Social Security Numbers (SSNs)

In the United States, everyone is issued a Social Security Number (SSN), which ends up being used as your unique identifier in many circumstances; therefore, it is often request-ed of people on forms. It always contains three digits, followed by two digits, followed by four digits. Usually when displayed it has dashes between the three sections; however, people sometimes leave these off.

It is possible to go one step further when validating. None of the three sections can be filled completely with zeros. Also, at this point in time the first three digits (which are an area code) cannot be higher than 772 because numbers higher than that have not been allocated yet. Eventually, after that allocation begins, scripts will need to be updated to allow for higher numbers. Listing 11.3.1 presents the SSN standardization and valida-tions routines.

Listing 11.3.1 **Social Security Number Library**

```php
<?php
// A function that will accept US SSNs
// and standardize them to xxx-xx-xxxx format.
function standardize_ssn($ssn) {
    // First, remove all non-digits from the string
    $s = preg_replace('/[^0-9]/', '', $ssn);

    // Now, break it into it's appropriate parts and insert dashes.
    return substr($s, 0, 3) . '-' . substr($s, 3, 2) . '-' . substr($s, 5);
}

// A function to check for SSN validity, requires a standardized number
function validate_ssn($ssn) {
    // First split the number into 3 parts:
    $parts = explode('-', $ssn);

    // If any part is all 0's - Invalid
    foreach ($parts as $p) {
        if ($p == 0) {
```

Listing 11.3.1   **Continued**

```
            return false;
        }
    }

    // If the first part is greater than 772 (May need updated in future)
    if ($parts[0] > 772) {
        return false;
    }

    // Finally, if the final part is not 4 characters, it is invalid
    if (strlen($parts[2]) != 4) {
        return false;
    }

    // Otherwise, we made it, it's valid.
    return true;
}

// Standardize & validate some SSN:
$ssn = array('774 35 4688', '354-00-0103', '123456789', 'Hello');
foreach ($ssn as $num) {
    $st = standardize_ssn($num);
    $valid = validate_ssn($st);
    $output = $valid ? 'Valid' : 'Invalid';
    echo "<p>{$st} - {$output}</p>\n";
}
?>
```

If you need to, you can get even more strict about checking valid SSNs by visiting the Social Security Administration's website at http://ssa.gov/. There they maintain a large list of every currently valid area code, as well as the highest two-digit number that has been assigned in that area code (following an odd assignment scheme). This is updated monthly, so a script could be created that reads this file, parses the data from it, and builds a lookup table for truly valid SSNs.

11.4 Numbers

When dealing with numbers, such as monetary amounts, no generic validation really can be done. Instead you need to check the number entered against the range of numbers that is valid for that specific input. We can, however, create a function to standardize any numbers that we are given. The format we will standardize on is the one most databases will request numbers in. This is without any spaces or commas in them, and optionally with a "-" in front for negative numbers. We will also allow for an optional parameter of how many decimal places to keep, automatically rounding the number for us.

PHP can and will automatically convert a string into a number when used; however, commas, spaces, and other things will often confuse it. Listing 11.4.1 solves all those problems by always giving you a valid number.

Listing 11.4.1 **General Number Validation Library**

```php
<?php
// A function that will accept and clean up number strings
function standardize_number($num, $precision = false) {
    // First, remove all non-digits, periods, and - signs from the string
    $num = preg_replace('/[^-.0-9]/', '', $num);

    // Now remove any -'s that are in the middle of the string:
    $num = preg_replace('/(?<=.)-/', '', $num);

    // We now have a valid string that PHP will properly consider a number.
    // If a precision was asked for, round accordingly:
    if ($precision !== false) {
        $num = round($num, $precision);
    }

    return $num;
}


// Standardize some number strings:
$nums = array('123.4643', 'Hello I bought 42 flowers for you.',
              '-344-345.424', '+544,342.566');
foreach ($nums as $num) {
    $st = standardize_number($num, 2);
    echo "<p>{$num} = {$st}</p>\n";
}
?>
```

11.5 Credit Card Numbers

If dealing with any sort of commerce website, you will need to take credit card numbers. Credit card companies have built a verification system into the card numbers, which makes the verification process possible. After standardizing a credit card number to be a string of all numbers with no spaces, two sets of validation can be done.

First, there are specific rules for different credit card companies as follows:

- Visa—Start with a 4, 13 or 16 digits long
- MasterCard—Start with 51-56, 16 digits long
- American Express—Start with 34 or 37, 15 digits long
- Discover—Start with 6011, 16 digits long

Finally then, there is an algorithm that all cards must pass known as Mod 10. This is a straightforward algorithm that lets you know whether the digits provided could be a possible credit card. It works as follows. First you need to reverse the digits and then multiply every other value by 2. Next add all digits together; however, if through multiplication a number is now 10 or larger, instead add its digits together. So a 7 gets doubled to 14, but then is equal to 1+4=5. After all these digits are added together, if the result is perfectly divisible by 10, it is a potentially valid credit card number. All these rules are combined into a couple of functions presented in Listing 11.5.1.

Listing 11.5.1   **Credit Card Number Library**

```php
<?php
// A function that will accept and clean up CC numbers
function standardize_credit($num) {
    // Remove all non-digits from the string
    return preg_replace('/[^0-9]/', '', $num);
}


// A function to check the validity of a CC number
// It must be provided with the number itself, as well as
// a character specifying the type of CC:
// m = Mastercard, v = Visa, d = Discover, a = American Express
function validate_credit($num, $type) {
    // First perform the CC specific tests:
    // Store a few evaluations we will need often:
    $len = strlen($num);
    $d2 = substr($num,0,2);

    // If Visa must start with a 4, and be 13 or 16 digits long:
    if ( (($type == 'v') && (($num{0} != 4) ||
            !(($len == 13) || ($len == 16)))) ||
    // If Mastercard, start with 51-56, and be 16 digits long:
        (($type == 'm') && (($d2 < 51) ||
            ($d2 > 56) || ($len != 16))) ||
    // If American Express, start with 34 or 37, 15 digits long:
        (($type == 'a') && (!(($d2 == 34) ||
            ($d2 == 37)) || ($len != 15))) ||
    // If Discover: start with 6011 and 16 digits long
        (($type == 'd') && ((substr($num,0,4) != 6011) ||
            ($len != 16))) ) {
        // Invalid card:
        return false;
    }

    // If we are still here, then time to manipulate and do the Mod 10
    // algorithm.  First break the number into an array of characters:
    $digits = str_split($num);
```

Listing 11.5.1 **Continued**

```php
    // Now reverse it:
    $digits = array_reverse($digits);

    // Double every other digit:
    foreach(range(1, count($digits) - 1, 2) as $x) {
        // Double it
        $digits[$x] *= 2;

        // If this is now over 10, go ahead and add its digits, easier since
        // the first digit will always be 1
        if ($digits[$x] > 9) {
            $digits[$x] = ($digits[$x] - 10) + 1;
        }
    }

    // Now, add all this values together to get the checksum
    $checksum = array_sum($digits);

    // If this was divisible by 10, then true, else it's invalid
    return (($checksum % 10) == 0) ? true : false;
}

// Check various credit card numbers:
$nums = array(
    '344 2345 3466 4577' => 'a', '3794 2345 3466 4577' => 'a',
    '4938748398324' => 'v', '4123-1234-5342' => 'v',
    '51847293 84567434' => 'm', '5723x2345x2345x6161' => 'm',
    '6011 6011 6011 6011' => 'd', '6012 392563242423' => 'd',
    );

foreach ($nums as $num => $type) {
    $st = standardize_credit($num);
    $valid = validate_credit($st, $type);
    $output = $valid ? 'Valid' : 'Invalid';
    echo "<p>{$st} - {$type} = {$output}</p>\n";
}
?>
```

11.6 Dates

Because PHP provides a number of excellent date tools, very little work is needed to standardize or validate dates. In particular, the `strtotime()` function converts most string representations of dates into UNIX timestamps. If it fails, it returns `false`. Given the power of this tool, it is rare that you ever need to use anything else. Once converted to a timestamp (if it works), you can use `date()` to format it into whatever visual display you prefer to standardize on, as demonstrated in Listing 11.6.1

Listing 11.6.1   **Using `strtotime()` and `date()` for Date Standardization and Validation**

```php
<?php
// Run against various dates
$dates = array('Dec 3 1973', '12/3/73', '1973-12-3',
    '1/0/2005', '3/32/2004', '0/1/0', '12/3/973', '2/31/2006', '13/30/05');

// Initialise the timezone settings, and loop over all the values:
date_default_timezone_set('America/New_York');
foreach ($dates as $d) {
    // Convert it & validate at the same time:
    $output = strtotime($d);
    // Prepare the display, either 'BAD DATE' or a formatted version
    $disp = ($output === false) ? 'BAD DATE' : date('m/d/Y', $output);
    echo "<p>{$d} = {$disp}</p>\n";
}
</?>
```

Note that `strtotime()` has some features that may be confusing at first. It allows any month to be specified with up to 31 days; however, if the month shouldn't allow 31 days, it automatically increments to make a valid date. So 11/31/2005 will come back as 12/1/2005. It also allows for a 0 to be specified for the day of a month (to which it responds with the last day of the previous month). A zero for the month means December and a zero for the year means 2000.

11.7 Email Accounts

Email accounts follow a set pattern of what is allowed. An email address must start with a character, number, underscore, or dash. It can then have any number of those characters plus periods. An "at" sign (@) follows that and then the domain name. Domain names consist of any number of "words" made of characters, digits, and dashes separated by periods. The final suffix must be between two and six characters long. (Some programmers erroneously check for only a two- or three-character end, but that doesn't take into account new top-level domains such as .museum.) Listing 11.7.1 still allows for an invalid, but short enough, top-level domain, such as .books; however, it is much simpler than doing a full lookup of the now rather long list of valid domains.

Listing 11.7.1   **Email Address Validation**

```php
<?php
// A function to check validity of email accounts:
function validate_email($address) {
```

Listing 11.7.1 **Continued**

```
    // Check against a massive regex for validity ...
    return preg_match(
        '/^[a-z0-9_-][a-z0-9._-]+@([a-z0-9][a-z0-9-]*\.)+[a-z]{2,6}$/i',
        $address);
}

// Run against various email accounts
$email = array('author@eliw.com', 'bob_123.3@a.b.c.r5-5.museum',
    'mrmrmr@bob.lawnmower', '$bob$@gmail.com', 'bob@gmail');

// Loop over these values, determine if they are valid emails or now.
foreach ($email as $e) {
    // Validate:
    $output = validate_email($e);
    // Prepare the display, either 'BAD' or 'GOOD'
    $disp = ($output == false) ? 'BAD' : 'GOOD';
    echo "<p>{$e} = {$disp}</p>\n";
}
?>
```

This of course only checks to see whether the email address, as entered, could be valid. It also allows for only the most common setups. A few variations might exist that you may need to add. Specifically an IP address can be included as the hostname if it is surrounded by square brackets and it is possible for the username to be surrounded by double-quotes to allow spaces within it. These are uncommon practices, however, in the current state of the Internet.

Doing more advanced work to truly detect whether an email account exists is handled in section 16.2 in Chapter 16, "Email."

11.8 URLs

If you have a web form where you are asking users for their home sites, it might be worthwhile to do a quick validation of this URL just to determine whether it appears to be valid. There are really two levels of checking the validity of a URL. One is just using parse_url() to attempt to parse the URL for you and do some basic sanity checking on some of the constituent parts.

Second, you may want to actually try to contact the web server and request the URL to see whether it truly exists. However, do realize that this may be a flawed test because the server could just be down at the moment that the URL was given to you. The standardization and validation routines are presented in Listing 11.8.1.

Listing 11.8.1   **URL Standardization and Validation Library**

```php
<?php
// A function to do a sanity check on a URL ... Since we are assuming
// that this is coming from user input, we will require it be a full
// URL, and not a relative one
function validate_url($url) {
    // Use parse_url to break the URL into parts for us:
    $up = parse_url($url);

    // If scheme, host, or path don't exist, or complete failure: INVALID
    if (!$up || !$up['scheme'] || !$up['host'] || !$up['path']) {
        return false;
    }

    // If the scheme is anything besides http(s) or ftp: Fail
    if (!( ($up['scheme'] == 'http') ||
           ($up['scheme'] == 'https') ||
           ($up['scheme'] == 'ftp'))  ) {
        return false;
    }

    // We made it here, it looks good to us.
    return true;
}

// Function that will actually take a url, and attempt to contact the server
// if it can't access the remote file, it returns false, else true.
function check_url($url) {
    // Request only the headers, no reason to download the whole file
    // Note that this call will only handle https connections if PHP was
    //   compiled with SSL support.
    $output = @get_headers($url);

    // Return appropriately
    return $output ? true : false;
}

// Test a few URLs
$urls = array('http://eliw.com/', 'http://php.net/get_headers',
    'gopher://bob.com/', 'https://lawn.tractor/models/1.php',
    'http://hubblesite.org/news/2006/01/', 'http://digg.com/');

// Loop over these, check if they appear valid, if they do, try to access
foreach ($urls as $r) {
    // If this does not validate:
    if (!(validate_url($r))) {
```

Listing 11.8.1   **Continued**

```
        // Set the display accordingly:
        $disp = 'Did not validate!';
    } else {
        // Try to access it, and set display accordingly
        $disp = check_url($r) ? 'GOOD!' : 'Could not contact...';
    }

    // Display this
    echo "<p>{$r} = {$disp}</p>\n";
}
?>
```

This validation routine specifically checks against only http, https, and ftp URLs, although of course other valid URL schemes exist, such as mailto, gopher, and others. This is being done for a few reasons. The primary reason is that the three we are allowing are the most common by far of URLs used today, especially in the context that this validation would be used in such as checking the input of a user. Another reason is that we want the URLs we are validating to also be able to be checked. The current method of checking involves the use of get_headers() to see whether the website is up and working. This would not work for a mailto link, nor would it work for gopher, which is an unsupported standard at this point in time.

You may also notice that the check_url() function will not work if it is passed an ftp site, although we are validating them as valid. Testing whether an ftp URL is valid is more difficult because ftp doesn't support the equivalent of HTML's HEAD command. Therefore if you wanted to update check_url() to actually handle ftp requests as well, the function would have to scan the URL given it for an ftp and then actually attempt to download the file specified.

12

Sessions and User Tracking

J UST AS WITH FORM DATA INPUT AND HANDLING, PHP provides an excellent and seamless interface to the common methods of tracking user sessions. This chapter starts with a description of cookies, expanding the concept to sessions, and finishes with some practical examples. For those unfamiliar with cookies and the PHP session mechanism, see the PHP documentation http://php.net/manual/features.cookies.php and http://php.net/manual/features.sessions.php.

As with all tools, there are good uses and bad uses. Sessions, cookies, and user tracking have had their share of bad press. However, they are an absolutely necessary component to provide the user with an excellent web experience and to implement the functionality of most services provided on the Internet. When properly implemented, the content provider can maintain a secure environment for the exchange of information and services.

Quick Hits

▶ **Set a cookie:**

```
$success = setcookie($name, $value);
```

Set the cookie $name with $value, returning true if successful. Please note: Cookies must be set before any output occurs from the script.

Full documentation: http://php.net/setcookie

▶ **Start a session:**

```
session_start();
```

Start a PHP session. If you want the session to be cookie-based, this must be called before any output occurs.

Full documentation: http://php.net/session_start

▶ **Delete all data associated with a session:**

```
$success = session_destroy();
```

All information associated with the current session is deleted. However, the session itself still exists; the session id must be disassociated from the current page before the session is closed, either by unsetting it with `setcookie()` or removing it from the query string.

Full documentation: http://php.net/session_destroy

▶ **Get or set the session id:**

```
$id = session_id();
```

```
$id = session_id($newid);
```

Retrieves or sets the session id string. The id is useful for adding to URLs or storing in some other structure.

Full documentation: http://php.net/session_id

12.1 Using Cookies to Remember Data

Cookies have been part of the Internet since the Netscape browser introduced them in 1995. Since then, they have been the topic of many long discussions concerning privacy issues, most all of which have been resolved today. Some people, however, still set their browsers to not accept cookies, and therefore it is important that you do not rely on cookies 100% of the time, or, if you do, make sure to let the user know this.

So, what are cookies in terms of a web browser? Simply put, they are bits of data that are passed from the server to the browser and that the browser stores. The browser then passes these pieces of data back whenever it visits that web page (or more usually, website) again. Essentially cookies are a way of storing variables on the remote user's machine so that they can be sent back every time the user contacts you. This way it is possible to maintain state data even after the browser has been closed and the connection is gone.

A common good use of cookies is, for example, holding display configurations. If a user wants to see the text bigger or smaller, he can do that, and the browser can remember this in the future. Cookies can also be used in user tracking by providing a unique code to the browser and therefore seeing that code returned any time that specific browser returns to a page on your site. A weather or movie times website might use a cookie to remember your ZIP Code to always show you local information only. Finally, cookies are often used to store a user's username for a website (but not the password!) so that the username information can be automatically filled in every time the user visits that website.

PHP makes it easy to set a cookie using the `setcookie()` command and always returns cookie data to you in the superglobal array `$_COOKIE`. When setting a cookie, you can just give a name and a value; however, more options are available. You can set the time when a cookie will expire via a UNIX time stamp. If this is not set, the cookie will expire as soon as the browser is closed. You can also set the path on your web server for which the cookie will be returned. By default, a cookie is returned only if you are in the same subdirectory in which the cookie was set. Set this to "/" to have it returned for your entire website. Finally you can also set the hostname to which cookies are returned. This defaults to the exact server name from which the cookie was sent. Often you want to change this to be returned to more of your websites. Setting it to ".urlexample.com", for example, means that it will be sent to urlexample.com, plus www.urlexample.com, images.urlexample.com, and so on. You cannot set a cookie to be returned to a website completely different from the one you are on; it must be the same website or a subdomain higher. You similarly cannot set a cookie to be returned to all of ".com", because, again, that would allow the cookie to be given out to a website not within your own subdomain.

Listing 12.1.1 creates a simple web page that, through the use of cookies, will remember some basic user configuration.

Listing 12.1.1 **Using Cookies**

```php
<?php
// This script does three functions based upon the input.
// If it finds cookies are provided, it just displays the information.
// If it finds a POST command sent to it, it turns those into cookies,
//    and then displays the same information
// If it finds neither, it presents a form to receive the data with.

// Check if we have both the cookies that we care for:
if (isset($_COOKIE['firstname']) && isset($_COOKIE['zipcode'])) {
    // We found the cookies, so just print the standard output
    print_standard_output($_COOKIE['firstname'], $_COOKIE['zipcode']);
}
// Else, if we received a form POST with this data:
elseif (isset($_POST['firstname']) && isset($_POST['zipcode'])) {
    // First we need to create these as cookies.
    // First create 'firstname', which will only last until the browser is
    //  killed and only return to this subdirectory.
    setcookie('firstname', $_POST['firstname']);

    // Determine our subdomain without having to know it:
    $parts = explode('.', $_SERVER['HTTP_HOST']);
    $cp = count($parts);
    // If a 1 part hostname, like 'localhost', don't bother:
    if ($cp == 1) { $subdomain = ''; }
    // Otherwise, generate our subdomain by using the last 2 parts
    else { $subdomain = ".{$parts[$cp-2]}.{$parts[$cp-1]}"; }

    // Now create 'zipcode', which returns to our whole subdomain, to the
    //  entire website, (from '/'), and which doesn't expire for 30 days.
```

Listing 12.1.1 **Continued**

```php
    setcookie('zipcode', $_POST['zipcode'], time()+(30*24*3600),
        '/', $subdomain);

    // Now, also, just print the standard output:
    print_standard_output($_POST['firstname'], $_POST['zipcode']);
}
// We didn't have anything, so make a form so they can provide data.
else {
    echo "
<form action=\"{$_SERVER['PHP_SELF']}\" method=\"POST\">
<p>What is your first name? <input type=\"text\" name=\"firstname\" /></p>
<p>What is your zipcode? <input type=\"text\" name=\"zipcode\" /></p>
<p><input type=\"submit\" /></p>
</form>
";
}


// The standard output:
function print_standard_output($name, $zip) {
    echo "
<p>Welcome back {$name}!  Perhaps you would like to see things
 happening near your home zipcode ({$zip}) ?</p>
";
}
?>
```

First, you do need to know that all cookies must be set before any output comes from your script. This is because cookies are headers and must come before the body of the request. If you need to set cookies in the middle of a page, you will need to use JavaScript to do so.

Something else to know is that the $_REQUEST superglobal contains all the cookies (as well as the GET and POST data). This would allow us to change the preceding script to be written more simply because we wouldn't care whether the data came from a POST or a cookie; all that would matter is that we received it. To do this we would need to reset the cookie each time. This is a common practice, though, because if you want a cookie that has an expiration time, with every access to the server you usually want to update that expiration time anyway. Given all this we could rewrite Listing 12.1.1 as Listing 12.1.2.

Listing 12.1.2 **Accessing Cookie Values Through** $_REQUEST

```php
<?php
// This script has two functions, either ask for data, or display data.
// Check if we have both variables we care about:
```

Listing 12.1.2   **Continued**

```
if (isset($_REQUEST['firstname']) && isset($_REQUEST['zipcode'])) {
    // Update or create the cookies, all set to expire in 1 hour:
    setcookie('firstname', $_REQUEST['firstname'], time()+3600);
    setcookie('zipcode', $_REQUEST['zipcode'], time()+3600);

    // Now, also, just print the standard output:
    echo "
<p>Welcome back {$_REQUEST['firstname']}! Perhaps you would like to see
 things happening near your home zipcode ({$_REQUEST['zipcode']}) ?</p>
";
} else {
    // We have nothing, so make a form so they can provide data.
    echo "
<form action=\"{$_SERVER['PHP_SELF']}\" method=\"POST\">
<p>What is your first name? <input type=\"text\" name=\"firstname\" /></p>
<p>What is your zipcode? <input type=\"text\" name=\"zipcode\" /></p>
<p><input type=\"submit\" /></p>
</form>
";
}
?>
```

12.2 Saving User Data with Sessions

The major drawbacks of using cookies for data storage are that you rely on the person allowing the cookie in the first place, and the amount of data you can store is somewhat limited. PHP sessions are a solution to those problems and many more. Sessions are a way of storing data locally within the web server and tying it to a specific user of the website. They are not meant to be permanent by their nature and instead are meant to persist through a "session"—that is, as long as a web browser is open.

They work by storing PHP variables on the back end and then presenting the client with a session id. This is usually via a cookie but can also be via a GET parameter in the URL. By calling session_start(), PHP takes care of all this for you. After doing that, you can reference session variables by the superglobal $_SESSION, and any changes you make to $_SESSION will be automatically updated when the page is finished.

Sessions are an excellent way, for example, to track a user who has used a username/password to log in to your website. You can start a session for the user, store data that she has successfully logged in, and therefore not prompt the user for a password again.

Listings 12.2.1, 12.2.2, and 12.2.3 present an example of a mini website with logins. Three separate web pages make up the site: A login page, which redirects you if you are already logged in; a "view" page that shows you some information, including session information; and finally an "edit" page that allows you to create this session data.

Listing 12.2.1   **Website Login Example—The Login Page, Filename: login.php**

```php
<?php
// The login page -- First check if the user has requested to log-off
$error = '';
session_start();
if (isset($_GET['logoff'])) {
    // We need to completely destroy the session.  First the data:
    $_SESSION = array();

    // If a session cookie exists, tell the browser to destroy it
    //   (give it a time in the past)
    if (isset($_COOKIE[session_name()])) {
        setcookie(session_name(), '', time()-1000, '/');
    }

    // Finally, finialize the session destruction:
    session_destroy();
}
// Secondly, see if the user is already logged in.
elseif (isset($_SESSION['valid']) && $_SESSION['valid']) {
    // Bounce them to the view page:
    header('Location: view.php');
    exit();
}
// 3rd, see if they attempted to log in:
elseif (isset($_POST['user']) || isset($_POST['pass'])) {
    // Just allowing a couple of fake users here, in real life you would
    //   probably be reading this information from a database.
    $user = isset($_POST['user']) ? $_POST['user'] : '';
    $pass = isset($_POST['pass']) ? $_POST['pass'] : '';
    if ( ( ($user == 'tanderson') && ($pass == 'Z1ON0101') ) ||
         ( ($user == 'asmith') && ($pass == 'brawl') ) ) {
        // user/pass is good, Store this fact in the session
        $_SESSION['valid'] = 1;
        $_SESSION['user'] = $_POST['user'];

        // and direct them to the main page
        header('Location: view.php');
        exit();
    } else {
        // Prepare an error statement:
        $error = 'Username & Password do not match, please try again';
    }
}
// Otherwise, let's ask them to log in:
?>
```

Listing 12.2.1 **Continued**

```
<!DOCTYPE html PUBLIC "-//W3C//DTD XHTML 1.0 Strict//EN"
    "http://www.w3.org/TR/xhtml1/DTD/xhtml1-strict.dtd">
<html xmlns="http://www.w3.org/1999/xhtml">
<head><title>Login</title>
<meta http-equiv="Content-Type" content="text/html; charset=iso-8859-1" />
<style>
form { border: 1px solid black; padding: 10px; }
#error { color: #FF0000; font-weight: bold; }
</style>
</head>
<body>
<?php // If we had an error:
if ($error) { echo "<p id=\"error\">{$error}</p>\n"; }
?>
<form action="<?= $_SERVER['PHP_SELF'] ?>" method="post">
<p>Welcome to our website, you need to log in:</p>
<p>Username: <input type="text" name="user" value="<?= @$user ?>"><br />
Password: <input type="password" name="pass" value="<?= @$pass ?>"></p>
<p><input type="submit" value="Login" /></p>
</form>
</body>
</html>
```

Listing 12.2.2 **Website Login Example—The Information View Page, Filename:
            view.php**

```
<?php
// The View page
//  First we need to check if they are logged in, and if not, make them:
session_start();
if (!(isset($_SESSION['valid']) && $_SESSION['valid'])) {
    // Back to login for you
    header('Location: login.php');
    exit();
}

// Now, set some default values in case they haven't told us anything yet:
$fname = isset($_SESSION['name']) ? $_SESSION['name'] : '[Unknown]';
$fcolor = isset($_SESSION['color']) ? $_SESSION['color'] : '[Unknown]';
?>
<!DOCTYPE html PUBLIC "-//W3C//DTD XHTML 1.0 Strict//EN"
    "http://www.w3.org/TR/xhtml1/DTD/xhtml1-strict.dtd">
<html xmlns="http://www.w3.org/1999/xhtml">
<head><title>View</title>
```

Listing 12.2.2   **Continued**

```
<meta http-equiv="Content-Type" content="text/html; charset=iso-8859-1" />
</head>
<body>
<p>This is our website, thanks for logging in!</p>
<p>You've told us that your Full Name is <?= $fname ?></p>
<p>We somehow also know that your favorite color is <?= $fcolor ?></p>
<p>Options: | <a href="edit.php">Edit Data</a> |
<a href="login.php?logoff=true">Log Off</a> |</p>
</body>
</html>
```

Listing 12.2.3   **Website Login Example—The Edit Information Page, Filename: edit.php**

```php
<?php
// The Edit page
//  First we need to check if they are logged in, and if not, make them:
session_start();
if (!(isset($_SESSION['valid']) && $_SESSION['valid'])) {
    // Back to login for you
    header('Location: login.php');
    exit();
}

// Secondly, see if this was a post, if so, save the data into the session
$msg = '';
if (count($_POST)) {
    // Save the data
    $_SESSION['name'] = $_POST['fname'];
    $_SESSION['color'] = $_POST['fcolor'];

    // Prepare a message
    $msg = 'Your data was saved.';
}
?>
<!DOCTYPE html PUBLIC "-//W3C//DTD XHTML 1.0 Strict//EN"
    "http://www.w3.org/TR/xhtml1/DTD/xhtml1-strict.dtd">
<html xmlns="http://www.w3.org/1999/xhtml">
<head><title>Edit</title>
<meta http-equiv="Content-Type" content="text/html; charset=iso-8859-1" />
<style>
form { border: 1px solid black; padding: 10px; }
#note { color: #00CC00; font-weight: bold; }
</style>
</head>
<body>
```

Listing 12.2.3   **Continued**

```php
<?php // If we have a message:
if ($msg) { echo "<p id=\"note\">{$msg}</p>\n"; }
?>
<p>Here you can edit data that will remain valid for this
   browsing session.</p>
<form action="<?= $_SERVER['PHP_SELF'] ?>" method="post">
<p>What is your full name?
<input type="text" name="fname" value="<?= @$_SESSION['name'] ?>" /></p>
<p>What is your favorite color?
<input type="text" name="fcolor" value="<?= @$_SESSION['color'] ?>" /></p>
<p><input type="submit" value="Save my preferences" /></p>
</form>
<p>Options: | <a href="view.php">View Data</a> |
<a href="login.php?logoff=truc">Log Off</a> |</p>
</body>
</html>
```

Do note of course that this session data, the way that this simple example has been designed, will in fact disappear forever after the browser is closed and the session expires. If you truly want to save any of this information permanently, it should be stored in a database or something similar. Sessions are good for keeping state information, such as remembering basic configuration from the database without having to query the database on every page or for items such as shopping carts.

12.3 Customizing Display Settings for a User

A common feature of websites, both for usability and for just providing a good user experience, is to allow the user to customize the display of the website. This can be as simple as offering different font sizes and color schemes, or it can be much more complicated. The most effective way to accomplish this is through the use of alternative style sheets. If your entire website is written in proper XHTML without any styling markup, the CSS can completely control how the page looks.

Although there is a mechanism for intrinsically supporting an alternative style sheet built into the XHTML specifications, this is unfortunately not very well supported in current browsers. Therefore it is best to handle the switching of style sheets yourself.

If you have a website that requires users to log in, you could save their preferences with their user data and read it whenever they log in. There is another, perhaps easier, way to allow users to control their displays without having to use logins. That is to simply set a cookie on the user's computer that will remember the user's display setting.

Listings 12.3.1, 12.3.2, and 12.3.3 present a simple example of this: one web page with two style sheets that can be used and a mechanism for switching between them. This can be expanded easily into multiple style sheets, and the code can be placed into a library to be used on every page.

Listing 12.3.1   **Display Format Switching: PHP Script**

```php
<?php
// If a stylesheet has been provided, either by GET or via COOKIE, use it
//  else use a default & ensure that GET overrides a cookie
$style = isset($_GET['style']) ? $_GET['style'] :
            ( isset($_COOKIE['style']) ? $_COOKIE['style'] : 'basic' );

// In either case, now forceably set a cookie to refresh it's timeout ...
//  make it last 30 days from now:
setcookie('style', $style, time()+3600*24*30, '/');
?>
<!DOCTYPE html PUBLIC "-//W3C//DTD XHTML 1.0 Strict//EN"
    "http://www.w3.org/TR/xhtml1/DTD/xhtml1-strict.dtd">
<html xmlns="http://www.w3.org/1999/xhtml">
<head><title>Our News Page</title>
<meta http-equiv="Content-Type" content="text/html; charset=iso-8859-1" />
<style>
@import url("<?= $style ?>.css");
</style>
</head>
<body>
<div id="selector">Style Selector:
<!--
<a href="<?= $_SERVER['PHP_SELF'] ?>?style=large">A</a>
<a href="<?= $_SERVER['PHP_SELF'] ?>?style=basic">a</a>
-->
<a href="<?= $_SERVER['PHP_SELF'] ?>?style=12c03c">A</a>
<a href="<?= $_SERVER['PHP_SELF'] ?>?style=12c03b">a</a>
</div>
<h1>Welcome to our news website!<br />
You may find the following articles interesting:</h1>
<div class="article">
<h2>Aliens from Mars invade!</h2>
<p>"We have been waiting long for this day.", stated a martian using a
 translation device that had been specifically designed for this purpose.
 "We do not come in peace!"</p>
</div>
<div class="article">
<h2>New litter box for cats developed.</h2>
<p>There is a new product on the market, and it's a high tech litter box.
 Yes, no more will you need to scoop and refill litter, because this cat
 box uses lasers to vaporize all waste that is placed within it.  Side
 effect odors are still being worked out.</p>
</div>
</body>
</html>
```

Listing 12.3.2 Display Format Switching: Basic CSS File, Filename: basic.css

```css
/* Basic page definitions: */
body {
    background-color: #FFFFFF;
    font-family: Geneva, Arial, Helvetica, sans-serif;
    font-size: 10px;
}
/* The selector */
div#selector {
    position: absolute;
    top: 5px;
    right: 5px;
    padding: 5px;
    border: 1px solid black;
}
/* The page title */
h1 {
    font-size: 24px;
    text-align: center;
    color: #003300;
}
/* The news articles */
div.article {
    border: 1px solid red;
    padding: 0px;
    margin: 10px;
}
/* The title of the story: */
div.article h2 {
    background-color: #99CC00;
    font-size: 12px;
    text-align: left;
    padding: 2px;
    margin: 0px;
}
/* The text of the story */
div.article p {
    margin: 0px;
    padding: 5px 5px 5px 25px;
}
```

Listing 12.3.3 Display Format Switching: Alternative CSS File, Filename: large.css

```css
/* Large Version page definitions: */
body {
    background-color: #FFFFFF;
```

Listing 12.3.3   **Continued**

```css
    font-family: Geneva, Arial, Helvetica, sans-serif;
    font-size: 14px;
}
/* The selector */
div#selector {
    position: absolute;
    top: 5px;
    right: 5px;
    padding: 7px;
    border: 2px solid black;
}
/* The page title */
h1 {
    font-size: 36px;
    text-align: center;
    color: #003300;
}
/* The news articles */
div.article {
    border: 3px solid red;
    padding: 0px;
    margin: 10px;
}
/* The title of the story: */
div.article h2 {
    background-color: #99CC00;
    font-size: 16px;
    text-align: left;
    padding: 7px;
    margin: 0px;
}
/* The text of the story */
div.article p {
    margin: 0px;
    padding: 10px 10px 10px 35px;
}
```

12.4 Creating a Library for Tracking a User Through Your Website

Web server log files do not give you a true path that a single user has taken through your website. Although there are techniques to approximate this from the log file, they are very rough. Therefore if you truly want to know paths that users are taking, you need to track them yourself.

The easiest way to do this is again via sessions. By creating a PHP session, you can store on each page the URL that the particular session was accessing. This could be stored in a database or could be written to a custom log file. By doing this you will get a much more accurate picture as to how your website is being used. Listing 12.4.1 shows a method of doing this using a database. This example assumes the use of MySQL. Following is the table that we will create.

Listing 12.4.1   **SQL Code**

```
CREATE TABLE 'web_tracker' (
    'hit' BIGINT UNSIGNED NOT NULL AUTO_INCREMENT ,
    'session' CHAR( 32 ) NOT NULL ,
    'addid' CHAR( 40 ) NOT NULL ,
    'url' VARCHAR( 512 ) NOT NULL ,
    'refer' VARCHAR( 512 ) ,
    'stamp' TIMESTAMP DEFAULT CURRENT_TIMESTAMP NOT NULL ,
    PRIMARY KEY ( 'hit' )
) TYPE = MYISAM ;
```

Note that while collecting this, we end up using both the session id and our own unique id together to try to denote a specific machine. This will hopefully truly create a unique situation for us. We will use the same technique that we did in Listing 1.11.1, "Generating a Unique Identifier," in Chapter 1, "Strings." Also, we will capture the referring page on a fresh hit to our website, letting us know where each person came from when examining the data later. Listing 12.4.2 should be included on every page of the website.

Listing 12.4.2   **Include File for User Tracking**

```php
<?php
// This is our include file.  Include it on every page in your website, and
//  it handles tracking the user for you.  Start by opening our session...
session_start();

// If the additional id is not present, then this is a new session.
//  Generate a 40 character unique identifier using the function created
//  in Listing 1.11.1. This combined with the session id, with hope to serve
//  as a TRUE unique ID.
$refer = 'NULL';
if (!isset($_SESSION['addid'])) {
    $_SESSION['addid'] = sha1($_SERVER['HTTP_USER_AGENT'] .
        $_SERVER['REMOTE_ADDR'] . time() . rand());

    // Also, since this is the 'first visit', let's store the referrer
    $refer = "'{$_SERVER['HTTP_REFERER']}'";
}
```

Listing 12.4.2 **Continued**

```
// Open a database connection (Update these with your own DB server info)
$db = mysql_connect('localhost', 'my_user', 'my_password')
    or die('DB Failure: ' . mysql_error());
mysql_select_db('my_database');

// Do the insert:
$sid = session_id();
mysql_query("
    insert into web_tracker
        (session, addid,
         url, refer)
    values
        ('{$sid}', '{$_SESSION['addid']}',
         '{$_SERVER['REQUEST_URI']}', {$refer})
    ");
?>
```

After you have collected all this data, you can manipulate it however you want. You can look at individual users' paths, average length of stay on the website, or much more. A few things should be noted about this, however. First, unless you force your pages to never be cached by a local browser, a user can click on the Back button, and you will not notice this activity because the PHP does not get run again. Second, you never know when the user has left your website nor where the user went. If you want to know these two things, you need to make sure that all external links actually bounce through a web page on your server, which will allow you to track the access. This can have an additional benefit of allowing you to give disclaimers on the page you are bouncing through that the user is leaving the website, perhaps even with a timer to give the user a few seconds to change his mind.

12.5 Implementing a Simple Shopping Cart

The Web is filled with commercial websites selling their wares. All these websites share the concept of a shopping cart. As you browse the website you can add items to your shopping cart, and when you are ready to check out it will remember them.

A simple shopping cart is no more than a PHP session that keeps track of all the items that someone has clicked on to buy. It is then useful to have a page allowing you to review your shopping cart, make changes, and, eventually, check out. Listings 12.5.1, 12.5.2, and 12.5.3 implement a simple shopping cart.

Listing 12.5.1 **Shopping Cart—Product Information Database, Filename: products.php**

```
<?php
// Just an included file with our product data.  Normally you would read
//  this data in from a database.  You would probably also store much more
```

Listing 12.5.1   **Continued**

```
//  data such as pictures and full product specifications.  For this
//  example we are going much simpler:
$products = array(
    'x563942' => array('desc' => 'Xcast gaming console', 'price' => 674.99),
    'x583954' => array('desc' => 'Xcast controller', 'price' => 24.99),
    'g7' => array('desc' => 'Xcast game: Deaf Fury', 'price' => 45.98),
    'g9' => array('desc' => 'Xcast game: C the Armadillo', 'price' => 19.95),
    's23' => array('desc' => 'Store brand Logo T-Shirt', 'price' => 12.97),
    'c997' => array('desc' => 'Gamerz Rool! Basecall Cap', 'price' => 5),
    );
?>
```

Listing 12.5.2   **Shopping Cart—Product View Page, Filename: view.php**

```
<?php
// Our products page
//  We will display all the products and allow people to choose them:
session_start();

// Include the products library
require 'products.php';

// If we were given an item to add to our cart, do so:
if (isset($_GET['add'])) {
    @$_SESSION['cart'][$_GET['add']]++;
}


// Calculate the total items, and total value, of our cart:
$total_num = 0;
$total_value = 0;
foreach (@$_SESSION['cart'] as $id => $count) {
    $total_value += $products[$id]['price'] * $count;
    $total_num += $count;
}
?>
<!DOCTYPE html PUBLIC "-//W3C//DTD XHTML 1.0 Strict//EN"
    "http://www.w3.org/TR/xhtml1/DTD/xhtml1-strict.dtd">
<html xmlns="http://www.w3.org/1999/xhtml">
<head><title>View Products</title>
<meta http-equiv="Content-Type" content="text/html; charset=iso-8859-1" />
<style>
table { border-collapse: collapse; }
.num { text-align: right; }
#cart { float: right; text-align: center; }
td, th, div { border: 1px solid black; padding: 4px;}
```

Listing 12.5.2 **Continued**

```css
.button {
    display: block; padding: 2px 5px; background-color: #0000FF;
    color: white; text-decoration: none;
    border-style: solid; border-width: 4px;
    border-bottom-color: #000099; border-right-color: #000099;
    border-top-color: #0066FF; border-left-color: #0066FF;
}
</style>
</head>
<body>
<div id="cart">Items in your cart: <?= $total_num ?>
<br />Total value of cart: <?= $total_value ?>
<br /><a href="cart.php">View your cart</a>
</div>
<p>Please choose what products you may desire below:</p>
<table>
 <tr><th scope="col">Item</th><th scope="col">Name</th>
 <th scope="col">Price</th><th scope="col">Buy it!</th></tr>
<?php
// Loop through all the products and give the options:
$counter = 0;
foreach ($products as $id => $p) {
    // Echo out a table row with this data:
    $counter++;
    echo "<tr><td>{$counter}</td><td>{$p['desc']}</td><td class=\"num\">",
        number_format($p['price'],2), "</td>";

    // Finish off the row by creating a 'Add to Cart' button ...
    echo "<td><a class=\"button\"
href=\"{$_SERVER['PHP_SELF']}?add={$id}\">Add to Cart</a></td></tr>\n";
}
?>
</table>
</body>
</html>
```

Listing 12.5.3 **Shopping Cart—View and Modify the Cart, Filename: cart.php**

```php
<?php
// The shopping cart page itself
session_start();

// Include the products library
require 'products.php';
```

Listing 12.5.3   **Continued**

```php
// If we were asked to clear the cart, do so immediately.
if (@$_POST['submit'] == 'Clear Cart') {
    unset($_SESSION['cart']);
}
// Otherwise if we have been presented with an update, handle it:
elseif (isset($_POST['update'])) {
    // Loop over all the updates
    foreach ($_POST['update'] as $id => $val) {
        // Only update if the value is numeric or blank - Otherwise ignore.
        $val = trim($val);
        if (preg_match('/^[0-9]*$/', $val)) {
            // If the value is 0 or blank, remove it:
            if ($val == 0) {
                unset($_SESSION['cart'][$id]);
            } else {
                // Otherwise, just reset to the new number
                $_SESSION['cart'][$id] = $val;
            }
        }
    }
}
?>
<!DOCTYPE html PUBLIC "-//W3C//DTD XHTML 1.0 Strict//EN"
    "http://www.w3.org/TR/xhtml1/DTD/xhtml1-strict.dtd">
<html xmlns="http://www.w3.org/1999/xhtml">
<head><title>Shopping Cart</title>
<meta http-equiv="Content-Type" content="text/html; charset=iso-8859-1" />
<style>
table { border-collapse: collapse; }
.num { text-align: right; }
td, th, div { border: 1px solid black; padding: 4px;}
</style>
</head>
<body>
<p>The following is in your shopping cart:</p>
<form action="<?= $_SERVER['PHP_SELF'] ?>" method="post">
<table>
 <tr><th scope="col">Item</th><th scope="col">Name</th>
 <th scope="col">Price</th><th scope="col">Qty</th></tr>
<?php
// Loop through all of the current cart:
$counter = 0;
$total = 0;
if (@is_array($_SESSION['cart'])) {
    foreach ($_SESSION['cart'] as $id => $c) {
```

Listing 12.5.3 **Continued**

```
        // Echo out a table row with this data:
        $counter++;
        echo "<tr><td>{$counter}</td><td>{$products[$id]['desc']}</td>",
            "<td class=\"num\">", number_format($products[$id]['price'],2),
            "</td><td><input type=\"text\" size=\"3\" class=\"num\" ",
            "name=\"update[{$id}]\" value=\"{$c}\" /></td></tr>\n";

        // Update our total
        $total += $products[$id]['price'] * $c;
    }
}

// Now echo out the 'total' line, and the 'update/buy options'.
// NOTE:  As it currently stands this Buy button doesn't do anything.
//   That will need implemented to your own personal system.
?>
<tr class="num"><td colspan="3">Total:</td>
 <td><?= number_format($total,2) ?></td></tr>
<tr class="num"><td colspan="4">
<input type="button" value="Keep Shopping"
 onclick="javascript:window.location.href='view.php'" />
<input type="submit" name="submit" value="Update Quantities" />
<input type="submit" name="submit" value="Clear Cart"
 onclick="return confirm('Are you sure you wish to empty your cart?')" />
<input type="button" value="Buy" />
</td></tr>
</table>
</form>
</body>
</html>
```

This example is complete except for the actual purchasing process, which would need to be custom made to your own system. The entire shopping cart process relies completely on session data in this example, and therefore there is no need for the user to have an account in order to shop.

12.6 Passing Session Data Between Two Servers

One intrinsic limitation of PHP sessions is that they are unique to that particular web server. If you have reason to use more than one web server and yet need to share data between them since they are related, sessions will let you down.

There is, however, a trick you can use to accomplish this, though it should not be done if you are storing any sensitive data in the session. This will also only work if both machines share the same subdomain. You can convert all the session data from one server into a cookie that you tell to be presented to all machines in your subdomain. Then the other server can pick up that cookie and convert the data back into a user session, as shown in Listing 12.6.1.

Listing 12.6.1 **Sharing Session Data Between Machines on a Subdomain**

```php
<?php
// A library to pass session data between two servers on the same subdomain:

// A function to convert a session into a cookie:
function session_2_cookie() {
    // Serialize, and base64 encode the session data:
    $output = base64_encode(serialize($_SESSION));

    // Now, send this as a cookie to our entire domain:
    setcookie('sessionpass', $output, false, '/', garner_subdomain());
}

// A function that will accept this cookie, and turn it back into a session
function cookie_2_session() {
    // Make sure that the session has started:
    @session_start();

    // Unserialize and unencode the cookie, saving it directly into
    //  the SESSION vars:
    $_SESSION = unserialize(base64_decode(@$_COOKIE['sessionpass']));
}

// A support function that will determine our subdomain for us without
//  having to know it:
function garner_subdomain() {
    // Explode the HOST into it's constituent parts:
    $parts = explode('.', $_SERVER['HTTP_HOST']);
    $cp = count($parts);

    // If a 1 part hostname like 'localhost' don't bother with a subdomain:
    if ($cp == 1) { $subdomain = ''; }
    // Otherwise, generate our subdomain by using the last 2 parts
    else { $subdomain = ".{$parts[$cp-2]}.{$parts[$cp-1]}"; }

    return $subdomain;
}

// Quick test:
// If GET next doesn't exist, then create a blank session, and add a value:
if (!(isset($_GET['next']))) {
    // Start the session
    session_start();
```

Listing 12.6.1 **Continued**

```
    // Blow away the current values:
    $_SESSION = array();

    // Add a single value:
    $_SESSION['test'] = 'Hello World';

    // Now convert the session into a cookie:
    session_2_cookie();

    // Now for testing, redirect immediately back to the same webpage:
    header("Location: {$_SERVER['PHP_SELF']}?next=true");
} else {
    // We are in the redirected mode, pretend to be a different server:
    // Convert the cookie back into a session:
    cookie_2_session();

    // And now output the value from it:
    echo "<p>{$_SESSION['test']}</p>";
}
?>
```

Now the test case with those functions is somewhat contrived but will show you how it would work, even with being on the same web server. Typically if you were going to use this, just before you would redirect someone to the "other server," you would first convert the session to a cookie. Then on the other end you would do the opposite. If you were in a situation where someone could jump back and forth at any point, you would need to have every page regenerating the cookie if the data changes and looking for the cookie to exist. However, at this point you might as well just use the cookie for storage and not bother with the session.

Note the use of the base64 encoding; this accomplishes two things. It ensures that the data is clean to send as a cookie (no high ASCII characters, no quotes, and so on). And, just as important, it obfuscates what would otherwise be a very readable (and therefore editable) PHP serialize output. That would allow the user to edit that and end up adding/changing data in your session.

Note

It is possible to end up sharing data between completely different domains as well as through the use of a shared data server. All web servers that need to have the same shared data can connect to this shared data server via whatever protocol is specified by the data server and retrieve or set the data that they need. This is similar to how the "one sign-on" web services work such as Microsoft Passport.

12.7 Parsing Specific Browser Information from Log Files

Many third-party applications are available for parsing web server log files and giving you no end of statistics from them. However, there is still much that you may want to do on your own to augment what these generic packages will do for you. For example, one often overlooked thing is the variations in certain versions of web browsers. Standard statistics packages will often group, for example, IE 5.0 and 5.5 together as 5.x, even though they are significantly different browsers. For that matter, there is the situation with all the different versions of Mozilla. Each of which has its own variations—plus the fact that certain versions of Firefox, Mozilla, and Netscape, are actually the same rendering engine. At the same time, Mozilla on a PC or on a Mac, is the same rendering engine and produces the same pages.

Therefore, Listing 12.7.1 creates some software that will know about these and give a better picture of your web traffic, letting you truly know what versions of browsers are hitting your website and therefore who you need to be serving with your XHTML and CSS.

Listing 12.7.1 **Parsing Browser Information from Log Files**

```php
<?php
// Declare some basic variables
$matches = array();
$names = array();

// Open the logfile for reading - Modify this to open your own file
//  in 'combined' log format.
if (!($fp = @fopen('access.log', 'r'))) {
    die("File open failed for the access log");
}

// Now loop through the file reading one line at a time:
while ($logline = fgets($fp)) {
    // Parse the logfile line:
    if (preg_match('/^(\S+) (\S+) (\S+) \[([^\]]+)\] "([^"]+)" (\S+)' .
            ' (\S+) "([^"]*)" "([^"]*)"$/', $logline, $matches)) {
        // Save the agent type, and prepare for finding OS type:
        $agent = $matches[9];
        $ostype = '';

        // Loop through all choices checking against the OS string
        if (strpos($agent, 'Win') !== false) { $ostype = 'Windows'; }
        elseif (strpos($agent, 'Mac') !== false) { $ostype = 'Macintosh'; }
        elseif (preg_match('/X11|Linux/', $agent)) { $ostype = 'Unix'; }
        else { $ostype = 'Other OS'; }
```

Listing 12.7.1   **Continued**

```php
// Go through all choices checking against the agents
// The order is important, so that 'greedier' comparisons later
//   don't grab too much.
$results = array();

// Find IE
if (preg_match('/MSIE ([0-9.]+)/', $agent, $results)) {
    @$names["IE {$results[1]} - $ostype"]['count']++;
// Safari
    } elseif (preg_match('/Safari\/([0-9.]+)/', $agent, $results)) {
    @$names["Safari {$results[1]}"]['count']++;
    @$names["Safari {$results[1]}"]['subs'][$ostype]++;
// Konqueror
} elseif (preg_match('/Konqueror\/([0-9.]+)/',$agent, $results)) {
    @$names["Konqueror {$results[1]}"]['count']++;
    @$names["Konqueror {$results[1]}"]['subs'][$ostype]++;
// Opera
} elseif (preg_match('/Opera\/?([0-9.]+)/',$agent, $results)) {
    @$names["Opera {$results[1]}"]['count']++;
    @$names["Opera {$results[1]}"]['subs'][$ostype]++;
// Mozilla, modern with a rv statement
} elseif (preg_match('/rv:([a-z0-9.]+)/',$agent, $results)) {
    @$names["Mozilla {$results[1]}"]['count']++;
    // See WHAT version of Mozilla this really is
    $spec = array();
    if (preg_match('/Netscape6?\/([0-9.]+)/',$agent, $spec)) {
        @$names["Mozilla {$results[1]}"]['subs']
            ["Netscape {$spec[1]} - {$ostype}"]++;
        } elseif (preg_match('/(?:Firefox|Firebird|Phoenix)\/([0-9.]+)/',
            $agent, $spec)) {
        @$names["Mozilla {$results[1]}"]['subs']
            ["Firefox {$spec[1]} - {$ostype}"]++;
    } else {
        @$names["Mozilla {$results[1]}"]['subs']
            ["Mozilla {$results[1]} - {$ostype}"]++;
    }
// Old Netscape
} elseif (preg_match('/Mozilla\/([0-9.]+)/',$agent, $results)) {
    @$names["Netscape {$results[1]}"]['count']++;
    @$names["Netscape {$results[1]}"]['subs'][$ostype]++;
// Some grabbing agents that we regularly see.
} elseif (preg_match('/[Gg]oogle|Java|msn/', $agent)) {
    @$names['Known non-browsers']['count']++;
// Well, everything else is an 'other'
} else {
```

Listing 12.7.1   **Continued**

```php
            @$names['Other Browsers']['count']++;
            @$names['Other Browsers']['subs'][$ostype]++;
        }
    }
}

// Clean up after ourselves, close the file pointer
fclose($fp);

// Before we start outputting anything, lets prepare our data for printing.
// Add things up for a total:
$total = 0;
foreach ($names as $one => $val) { $total += $val['count']; }

// Sort the data by most hits
function compare($a, $b) {
    if ($a['count'] == $b['count']) { return 0; }
    else return (($a['count'] < $b['count']) ? 1 : -1);
}
uasort($names, 'compare');

// Lets start our web page
?>
<!DOCTYPE html PUBLIC "-//W3C//DTD XHTML 1.0 Strict//EN"
    "http://www.w3.org/TR/xhtml1/DTD/xhtml1-strict.dtd">
<html xmlns="http://www.w3.org/1999/xhtml">
<head><title>Specific Browser Statistics</title>
<style>
body {
    font-family: Geneva, Arial, Sans Serif;
    background-color: #ECECEC;
    text-align: center;
    font-size: 11px;
}
table {    border: 2px solid black; }
th, td {
    border: 1px solid black;
    padding: 1px;
    margin: 1px;
}
td { text-align: right; }
.sm { font-size: 10px; }
.name {    text-align: left; }
table.sub {
    background-color: #E0E0E0;
```

Listing 12.7.1 **Continued**

```
      margin-left: 10px;
}
</style>
</head>
<body>
<h1>Specific Browser Statistics</h1>
<table><tr>
<th scope="col" width="1%" style="background-color: #999999">No.</th>
<th scope="col" colspan="2" style="background-color: #CCCC00">Hits</th>
<th scope="col" style="background-color: #9999FF">Browser</th>
<th scope="col" style="background-color: #CC00CC">Cuml</th>
</tr><tr><td colspan="5"></td></tr>
<?php
// Loop through all specifics ...
$count = 1;
$cuml = 0;
foreach ($names as $one => $val) {
    // The Number
    echo '<tr><th scope="row">', $count++, "</th>\n";
    // The Count
    echo "<td>{$val['count']}</td>\n";
    $cuml += $val['count'];
    // The Percent
    printf("<td>  %.2f%%</td>\n", 100.00 * ($val['count'] / $total));
    // The Name
    echo "<td class=\"name\">  {$one}";

    // If it has subs ...
    if (isset($val['subs'])) {
        // Print them
        echo "<table class=\"sub sm\">\n";

        // Sort them ...
        arsort($val['subs']);
        foreach ($val['subs'] as $sb => $sbnum) {
            // The hits
            echo "<tr><td>  {$sbnum}</td>\n";
            // The %
            printf("<td class=\"sm2\">  %.2f%%</td>\n",
                100.00 * ($sbnum / $val['count']));
            // The Name
            echo "<td class=\"name\">  {$sb}</td>\n";
            echo "</tr>\n";
        }
        echo "</table>";
    }
```

Listing 12.7.1   **Continued**

```
    // Finish the Name
    echo "</td>\n";

    // The cuml %
    printf("<td>  %.2f%%</td>\n", 100.00 * ($cuml / $total));
    print "</tr>\n";
}

// End everything up ...
?>
</table>
</body>
</html>
```

As written, this will always read from a certain log file and create the output. If you wanted to use this on a regular basis, you would probably want to set it to run once a night on your log file and save the output of it to a static HTML file because it could take a while to run on a large log file.

Whenever you are using this and start to see a large number of "other" statements, you will need to discover what these others are and update the script to detect those. They may be new browsers on the market, or they may be various bots that you just need to include in the "known bots" section. The real trick is looking specifically at the user agent lines that are generated and discovering what part of them is a unique identifier that you can key off of without being too greedy.

Caution

Any data generated by the client, such as user agent strings, should always be treated as suspect information; such information can easily be faked or "spoofed" by anyone who feels the need to do so.

13

Web Services and Other Protocols

BECAUSE PHP IS SO CLOSELY ASSOCIATED with web development and information delivery, interfaces have been developed that allow PHP to access many more Internet protocols than just HTTP. In general, protocol interfaces are implemented in two ways: either as a protocol-specific library or by using PHP's inherent input/output facilities. Examples of protocol-specific libraries are the LDAP or SOAP interfaces, both discussed in this chapter. Perusing through the online PHP manual will reveal whether a library or extension exists for any desired protocol.

Chapter 9, "Web Page Creation/XHTML/CSS," provided examples of accessing Internet protocols using PHP's inherent input/output system by accessing HTTP-based services in basic file operations. HTTP is not the only protocol that can be accessed in this fashion; the FTP protocol and the secure protocols, HTTPS and FTPS, can be accessed in a similar fashion. Using standard URL syntax, the standard file functions, such as `file_get_contents()` and `fopen()`, can be used to access information with any of these protocols. The section 13.4, "Connecting to an FTP Server," later in this chapter demonstrates how to access FTP-located files in this manner. A list of all the protocols supported can be found in Appendix M of the PHP online reference, http://php.net/manual/wrappers.php.

If you find that there are no preexisting libraries or any built-in support for a particular protocol, there is no need to despair. PHP provides an extensive set of general input/output functions, called the *stream functions*. Streams are in fact how protocol support is integrated into the PHP input/output system. Section 13.6, "Using Sockets to Connect to an Internet Server," later in the chapter demonstrates how to use streams to interface with—you guessed it—HTTP servers.

Quick Hits

▶ Get the host name of a given IP address:

```
$hostname = gethostbyaddr($ipaddress);
```

Simply, the host name assigned the specified IP address is returned. Note that this operation can potentially be time-consuming if done many times.

Full documentation: http://php.net/gethostbyaddr

▶ Get the IP address of a given host name:

```
$ipaddress = gethostbyname($hostname);
```

The given host name is resolved into its IP address.

Full documentation: http://php.net/gethostbyname

▶ Get an Internet service port number by name:

```
$port = getservbyname($service);
```

Retrieves the port number associated with the specified network service.

Full documentation: http://php.net/getservbyname

▶ Get an Internet service name from a port:

```
$name = getservbyport($port, $protocol);
```

The name of the service running on the specified port is returned. The $protocol should be tcp or udp.

Full documentation: http://php.net/getservbyport

▶ Parse the components of a URL:

```
$components = parse_url($string);
```

This function attempts to parse the given string, returning an associative array containing one or more of the following keys: scheme, host, port, user, pass, path, query, fragment. If no parsing can be accomplished, false is returned.

Full documentation: http://php.net/parse_url

▶ Encode/decode a string for use in a URL:

```
$urlready = urlencode($normalstring);

$normalstring = urldecode($urlready);
```

These functions encode/decode strings to make them usable in a URL, in which all nonalphanumeric characters are encoded using the "%XX" format and "+" for spaces.

Full documentation: http://php.net/urlencode and http://php.net/urldecode

▶ Build and URL query string:

```
$query = http_build_query($array);
```

This function builds a URL-encoded query string from the given array, ready for appending to a URL after the "?".

Full documentation: http://php.net/http_build_query

13.1 Submitting a POST **HTTP Request with cURL**

Situations exist where you may need, in the middle of a PHP script, to send data to another server and retrieve the response. This is often the case when dealing with a third-party vendor, such as a payment company, data provider, and so on. Accomplishing this is easy to do with GET strings because you can just generate the string needed by hand and call it via `file_get_contents()` as a URL. (Or even using `http_build_query()` to help you create your data request.)

However, the situation is not as simple when you need to do a POST. POST commands go to a regular URL, but the data is sent separately as part of the request headers. The regular PHP URL wrappers cannot handle this. Therefore it is easiest to use the PHP cURL extension, which allows for complex interactions with Internet protocols.

> **Note**
>
> It is also possible to handle POST arguments via directly connecting to the server with sockets or an
> `fopen()` command and sending the POST data manually.

Listing 13.1.1 creates a function that handles doing a POST for you, just by passing it the URL to contact, as well as the POST data. The POST data should be in the same format that `http_build_query()` produces, and therefore we will make sure to use it.

Listing 13.1.1 **Using cURL for HTTP POST Operations**

```php
<?php
// Create a function to handle the posting of data
function http_post($url, $post) {
    // Initialize a cURL session:
    $c = curl_init();

    // Set the URL that we are going to talk to:
    curl_setopt($c, CURLOPT_URL, $url);

    // Now tell cURL that we are doing a POST, and give it the data:
    curl_setopt($c, CURLOPT_POST, true);
    curl_setopt($c, CURLOPT_POSTFIELDS, $post);

    // Tell cURL to return the output of the page, instead of echo'ing it:
    curl_setopt ($c, CURLOPT_RETURNTRANSFER, true);

    // Now, execute the request, and return the data that we receive:
    return curl_exec($c);
}

// Create some data that we want to send as a post:
$fields = array('data' => 'Jonathan Swift', 'idx' => 5783);
```

Listing 13.1.1   **Continued**

```
// Actually perform the post to a url:
echo http_post('http://example.com/script.php', http_build_query($fields));
?>
```

cURL can handle many advanced Internet protocols and is extremely powerful. This is just a small taste of what it can do. To discover more, read the documentation at http://php.net/curl.

> **Note**
>
> cURL support in PHP relies on the libcurl library, which must be obtained and compiled into PHP, as well as enabling the extension, which does not exist by default either. More information on how to accomplish these tasks is available in the PHP documentation at http://php.net/curl.

13.2 Communicating with an LDAP Server

LDAP stands for the *Lightweight Directory Access Protocol*. It is used to talk with directory services for retrieving and modifying data. It is not a relational database system. LDAP is simply a system that provides a hierarchical organization of data. LDAP's most common use currently is for corporate address and email books, allowing for all information about each employee to be stored and retrieved as needed.

PHP provides commands to communicate to an LDAP server that are easy to use. A typical set of commands would be to connect to the server, bind (authenticate), search for some data, and then handle the data. The only problem is that the structure of each LDAP server is completely different based on how the administrator set it up, just like every database system is different. Therefore, you must understand the structure of the tree hierarchy of that LDAP server to work with it.

In Listing 13.2.1, we connect to a fictional LDAP server that just has three levels of hierarchy with the top one being c = Country Code, then under that o = Organization, and then below that un = User Name. (Nominally, of course, there would be more information beneath that level; however, this is all we need for our example.)

Listing 13.2.1   **Accessing an LDAP Server**

```
<?php
// Ok, begin by connecting to the ldap server.
if (!($lc = ldap_connect('ldap.example.com'))) {
    die("ERROR: Can't connect to the LDAP server\n");
}

// Now, do an anonymous bind (read only access)
ldap_bind($lc);
```

Listing 13.2.1   **Continued**

```
// Now, we are going to search for anyone in the IT department
// with a username starting with 'e'
$res = ldap_search($lc, 'o=Information Technology, c=US', 'un=e*');

// Now, let's read all results from our search:
$data = ldap_get_entries($lc, $res);

// Loop over them all, echoing the data out:
for ($i=0; $i < $data['count']; $i++) {
    echo "Full entry (distinguished name - dn): {$data[$i]['dn']}<br />\n";
    echo "Username: {$data[$i]['un'][0]}<br />\n";
}
?>
```

Like many other extensions of the language, LDAP support must be compiled into the server (or enabled on Windows) before you can use it. Also, we have only scratched the surface of what the full LDAP extension can do. To explore more, read the documentation at http://php.net/ldap.

13.3 Using Web Services Via SOAP

SOAP is a protocol commonly used to communicate with web services, typically over an HTTP connection. Web services are a way for machines to provide functions that can be called remotely from any other machine. This provides great flexibility because a service can exist in one place, and the entire world can access it. A number of free and commercial web services exist on the Web, such as ZIP Code lookups, credit reports, and so on. Google, Amazon, and eBay all provide SOAP functions to manipulate their data.

At its heart, SOAP is an XML-based protocol. A file exists (WSDL—Web Services Description Language) that explains what functions a server offers. A client then connects sending a request in XML and then the server responds in XML as well. PHP provides a SOAP extension that takes care of most of this for you, allowing you to easily create and access SOAP web services. To begin our exploration, let's create a simple SOAP server that provides mathematical functions. The first thing that we need to do is create some WSDL that says what our web service will provide. This is used by both the server and clients to configure themselves. For our simple web service, we end up with the WSDL file shown in Listing 13.3.1.

Listing 13.3.1   **SOAP Example: The Service Description—Filename: math.wsdl**

```
<?xml version="1.0"?>
<definitions xmlns="http://schemas.xmlsoap.org/wsdl/"
    xmlns:xsd="http://www.w3.org/2001/XMLSchema"
    xmlns:tns="http://example.com/soap/math.php"
    xmlns:soap-env="http://schemas.xmlsoap.org/wsdl/soap/"
```

Listing 13.3.1 **Continued**

```
  xmlns:wsdl="http://schemas.xmlsoap.org/wsdl/"
  xmlns:soapenc="http://schemas.xmlsoap.org/soap/encoding/"
  targetNamespace="http://example.com/soap/math.php">

<message name="mInput">
  <part name="a" type="xsd:float"/>
  <part name="b" type="xsd:float"/>
</message>

<message name="mOutput">
  <part name="return" type="xsd:float"/>
</message>

<portType name="MathServicePortType">
  <operation name="add">
    <input message="tns:mInput"/>
    <output message="tns:mOutput"/>
  </operation>
  <operation name="divide">
    <input message="tns:mInput"/>
    <output message="tns:mOutput"/>
  </operation>
</portType>

<binding name="MathServiceBinding" type="tns:MathServicePortType">
  <soap-env:binding xmlns="http://schemas.xmlsoap.org/wsdl/soap/"
      style="rpc" transport="http://schemas.xmlsoap.org/soap/http"/>
    <operation xmlns:default="http://schemas.xmlsoap.org/wsdl/soap/"
        name="add">
      <input xmlns:default="http://schemas.xmlsoap.org/wsdl/soap/">
        <soap-env:body xmlns="http://schemas.xmlsoap.org/wsdl/soap/"
            use="encoded"
            encodingStyle="http://schemas.xmlsoap.org/soap/encoding/"/>
      </input>
      <output xmlns:default="http://schemas.xmlsoap.org/wsdl/soap/">
        <soap-env:body xmlns="http://schemas.xmlsoap.org/wsdl/soap/"
            use="encoded"
            encodingStyle="http://schemas.xmlsoap.org/soap/encoding/"/>
      </output>
    </operation>
    <operation xmlns:default="http://schemas.xmlsoap.org/wsdl/soap/"
        name="divide">
      <input xmlns:default="http://schemas.xmlsoap.org/wsdl/soap/">
        <soap-env:body xmlns="http://schemas.xmlsoap.org/wsdl/soap/"
            use="encoded"
```

Listing 13.3.1 **Continued**

```
                encodingStyle="http://schemas.xmlsoap.org/soap/encoding/"/>
        </input>
        <output xmlns:default="http://schemas.xmlsoap.org/wsdl/soap/">
          <soap-env:body xmlns="http://schemas.xmlsoap.org/wsdl/soap/"
              use="encoded"
              encodingStyle="http://schemas.xmlsoap.org/soap/encoding/"/>
        </output>
      </operation>
    </binding>

  <service name="MathServiceService">
    <port xmlns:default="http://schemas.xmlsoap.org/wsdl/soap/"
        name="MathServicePort"
        binding="tns:MathServiceBinding">
      <soap-env:address xmlns="http://schemas.xmlsoap.org/wsdl/soap/"
          location="http://example.com/soap/math.php"/>
    </port>
  </service>
</definitions>
```

This is a foreboding file, and one you might not want to undertake writing yourself. That is understandable. Because of that, there are many options online for programs that will write WSDL for you, and even some code that people have contributed that will endeavor to write WSDL for you from your PHP files. A few searches on the Web will provide these tools for you. Explaining all the parts of this file is beyond the scope of this book.

Now that we have our WSDL, its complexity allows for the server to be created easily. In Listing 13.3.2 we create a class, define methods in the class that will be our SOAP accessible functions, and then tell PHP to use that class as the web service.

Listing 13.3.2 **SOAP Example: Math SOAP Service Definition—Filename: math.php**

```php
<?php
// Create our service as a class:
class MathService {
    // A Function to add two numbers together:
    function add($a, $b) {
        return $a + $b;
    }

    // A Function to divide a by b:
    function divide($a, $b) {
        return $a / $b;
    }
}
```

Listing 13.3.2 **Continued**

```
// Instantiate the new Soap Server
$ss = new SoapServer("http://example.com/soap/math.wsdl");

// Set it to have the functions of this class:
$ss->setClass('MathService');

// And handle any request that came in:
$ss->handle();
?>
```

Now, Listing 13.3.3 creates a SOAP client that connects to this service and requests some functions to be run.

Listing 13.3.3 **SOAP Example: Using the Service**

```
<?php
// Connect to the Soap server via the wsdl file.
$sc = new SoapClient("http://example.com/soap/math.wsdl");

// Add two numbers.
$answer = $sc->add(3, 4);
echo "3 plus 4 is: {$answer}<br />\n";

// And Divide
$answer = $sc->divide(42, 7);
echo "42 divided by 7 is: {$answer}<br />\n";
?>
```

It does need to be stated that SOAP is an extension to PHP 5 and thus, although part of the base system, you do need to specify that it is included when compiling PHP. On Windows you need to include it in the configuration file. To get more details on activating SOAP for your PHP install or for more information on what SOAP can do, visit http://php.net/soap.

13.4 Connecting to an FTP Server

There are many ways to connect to an FTP server in PHP. One is using the cURL package, discussed in Section 13.1, "Submitting a POST HTTP Request with cURL," earlier in the chapter, which not only handles the POST submissions talked about there but can do FTP as well. Another, is with the specific FTP extension that exists in PHP; this is discussed in more depth in the upcoming Section 13.5, "Creating a PHP-Based FTP Client."

The easiest way to connect to an FTP server, however, is to use PHP's basic file commands, such as file_get_contents() and file_put_contents(), and pass them a fully qualified ftp URL, just like would be used in a web browser. The format of this is as follows:

```
ftp://user:password@example.com/directory/file.ext
```

where, of course, you replace the user and password with the ones that you need for your situation (or leave them off for anonymous access), replace example.com with the host you are connecting do, and then similarly change the directories and filename. This makes putting or receiving a file a simple one-line operation in PHP as shown in Listing 13.4.1

Listing 13.4.1 **Accessing an FTP Service Using Basic File Operations**

```php
<?php
// Let's connect to our server and put a file...
file_put_contents('ftp://user:pass@example.com/storage.txt',
    'Hello there Mr. FTP Server!');

// Now let's read that data back in:
$data = file_get_contents('ftp://user:pass@example.com/storage.txt');

// And echo it back out:
echo $data;
?>
```

13.5 Creating a PHP-Based FTP Client

Although Listing 13.4.1 is easy to use, it is limited to just being used for putting, or retrieving files, one at a time. There are times when you need to do more with an FTP server, such as getting directory listings, making directories, deleting files, putting multiple files at once, and so on.

The best way to accomplish all these tasks in PHP is to use the FTP extension that is built into it. (Note that the FTP extension is enabled by default in Windows builds of PHP but must be specifically compiled into other versions.)

To fully explore the possibilities that the FTP extension provides, Listing 13.5.1 is a basic FTP client written in PHP. This script is designed to be run from the command line, using the command-line version of PHP to execute it instead of through a web server.

Listing 13.5.1 **Basic Command Line FTP Client**

```php
<?php
// Basic FTP client software.

// Start by preparing to read from stdin.
$stdin = fopen('php://stdin', 'r');
```

Listing 13.5.1 **Continued**

```php
$server = false;
$mode = FTP_ASCII;

// Declare all currently valid commands:
$commands = array('open', 'close', 'quit', 'exit', 'cd', 'ls', 'dir',
    'pwd', 'get', 'put', 'ascii', 'binary', 'bin', 'delete', 'del');

// If parameters were provided, assume they are host, user, pass
if ($argc > 1) {
    // Remove the filename from the line
    array_shift($argv);
    // Now call the open function to handle this:
    _open($argv);
}

// Now, Sit and loop forever, taking user input and handling it.
while (true) {
    // First of all, give the prompt:
    echo 'phpftp> ';

    // Now accept User Input
    $line = trim(fgets($stdin));

    // Only if the line contained anything, continue:
    if ($line) {
        // Split the line into an array of space separated entries:
        $opts = explode(' ', $line);
        $cmd = strtolower(array_shift($opts));

        // Take the first entry as a command, and execute the appropriate
        //  function, but first make sure it is a valid command!
        if (!in_array($cmd, $commands)) {
            echo "! Command not supported.\n";
        }
        // If server is false, only allow 'open'
        // Otherwise, don't allow open!
        elseif (($server xor ($cmd != 'open')) && ($cmd != 'quit')
                && ($cmd != 'exit')) {
            echo "! Invalid server status for this command.\n";
        } else {
            // Otherwise, we can execute whatever command they gave us.
            // Just call it as a function name, it will exist at this point!
            $func = "_{$cmd}";
            $func($opts);
        }
}
```

Listing 13.5.1 **Continued**

```php
    }
}

// Now declare a function for each command!

// To open a connection:
function _open($opts) {
    global $server, $stdin;

    // Prepare to open the connection, prompt for missing items such as host:
    if (!isset($opts[0])) {
        echo '? Host: ';
        $opts[0] = trim(fgets($stdin));
    }

    // And Username:
    if (!isset($opts[1])) {
        echo '? User: ';
        $opts[1] = trim(fgets($stdin));
    }

    // And Finally, password -- Note that this will be visible on the screen
    if (!isset($opts[2])) {
        echo '? Pass: ';
        $opts[2] = trim(fgets($stdin));
    }

    // Now we have what we need, attempt to open!
    if (!($server = @ftp_connect($opts[0]))) {
        echo "! Error, cannot connect to host!\n";
        $server = false;
    } else {
        // We connected, try to login
        if (!(@ftp_login($server, $opts[1], $opts[2]))) {
            echo "! Error, Username/Password not accepted!\n";
            ftp_close($server);
            $server = false;
        } else {
            // It worked, let 'em know!
            echo "- Connected to {$opts[0]}\n";

            // Try to let them know the type of server as well:
            if ($type = ftp_systype($server)) {
                echo "- Server type: {$type}\n";
            }
```

Listing 13.5.1 **Continued**

```
            // Set the mode to Ascii & go ahead and let them know
            //  what directory they are in:
            _ascii(0);
            _pwd(0);
        }
    }
}

// To close a connection:
function _close($opts) {
    @ftp_close($GLOBALS['server']);
    $GLOBALS['server'] = false;
    echo "- Connection Closed.\n";
}

// To change directories
function _cd($opts) {
    // Try to change to the directory that they specified:
    if (!(@ftp_chdir($GLOBALS['server'], @$opts[0]))) {
        echo "! Error, Failed to change directory\n";
    }

    // In either case, give them their current directory:
    _pwd(0);
}

// To quit the program!
function _exit($opts) {
    // If we are currently connected, close first:
    if ($GLOBALS['server']) {
        _close(0);
    }
    echo "- Goodbye!\n";
    exit();
}
function _quit($opts) {
    _exit($opts);
}

// To get a directory listing:
function _ls($opts) {
    // Use rawlist to get a nicely formatted version from the server.
    // Pass the opts all collapsed into one string if the person used them:
    $optstring = implode(' ', $opts);
    if ($res = ftp_rawlist($GLOBALS['server'], $optstring)) {
        foreach ($res as $r) { echo "{$r}\n"; }
```

Listing 13.5.1 **Continued**
_____

```php
        } else {
            // Give an error statement
            echo "! Error, could not generate directory listing\n";
        }
    }
    function _dir($opts) {
        _ls($opts);
    }

    // To figure out what directory you are in:
    function _pwd($opts) {
        // Get the current directory, and echo it:
        $cwd = ftp_pwd($GLOBALS['server']);
        echo "- Current directory: {$cwd}\n";
    }

    // To get a file from the remote host, and save it locally.
    function _get($opts) {
        // If we don't have any options, give an error
        if (!($opts)) {
            echo "! Error, no file specified\n";
        } else {
            // If we don't have a second option, assume a desire to
            // save the file into the current directory, with the same name
            if (!isset($opts[1])) {
                $opts[1] = basename($opts[0]);
            }

            // Now, attempt to save the file.
            if (!@ftp_get($GLOBALS['server'], $opts[1], $opts[0],
                    $GLOBALS['mode'])) {
                echo "! Error - Could not download file\n";
            } else {
                echo "- Data saved to file: {$opts[1]}\n";
            }
        }
    }

    // To put a local file to the remote host:
    function _put($opts) {
        // If we don't have any options, give an error
        if (!($opts)) {
            echo "! Error, no file specified\n";
        } else {
            // If we don't have a second option, assume a desire to
            // save the file into the current directory, with the same name
```

Listing 13.5.1   **Continued**

```php
        if (!isset($opts[1])) {
            $opts[1] = basename($opts[0]);
        }

        // Now, attempt to save the file.
        if (!@ftp_put($GLOBALS['server'], $opts[1], $opts[0],
                $GLOBALS['mode'])) {
            echo "! Error - Could not upload file\n";
        } else {
            echo "- Data uploaded to file: {$opts[1]}\n";
        }
    }
}

// To Change the transfer mode to ASCII
function _ascii($opts) {
    // Just change it, and echo
    $GLOBALS['mode'] = FTP_ASCII;
    echo "- Transfer mode: ASCII\n";
}

// To Change the transfer mode to Binary
function _binary($opts) {
    // Just change it, and echo
    $GLOBALS['mode'] = FTP_BINARY;
    echo "- Transfer mode: Binary\n";
}
function _bin($opts) {
    _binary($opts);
}

// Allow for deleting of files
function _delete($opts) {
    // If we don't have any options, give an error
    if (!($opts)) {
        echo "! Error, no file specified\n";
    } else {
        // Now, attempt to delete the file
        if (!@ftp_delete($GLOBALS['server'], $opts[0])) {
            echo "! Error - Could not delete file\n";
        } else {
            echo "- File Deleted: {$opts[0]}\n";
        }
    }
}
```

Listing 13.5.1 **Continued**

```
function _del($opts) {
    _delete($opts);
}
?>
```

To accomplish the task of creating a fully functional (though basic) FTP client in PHP, start by beginning to converse with the operating system's input by opening php://stdin. This is the equivalent in other languages of reading from stdin, and is how you accept input from the user. It then enters a loop waiting for input and doing some basic sanity checks on the command it was given, and then proceeds to perform the task requested of it.

It creates a set of its own internal functions to map to the various commands and is almost a direct one-for-one mapping for the functions provided in the FTP extension The only difference is that the client does some extra error checking to give useful responses back to the user. Of note about the code itself: The use of a variable to hold function names, as discussed in Chapter 6, "Functions," is implemented.

In the end this creates a functional FTP client that has been written completely in PHP. It is missing some more advanced features, and even some basic ones (such as the creation and removal of directories), but gives a fairly complete example of how powerful the FTP extension for PHP is.

13.6 Using Sockets to Connect to an Internet Server

If you need to talk to an Internet service other than the ones mentioned so far, such as http, ftp, SOAP, and so on, you will need to directly access this service via TCP or UDP sockets. This is a raw connection to another server, and you must know the details of the protocol you will be dealing with to properly send commands and receive data from them.

PHP provides a number of ways to talk with Internet servers, including a fsockopen() function and an entire BSD sockets extension that can be used. However, as of PHP 5, the streams extension has been greatly enhanced and is the preferred way to talk with Internet servers because it is highly configurable and powerful.

To demonstrate this, Listing 13.6.1 is a small application that uses stream_socket_client() to connect to the free Internet Time Service provided by NIST. The time service works as follows: A TCP connection is made to port 13 on one of the NIST servers. When a connection is successfully created, the server immediately sends the response back with the current time.

Listing 13.6.1   **Accessing the NIST Time Service**

```php
<?php
// Open a connection to NIST's time server, or die
if (!($tp = stream_socket_client('tcp://time.nist.gov:13', $err, $str))) {
    exit("ERROR: Failed to connect - {$err} - {$str}\n");

    exit("ERROR: Failed to connect - {$err_num} - {$err_string}\n");
}

// Ignore the first line of output, it is blank:
fgets($tp);

// Now echo out the second line, it is the date string:
echo trim(fgets($tp));

// Close the connection
fclose($tp);
?>
```

To find out more information about the stream functions, see http://php.net/stream.

13.7 Creating Your Own Basic Web Server

Purely as an example of what you can do in PHP using the stream and socket function-ality, we will create a web server in PHP. Listing 13.7.1 will be a basic web server, serv-ing only GET requests and basic file types. Given that it will be written in PHP, however, we will add an easy feature: Every file served through this web server will be treated as PHP and parsed for commands. After all, why else would you write a web server in PHP except to run PHP in it?

To make this web server, we'll start by creating our service on a specific port and IP address. In Listing 13.7.1, it is set to the local loopback address 127.0.0.1 and port 8088 to not conflict with any other web server on the same machine. We then listen for con-nections. To handle more than one client connection at a time, when a connection comes in, we will launch a new process using pcntl_fork(). This creates a new process that can handle the request and return the data, leaving the parent/server process to immediately be ready to accept another connection.

This setup will not scale well; someone could easily bring down your machine by rapidly connecting to the machine, causing you to spawn thousands of processes. If this server was ever put into production, it would at the very least need to have a limiting factor built into it, keeping the number of processes to a certain maximum. Of course, after that there are many other issues with this basic web server in terms of performance, features, and so on. However, it gives a good overview of how to write an Internet server.

Listing 13.7.1   **Basic PHP HTTP Server**

```php
<?php
// A barebones, basic, php webserver

// First let's insert some basic configuration, at the top of the file
//   where it is easy to edit
$port = 8088;
$host = '127.0.0.1';
$docroot = '/html';

// Ensure that our server will never timeout
set_time_limit(0);

// Start off by listening to our designated port:
if (!($server = stream_socket_server("tcp://{$host}:{$port}",
        $err_num, $err_string))) {
    exit("ERROR: Failed to Open Server - {$err_num} - {$err_string}\n");
}

// Now, begin a permanent loop
for (;;) {
    // Listen for a new connection and don't timeout:
    $client = stream_socket_accept($server, -1);

    // If we truly got a client connection, and not an error:
    if ($client) {
        // Attempt to fork a new process, so that the server can
        //   still accept new connections.
        $pid = pcntl_fork();

        // If an error happened:
        if ($pid == -1) {
            exit("ERROR: Could not create new process!");
        }
        // Else, if we are in the child
        elseif (!$pid) {
            // Read the first line of the request
            //   (The only line we are going to bother with)
            $command = fgets($client, 2048);

            // Read the rest of the request; however, we are going to ignore
            //   it - Given we are being such a simple web server. We need to
            //   read all lines presented, until we get a blank line or
            //   error, that means the request is done.
            while($line = fgets($client, 2048)) {
                if (trim($line) === '') { break; }
            }
```

Listing 13.7.1 **Continued**

```
            // Now, divide up the request string into it's parts:
            $request = explode(' ', $command);

            // If the Request is not GET tell them we cannot do that.
            if ($request[0] != 'GET') {
                // Respond that we do not support this
                @fwrite($client,
"HTTP/0.9 501 Not Implemented
Server: Bare-Basic-PHP-WebServer
Content-Type: text/html

<html><head><title>501 Not Implemented</title></head>
<body><h1>501 Not Implemented</h1>
<p>This is a very basic web server that only implements GET</p>
</body></html>");
                // Close the connection
                fclose($client);
                // And exit the child
                exit();
            }

            // Attempt to split any GET parameters out of the request:
            $parts = explode('?', $request[1]);

            // If the request ends in '/', assume index.php
            if ($parts[0]{strlen($parts[0])-1} == '/') {
                $parts[0] .= 'index.php';
            }

            // Now, if the file requested cannot be found in document root:
            if (!is_file($docroot . $parts[0])) {
                // Respond with a 404 error - We can't find the document:
                @fwrite($client,
"HTTP/0.9 404 Not Found
Server: Bare-Basic-PHP-WebServer
Content-Type: text/html

<html><head><title>404 Not Found</title></head>
<body><h1>404 Not Found</h1>
<p>We looked, but the file you requested was nowhere to be found!</p>
</body></html>");
                // Close the connection
                fclose($client);
                // And exit the child
                exit();
            }
```

Listing 13.7.1   **Continued**

```php
        // Finally, we are ALMOST ready
        // We just need to decide what filetype to return:
        $path = pathinfo($parts[0]);
        switch ($path['extension']) {
            // For the image types:
            case 'gif':
            case 'png':
            case 'jpg':
                $mime = "image/{$path['extension']}";
                break;
            // Text Types:
            case 'html':
            case 'xml':
            case 'css':
                $mime = "text/{$path['extension']}";
                break;
            // Javascript:
            case 'js':
                $mime = 'application/x-javascript';
                break;
            // Special case for PHP files:
            case 'php':
                $mime = 'text/html';
                break;
            // Give a generic answer for everything else:
            default:
                $mime = 'application/octet-stream';
        }

        // We know the mime type to return, prep the GET variables
        if (isset($parts[1])) {
            // Parse them into $_GET just like PHP would have
            parse_str($parts[1], $_GET);
        }

        // Now, INCLUDE the file, no matter what the type.  This is a
        //  PHP webserver, so we are going to assume that EVERY file
        //  might have some embedded PHP in it.  Capture the output
        //  via buffering
        ob_start();
        include "{$docroot}{$parts[0]}";
        $output = ob_get_contents();
        ob_end_clean();

        // Ok, time to return everything!
```

Listing 13.7.1   **Continued**

```
            $length = strlen($output);
            @fwrite($client,
"HTTP/0.9 200 Ok
Server: Bare-Basic-PHP-WebServer
Content-Type: {$mime}
Content-Length: {$length}

{$output}");

            // Since we aren't supporting Keep-Alive, close the connection
            fclose($client);
            exit();
        }
    }
    // We are in the parent here, just about to restart our loop, make sure
    //  that the parent closes the client connection.
    @fclose($client);
}
?>
```

Note that this program as designed will run forever and will need to be manually killed off. When calling `pcntl_fork()`, your process splits into two identical copies with only a slight difference. In the parent, the call to `pcntl_fork()` returns the process id of the child. In the child, it returns 0. This allows you to then run different code depending on whether the current process is the parent or the child of the fork.

> **Caution**
>
> The `pcntl` (process control) functions of PHP are not available on Windows, because Windows has a different process model than UNIX. Also, even on UNIX they are not compiled into the server by default and must be specifically included upon compilation. To learn more about these functions and how to enable them, visit http://php.net/pcntl.

14

Relational Databases

IN WEB ENVIRONMENTS, DATABASES ARE as ubiquitous as blades of grass in a meadow. Web applications such as photo archives, blogs, podcasts, forums, retail sites, and portals are all driven by databases. As you might expect, the theory and application of database development is a wide field. However, to start using a database, you need only understand a few basic concepts and operations.

The most common type of database in use today are relational databases. In the most basic view, a relational database is simply a table of rows and columns, as shown in Table 14.1.

Table 14.1 **A Simple Database**

ID	First Name	Second Name	Street Address	ZIP Code
822382	Joe	Smith	119 Main Street	90099
793849	Alice	Jones	9232 Song Way	09925

You can think of each row as containing some "item," and the columns in that row are parameters describing that item. In database terminology, each row is a *record* and each column is a *field*. In Table 14.1, each item is a person, described by name, address, and unique identifier. A database column is defined to contain a specific type of data: strings, integers, dates, booleans, and so on. The basic database operations include creating tables, defining columns, adding rows, deleting rows, changing values of a row, and searching for rows that match some condition.

Almost always, a database is accessed through a database server: a machine running the database software. Hence, to use a database, a connection must be established to such a server. After a connection is made, the database is sent commands, called *queries*, to which the database returns a result, usually in tabular form. Different database systems implement different methods of communicating with them. Today, all readily accessible relational database systems use a language known as SQL. Each system has its own variation on the basic SQL syntax, however, and these need to be known to you to operate within that database.

For PHP to access a database, an interface library must be provided. Fortunately, interfaces for most of the popular database systems exist, including Oracle, Sybase, MySQL, Microsoft SQL Server, and PostgreSQL. For many of these interfaces, you must explicitly install them. PHP also includes an interface to SQLite, a file-based database system that requires no separate database server (see Section 14.6, "Communicating with SQLite," later in this chapter). Finally, as of version 5.1, a database abstraction library, called PHP Data Objects (PDO), has been implemented, allowing a common set of functions to be used to access a number of different databases. PDO is examined in Section 14.8, "Using an Abstraction Layer to Communicate with a Database (PDO)," later in this chapter.

The following sections go through the process of accepting data from a user, cleaning up or "untainting" the data to ensure security, inserting a value, and then selecting data back out and assigning the results in an associative array while checking for errors during the whole procedure.

14.1 Communicating with MySQL

MySQL is one of the most popular databases used with PHP, and PHP 5 includes a new access library for it—MySQLi, which stands for MySQL Improved. Both a functional interface library and an object-oriented class definition have been provided. For a full description of the library, see http://php.net/mysqli. For our example, the functional interface will be used. Listing 14.1.1 presents the SQL to create and initialize our example table. Listing 14.1.2 is the PHP script demonstrating how to manipulate the table.

Listing 14.1.1 **SQL to Create the Table**

```
create table tools (
    id   int          not null auto_increment primary key,
    desc varchar(255) not null,
    qty  int          not null
) ENGINE=MyISAM ;

insert into tools (desc, qty) values ('Screwdriver', 10);
insert into tools (desc, qty) values ('Tablesaw', 1);
insert into tools (desc, qty) values ('Router', 2);
```

Listing 14.1.2 **PHP Code to Access the MySQL Database**

```php
<?php
// Open the database connection
if (!($db = mysqli_connect('localhost', 'guest', 'secret', 'dbname'))) {
    // Handle errors
    die('SQL ERROR: Connection failed: ' . mysqli_error($db));
}
```

Listing 14.1.2 **Continued**

```
// Prepare a SQL insert: assume we received the description from the user
$desc = 'Mortising Machine';
$escaped = mysqli_escape_string($desc);
$sql = "insert into tools (desc, qty) values ('{$escaped}', 0)";

// Do the insertion:
if (!(mysqli_query($db, $sql))) {
    // Give an error statement:
    die('SQL INSERT ERROR: ' . mysqli_error($db). " - Query was: {$sql}");
}

// Select data from the table:
$sql = 'select id, desc from tools order by id asc';
if (!($result = mysqli_query($db, $sql))) {
    // Give an error statement:
    die('SQL SELECT ERROR: ' . mysqli_error($db). " - Query was: {$sql}");
}

// Read all the data back in as associative arrays
while ($row = mysqli_fetch_assoc($result)) {
    echo "{$row['id']}. {$row['desc']}<br />\n";
}

// Now close the connection
mysqli_close($db);
?>
```

In Listing 14.1.2, we start off by making a connection to the desired database. The arguments to the `mysqli_connect()` call will need to be modified to access your particular database. After connecting, nearly all further interaction with the database is done by SQL queries sent by the `mysqli_query()` call. After each query, the result of the call is checked to make sure that the query was successfully sent. If the query requested results to be returned, the `mysqli_fetch_assoc()` call is used to return any results in an associative array. For our example, we make two queries: one to insert a new row and one to retrieve information from the table. Finally, the connection is closed.

Listing 14.1.2 demonstrates the basic set of operations that hold true for most relational databases: A connection is made, a set of SQL queries is sent and the results retrieved, and finally the connection is closed. Due to the power of the SQL language itself, the presented functions will handle most basic database applications. Most of the other functions in the interface library involve setting and retrieving the state of a database or for optimizing the connection.

14.2 Communicating with Oracle

Oracle is one of the oldest and most established database systems in use today. Hence, it has its share of idiosyncrasies. From PHP's point of view there are a few things to remember. Primarily, there is not a single function call to handle SQL commands. You need to first parse the SQL with `oci_parse()`, execute it with `oci_execute()`, and then finally, if it was an insert or update, commit the results with `oci_commit()`. Also, like Sybase, there is not a built-in function for escaping strings, so that needs to be done manually. For a full description of the library, see http://php.net/oci8. Listing 14.2.1 provides the Oracle-specific SQL for creating an initializing a table. As in Listing 14.1.2, Listing 14.2.2 provides the PHP script demonstrating some basic operations on the created table: connecting to the database, inserting new data, retrieving data, and closing the connection.

Listing 14.2.1   **SQL to Create an Oracle Table**

```
create sequence TOOLS_ID
start with 1
increment by 1
nomaxvalue
go

create table TOOLS (
    ID   number(10)   not null,
    DESC varchar2(255) not null,
    QTY  number(8)     not null
    constraint TOOLS_PK primary key(ID)
)
go

create or replace trigger TOOLS_IDTRIG
before insert on TOOLS
for each row
begin
select TOOLS_ID.nextval into :new.ID from dual;
end;
go

insert into tools (DESC, QTY) values ('Screwdriver', 10)
go
insert into tools (DESC, QTY) values ('Tablesaw', 1)
go
insert into tools (DESC, QTY) values ('Router', 2)
go
```

Listing 14.2.2   **PHP Code to Access the Oracle Database**

```php
<?php
// Open the database connection
if (!($db = oci_connect('GUEST', 'secret', 'SERVICE.NAME'))) {
    // Handle errors
    die('SQL ERROR: Connection failed: ' . oci_error());
}

// Switch to the appropriate schema that we want to deal with:
$sql = 'alter schema set current_schema=SCHEMANAME';

// Parse & Execute this statement:
$stmt = oci_parse($db, $sql) or die ("SQL ERROR: " . oci_error($db));
oci_execute($stmt) or die ("SQL ERROR: " . oci_error($stmt));

// Prepare a SQL insert: assume we received the description from the user
$desc = 'Mortising Machine';
$escaped = str_replace("'", "''", $desc);
$sql = "insert into TOOLS (DESC, QTY) values ('{$escaped}', 0)";

// Do the insertion, making sure to commit afterwards!
$stmt = oci_parse($db, $sql) or die ("SQL ERROR: " . oci_error($db));
oci_execute($stmt) or die ("SQL ERROR: " . oci_error($stmt));
oci_commit($db) or die ("SQL ERROR: " . oci_error($db));

// Select data from the table:
$sql = 'select ID, DESC from TOOLS order by ID asc';
$stmt = oci_parse($db, $sql) or die ("SQL ERROR: " . oci_error($db));
oci_execute($stmt) or die ("SQL ERROR: " . oci_error($stmt));

// Read all the data back in as associative arrays
while ($row = oci_fetch_assoc($stmt)) {
    echo "{$row['id']}. {$row['desc']}<br />\n";
}

// Now close the connection
oci_close($db);
?>
```

14.3 Communicating with PostgreSQL

PostgreSQL is another open source relational database system often used by PHP programmers. It is a full-featured system and has a long history dating back to 1986. For a full description of the library, see http://php.net/pgsql. As in the previous sections,

Listing 14.3.1 is the PostgreSQL–specific SQL to create and initialize the example table. Listing 14.3.2 is the PHP script to connect, insert data, retrieve data, and close the connection.

Listing 14.3.1 SQL to Create the PostgreSQL Table

```
create table tools (
    id    serial,
    desc varchar(255) not null,
    qty  int          not null,
    primary key(id)
);


insert into tools (desc, qty) values ('Screwdriver', 10);
insert into tools (desc, qty) values ('Tablesaw', 1);
insert into tools (desc, qty) values ('Router', 2);
```

Listing 14.3.2 PHP Code to Access the PostgreSQL Database

```php
<?php
// Open the database connection
if (!($db = pg_connect(
        'host=localhost dbname=dbname user=guest password=secret'))) {
    // Handle errors
    die('SQL ERROR: Connection failed: ' . pg_last_error($db));
}

// Prepare a SQL insert: assume we received the description from the user
$desc = 'Mortising Machine';
$escaped = pg_escape_string($desc);
$sql = "insert into tools (desc, qty) values ('{$escaped}', 0)";

// Do the insertion:
if (!(pg_query($db, $sql))) {
    // Give an error statement:
    die('SQL INSERT ERROR: ' . pg_last_error($db). " - Query was: {$sql}");
}

// Select data from the table:
$sql = 'select id, desc from tools order by id asc';
if (!($result = pg_query($db, $sql))) {
    // Give an error statement:
    die('SQL SELECT ERROR: ' . pg_last_error($db). " - Query was: {$sql}");
}

// Read all the data back in as associative arrays
while ($row = pg_fetch_assoc($result)) {
```

Listing 14.3.2 **Continued**

```php
        echo "{$row['id']}. {$row['desc']}<br />\n";
    }

// Now close the connection
pg_close($db);
?>
```

14.4 Communicating with Sybase

Sybase is a popular commercial database system that has fairly large penetration in the market. There are a few specific things to note when dealing with Sybase. First, Sybase does not have its own specific escape function to clean data for you. Therefore you need to handle this yourself by replacing all occurrences of single quotes (') with two single quotes (''). Also note that you cannot specify the database you want to work with in the connection statement and therefore you must specify it afterward. Finally know that there is not a specific function to return the last error that happened. Instead there is sybase_get_last_message(), which returns the last message from the database whether it was an error or not, therefore sometimes giving you some interesting results. For a full description of the library, see http://php.net/sybase. As done previously, Listing 14.4.1 is the SQL to create and initialize the example table. Listing 14.4.2 is the PHP script to connect, insert data, retreive data, and close the connection to the Sybase database.

Listing 14.4.1 **SQL to Create the Sybase Table**

```sql
create table tools (
    id    int        identity,
    desc varchar(255) not null,
    qty   int         not null,
)
go

insert into tools (desc, qty) values ('Screwdriver', 10)
go
insert into tools (desc, qty) values ('Tablesaw', 1)
go
insert into tools (desc, qty) values ('Router', 2)
go
```

Listing 14.4.2 **PHP Code to Access the Sybase Database**

```php
<?php
// Open the database connection
if (!($db = sybase_connect('servername', 'guest_user', 'secret'))) {
```

Listing 14.4.2 **Continued**

```
    // Handle errors
    die('SQL ERROR: Connection failed: ' . sybase_get_last_message());
}

// Now switch to the proper database:
if (!(sybase_select_db('dbname'))) {
    // Handle errors
    die('SQL ERROR: Database Selection failed: ' .
        sybase_get_last_message());
}


// Prepare a SQL insert: assume we received the description from the user
$desc = 'Mortising Machine';
$escaped = str_replace("'", "''", $desc);
$sql = "insert into tools (desc, qty) values ('{$escaped}', 0)";

// Do the insertion:
if (!(sybase_query($sql))) {
    // Give an error statement:
    die('SQL INSERT ERROR: ' . sybase_get_last_message().
        " - Query was: {$sql}");
}

// Select data from the table:
$sql = 'select id, desc from tools order by id asc';
if (!($result = sybase_query($sql))) {
    // Give an error statement:
    die('SQL SELECT ERROR: ' . sybase_get_last_message().
        " - Query was: {$sql}");
}

// Read all the data back in as associative arrays
while ($row = sybase_fetch_assoc($result)) {
    echo "{$row['id']}. {$row['desc']}<br />\n";
}

// Now close the connection
sybase_close($db);
?>
```

14.5 Communicating with Microsoft SQL Server

At one point Microsoft's SQL Server shared a code base with Sybase, and therefore today they are still similar. For a full description of the library, see http://php.net/mssql. Listing 14.5.1 is the SQL needed to create and initialize the example table. Listing 14.5.2 is the PHP script to connect to the database, insert new data, retrieve data, and close the connection.

Listing 14.5.1   **SQL to Create the Microsoft SQL Server Table**

```
create table tools (
    id    int          identity,
    desc varchar(255) not null,
    qty  int          not null,
)
go

insert into tools (desc, qty) values ('Screwdriver', 10)
go
insert into tools (desc, qty) values ('Tablesaw', 1)
go
insert into tools (desc, qty) values ('Router', 2)
go
```

Listing 14.5.2   **PHP Code to Access the Microsoft SQL Server Database**

```
<?php
// Open the database connection
if (!($db = mssql_connect('servername', 'guest_user', 'secret'))) {
    // Handle errors
    die('SQL ERROR: Connection failed: ' . mssql_get_last_message());
}

// Now switch to the proper database:
if (!(mssql_select_db('dbname'))) {
    // Handle errors
    die('SQL ERROR: Database Selection failed: ' .
        mssql_get_last_message());
}

// Prepare a SQL insert: assume we received the description from the user
$desc = 'Mortising Machine';
$escaped = str_replace("'", "''", $desc);
$sql = "insert into tools (desc, qty) values ('{$escaped}', 0)";
```

Listing 14.5.2   **Continued**

```php
// Do the insertion:
if (!(mssql_query($sql))) {
    // Give an error statement:
    die('SQL INSERT ERROR: ' . mssql_get_last_message() .
        " - Query was: {$sql}");
}

// Select data from the table:
$sql = 'select id, desc from tools order by id asc';
if (!($result = mssql_query($sql))) {
    // Give an error statement:
    die('SQL SELECT ERROR: ' . mssql_get_last_message() .
        " - Query was: {$sql}");
}

// Read all the data back in as associative arrays
while ($row = mssql_fetch_assoc($result)) {
    echo "{$row['id']}. {$row['desc']}<br />\n";
}

// Now close the connection
mssql_close($db);
?>
```

14.6 Communicating with SQLite

SQLite is a serverless database system included in PHP 5. With SQLite you can access local files as if they were databases and have a full set of standard SQL functions at your disposal. To learn more about SQLite itself, visit the SQLite home page: http://sqlite. org/. To discover more functionality of the PHP SQLite interface, see http://php.net/ sqlite. SQLite comes prebundled with PHP 5; however, it is not enabled by default, so you will need to edit the php.ini file to enable it.

Because an SQLite database is accessed through the PHP interface, we need to modify our example slightly. Instead of simply providing the SQL to create and initialize the example table, Listing 14.6.1 is actually a PHP script to do the creating and initialization. Listing 14.6.2 is more inline with the previous sections; it is also a PHP script that connects, inserts new data, retrieves data, and closes the connection to our example database.

Listing 14.6.1   **Creating SQLite Tables Within PHP**

```php
<?php
// Open the database:
if (!($db = sqlite_open('tools.db'))) {
```

Listing 14.6.1 **Continued**

```php
    // Handle errors
    die('SQL ERROR: Open failed: ' .
        sqlite_error_string(sqlite_last_error($db)));
}

// Prepare the database creation:
$sql = "
create table tools (
    id    integer  primary key,
    desc text      not null,
    qty  integer   not null
);

insert into tools (desc, qty) values ('Screwdriver', 10);
insert into tools (desc, qty) values ('Tablesaw', 1);
insert into tools (desc, qty) values ('Router', 2);
";

// Create it all:
if (!(sqlite_exec($db, $sql))) {
    // Give an error statement:
    die('SQL ERROR: ' . sqlite_error_string(sqlite_last_error($db)) .
        " - Query was: {$sql}");
} else {
    echo 'SUCCESS!';
}

// Now close the database
sqlite_close($db);
?>
```

Listing 14.6.2 **PHP Code to Access the SQLite Database**

```php
<?php
// Open the database:
if (!($db = sqlite_open('tools.db'))) {
    // Handle errors
    die('SQL ERROR: Open failed: ' .
        sqlite_error_string(sqlite_last_error($db)));
}

// Prepare a SQL insert: assume we received the description from the user
$desc = 'Mortising Machine';
$escaped = sqlite_escape_string($desc);
$sql = "insert into tools (desc, qty) values ('{$escaped}', 0)";
```

Listing 14.6.2 **Continued**

```php
// Do the insert
if (!(sqlite_query($db, $sql))) {
    // Give an error statement:
    die('SQL ERROR: ' . sqlite_error_string(sqlite_last_error($db)) .
        " - Query was: {$sql}");
}

// Select data from the table:
$sql = 'select id, desc from tools order by id asc';
if (!($result = sqlite_query($db, $sql))) {
    // Give an error statement:
    die('SQL ERROR: ' . sqlite_error_string(sqlite_last_error($db)) .
        " - Query was: {$sql}");
}

// Read all the data back in as associative arrays
while ($row = sqlite_fetch_array($result)) {
    echo "{$row['id']}. {$row['desc']}<br />\n";
}

// Now close the connection
sqlite_close($db);
?>
```

14.7 Communicating with Databases Through ODBC

ODBC is a database connection abstraction layer. It allows you to use a standard set of functions to communicate to any database that supports an ODBC connection. The ODBC interface on your machine must be configured with the proper datasource information that tells it what actual database to connect and talk to. For a full description of the library, see http://php.net/odbc. Because this example is not database specific, we do not present the SQL to create and initialize the example table; use the listing from a previous section that is appropriate to the database in use. Listing 14.7.1 is the PHP script to connect to, insert new data, retrieve data, and close the connection.

Listing 14.7.1 **Accessing a Database Using ODBC**

```php
<?php
// Open the database connection
if (!($db = odbc_connect('datasource', 'guest_user', 'secret'))) {
    // Handle errors
    die('SQL ERROR: Connection failed: ' . odbc_errormsg());
}
```

Listing 14.7.1 **Continued**

```
// Prepare a SQL insert: assume we received the description from the user
$desc = 'Mortising Machine';
$escaped = str_replace("'", "''", $desc);
$sql = "insert into tools (desc, qty) values ('{$escaped}', 0)";

// Do the insertion:
if (!(odbc_exec($db, $sql))) {
    // Give an error statement:
    die('SQL INSERT ERROR: ' . odbc_errormsg($db) . " - Query was: {$sql}");
}

// Select data from the table:
$sql = 'select id, desc from tools order by id asc';
if (!($result = odbc_exec($db, $sql))) {
    // Give an error statement:
    die('SQL SELECT ERROR: ' . odbc_errormsg($db) . " - Query was: {$sql}");
}

// Read all the data back in as associative arrays
while ($row - odbc_fetch_array($result)) {
    echo "{$row['id']}. {$row['desc']}<br />\n";
}

// Now close the connection
odbc_close($db);
?>
```

14.8 Using an Abstraction Layer to Communicate with a Database (PDO)

PHP 5.1 includes an inclusive abstraction object called PHP Data Objects (PDO). Using PDO you can communicate with many different types of databases. As of this writing, PDO supports SQL Server, Sybase, Interbase, Informix, MySQL, Oracle, ODBC, PostgreSQL, and SQLite. By using PDO, you can theoretically write code once, and just by changing the connect string have it work on any other database without making any changes.

Note that PDO is a *database access* abstraction layer; it provides a common set of functions to access different databases. PDO is not a *database* abstraction layer; the SQL used in queries, column type definitions, table management, and so on still need to be tailored to specific database idiosyncrasies, if need be. For a full description of the library, see http://php.net/pdo.

To use PDO, a couple of directives must be present in your system's php.ini file. If using a standard distribution in UNIX, the directive would be extension pdo.so, or under Windows, extension `php_pdo.dll`. This enables general PDO support. Next, you must enable PDO support for the specific databases that you will be using with PDO. For example, if you want to access a MySQL database using PDO, you must add the directive extension `pdo_mysql.so` (for UNIX) or extension `php_pdo_mysql.dll` (for Windows) to the php.ini file. You may add as many databases as you want. As with all installation issues, see http://php.net/pdo for details and a list of available PDO database drivers.

In Listing 14.8.1 we are choosing to demonstrate PDO by accessing the SQLite database created in section 14.6. Note that to do this we need to specify that we want to use an older version of SQLite, version 2, by stating `sqlite2` in the connection string. If we just state `sqlite`, it will create an SQLite v3 database, which the older direct SQLite functions such as `sqlite_query()` cannot access. The direct SQLite functions operate on SQLite v2 databases only.

Listing 14.8.1 **Using PDO to Access an SQLite Database**

```php
<?php
// Open the database:
if (!($db = new PDO('sqlite2:tools.db'))) {
    // Handle errors
    $errinfo = $db->errorInfo();
    die('SQL ERROR: Open failed: ' . $errinfo[2]);
}

// Prepare a SQL insert: assume we received the description from the user
$desc = 'Jointer';
$escaped = str_replace("'", "''", $desc);
$sql = "insert into tools (desc, qty) values ('{$escaped}', 0)";

// Do the insert
if (!($db->query($sql))) {
    // Give an error statement:
    $errinfo = $db->errorInfo();
    die('SQL INSERT ERROR: ' . $errinfo[2] . " - Query was: {$sql}");
}

// Select data from the table:
$sql = 'select id, desc from tools order by id asc';
if (!($result = $db->query($sql))) {
    // Give an error statement:
    $errinfo = $db->errorInfo();
    die('SQL SELECT ERROR: ' . $errinfo[2] . " - Query was: {$sql}");
}

// Read all the data back in as associative arrays
while ($row = $result->fetch()) {
```

Listing 14.8.1   **Continued**

```
    echo "{$row['id']}. {$row['desc']}<br />\n";
}

// Now close the connection
unset($db);
?>
```

14.9 Implementing an SQLite Based Blog

Blogs have become a popular method of producing content on the Web. Many different software packages can handle this for you; however, they are not difficult concepts to create yourself if you want. The listings in this section create a simple blog that saves its data into an SQLite database.

The example uses a basic plain-text password to allow inserting or editing entries, and it automatically displays only the last five blog entries. Of course, afterward additional pages could be created to read from the same database file and generate other archive pages, or individual pages for each blog entry.

First, Listing 14.9.1 creates a library file that helps us talk with our database.

Listing 14.9.1   **Utility Library for Accessing the Blog—Filename: bloglib.php**

```php
<?php
// This is a small header file that will connect to the database for us
//  and provide some convenience functions:

// An error handling routine
function blog_error($pdo) {
    // Read the error, and exit printing it to the screen:
    $errinfo = $pdo->errorInfo();
    die("SQL ERROR: {$errinfo[2]}");
}

// Provide a function that connects to the database for us:
function blog_connect() {
    // Open the database:
    if (!($pdo = new PDO('sqlite:blog.db'))) {
        bloq_error($pdo);
    }

    // Return the connection
    return $pdo;
}

// A function that will do queries for us, taking care of error trapping
function blog_query($pdo, $sql) {
```

Listing 14.9.1   **Continued**

```
    // Run the query:
    if (!($results = $pdo->query($sql))) {
        blog_error($pdo);
    }

    // Return the results
    return $results;
}
?>
```

Given that this is SQLite that we are using, we don't have a generic front-end database system to use to generate our database and table. Therefore, Listing 14.9.2 creates an "initialize" script that does that for us. We will add a small amount of logic to try to make sure that it only gets run once.

Listing 14.9.2   **Initialize the Blog Database—Filename: bloginit.php**

```
<?php
// This script initializes our blog database for us, making sure
//  that everything exists.
require_once 'bloglib.php';

// If the file already exists, exit with an error:
if (file_exists('blog.db')) {
    die("ERROR: Database Already exists");
}

// Open the database:
$db = blog_connect();

// Now, create our blog table, only need the one
blog_query($db, "
    create table blog (
        id      integer  primary key,
        date    text     not null,
        what    text     not null
    )
");

// Now close the connection
unset($db);
?>
```

Finally we can create the blog itself, a single web page that displays the blog and submits back to itself for updates, as shown in Listing 14.9.3.

Listing 14.9.3 **The Blog Page**

```php
<?php
// This is the actual blog script itself.  Do some database prep:
require_once 'bloglib.php';
$db = blog_connect();

// Now first of all, see if we were posted to.
if (count($_POST)) {
    // Ok, handle doing the insert or update that was requested.
    // Check the password!
    if ($_POST['pass'] != 'letmein') {
        die('ERROR: Unauthorized Access');
    }

    // Ok, we are here, so handle it.
    if (trim($_POST['what'])) {
        // Prep the date
        date_default_timezone_set('America/New_York');
        $ddate = date("M j, Y  h:i a");

        // Prep the data, and insert it.
        $wwhat = sqlite_escape_string(trim($_POST['what']));
        blog_query($db, "
            insert into blog (date, what)
            values ('{$ddate}', '{$wwhat}')
            ");
    }
}
?>
<!DOCTYPE html PUBLIC "-//W3C//DTD XHTML 1.0 Strict//EN"
    "http://www.w3.org/TR/xhtml1/DTD/xhtml1-strict.dtd">
<html xmlns="http://www.w3.org/1999/xhtml">
<head><title>Mini-Blog!</title>
<style>
div.entry {
    border: 1px solid red;
    padding: 0px 5px;
    margin: 0px 0px 30px 0px;
}
div.date {
    float: right;
    font-size: 80%;
}
</style>
</head>
<body>
<h1>The Blog!</h1>
```

Listing 14.9.3 **Continued**

```php
<?php
// We need to prepare to display the blog.  Read in the last 5 entries:
$rs = blog_query($db, "
    select date, what
    from blog
    order by id desc
    limit 5
");

// Now loop through them all, printing them out
while ($row = $rs->fetch()) {
    echo "<div class=\"entry\">{$row['what']}
<div class=\"date\">{$row['date']}</div></div>\n";
}

// Now quickly give them the ability to add a new entry:
?>
<form action="<?= $_SERVER['PHP_SELF'] ?>" method="post">
New Entry:
<input name="what" type="text" id="what" size="60" />
  Passcode:
<input name="pass" type="password" id="pass" size="10" maxlength="10" />
 
<input type="submit" name="Submit" value="Update" />
</form>
</body>
</html>
<?php
// Now close the connection
unset($db);
?>
```

As you can see, this is a basic blog. It uses a plain text password as an attempt to stop other users from entering data. It displays only five entries and has no way to view old entries. It also doesn't scrub the data that you are sending it (looking for HTML or BBcode as described in Chapter 10, "Web Form Handling"), assuming that because you are the one adding to the blog, you will make sure that you don't do anything bad. It uses page refreshing and a basic POST to update the form, where it could have used Ajax to make it seamless. It could even give you options to edit the existing entries. Finally you may want to provide a way for the blog to show previous entries that have dropped off the list.

All these features are enhancements that you can add or modify after you have a basic system like this. That is one of the better tenants of web programming: Build the simplest version of the tool that you can and expand from there until it is at a state you are happy with.

15

Other Data Storage Methods

FOR LARGE, INTERRELATED DATASETS THAT NEED to be accessible by many different sources, databases are a fine solution. However, more often than not, applications only use information that is not very extensive, needs to be accessed quickly, and is easily portable. For such data, the overhead of using a database is not necessary and most likely not efficient.

Fortunately, PHP provides a number of functions that make the storage and retrieval of data convenient, fast, and portable. This chapter explores a number of techniques, ranging from the traditional methods of writing and reading explicitly formatted files, to PHP-specific functions that allow you to save and restore PHP variables exactly as they were defined.

Quick Hits

▶ Save any variable as a string and recover it again:

```
$string = serialize($somevariable);
```

```
$variable = unserialize($string);
```

This pair of functions creates a string representation of any variable type, except resources. The original variable can then be recovered.

Full documentation: http://php.net/serialize and http://php.net/unserialize

▶ Create and read comma-separated format files:

```
$stringlength = fputcsv($file, $array, $delimiter);
```

```
$array = fgetcsv($file, $maxlength, $delimiter);
```

These functions write and read a single line from an opened file, using the specified delimiter, to separate the values in the array.

Full documentation: http://php.net/fputcsv and http://php.net/fgetcsv

▶ Write and read specially formatted files:

```
$stringlength = fprintf($file, $format, $variable1, …);
```

```
$array = fscanf($file, $format);
```

These functions write and read in files using the specified formatting.

Full documentation: http://php.net/fprintf and http://php.net/fscanf

▶ Write and read values using the URL query string format:

```
$urlquery = html_build_query($array);
```

```
parse_str($urlquery, $array);
```

These functions save and retrieve array values to and from the URL query string format.

Full documentation: http://php.net/html_build_query and http://php.net/parse_str

▶ Create PHP code that would define a variable:

```
$PHPstring = var_export($variable);
```

This function returns a string containing valid PHP that would re-create the passed variable.

Full documentation: http://php.net/var_export

15.1 Creating and Reading CSV files

Comma-separated values (CSV) is a common file format used for transferring data between two different systems. Most all spreadsheet software as well as database clients allow for data to be imported or exported as CSV. Variations on the specifics of the format need to be accounted for; however, the standard version states that commas separate all fields, and that optionally a field can be surrounded by double quotation marks.

The delimiter can change, as can the field enclosure, but that for the most part, covers the changes that can occur. Fortunately, PHP provides a pair of functions that make handling CSV files easy: `fgetcsv()` and `fputcsv()`. These two functions work directly with file handles and take care of everything for you. Through optional fields, you can specify a delimiter other than comma and a different enclosure other than a double-quote. Listing 15.1.1 shows an example.

Listing 15.1.1 **Writing and Reading CSV**

```php
<?php
// Define three arrays of data that we wish to write to disk,
//   each in a similar format:
$line1 = array(27, 'Sally had a dog', 0.567, 'a');
$line2 = array(42, "See\nJane\nrun", 1.7, 'f');
$line3 = array(3, 'Once upon a "mid-day" sunny ...', 3.14, 'p');

// Now open a CSV file to write these out to:
$csv = fopen('test.csv', 'w');
```

Listing 15.1.1   **Continued**

```
// And put these lines in it as csv:  Will output similar to:
// 27,"Sally had a dog",0.567,a
fputcsv($csv, $line1);
fputcsv($csv, $line2);
fputcsv($csv, $line3);

// Now close the file.
fclose($csv);

// Now let's open it back up to read from it:
$readcsv = fopen('test.csv', 'r');

// Read in each line, and dump it to the screen ... each line will be
// an array holding one entry per CSV value:
echo "<pre>";
while ($line = fgetcsv($readcsv)) {
    print_r($line);
}
echo "</pre>";

// Close the file:
fclose($readcsv);
?>
```

Even though we have carriage returns and double quotes in our string, that doesn't adversely affect the conversion. PHP automatically handles these for you. Carriage returns are not seen as the end of a CSV line if they are in the middle of an enclosed string. Similarly, double quotes are in fact, doubled, to mean that a real double quote should appear. Therefore "" is added to the file to make a single one be read back in later.

If you need to access files with different parameters, this is fairly straightforward. Let's say that you had a file separated by |'s, and had single quotes as an enclosure. In that case, you would use the following lines to read/write the data. (Note that you need to provide a maximum length to the line to fgetcsv() if you specify alternate characters):

```
fputcsv($csv, $line1, '|', "'");
$line = fgetcsv($csv, 2048, '|', "'");
```

15.2 Using Custom Text Files for Storage

Most of the time if you need to store data in plain text files, CSV is the easiest method to use. However there will be times that, for whatever reason, a special format is required. For example, you might end up with a file stored in a different format, and you need to read from it.

Handling this is not that difficult, especially through the application of `fscanf()` and `fprintf()`, which are similar to their C counterparts of the same names. With these functions you pass them a string with special formatting commands embedded that all begin with a percent sign. These commands tell the functions how to format the data when printing, or conversely how to expect it to be formatted when reading it back in.

The options that exist with these functions are extensive and can be fully explored at http://php.net/sprintf.

The most common things that you will use, however, are straightforward. The format of each typical formatting command is `%n.mc`. Where n is the minimum number of characters that should be output (padded by spaces), and m is the number of decimal digits displayed (precision) for floating-point numbers, or a maximum number of characters displayed for strings. The c is a single character that defines the type of the variable being output/read-in, the common ones being d for integers, f for floating-point numbers, and s for strings.

A few variations also exist. If you begin n with a 0, the output will be padded with 0's instead of spaces. Also if you put a - after that number, it will be left-justified instead of the default right justification.

Using these tools at your disposal, it can be easy to read and write custom format files, as shown in Listing 15.2.1.

Listing 15.2.1 **Using Custom Text Files for Data Storage**

```php
<?php
// We are going to read/write from a file that has the following format:
// line 1 will be a 7 digit number (zero padded) followed immediately by
//     a string of any length.
// line 2 will be a 3 character code, followed by *, then a left-justified
//     string no longer than 40 characters, a space, and then a float value

// Define the data that we will be writing:
$num = 27;
$str = 'An entry into this data file';
$code = 'AxH';
$left = 'Data Validated';
$val = 5.6789;

// Now open a data file to write these out to:
$dat = fopen('test.dat', 'w');

// And put this data into it in the custom format described:
// First line, a zero padded 7 digit number followed immediately by a string
fprintf($dat, "%07d%s\n", $num, $str);

// Second line, 3 character code, *, 40 char left-just string, space, float
fprintf($dat, "%3s*%-40s %f\n", $code, $left, $val);
```

Listing 15.2.1   **Continued**

```
// Now close the file.
fclose($dat);

// Now let's dump the file to the screen to see what it looks like:
echo "<pre>File Contents:\n";
readfile('test.dat');

// Now let's open it back up to read from it:
$readdat = fopen('test.dat', 'r');
echo "\n\nFile Data:\n";

// Read back in the first line using a similar format string.
fscanf($readdat, "%07d%[^\n]", $n1, $s2);
echo "Number = '{$n1}'\nString = '{$s2}'\n";

// And now the second line:
fscanf($readdat, "%3s*%40[^\n] %f\n", $c3, $l4, $v5);
echo "Code = '{$c3}'\nLeft-String = '{$l4}'\nFloat = '{$v5}'";
echo "</pre>";

// Close the file:
fclose($readdat);
?>
```

Looking at that code, you will notice that the format strings used for fprintf() and fscanf() are actually slightly different. This is because of an odd effect that fscanf() has built into it. It by default stops scanning for any string, upon the first whitespace that it finds. This therefore breaks any attempt at using "%s" to read back in most strings.

To solve this, fscanf() allows you to specify character classes in regex-like fashion as a matching scheme instead of giving a format code (such as s or d). Therefore, to match all of a given string, we can specify [^\n], which matches everything that is not a carriage return, which of course will not exist because fscanf() reads in only one line at a time. After that small change to our scan lines, we are reading the data back in that we originally put there.

15.3 Accessing and Updating DBM-Style Databases

DBM (or *Berkeley DB*) style databases have been in existence for a long time. They are locally stored files that contain data for you in an easy to access manner. They are not, however, relational databases as most people are used to dealing with. There are no table structures, no rows of data, and so on. All that a DBM-style database handles is the storing of keys and values for those keys. In many ways you can look at a DBM database as being a PHP associative array, just stored on your disk.

You need to know a few basic commands to work with DBM databases. dba_open() opens a database for reading/writing. dba_replace() replaces or inserts a key/value pair for you. dba_fetch() returns a value based on the key provided. Finally, dba_close() finishes working with a DBM database and commits changes back to the disk. The next example works like a configuration file for a piece of software, holding information for the software to use. Listing 15.3.1 is a PHP script that allows us to edit these values. Then any other script could read this data in as needed.

Listing 15.3.1 **Accessing DBM-Formatted Files**

```php
<?php
// Open the file for both reading&writing access:  Using 'inifile' format.
$db = dba_open('config.db3', 'c', 'inifile');

// Now, if we were 'posted' to, assume an update:
if (count($_POST)) {
    // Save each option into the database overriding what was already there
    dba_replace('fore', $_POST['fore'], $db);
    dba_replace('back', $_POST['back'], $db);
    dba_replace('size', $_POST['size'], $db);
}

// Now, in either case, read in the three config items and store them in
// php variables ... default to known values if they don't exist: )
$fore = dba_fetch('fore', $db);
if (!($fore)) { $fore = 'black'; }
$back = dba_fetch('back', $db);
if (!($back)) { $back = 'white'; }
$size = dba_fetch('size', $db);
if (!($size)) { $size = '12px'; }
?>
<!DOCTYPE html PUBLIC "-//W3C//DTD XHTML 1.0 Strict//EN"
    "http://www.w3.org/TR/xhtml1/DTD/xhtml1-strict.dtd">
<html xmlns="http://www.w3.org/1999/xhtml">
<head>
<title>Configuration</title>
<meta http-equiv="Content-Type" content="text/html; charset=iso-8859-1" />
<style>
body {
    color: <?= $fore ?>;
    background-color: <?= $back ?>;
    font-size: <?= $size ?>;
}
</style>
</head>
<body>
<form action="<?= $_SERVER['PHP_SELF'] ?>" method="post" name="myform">
```

Listing 15.3.1 **Continued**

```
<p>Foreground color?
  <input type="text" name="fore" value="<?= $fore ?>" /></p>
<p>Background color?
  <input type="text" name="back" value="<?= $back ?>" /></p>
<p>Font size? <input type="text" name="size" value="<?= $size ?>" /></p>
<input value="Save Config" type="submit" />
</form>
</body>
</html>
```

When opening the file we passed in two extra parameters. The `'c'` is a useful parameter that creates the database if needed, plus allows both read and write access at the same time. The final parameter `'inifile'` describes the type of DBM handler that will be used. There are a number of different handlers and therefore database types. It is recommended that you download, compile, and install a more sophisticated database handler, such as `'db4'` from Sleepycat software, or either of the open source varieties `'gdbm'` (GNU database manager) or `'qdbm'` (Quick Database Manager). The `'inifile'` type that we used is one that is built into PHP 5. It emulates Microsoft style .ini files (the same format as the php.ini file).

For more information about how to compile and install this extension and the variations on it, visit http://php.net/dba.

15.4 Storing Data Via Serialize and Unserialize

PHP has a set of functions, `serialize()` and `unserialize()`, that convert a PHP variable into a storable (text) format and convert it back again. These functions are often used to store variables into databases, pass them between programs, or other such purposes. However, it also makes it easy to store this data into a file and read it back in again.

Simply create your data structure in memory via whatever method desired, serialize it, save it to disk, read it back in, and unserialize it. After that process you can access it just like it was in the first place. Listing 15.4.1 demonstrates a simple use of the serialize functions.

Listing 15.4.1 **Using** `serialize()` **and** `unserialize()` **for Data Storage**

```
<?php
// Create a data structure in memory.
$orig = array(
    array('name' => 'Dierdre', 'category' => 5),
    array('name' => 'Cheryl', 'category' => 3, 'spouse' => 'Bob'),
    array('name' => 'Fergus', 'category' => 3, 'spouse' => 'Glynis'),
    array('name' => 'Jonathas', 'category' => 2, 'spouse' => 'Amalia'),
```

Listing 15.4.1   **Continued**

```
      array('name' => 'SCA', 'type' => 'group', 'year' => 34)
      );

// Write it to a file, serialized, using locking to avoid conflicts
file_put_contents('output.ize', serialize($orig), LOCK_EX);

// Now read it all back in and unserialize it at the same time:
$new = unserialize(file_get_contents('output.ize'));

// Echo out the first entry's name ('Dierdre')
echo "First entry is: {$new[0]['name']}<br />";

// Now just go ahead and dump the entire structure to the screen:
echo '<pre>';
var_dump($new);
echo '</pre>';
?>
```

When used with basic data structures, `serialize()` is convenient and simple to use. However, the real power of these functions lies in the fact that they can also be used to create storable, or persistent, versions of objects as well. When serializing objects, both the properties and methods of the object are preserved, allowing object-oriented applications a method of saving potentially highly complex data using this pair of functions.

It is important to note that one data type cannot be serialized: resources. As you may remember, resources are, in general, variables that refer to things external to PHP, such as opened files or database connections. Because classes often create objects that use resources, PHP provides two "magic" methods that every object shares: `__sleep()` and `__wakeup()`. The former is called whenever an object is serialized, and the latter is called when an object is unserialized. These methods are provided to allow an object to close resources, such as database connections, when serialized and to reopen any needed resources when unserialized.

15.5 Automatically Creating and Updating PHP Include Files

There are times when you have some configuration data that your script needs to access, and the easiest way to store and use that is of course to just place it in a PHP file and include it. That way it is just part of your program, and the data is immediately ready to access.

Normally, this would involve you having to update that configuration file by hand whenever anything changes. This does not need to be the case, however, because PHP provides a function called `var_export()` that turns any PHP variable back into valid

PHP code. Therefore by applying this you could update your configuration data, saving it back to the file. You could even use this to store other forms of data as a quick and easy method as shown in Listing 15.5.1.

Listing 15.5.1   **Using** `var_export()` **to Save Data**

```php
<?php
// Include our file:
$data = array();
@include 'config.php';

// If we were asked to make changes, then do so:
if (count($_POST)) {
    // Just update/add the value to the 'data' array
    $data[$_POST['name']] = $_POST['val'];

    // Now save it to disk, create the 'full' file wrapping it in valid PHP
    $file = "<?php\n\$data = " . var_export($data, true) . ";\n?>\n";
    file_put_contents('config.php', $file, LOCK_EX);
}

// Echo out the current data
echo "<pre>Current Data is:\n\n";
print_r($data);
echo "</pre>\n";
?>
<form action="<?= $_SERVER['PHP_SELF'] ?>" method="post" name="myform">
<p>Key: <input type="text" name="name" value="" /></p>
<p>Value: <input type="text" name="val" value="" /></p>
<input value="Save Data" type="submit" />
</form>
```

As written, this is very simplistic and only inserts single-dimensional strings. However, you can see the basic concept. Any PHP data can be re-created/stored in this manner, allowing for PHP files that "rewrite themselves" and all the power (and danger) that comes with that.

16

Email

Email is the "killer app" of the Internet (though some may claim it is WWW). Amazing numbers of email messages get sent across the Internet every day. Inevitably, you will need to write code that deals with email. As is obvious to the most casual observer, email has two aspects: sending and receiving. In PHP, sending email is straightforward using the `mail()` function. Most of this chapter deals with formatting and sending mail. On the other hand, receiving and managing email is a much larger issue. The technical details of receiving email are well supported through the IMAP interface (see http://php.net/imap). However, the IMAP module is not part of the default installation and requires an external library that does have some installation constraints and therefore will not be covered in this book.

Quick Hits

▶ Send an email:

```
$success = mail($to, $subject, $message, $extra_headers);
```

This function sends an email to the specified recipients. Many examples in this chapter use `mail()`. Other mail headers, such as "From", "Cc", and "Bcc" can be specified in the optional parameter `$extra_headers`.

Full documentation: http://php.net/mail

▶ Make sure that lines of text are not too long for the mail standard:

```
$chunks = chunk_split($text);
```

When including attachments, for example, it is necessary to make sure that line lengths are less than 76 characters long. This function appropriately formats such information to fit the email standards.

Full documentation: http://php.net/chunk_split

▶ Encode/decode string in MIME base64 format:

```
$readyformail = base64_encode($attachment);

$attachment = base64_decode($fromemail);
```

To send binary data in email, these routines encode the data into a character-based format that will survive email transport.

Full documentation: http://php.net/base64_encode and http://php.net/base64_decode

16.1 Sending Email (Text/HTML/Dual Format/Inline Images/Attachments)

Today many different types of email get sent. Sometimes email contains file attachments, inline images, dual format (text/HTML), and so on. Sending each of these more complicated mail formats requires knowledge of how the MIME mail standard works. To understand how to send each variation that may exist on an email, we will start with the simplest examples and move to the more complicated.

To begin, you need to know how to send a basic text email message. This is accomplished through the use of the mail() command. In its most basic usage, you pass it a string of recipients, the subject, and the message to be sent. There is also a fourth parameter, which contains any additional mail headers that you want to specify. Listing 16.1.1 uses this just to specify whom the email is from and the software that sent it.

Listing 16.1.1   **Basic Use of the** mail() **Function**

```php
<?php
// Prepare by setting a timezone, mail() uses this.
date_default_timezone_set('America/New_York');

// Save some values to send in email, these might have come from any source:
$to = 'example@eliw.com';
$subject = 'A sample email - Text Only';

// Define the headers we want passed.  Note that they are separated by \r\n
$headers = "From: php@example.com\r\nX-Mailer: Custom PHP Script";

// Now the body of the message:
$body = "This is our sample email.\n\nHello World!\n\nThat's it for now.";

// Finally, send the email
mail($to, $subject, $body, $headers);
?>
```

As you can see, sending an email is basic and easy to accomplish. You can add more people to receive this email by either adding their addresses, comma separated, to the $to variable, or by adding cc: or bcc: headers.

Basic text email is fine, but more often these days we want to send HTML email. Now you can just set the body of the email to have HTML in it and add one additional header of Content-type: text/html and have it work. This causes problems, though, if someone is using a mail client that cannot understand HTML email. Therefore it is usually best to send any HTML email as dual format. This means providing both a text and an HTML version in the same email. The client can then choose which version to display. This is accomplished via stating a content type of multipart/alternative and giving a boundary string that denotes the different areas of the email, which in turn also specify their own content types (see Listing 16.1.2).

In these examples we are using \r\n as the line separator for mail headers so that these scripts will work from a Windows machine. If you are running this on a UNIX box, you can change those to \n.

Listing 16.1.2   **Sending a Simple HTML Mail**

```php
<?php
// Prepare by setting a timezone, mail() uses this.
date_default_timezone_set('America/New_York');

// Save some values to send an email, these might have come from any source:
$to = 'example@eliw.com';
$subject = 'A sample email - Dual Format';

// Create a boundary string.  It needs to be unique (not in the text) so ...
// We are going to use the sha1 algorithm to generate a 40 character string:
$sep = sha1(date('r', time()));

// Define the headers we want passed.  Note that they are separated by \r\n
$headers = "From: php@example.com\r\nX-Mailer: Custom PHP Script";

// Add in our content boundary, and mime type specification:
$headers .=
    "\r\nContent-Type: multipart/alternative; boundary=\"PHP-alt-{$sep}\"";

// The body of the message.  Use the separator with -- in front of it to
//  mark the beginning of each section, and then provide the content type.
//  A blank line beneath that will define the beginning of the content.
//  At the end finish with the separator again, but this time with a --
//  after it as well.
$body =<<<EOBODY
--PHP-alt-{$sep}
Content-Type: text/plain

This is our sample email message

Hello World!
```

Listing 16.1.2   **Continued**

```
That's it for now

--PHP-alt-{$sep}
Content-Type: text/html

<p>This is our sample email message</p>
<h2>Hello World!</h2>
<p>That's it for now.</p>

--PHP-alt-{$sep}--
EOBODY;

// Finally, send the email
mail($to, $subject, $body, $headers);
?>
```

Figure 16.1.1 shows schematically how the email is laid out. The important feature to note is that the content type of the message itself is sent as a mail header, while the content types of the individual components of the message are embedded in the message itself. As a general rule, the simpler versions of the email message (such as text) should be listed first, so that non–MIME compliant email readers will see them before potentially confusing complicated formats.

Basic HTML email is good; however, a few variations still can exist. One that we have not discussed yet is handling attachments. Attachments are files included in the email and typically are desired to be available whether they are read via text or HTML. To do this, we need to use the multipart/mixed MIME type that specifies that mixed types will be included in the email.

At the same time, however, we still want to include the alternate MIME type to give both a text and HTML version of the email. This is accomplished by embedding types within each other and using multiple different boundary separators. Because each part of a multiple MIME can specify its content type (such as text/plain), it can also choose to display a multipart type.

Hence in this situation, we will make the primary MIME type be multipart/mixed so that we can do an attachment or two. But inside it we will have a multipart/ alternative that will specify our two versions of the text. To actually do the included attachments, we will read in the data from the file, encode it into base64 so that it can survive the transport through email, and then include it specifying that it is an attachment. To make sure that it matches the MIME specifications we will use chunk_ split(), which breaks up the string into 76-character-long segments, placing a carriage return after each line. Listing 16.1.3 shows how all this is put together.

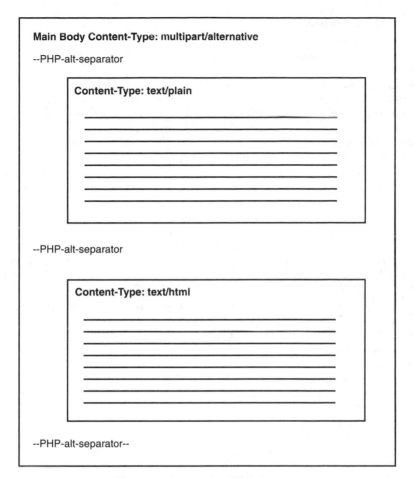

Figure 16.1.1   Basic HTML layout.

Listing 16.1.3 **HTML Email with an Attachement**

```php
<?php
// Prepare by setting a timezone, mail() uses this.
date_default_timezone_set('America/New_York');

// Save some values to send an email, these might have come from any source:
$to = 'example@eliw.com';
$subject = 'A sample email - Dual Format plus attachment';

// Create a boundary string.  It needs to be unique (not in the text) so ...
// We are going to use the sha1 algorithm to generate a 40 character string:
$sep = sha1(date('r', time()));
```

Listing 16.1.3 **Continued**

```
// Define the headers we want passed.
$headers = "From: php@example.com\r\nX-Mailer: Custom PHP Script";

// Add in our primary content boundary, and mime type specification:
$headers .=
    "\r\nContent-Type: multipart/alternative; boundary=\"PHP-alt-{$sep}\"";

// Read in our file attachment
$attachment = file_get_contents('attachment.zip');

// Base64 encode it so that the potentially binary file can safely be sent
// over email, which is a text based protocol.
$encoded = base64_encode($attachment);

// Now use chunk_split to automatically break this into lines that are at
//  most 76 characters wide.  This is needed to match the email protocol.
$attached = chunk_split($encoded);

// Now the body of the message.  Separate each original part (message from
//  attachments) with the first separator.  Then within that giving
//  alternatives with the second separator.
$body =<<<EOBODY
--PHP-mixed-{$sep}
Content-Type: multipart/alternative; boundary="PHP-alt-{$sep}"

--PHP-alt-{$sep}
Content-Type: text/plain

This is our sample email message

Hello World!

That's it for now

--PHP-alt-{$sep}
Content-Type: text/html

<p>This is our sample email message</p>
<h2>Hello World!</h2>
<p>That's it for now.</p>

--PHP-alt-{$sep}--

--PHP-mixed-{$sep}
Content-Type: application/zip; name="attachment.zip"
```

Listing 16.1.3 **Continued**

```
Content-Transfer-Encoding: base64
Content-Disposition: attachment

{$attached}
--PHP-mixed-{$sep}--
EOBODY;

// Finally, send the email
mail($to, $subject, $body, $headers);
?>
```

Figure 16.1.2 shows schematically how this message is laid out. We specified that we wanted `multipart/mixed`. We then specified that the first part of our mixed type was a `multipart/alternative` and continued just like in Listing 16.1.2. We then closed off that section and continued with our mixed type to include the attachment.

It could also be possible to embed an attachment block inside one of the alternative sections. This would have the effect of making the attachment accessible only to that display mode. In this way, for example, you could make an email that if viewed via HTML had no attachments, but via text would indeed have one.

As a related topic, nothing stops you from including references in your HTML to a remote site. This allows for things such as the inclusion of graphics. From the user's perspective, this is actually convenient because the graphics are not downloaded until the message is actually viewed. It also can allow for a graphic to change. A good use of this is a sales flyer. If the price of a product were a graphic, the graphic could be updated to reflect a change in price or to let the user know that the product is sold out without having to send out another email message.

There are also a number of disadvantages to referencing images instead of including them in the email. If your web server is down or connectivity is slow, the user may receive your email but none of the graphics. Worse, many email clients have begun blocking images from emails where the source is unknown to the client. Because the client has to make a connection to the server at the time of reading, the sender can garner information just like from a standard website. One nefarious use of this has been for spammers. They will send out thousands of emails with an HTML graphic in them and a unique code. If the user opens the HTML email, the unique code is sent to the spammer as part of the image request and then the spammer knows that he has discovered a valid email address.

Therefore, if you are including small graphics, you may want to imbed them into your email. Do not do this with large files because it will make for unwieldy emails. Embedding images is done in a similar way to attachments, by base64 encoding them. However, this time we use the mime type of `multipart/related` to specify that this "attachment" of sorts is actually related to the HTML message.

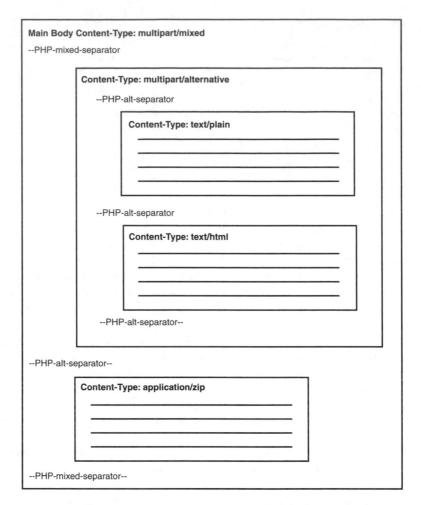

Figure 16.1.2   HTML mail layout with attachment.

Unlike an attachment, which is specified via the `Content-Disposition: attachment` line, the inline data is given a content ID. This content ID, specified such as `Content-ID: foo-bar-2`, allows for the HTML to embed the content via the command `cid: foo-bar-2`. Now using this, we can rewrite Listing 16.1.3 to also include an embedded graphic for the HTML, while still offering the attachments and a text version. This will of course require three different boundary separators, as well as the content ID that also needs to be unique. As shown in Listing 16.1.4, we are just going to generate the separator string once and append to it as needed to get our different strings.

Listing 16.1.4   **Using Embedded Images in HTML Email**

```php
<?php
// Prepare by setting a timezone, mail() uses this.
date_default_timezone_set('America/New_York');

// Save some values to send an email, these might have come from any source:
$to = 'example@eliw.com';
$subject = 'A sample email - Dual Format plus attachment plus inline';

// Create a boundary string.  It needs to be unique (not in the text) so ...
// We are going to use the sha1 algorithm to generate a 40 character string:
$sep = sha1(date('r', time()));

// Define the headers we want passed.
$headers = "From: php@example.com\r\nX-Mailer: Custom PHP Script";

// Add in our primary content boundary, and mime type specification:
$headers .=
    "\r\nContent-Type: multipart/mixed; boundary=\"PHP-mixed-{$sep}\"";

// Prepare our attachment file - Read it in, encode it and split it
$attached = chunk_split(base64_encode(file_get_contents('attachment.zip')));

// Also now prepare our inline image - Also read, encode, split:
$inline = chunk_split(base64_encode(file_get_contents('figure.gif')));

// Now the body of the message.
$body =<<<EOBODY
--PHP-mixed-{$sep}
Content-Type: multipart/alternative; boundary="PHP-alt-{$sep}"

--PHP-alt-{$sep}
Content-Type: text/plain

Hello Investors!

We sold 2 million units this quarter, and expect greater sales in the
next few months.  $300 of profit was earned per unit, making us the
most profitable company in the market today.

That's it for now.  Stay tuned for more announcements.

--PHP-alt-{$sep}
Content-Type: multipart/related; boundary="PHP-related-{$sep}"
```

Listing 16.1.4 **Continued**

```
--PHP-related-{$sep}
Content-Type: text/html

<h2>Hello Investors!</h2>
<p>You may wish to look at the excellent numbers
 that we are generating:<br />
<img src="cid:PHP-CID-{$sep}" /></p>
<p>That's it for now.  Stay tuned for more announcements.</p>

--PHP-related-{$sep}
Content-Type: image/gif
Content-Transfer-Encoding: base64
Content-ID: <PHP-CID-{$sep}>

{$inline}
--PHP-related-{$sep}--

--PHP-alt-{$sep}--

--PHP-mixed-{$sep}
Content-Type: application/zip; name="attachment.zip"
Content-Transfer-Encoding: base64
Content-Disposition: attachment

{$attached}
--PHP-mixed-{$sep}--
EOBODY;

// Finally, send the email
mail($to, $subject, $body, $headers);
?>
```

The ordering of the nested separators is important. The ordering needs to logically "make sense" to the client so that the client can understand how it is structured and display all the information. So in this case, we have nested the levels as shown in Figure 16.1.3.

As illustrated, we are stating that we have a mixed email with two parts: an "alternative," and an attachment. Then within the alternative, there are two options: the plain text, and a "related" block. The related block has HTML in it, with an imbedded image. It all fits together logically and can be understood by the browser.

When creating multipart messages, you need to pay extra attention to the carriage returns that you use. Each boundary requires a carriage return before and after it. This means that if you have two separators right after each other, you need a blank line between them. Otherwise, there is only one carriage return trying to fill the roles of both "ending return" to the first separator and "opening return" to the latter one. This cannot be, and the client will get confused. In general, extra carriage returns before a separator should not cause any problems. Extra carriage returns after a separator and before any header tags, however, are not allowed.

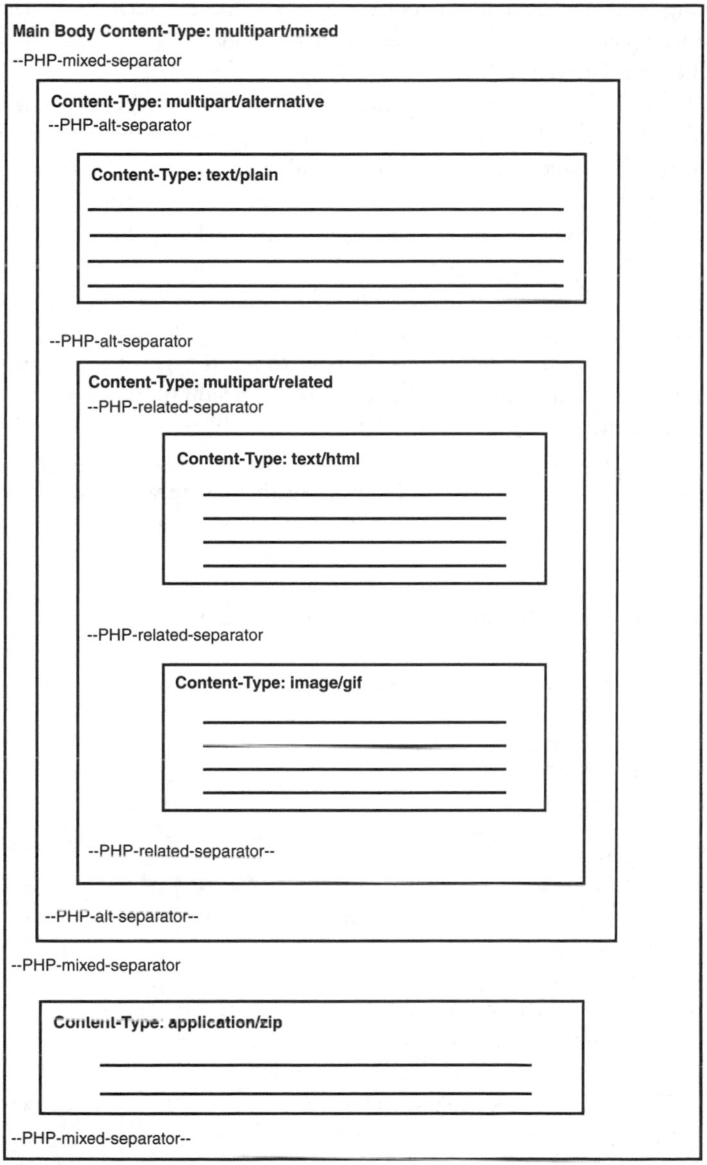

Figure 16.1.3   HTML mail layout with attachment and embedded image.

16.2 Determining Whether an Email Account Exists

A common web application is having users sign up for some service. Often you want to confirm whether the given email truly exists. Realistically, there is only one accurate way of determining whether an email account exists and is active. You must actually send an email to the user and require that the user either respond to it or click a link in it to verify that the user received the email.

Using a link is the better solution because automatic responders could take care of responding to your query. But most of the time, a real person clicks the link. All you need to do is include some information in that link that will identify who the user is. For example, when someone first enters an email address on a web page, the address is stored in a table along with a uniquely generated number. This number is then passed back on the link.

The example in this section uses a simpler solution, not relying on any data storage in the first place. When given the email address, we will manipulate it in various ways before returning it. Then on returning to the confirmation page, the manipulations are reversed to see whether the email is valid. This will be accomplished via a basic mechanism. We will take the email given to us and create a hash value from it, in this case using md5(). However, we will first prepend a value to the string before creating the hash. This way, someone would have to know what that string was to duplicate the hash. First, Listing 16.2.1 creates a web page that takes the user's email address and generates the email.

Listing 16.2.1 **Creating an Email with a Confirmation Link**

```php
<?php
// If we had a POST element called 'email', then we need to prep and send:
if (isset($_POST['email'])) {
    // Make sure it wasn't blank:
    $email = trim($_POST['email']);
    if ($email) {
        // Prepare by setting a timezone, mail() uses this.
        date_default_timezone_set('America/New_York');

        // Take the address given, prepend a magic string, and hash it:
        $hashed = md5('magic_string' . $email);

        // Make the email address ready to be sent via, well, email:
        $prepped = urlencode($email);

        // Generate the email message that these people need to verify:
        // For simplicity, doing this as pure text email at this point.
        mail($email, 'Please verify your email address', "
Someone has entered your email address into our form.
```

Listing 16.2.1 **Continued**

```
If it was you, and you wish to verify your address, please click the
following link:
http://example.com/verify.php?e={$prepped}&h={$hashed}
", 'From: php@example.com');

        // Let them know that this email is sent.
        echo "
<p>A verification email has been sent to {$email},
 please following the instructions included in it.</p>
";
    }
}
?>
<form action="<?= $_SERVER['PHP_SELF'] ?>" method="post" name="f1">
<p>What is your email address? <input name="email" type="text" /></p>
<p><input type="submit" /></p>
</form>
```

Now Listing 16.2.2 accepts the data from this link and attempts to reverse engineer the hash provided for it.

Listing 16.2.2 **Verifying an Email Confirmation—Filename: verify.php**

```
<?php
// This is the verification script
// We need to check if we got the appropriate fields
if (isset($_GET['e']) && isset($_GET['h'])) {
    // Attempt to create an identical hash using the same magic string
    $hashed = md5('magic_string' . $_GET['e']);

    // If the new hash equals what was passed in
    if ($hashed == $_GET['h']) {
        // They have passed muster.  Let them know this.  In a real
        //  application you would need to save this fact and continue in
        //  the process at this point.
        echo "<p>Your email has been validated.<p>\n";
    } else {
        // It didn't pass.
        echo "<p>Your email failed it's validation test.<p>\n";
    }
} else {
    echo "<p>Invalid page access!<p>\n";
}
?>
```

As it stands this is a simple algorithm. The email address is visible as part of the link, and it is a simple hash algorithm. Therefore if someone really wanted to he might be able to crack this. It would take some effort, though, and therefore this is a good solution for some basic authentication. Again, if more complicated methods are desired, storing data in a database and providing only a unique, random key to the client will give you the better solution that you need.

16.3 Creating a Mass Email Mailer

There are times when you may need to send out an email to many people. Perhaps your company sends out a newsletter to all its subscribers. In these cases you don't want to perform a loop of multiple calls to mail() because this is inefficient. Each call to mail() generates a separate call to sendmail on UNIX or a separate connection to an SMTP server on Windows.

There are two potential ways to handle this. Given that in these cases you usually don't want everyone's email address to appear in the To field, this limits the choices. If your list isn't too unwieldy, one simple option is to actually have a fake "to" address that the email is nominally sent to. This address would be yourself or preferably a mailing list type address that you tell your mail server to just ignore emails to such as mailing-list@example.com. Then include everyone else as a Bcc onto this message. The mail server will handle this Bcc, parsing it and ensuring that everyone on the list receives a copy. Our mass email is presented in Listing 16.3.1

Listing 16.3.1   **Mass Emailing by Using Bcc**

```php
<?php
// Prepare by setting a timezone, mail() uses this.
date_default_timezone_set('America/New_York');

// Create an array of email addresses that we are going to send to every
//   time this script is called.
$addresses = array('example@eliw.com', 'php@example.com',
    'crossbow@example.com', 'eliwhite@example.com',
    'SiegfriedFaust@example.com');

// Now in preparation for sending, convert all of these into a BCC list:
$list = implode(',', $addresses);

// Send the email to the 'dummy' address:
mail('mailing-list@example.com', 'Our next Newsletter Edition', "
    This is our next edition of our Newsletter.  Well, I guess
that about sums it up.  Not really much to say right now.
", "From: mailing-list@example.com\r\nBcc: {$list}");
?>
```

Again, although this works, the efficiency depends on the server and method by which the server handles this. The next option would be to handle this yourself. You can write code that would contact your local SMTP server directly and do the equivalent of the script presented in Listing 16.3.1, issuing many RCPT TO commands to send the message to many people but making the actual To header be something different.

However, the real power in connecting directly to the SMTP server is that you can make it appear that the message was sent solely to that specific user. This means it will not get picked up by some of the rudimentary spam filters. It also allows you to customize each message to the user efficiently, making only one connection to the SMTP server and pushing multiple emails through versus making numerous calls to mail(), each of which spawns a new connection. Listing 16.3.2. creates a function that does this for us. Taking an array of email addresses, the function makes it appear that each email is sent to only that user. It also inserts a footer into each message that includes the email address it was sent to. It would be easy to modify the function to make it customize other parts of the message itself. The function connects directly to the SMTP server, using the PHP Streams functionality, as explored in Section 13.6, "Using Sockets to Connect to an Internet Server," and Section 13.7, "Creating Your Own Basic Web Server," of Chapter 13, "Web Services and Other Protocols."

Listing 16.3.2 **Mass Emailing by Connecting Directly to an SMTP Server—Filename: mass_email.php**

```php
<?php
// Prepare by setting a timezone, mail() uses this.
date_default_timezone_set('America/New_York');

// A function that takes an array of email addresses, and a message to send.
//  and connects to a SMTP server, also specified, to deliver the content.
function mass_email($emails, $from, $subj, $message,
        $smtp, $moreheaders = '') {
  // First order of business is to connect to the SMTP server - port 25:
  if (!($sp = stream_socket_client("tcp://{$smtp}:25", $err_num,
        $err_string))) {
     exit("ERROR: Failed to connect - {$err_num} - {$err_string}\n");
  }

  // Read the response, we should be welcomed with a 220 response
  _check_response(fgets($sp), '220');

  // Now, be friendly and say hello .. Note we are using the server
  //  specified name ... If this is run from the command line, this will
  //  not exist and will need set specifically in some other fashion:
  $host = isset($_SERVER['HTTP_HOST'])
      ? $_SERVER['HTTP_HOST'] : 'example.com';
  fputs($sp, "HELO {$host}\n");
```

Listing 16.3.2   **Continued**

```php
    // And make sure that they claim this was ok (250 response)
    _check_response(fgets($sp), '250');

    // Now we can start looping, sending an email to each ...
    foreach ($emails as $e) {
        // Allow ourselves 10 seconds to complete this one email:
        set_time_limit(20);

        // Say who the email is from:
        fputs($sp, "MAIL FROM: {$from}\n");
        _check_response(fgets($sp), '250');

        // Now who is the email to:
        fputs($sp, "RCPT TO: {$e}\n");
        // In this case, a 'bad' response is ok.  It means they don't accept
        //  that particular email address as valid, so skip, and move on:
        if (_check_response(fgets($sp), '250', false)) {
            // Ok, we made it this far.  Prepare for the body
            fputs($sp, "DATA\n");
            _check_response(fgets($sp), '354');

            // Send headers, include the 'moreheaders' parameter if provided
            fputs($sp, "To: {$e}\nFrom: {$from}\nSubject: " .
                "{$subj}\n{$moreheaders}\n\n");

            // Now we can send the body:
            fputs($sp, $message);

            // And our custom footer
            fputs($sp, "\n\n-- Sent to: {$e} by the " .
                "PHP 5 in Practice Mass Mailer\n");

            // Now close the data with a single period on a line:
            fputs($sp, ".\n");
            _check_response(fgets($sp), '250');
        } else {
            // If we got here the recipient was bad.
            //  So reset our state to start fresh
            fputs($sp, "RSET\n");
            _check_response(fgets($sp), '250');
        }
    }

    // Close the connection, we are done!
    fputs($sp, "QUIT\n");
    fclose($sp);
```

Listing 16.3.2 **Continued**

```php
    // Before exiting, reset the time limit to its original value:
    set_time_limit(ini_get('max_execution_time'));
}


// A small utility function that we will use to check the response from the
//  server:  It checks response against the expected response.  If bail is
//  set to true, it was a BAD error and exits out.  Otherwise it just
//  returns false.
function _check_response($response, $expected, $bail = true) {
    // Compare the response to what was expected:
    if (strncmp($response, $expected, strlen($expected)) != 0) {
        // If we were told to bail, do so:
        if ($bail) {
            exit("ERROR: Bad Response\nExpected: {$expected}
Received: {$response}");
        } else {
            // Just return false so this can be handled
            return false;
        }
    }

    // If we made it here, return true
    return true;
}
?>
```

Listing 16.3.3 creates a short script that mass emails all these people with the custom-looking emails.

Listing 16.3.3 **Mass Email with Customized Messages**

```php
<?php
// Require the library:
require_once 'mass_email.php';

// Create an array of email addresses that we are going to send to every
//  time this script is called.
$addresses = array('example@eliw.com', 'php@example.com',
    'crosshow@example.com', 'eliwhite@example.com',
    'SiegfriedFaust@example.com');

// Send that mass email to everyone!
mass_email($addresses, 'The List <list@example.com>',
    'Our next Newsletter Edition', "
```

Listing 16.3.3 **Continued**

```
   This is our next edition of our Newsletter.  Well, I guess
that about sums it up.  Not really much to say right now.
", 'mail.example.com');
?>
```

You need to be aware of a few things in an application using this software as is. Currently, the script handles bad email addresses gracefully, at least it attempts to. If the server reports that an email address is not acceptable, the address is skipped and the next address is attempted. This is important if you have a large list with one bad email in the middle of it.

Given that we can detect this (as long as the SMTP server actually reports it), you could keep a count and automatically generate a report of failed addresses. Typically a server is going to fail only addresses that it somehow knows about, such as local accounts or perhaps blocked domains.

You may also find it worthwhile to note the use of set_time_limit() throughout the script. Essentially, it can take a while for the SMTP server to accept each email, perhaps a few seconds on a normal server or a bit longer on a busier server. Because of this, regular PHP timeouts may occur if you are sending to large lists. As written, the script gives itself 20 seconds for each email to complete and when done resets the time limit to handle the next address. If the SMTP server is too slow, this limit might need to be made larger to prevent unnecessary timeouts. Also, this function does not fail gracefully at all. It will completely stop what it is doing, leaving potentially a large portion of the list unprocessed. If this was a service that you relied on, it could be worthwhile to track what addresses were properly sent to so that the others could be attempted at a later time.

Listing 16.3.3 demonstrates a simple example of how to deal with an SMTP server. For more information about how SMTP works, see http://www.faqs.org/rfcs/rfc2821.

16.4 Implementing Basic Mailing List Software

Many open source or freeware mailing list management software programs are available right now. However, they all are complicated and full of features. Normally this is a good thing; however, at times a simple solution is best. What if, for example, you just needed to maintain a small mailing list for a group of friends?

A small set of PHP scripts using the mass email function of Listing 16.3.2 can in fact handle this for you. There is only one requirement to using it: You need to decide how to integrate it into your email system.

As currently written, Listing 16.4.1 wants to receive a full email (header and body) as standard input (stdin). It parses the header for certain lines, throws the rest away, and then sends copies out to everyone on the mailing list. This can be triggered in many different ways. You could have an email client reading email from the account call this script for each new message. On most UNIX systems you can create an extra account for the mailing list and have a `.forward` file that sends all email into this program. You could directly interface it with the mail server itself. You might even choose to just run this from the command line, entering the email from the command line and ending in Ctrl+D. Whatever solution you want to use, you need to discover the specifics of how exactly to enable it through the software you want to use.

In the end, what needs done is the same. Send the email message to the script as stdin, and the script will do the rest.

Listing 16.4.1 **Mail List Application**

```php
<?php
// Require the mass mailing library:
require_once 'mass_email.php';

// Create an array of email addresses of our subscribers.
// Create an array of email addresses of our subscribers.
$subscribers = array('example@eliw.com', 'php@example.com',
    'crossbow@example.com', 'eliwhite@example.com',
    'SiegfriedFaust@example.com', 'hyper@example.com');

// Now, first of all, the entire email (header/body) should be waiting
// for us as stdin.  So read it all into memory so we can process it.
$msg = file_get_contents('php://stdin');

// Now, we need to separate the header from the body, look for the first
// double line break to detect this - look for the Unix method: \n\n
// and the Windows style of \r\n for each break.
list($head, $body) = preg_split("/\n\n|[\r\n][\r\n]|[\r\n][\r\n]/", $msg, 2);

// Now there are various parts of the header that we need to know.
// It will be easier to parse each of these out of the header if we have
// separate lines, so split it as such:
$headlines = explode("\n", $head);

// Now, set some default values in case we can't determine some of these:
$from = 'familylist@example.com';
$subject = '[No Subject]';

// Now, loop through each header line - Save our data, and KILL the line.
foreach ($headlines as $key => $line) {
    // If this is 'from'
    if (strncasecmp($line, 'From:', 5) === 0) {
        // snag the From and store it:
        $from = trim(substr($line, 5));

        // Now destroy this one:
        unset($headlines[$key]);
    }
```

Listing 16.4.1   **Continued**

```php
        // Else if this is the Subject
        elseif (strncasecmp($line, 'Subject:', 8) === 0) {
            // Grab the subject line
            $subject = trim(substr($line, 8));

            // Now destroy the original.
            unset($headlines[$key]);
        }
    }
}

// We are read to rebroadcast this email to everyone with a few changes.
// We are going to leave the 'From', the same, but set a Sender: of the list
// address so that it is obvious that this was sent to/from the list.
// Also add a prefix to the subject so people know that it came from a list:
// Attempt to keep all other headers intact!

// Add in the Sender header to the line listing:
$headlines[] = 'Sender: familylist@example.com';

// Send that mass email to everyone!
mass_email($subscribers, $from, '[Family] ' . $subject,
    $body, 'mail.example.com',    implode("\n", $headlines) );
?>
```

Now of course you probably wouldn't want to have to edit this script each time you wanted to add someone to the mailing list. It would be worthwhile therefore to use some of the solutions from Chapter 14, "Relational Databases," or Chapter 15, "Other Data Storage Methods," to actually store the data in a separate location and have a web front-end that allows you to edit the list of who receives email.

Also, all mailing list software is different in exactly how it works. Each has its own method of handling messages and manipulating headers. Because this is a custom system and doesn't need to be generically powerful, you can make it do just exactly what you want it to do, and nothing more.

16.5 Protecting Email Addresses from Spam Collectors

Many spammers today use harvesting software that scours websites looking for email addresses on web pages. Once found, spammers start sending spam to these addresses. It is therefore beneficial to find some way to block them from doing this. Many techniques on how to do this are described on the Web—from basic methods such as adding the text "NOSPAM" into your email and hoping that human beings understand to remove it, to much more complex methods.

A standard tactic that we will explore here is to use JavaScript. Because most crawlers are not going to bother to execute any JavaScript on the page before trying to look for email addresses, this gives us a tool. We can print the link via JavaScript so that it isn't truly part of the page. This isn't enough though because the email address would still be visible in the JavaScript code.

The solution therefore is to convert the entire link into ASCII codes, save them in a JavaScript array, and then use JavaScript to turn it back into regular HTML. The only way that a script scanning the page would ever figure this out is if it does have a JavaScript engine in it and executes the page.

Listing 16.5.1 is a PHP function that generates the JavaScript automatically, making it easy to use.

Listing 16.5.1 **Generating Email Address in the Browser**

```php
<?php
// A function that will protect email addreses, by generating JavaScript,
//  which will in turn generate the Email Link!
function write_protected_email($address) {
    // Generate the full link:
    $link = "<a href=\"mailto:{$address}\">{$address}</a>";

    // Loop through the string, creating an array of codes:
    $codes = array();
    for ($i = 0; $i < strlen($link); $i++) {
        // Use 'ord' to convert the character to it's ascii value
        $codes[] = ord($link{$i});
    }

    // Ok, now echo out the JavaScript needed to recreate.
    // Essentially is just the array, and a loop to print it out:
    // Make the array first:
    $outputarray = implode(',', $codes);

    // Now echo it and we are done.
    echo "
<script>
var datapoints = new Array({$outputarray});
for (var i = 0; i < datapoints.length; i++)
  { document.write(String.fromCharCode(datapoints[i])); }
</script>
";
}

// Test this to see if it works:
write_protected_email('Francesca_Angelo@example.com');
?>
```

16.6 Creating a Watchdog Process to Send Email If a Web Page Changes

There are various useful reasons to be alerted when a web page changes, and the easiest way to be notified is via email. For example, you may want to know if the home page on your personal website changes. Why? So that if you know you didn't make the change that someone has recently hacked your site and you need to do something about it.

Similarly you may want to know when a page on a remote website changes. Perhaps it is a shopping page that is currently out of stock of the item you want, and you want to know immediately when the item is back in stock. It may even just be your favorite website that you visit often, and you want to know when something new exists.

Checking pages for modifications is fairly simple; however, there are a few things to take into account. First, you might think that you could just request the HTTP headers via the function get_headers() and look at the last modified time. The problem is that this is often not provided for dynamic web pages, and, even when it is provided, it cannot be trusted. Therefore, you really need to download the entire web page to check against.

Second, understand that there are two approved ways of going about this. One is to create a script that does a single check to see whether the page has changed since the script was last run. This script can then be fired off at an interval of your choice, via your operating system's scheduling mechanism (crontab on UNIX, Scheduled Tasks on Windows). The other option is to make a program that runs forever (until manually killed). It can loop, sleeping for an appropriate amount of time in between checks of the website. This can be more convenient if you just need to occasionally check a remote website and not do so until the end of time. It also, of course, is usable even if you do not have access to the scheduling facilities of the machine you are on.

Listing 16.6.1 is written as a command-line application, taking the URL to check, the email address to send notices to, and the number of seconds to wait between requests as arguments. It will run until manually killed. Making a scheduled version would require saving the downloaded web page to a file and only doing the loop in this program once.

Listing 16.6.1 **Page Checking**

```php
<?php
// This program will run 'forever' checking the status of a provided webpage

// Prepare by setting a timezone, mail() uses this.
date_default_timezone_set('America/New_York');

// Ensure that the email, URL, and seconds were provided:
if ($argc < 4) {
    exit("Proper Usage: {$_SERVER['PHP_SELF']} <email> <url> <frequency>");
}
```

Listing 16.6.1   **Continued**

```php
// We have the right number of parameters, let's assume they are correct:
$email = $argv[1];
$url = $argv[2];
$seconds = $argv[3];

// Make sure that we don't timeout:
set_time_limit(0);

// We need to do an initial grab of the URL:
$saved = @file_get_contents($url);

// Now, loop forever:
while (true) {
    // Sleep for X seconds before trying to access the page again:
    sleep($seconds);

    // Ok, get a new copy of the page:
    $new = @file_get_contents($url);

    // Compare them to see if there is any difference:
    if ($saved !== $new) {
        // The page changed!  First of all, save the 'new' as the 'saved'
        $saved = $new;

        // Now time to send that email!
        mail($email, "Page Changed - {$url}", "
The URL that I was told to watch:
{$url}

Appears to have changed.  I thought you might want to know that.

Your friend,
Automatic URL Watcher Robot
", "From: {$email}");
    }
}
?>
```

One enhancement that might be worth making to this script is the capability for it to detect a failed connection and not consider that a "change" to the website. As currently written, if the web server went down for just a few minutes, you would get two email messages. One would claim a change when it went down, and another when it came back up. Another useful enhancement would be to have the script report what the differences were that caused the alert. Such a report could be generated by either by the UNIX diff application, or by the script found in Listing 8.8.1, in Chapter 8, "Files and Directories."

17

XML

IT'S ALL YOU HEAR ABOUT THESE DAYS: XML—Extensible Markup Language. In over-simplified terms, XML is basically a syntax that allows for the exchange of textual information between applications. The information is arranged in a treelike structure that can be represented by PHP objects or accessed through Document Object Model (DOM) functions. Before proceeding on to PHP's resources for utilizing XML, a brief introduction to the syntax will be presented. For more information about XML and the technologies built on it, see http://www.w3.org/XML/.

Listing 17.0.1 is an XML document describing a contact list. Most of the rest of the chapter uses this XML document.

Listing 17.0.1 Basic XML Example: Contact List Description—Filename: contacts.xml

```
<?xml version='1.0' ?>
<contacts>
  <contact idx="37">
    <name>Ramsey White II</name>
    <category>Family</category>
    <phone type="home">301-555-1212</phone>
    <meta id="x634724" />
  </contact>
  <contact idx="42">
    <name>Stratis Kakadelis</name>
    <category>Friends</category>
    <phone type="home">240-555-1212</phone>
    <phone type="work">410-555-7676</phone>
    <email>skak@example.com</email>
    <meta id="y49302" />
  </contact>
  <contact idx="57">
    <name>Kelly Williamson</name>
    <category>Friends</category>
```

Listing 17.0.1 **Continued**

```
    <phone type="cell">443-555-9999</phone>
    <email>kwill@example.com</email>
    <email>dynky@tech.example.com</email>
    <meta id="w4r302" />
  </contact>
</contacts>
```

All XML documents must start with a line: `<?xml version='1.0' ?>`. This tag identifies the type of document that will follow, an XML document, and what version of the XML standard it is compliant with, in this case version 1.0. The rest of the document is made up of tags that are words surrounded by "<" and ">". Tags come in two forms: with values and without values. A tag with a value has the form `<tagname>value</tagname>`. The first tag is usually referred to as the *opening tag* while the matching tag after the value is called the *closing tag*. Note the forward slash, "/", in the closing tag. The value can be text or any number of other tags. In Listing 17.0.1, the value of the `<contacts>` tag is essentially the whole of the document. For a tag without a value, the syntax is simply `<tag />`. There is no closing tag; instead the tag itself has the forward slash as part of its syntax.

Tags can also have attributes. Attributes are defined as part of the tag as follows: `<tagname attribute="attributevalue">`. Both types of tags can have attributes, and a single tag can have any number of attributes assigned to it. In Listing 17.0.1, the tag `<phone>` has an attribute `type` defined with it.

As previously stated, a value of a tag can have other tags within it. These nested tags are called the *children tags* while the tag itself is the *parent tag* of the children. All XML documents must have a single parent tag that surrounds all the other content. In Listing 17.0.1, the topmost, or root, tag is called `<contacts>`.

> **Note**
>
> Now is a good time to remind you of the most important aspect of XML: XML is solely a syntax standard. The tag names and attributes associated with any tag are completely arbitrary. Tags have no meaning other than that attached to them by the developer of a particular XML document. XML is simply a method on which other standards can be defined using a common language. The most common example of this is XHTML. XHTML uses the XML syntax to define a document structure that web browsers understand. Another example, RSS feeds, is discussed in Section 17.5, "Creating an RSS File," and Section 17.6, "Creating an RSS Display Script for Websites," later in the chapter. The subject of defining and validating XML-based documents is discussed in Section 17.3, "Validating an XML document."

Quick Hits

▶ Read an XML file into an object variable:

```
$xml = simplexml_load_file($xmlfile);
```

This function returns an object with the same logical structure as represented by the XML file.

Full documentation: http://php.net/simplexml

▶ Read an XML file into a DOM object:

```
$dom = new DOMDocument();

$dom->load($filename);
```

This pair of functions creates a DOM object and then loads an XML file into the object structure.

Full documentation: http://php.net/dom

17.1 Parsing an XML File to Retrieve Data

PHP actually provides a number of different ways to access the data from an XML document. The XML, XMLReader, and DOM XML extensions all offer different unique ways in which to navigate through an XML document. Each has its own benefits and drawbacks, and is worth investigating. However, PHP 5 adds another extension, known as SimpleXML. This extension, as it sounds, makes it simple to access XML data and therefore will be the manner this book uses.

SimpleXML at its heart is one of two functions: `simplexml_load_string()`, which operates on an XML document already saved into a PHP variable, and `simplexml_load_file()`, which does the same from a file. Upon calling one of these functions SimpleXML returns an object that replicates the XML document. Each XML tag becomes a property of the object, nested accordingly. Perhaps the best way to illustrate this is via an example. Let's use the XML data file from Listing 17.0.1, which might be from a basic contact management system. Once parsed through SimpleXML, you can directly access any particular part of this data. Looking at Listing 17.1.1 it is evident how easy it would be to actually access this data once in this structure.

Listing 17.1.1 **Reading XML Files with SimpleXML**

```php
<?php
// Using SimpleXML, read the file into memory:
$xml = simplexml_load_file('contacts.xml');

// Let's print out a formatted version of some of this contact data:
// Start with an ordered list:
echo "<ol>\n";

// Loop over each contact:
foreach ($xml->contact as $c) {
```

Listing 17.1.1 **Continued**

```
    // Print their name:
    echo '<li>' . $c->name;

    // Now start an Unordered list for their phone numbers:
    echo '<ul>';

    // Loop over every phone number for this person:
    foreach ($c->phone as $p) {
        // Echo out a line including the type of number:
        // The attribute will be accesible as if it were an assoc array
        // entry.  Using the entry itself, will echo it's value.
        echo '<li>', ucfirst($p['type']), ': ', $p, '</li>';
    }

    // Close off the phone list:
    echo "</ul></li>\n";
}
?>
```

17.2 Performing Searches Through XML with XPath

Directly accessing and traversing through an XML document, as described in Listing 17.1.1, is handy when you know the exact format and ordering of the document in question. Often you may be presented with a document that has varying specifications. The data that you want to access might exist under multiple tags. Or you simply may have a large XML document and know that you want only one small piece of data from it.

In these cases, traversing the document tree may not be the best use of your time. Instead, you want to search through the document for the exact item (or items) that you need. This capability is available also through the SimpleXML extension. Within it, you can perform XPath searches. XPath is a standard for performing these kinds of searches through XML.

You perform a search via `xpath('searchstring')`. The basic format of an XPath search is of the form: "/x/y/z", where x, y, and z are nested XML tags, such as of the form: <x><y><z/></y></x>. Starting the XPath with a "/" as we did means that "x" had to be at the top level. Had that been left off, such as in "x/y/z", it would match that combination of elements at any depth in the XML structure.

Some common XPath queries are explained in the following list; these different queries can be combined in infinite combinations to generate powerful searches:

- x—Matches any tag named x
- x/y—Matches any tag named y, directly contained in a tag named x

- x/y/..—Similar to the preceding item but actually matches and returns tag x, instead of tag y

- x//y—Matches any tag named y that is a descendant of a tag named x (any number of levels deep)

- x[5]—Matches the fifth tag named x

- x[last()]—Matches the last tag named x

- x[@att]—Matches any tag named x, with an attribute named att

- x[@att="val"]—Matches any tag named x, with an attribute named att that has the value "val"

Many more options exist; these are just the most common. To discover more about XPath and all its various options, read the W3C's specification for XPath, found at http://www.w3.org/TR/xpath.

Listing 17.2.1 explores a few of these searches on the XML file from Listing 17.0.1.

Listing 17.2.1   **Example Searches of an XML Document**

```php
<?php
// Using SimpleXML, read the file into memory:
$xml = simplexml_load_file('contacts.xml');

// Xpath search to find all 'meta' tags no matter what the depth:
$meta = $xml->xpath('//meta');

// Loop over them and output their IDs
foreach ($meta as $m) {
    echo "Meta - {$m['id']}<br />\n";
}

// Find all email tags within a contact tag from the root of the XML document:
$email = $xml->xpath('/contacts/contact/email');

// Loop over them and output the email addreses:
foreach ($email as $e) {
    echo "Email - {$e}<br />\n";
}

// Finally, find any contact who has a cellphone number
$cell = $xml->xpath('contact/phone[@type="cell"]/..');

// Loop over them and output their names:
foreach ($cell as $c) {
    echo "Cell Contact - {$c->name}<br />\n";
}
?>
```

17.3 Validating an XML Document

As shown in the previous examples, it is important that you understand the structure of an XML document to properly process it. This is why the concept of XML validation exists. You can use various proto-languages to describe the allowable contents of an XML document. You can then take any XML document that is supposed to be of that format and verify that it in fact is.

Any commercial vendor or third-party application you are working with that provides an XML document will probably also provide a validation scheme as well. This way you can be sure that the data you receive (perhaps even the data that you send out) is valid before anything else is done with it.

The three main languages used to describe the contents of an XML file are DTD, Xml Schema, and RelaxNG. DTD was the original standard for doing this inherited from XML's SGML roots. Over the years it has become outdated and cannot fully work with all current XML capabilities (such as namespaces). Because of this we will not cover it in any more detail; however, know that you can validate against it in a similar fashion to the other ones shown in this chapter with the `validate()` method.

XML Schema is the new format provided by the W3C and is the most commonly used one today. It also happens to be in XML format, thereby using XML to describe XML. The third solution is RelaxNG, which is a standard developed by the OASIS organization in response to XML Schema. The claim was that XML Schema was more complicated than it needed to be and therefore a simpler language was needed. RelaxNG is catching on in popularity.

> **Note**
>
> Learning how to write in these validation languages is beyond the scope of this book and could be the topic of a book in itself. If you want to learn more about how to use these languages, visit the following websites:
>
> - XML Schema—http://www.w3.org/XML/Schema
> - RelaxNG—http://www.relaxng.org/
>
> Also, if you don't want to write your own and would rather have software do it for you, a number of packages will attempt to do that for you. One of the more popular of which is Trang, which can take an XML file and generate Schema, RelaxNG, or DTDs for you; see the website: http://thaiopensource.com/relaxng/trang.html.

PHP makes doing validation easy; however, you must use the DOM module to accomplish this. After loading an XML file into memory via creating a new `DOMDocument` object and then loading the file via `load()`, you can quickly validate. At that point a call can be made to either `relaxNGValidate()` or `schemaValidate()` passing them the filename (or URL) of a validation document. These will simply return a true or false, letting you know whether the validation was successful. If false is returned, PHP warnings will be generated that contain the errors that were found.

Following are a couple of sample validation documents designed for the test XML in Listing 17.0.1. First Listing 17.3.1 presents an example written in RelaxNG.

Listing 17.3.1   **A RelaxNG Document Defining a Contacts XML File—Filename: contacts.rng**

```
<?xml version="1.0" encoding="UTF-8"?>
<grammar ns="" xmlns="http://relaxng.org/ns/structure/1.0"
 datatypeLibrary="http://www.w3.org/2001/XMLSchema-datatypes">
  <start>
    <element name="contacts">
      <oneOrMore>
        <element name="contact">
          <attribute name="idx"><data type="integer"/></attribute>
          <element name="name"><text/></element>
          <element name="category"><text/></element>
          <zeroOrMore>
            <element name="phone">
              <attribute name="type"><text/></attribute>
              <text/>
            </element>
          </zeroOrMore>
          <zeroOrMore>
            <element name="email"><text/></element>
          </zeroOrMore>
          <element name="meta">
            <attribute name="id"><text/></attribute>
          </element>
        </element>
      </oneOrMore>
    </element>
  </start>
</grammar>
```

Listing 17.3.2 presents an example of what this same code would look like as an XML Schema.

Listing 17.3.2   **An XML Schema Document Defining a Contacts XML File—contacts.xsd**

```
<?xml version="1.0" encoding="UTF-8"?>
<xs:schema xmlns:xs="http://www.w3.org/2001/XMLSchema"
    elementFormDefault="qualified">
  <xs:element name="contacts" type="contactsType"/>
  <xs:complexType name="contactsType">
    <xs:sequence>
      <xs:element maxOccurs="unbounded" name="contact" type="contactType"/>
```

Listing 17.3.2 **Continued**

```
      </xs:sequence>
    </xs:complexType>
    <xs:complexType name="contactType">
      <xs:sequence>
        <xs:element name="name" type="xs:string"/>
        <xs:element name="category" type="xs:string"/>
        <xs:element name="phone" type="phoneType"
            minOccurs="0" maxOccurs="unbounded"/>
        <xs:element name="email" type="xs:string"
            minOccurs="0" maxOccurs="unbounded"/>
        <xs:element name="meta" type="metaType"/>
      </xs:sequence>
      <xs:attribute name="idx" use="required" type="xs:integer"/>
    </xs:complexType>
    <xs:complexType name="metaType">
      <xs:attribute name="id" use="required" type="xs:string"/>
    </xs:complexType>
    <xs:complexType name="phoneType">
      <xs:simpleContent>
        <xs:extension base="xs:string">
          <xs:attribute name="type" use="required" type="xs:string"/>
        </xs:extension>
      </xs:simpleContent>
    </xs:complexType>
</xs:schema>
```

Now that we have these files, we can run just a few lines of code to attempt to validate them against our XML document (see Listing 17.3.3). If everything is written correctly, it should pass!

Listing 17.3.3 **Performing XML Validation**

```php
<?php
// Using the DOM extension, load the XML file into memory:
$dom = new DOMDocument();
$dom->load('contacts.xml');

// Validate this against our RelaxNG file:
echo '<p>Checking against RelaxNG: ';
$pass = $dom->relaxNGValidate('contacts.rng');
echo $pass ? "Passes</p>\n" : "FAIL</p>\n";

// Validate this against our Schema file:
echo '<p>Checking against XML Schema: ';
```

Listing 17.3.3   **Continued**

```
$pass = $dom->schemaValidate('contacts.xsd');
echo $pass ? "Passes</p>\n" : "FAIL</p>\n";

// Just to show that we can, convert the DOM object into a SimpleXML one:
$xml = simplexml_import_dom($dom);
echo "<p>First Contact's name: {$xml->contact[0]->name}</p>\n";
?>
```

Note the last few lines of this example. Even though you have to use the DOM extension to do the validation, you can still use SimpleXML to access the data. SimpleXML provides a conversion function, `simplexml_import_dom()`, that takes a DOM object and creates a SimpleXML object from it for you.

17.4 Transforming XML into XHTML with XSLT

XSL Transformations (or XSLT) are a manner in which you can turn an XML document directly into XHTML for display in a web browser. This is done via the creation of an XSL file, which is the XML equivalent of a CSS style sheet. Within XSL files you can specify how you want the XML to be transformed.

It is worth noting that some web browsers have this capability built in; however, it can cause problems. Besides potential issues with buggy implementations, any older browser will not be able to understand this. Therefore, it is often better to perform transformations within PHP itself and just output the XHTML.

Transformations are made available in PHP 5 by the XSL extension. It comes by default with PHP 5; however, you may need to compile it into the system and/or enable it. Also, a full discussion of XSL, a powerful and potentially complex language, is beyond the scope of this book. To learn more about how to enable the XSL extension and to find links about XSL itself, visit http://php.net/xsl. The W3C reccomendation for XSLT can be found at http://www.w3.org/TR/xslt.

The basics of XSL, however, are not that difficult. If you know a few XSL commands, you can do much. First of all is

```
<xsl:template match="xpath_query">
```

This is the heart of the XSL file because it defines a template that will be applied to any tag that matches the XPath query given. (For more discussion on XPath, refer to Section 17.2, "Performing Searches Through XML with XPath.") Within a template, you will want to use the following regularly:

```
<xsl:value-of select="xpath_query">
```

This similarly uses an XPath query but retrieves the value of the object the query returns. This can be inserted into the rest of your layout. Finally, you need to also know how to use the following:

```
<xsl:apply-templates />
```

This command, when used inside one template, tells the transformation engine to parse any additional tags within this matched tag and to insert any templates that it finds for them in that location. So for example, in our XML example from Listing 17.0.1, we can define a template for "contacts" to give some overall display to the page and then a template for "contact". The contact template will be run for each instance of a "contact" tag. However, we need to tell the template for "contacts" to allow this, and where to allow this, by use of the `apply-templates` command.

These three commands let you do a lot of formatting to a simple XML file. Listing 17.4.1 is an XSL file that we will apply to our contacts XML.

Listing 17.4.1   **An XSLT Example—Filename: contacts.xsl**

```
<xsl:stylesheet version="1.0"
      xmlns:xsl="http://www.w3.org/1999/XSL/Transform">
  <xsl:output method="html" />
  <xsl:template match="contacts">
    <html><head><title>Contacts!</title></head><body>
    <div style="border: 2px solid blue; padding: 5px;">
      <h1>Contacts:</h1>
      <xsl:apply-templates />
    </div></body></html>
  </xsl:template>
  <xsl:template match="contact">
    <div style="border: 1px solid black; margin: 20px; padding: 5px;">
      <h2><xsl:value-of select="name" /></h2>
      <p>
        Home Phone: <xsl:value-of select="phone[@type='home']" /><br />
        Work Phone: <xsl:value-of select="phone[@type='work']" /><br />
        Cell Phone: <xsl:value-of select="phone[@type='cell']" /><br />
      </p>
    </div>
  </xsl:template>
</xsl:stylesheet>
```

Granted this is a straightforward use of XSL. If you investigate and learn more about it, you would find that it is a powerful tool to have in your developer's toolkit. It could almost be considered a full programming language because it is complete with the capability to create and access variables, as well as loop structures and conditional execution.

Now that our XSL file is created, it is truly just a matter of a few function calls to turn our XML, into HTML, as shown in Listing 17.4.2.

Listing 17.4.2 **Transforming XML to XHTML Using XLST**

```php
<?php
// Using the DOM extension, load the XML file into memory:
$dom = new DOMDocument();
$dom->load('contacts.xml');

// Now also load the XSL file as well:
$xsl = new DOMDocument();
$xsl->load('contacts.xsl');

// Create a new XSLT Processor
$proc = new XSLTProcessor;

// Import the XSL styles into this processor
$proc->importStyleSheet($xsl);

// Now transform the XML file and echo it to the screen!
echo $proc->transformToXML($dom);
?>
```

17.5 Creating an RSS File

RSS is a specific XML format that has been created for the sole purpose of syndicating "news" type information. It considers your information to be a channel and for that channel to have multiple items. Each item in turn can have certain information included, such as a title, URL, and description. RSS is used regularly now by news websites, blogs, and podcasts.

If you are interested in the full specification, to see all the options that exist, you should visit http://www.rssboard.org/, which hosts the current keepers of the standard. As an example, Listing 17.5.1 generates a small RSS feed from an array of news items.

Listing 17.5.1 **Generating RSS**

```php
<?php
// Create our array of news stories.
// These might have come from a database originally:
$news = array(
  array('Man hates politics', 'http://example.com/23423.php',
    'A man has been found that hates politics.  Politicians are surprised.'),
  array('Cat eats mouse', 'http://example.com/83482.php',
    'A cat was found eating a mouse.  The mouse was very surprised.'),
  array('Programmer gets hired', 'http://example.com/03912.php',
    'A programmer has received a telecommuting agreement, and is happy.'),
  );
```

Listing 17.5.1 **Continued**

```php
// Now, first to create our RSS feed, start with the appropriate header:
header('Content-type: text/xml');

// Echo out the opening of the RSS document.  These are parts that just
//  describe your website, and what the RSS feed is about:
echo '<?xml version="1.0" ?>';
echo <<<EORSS

<rss version="2.0">
  <channel>
    <title>Not So Nifty News Stories (NSNNS)</title>
    <link>http://example.com/nsnns.php</link>
    <description>The best news stories we can legally find!</description>
    <language>en-us</language>
    <copyright>Copyright 2006 - NSNNS</copyright>
    <webMaster>webmaster@example.com</webMaster>
    <generator>A Custom PHP Script</generator>
EORSS;

// Now that we've taken care of that, we can echo out each news item
// So just start looping through them!
foreach ($news as $item) {
    // Well, not much fancyness needed, just echo them out:
    echo <<<EOITEM

    <item>
      <title>{$item[0]}</title>
      <link>{$item[1]}</link>
      <description>{$item[2]}</description>
    </item>
EOITEM;
}

// Almost done.  Just need to print a few closing tags now and that's it:
echo <<<EOCLOSE

  </channel>
</rss>
EOCLOSE;
?>
```

As can be seen from examining the code, this script starts off with some data. In this case an array of data refers to various news stories including a title, a URL, and a description of the story. Using this data, it generates an RSS feed that describes all of this news. The data more likely would have come from a database in a real example.

17.6 Creating an RSS Display Script for Websites

RSS feeds are often used in nontraditional ways. Web browsers have various ways of displaying them, separate RSS software exists to read them, and even email clients are starting to display the output of the RSS.

With all this, though, one thing is often overlooked: simply reading in the RSS feed from another website and displaying it on your own website. Listing 17.6.1 creates a basic function that reads in a remote RSS feed, specified by a URL, and generates an HTML definition list from it, making the title a link and including the description. It also includes the title of the feed as a paragraph first.

If you want to use this in a live web page, you can wrap it inside a `<div>` tag to control/apply additional formatting.

Listing 17.6.1 **Display an RSS Feed**

```php
<?php
// Create a function that will turn an RSS feed, into a definition list:
function rss_dl($url) {
    // Begin by loading the RSS feed into SimpleXML:
    $rss = simplexml_load_file($url);

    // Ok, output the title of the feed just as a paragraph block.  People
    // can use stylesheets later to make it look as they wish:
    echo <<<EOSNIPPET
<p>
  <a href="{$rss->channel->link}">{$rss->channel->title}</a>
</p>
EOSNIPPET;

    // Now begin our definition list:
    echo "<dl>\n";

    // Loop through all items to make definition entries from them
    foreach ($rss->channel->item as $i) {
        // The title with link:
        echo "<dt><a href=\"{$i->link}\">{$i->title}</a></dt>\n";

        // The description as the dd
        echo "<dd>{$i->description}</dd>\n";
    }

    // End our list now, we are done
    echo "</dl>\n";
}
```

Listing 17.6.1 **Continued**

```
// Test this out:
rss_dl('http://acorn.atlantia.sca.org/calendar.xml');

// And try it again:
echo "<br /><br /><br />\n";
rss_dl('http://rss.cnn.com/rss/cnn_topstories.rss');
?>
```

18

Images

D UE TO ITS CLOSE ASSOCIATION WITH WEB PAGE GENERATION, an extensive set of libraries has been incorporated into PHP to create and manipulate images. The core set of routines is based on the GD library. Because of the large number of formats, the GD library is then enhanced by the inclusion of format-specific routines. Most of the common libraries are bundled with PHP. However, to use them, they need to be explicitly specified during compilation. For a full discussion, see the requirements section found at http://php.net/image.

The image model used is straightforward: Images are rectangular arrays of pixels. Graphics elements, such as lines, circles, and image data, are "painted" onto an image, only modifying those pixels directly affected by the element being drawn. At this point, it is good to note that text elements can also be drawn, as demonstrated by Listing 18.1.1.

The image library supports two color models: true color or palette-based. In a true color image each pixel is represented by three values: red, green, and blue components. Hence, an image can have as many colors as it has pixels. JPEG images are true color images. Palette-based images use only a single value to specify the color of each pixel. This value is an index into a table, or palette. Each entry in this table then specifies the red/green/blue components of that color. GIF images are palette-based images. PNG images can be either true color or palette-based. Regardless of image type, colors must first be "allocated" for an image before it can be used by any drawing function.

Images can also support *alpha transparency*. When a color is defined, its transparency can be specified. The amount of transparency controls how much of any color behind this color will show through; the effect is similar to looking through a colored window.

All image functions operate in pixel space, with the (0, 0) pixel located in the upper-left corner of the image. If data is in some other coordinate space, the user must first convert the data to pixel coordinates. You might want to refer to Section 5.8, "Matrix Math Execution Using Arrays," of Chapter 5, "Arrays," for efficient functions to deal with coordinate transformations.

Because they are common formats, all examples in this chapter read in only JPEG images and produce only PNG images. However, as noted previously, most popular image formats are supported by the image GD library. This is being done to demonstrate the various capabilities of GD. This also can be a common practice because PNG images do not suffer from compression artifacts like JPEGs do. If you open a JPEG and make some changes, such as adding text to it, and then output it as a JPEG again, you will not only cause compression artifacts on your text but will also be recompressing the JPEG causing more visible issues. If you find the need to output as a JPEG, a GIF, or any other format, simply change the content type that is being sent to the browser and call the appropriate image function to create the image in that format.

Caution

There is one additional piece of information that you might need when programming image producing applications. Because you are outputting an image content type you will just see a broken image if you have any errors or try to output any debugging information. To solve this you either need to change your content type to text/html or text/plain while debugging. Alternatively, write debugging statements to a log file and look for them there.

Quick Hits

▶ **Get information about what has been installed for the GD library:**

```
$array = gd_info();
```

This function returns an array of information about what format libraries and version have been installed in the PHP environment.

Full documentation: http://php.net/gd_info

▶ **Get the size of an image:**

```
list($width, $height, $type, $html) = getimagesize($imagefile);
```

The width, height, and format type for the specified image file are returned. Also, the HTML width and height attributes are returned in $html.

Full documentation: http://php.net/getimagesize

▶ **Create an image:**

```
$image = imagecreatetruecolor($width, $height);
```

```
$image = imagecreate($width, $height);
```

Create a true color or palette-based image.

Full documentation: http://php.net/imagecreatetruecolor and http://php.net/imagecreate

▶ **Read in an image file:**

```
$image = imagecreatefromjpg($imagefile);

$image = imagecreatefromgif($imagefile);

$image = imagecreatefrompng($imagefile);
```

Read the specified file into an image. Note that many more formats can be read.

Full documentation: http://php.net/imagecreatefromjpg, http://php.net/imagecreatefromgif, http://php.net/imagecreatefrompng

▶ **Prepare a color to use with an image:**

```
$color = imagecolorallocate($image, $red, $green, $blue);

$color = imagecolorallocatealpha($image, $red, $green, $blue, $alpha);
```

The color specified by $red, $green, $blue, and a specified transparency is created for the specified image. The color component values range from 0 to 255, whereas the alpha is from 0 to 127.

Full documentation: http://php.net/imagecolorallocate

▶ **Draw circles, ellipses, and arcs into an image:**

```
$success = imageellipse($image, $x, $y, $width, $height, $color);

$success = imagearc($image, $x, $y,
                    $width, $height,
                    $startangle, $endangle,
                    $color);
```

The (x,y) position is the center of figure. The (width, height) is the size of the element. The 0 degree angle is at the three o'clock position, increasing clockwise. Filled versions are available.

Full documentation: http://php.net/imageellipse and http://php.net/imagearc

▶ **Draw lines, rectangles, and polygons:**

```
$success = imageline($image, $x1, $y1, $x2, $y2, $color);

$success = imagerectangle($image, $x1, $y1, $x2, $y2, $color);

$success = imagepolygon($image, $points, $number, $color);
```

Draw either the line from (x1, y1) to (x2, y2) or the box bounded by (x1, y1), (x2, y2). For polygons, the points are specified by an array where $points[0] = x0, $points[1] = y0, and so on.

Full documentation: http://php.net/imageline and http://php.net/imagerectangle

▶ **Render text:**

```
$success = imagestring($image, $font, $x, $y, $string, $color);
```

The text starts at (x, y) using the specified font and color.

Full documentation: http://php.net/imagestring

▶ **Create text strings based on TrueType fonts:**

```
$bounding = imagettftext($image,
                         $fontsize, $angle,
                         $x, $y, $color,
                         $fontfile, $text);
```

Write the text using the TrueType font specified in `$fontfile`. The `$angle` specifies the direction the text will be written: 0 for normal, -90 from text going up-to-down, and so on. An array is returned of the bounding box that surrounds where the text was written. The function `imagefttext()` is available for use with FreeType2 fonts.

Full documentation: http://php.net/imagettftext and http://php.net/imagefttext

▶ **Copy part of an image into another image:**

```
$success = imagecopy($to, $from,
                     $to_x, $to_y,
                     $from_x, $from_y,
                     $width, $height);
```

This will copy a portion of image `$from` into image `$to`.

Full documentation: http://php.net/imagecopy

18.1 Generating Composite Images with Text

One easy and common task is to take an existing image and overlay some text onto it. There are many reasons you might want to do this. Perhaps you want to add automatic captions to your images or insert the title of a press release on the image taken from it. This can even be used in some cases to mark any image from your website as being specifically from your website with a copyright notice. That way if someone takes the image from you, the notice is blatantly there.

Listing 18.1.1 demonstrates this copyright example. The script simply opens from the filesystem, writes a copyright statement onto the image, and then returns the image. If you place this PHP file as part of an `<img src="" />` tag, you will see your image with the statement.

Listing 18.1.1 **Adding Copyright Text to an Image**

```php
<?php
// We are going to insert a copyright statement onto a graphic.
// Read the graphic into memory, this is a JPEG so we use that function:
$gfx = imagecreatefromjpeg('eli.jpg');

// Now, we want to place this statement at the bottom
// so we need to determine the dimensions of our image:
$width = imagesx($gfx);
$height = imagesy($gfx);

// Define our string we are going to print:
$statement = 'Copyright 2006 - eliw.com';
```

Listing 18.1.1 **Continued**

```
// We are going to use the basic built-in monospace fonts to write with:
// We would like to use font size of 3.  However, if that ends up being
// too wide for our image, we need to go smaller.  Therefore let's be
// smart and do some testing on various font sizes:
foreach (range(3, 1) as $fontsize) {
    // Calculate the width of a single character of this font:
    $fontw = imagefontwidth($fontsize);

    // Calculate the full width of this statement.
    $fullw = strlen($statement) * $fontw;

    // Is this, plus 4 to give spacing, less than our image?
    if ($fullw + 4 <= $width) {
        // Yay, it is.  Break out of this loop and continue with this size.
        break;
    }
}

// We need to know the height of a character of this font.
$fonth = imagefontheight($fontsize);

// We want two colors for this.  We need to display a black background
// and want white text on top of that.  Declare those colors via RGB:
$black = imagecolorallocate($gfx, 0, 0, 0);
$white = imagecolorallocate($gfx, 255, 255, 255);

// We are placing our text in the bottom right corner and we want to leave
// a 2 pixel space around our text, but need the black box to hit the edges
// of the image.  Therefore, draw the rectangle big enough to hold it.
imagefilledrectangle($gfx, // The graphics object to draw on
    $width - $fullw - 4,  // The X value of upper left corner
    $height - $fonth - 4, // The Y value of upper left corner
    $width,               // The X value of lower right corner
    $height,              // The Y value of lower right corner
    $black);              // The color

// Now, print this statement out in the bottom right corner.
imagestring($gfx,         // The graphics object to draw on
    $fontsize,            // The font size to use.
    $width - $fullw - 2,  // X value of upper left corner
    $height - $fonth - 2, // Y value of upper left corner
    $statement,           // The text to print
    $white);              // The color to do it with.

// We are now done with our manipulations.
```

Listing 18.1.1 **Continued**

```
// Let the browser know that we are going to output this as a PNG
header('Content-type: image/png');

// And then output our new image:
imagepng($gfx);
?>
```

Listing 18.1.1 explores a few neat concepts. You can see how easily a file is read into memory and then manipulated. You also can see how easy it is to output the file into a different format in the end when we output what was once a JPEG as a PNG. Dealing with text can be a little tricky, however. You need to determine the dimensions that the text will end up being on the screen and handle that accordingly. In this case we have also decided to draw a black background onto the screen first so that the text will always show up.

To deal with the dimensions in this case, it was realized that this script could be easily modified to take the filename from a GET string. Therefore it would be easy to add this copyright statement to any image on your website. However, what happens if the font is too large? We have a quick little loop that starts at the preferred size for the font and makes sure that it will fit. If it doesn't, it works its way smaller until it finds one that does fit.

Listing 18.1.1 uses the built-in fonts with PHP. There are five of them, and they are all monospaced. They are usable but not necessarily the prettiest ones. Also, there is not really any capability to apply variations to the text (such as bold or italic). The biggest problem in this case, however, is the lack of options in size. What happens in Listing 18.1.1 when size 1 text won't fit either? Well, it runs off the image, and you can't make it any smaller.

To solve all these issues, you can use TrueType or PS1 fonts. These give you much more flexibility but can be a little trickier to use. As an experiment Listing 18.1.2 rewrites Listing 18.1.1 to use TrueType fonts and its respective functions instead.

Listing 18.1.2 **Using TrueType Fonts to Write Text into an Image**

```
<?php
// We are going to insert a copyright statement onto a graphic.
// Read the graphic into memory, this is a JPEG so we use that function:
$gfx = imagecreatefromjpeg('eli.jpg');

// Now, we want to place this statement at the bottom
// so we need to determine the dimensions of our image:
$width = imagesx($gfx);
$height = imagesy($gfx);
```

Listing 18.1.2   **Continued**

```php
// Define our string we are going to print:
$statement = 'Copyright 2006 - eliw.com';
$font = 'arial';

// We are going to use truetype fonts, and would like a fontsize of 11
// If that ends up being too wide for our image, we need to go smaller.
foreach (range(11, 1) as $fontsize) {
    // Calculate the bounding box of this text
    $box = imagettfbbox($fontsize, 0, $font, $statement);

    // Use the lower left X (0) and the upper right X (4) to calculate width
    $fontw = abs($box[4] - $box[0]);

    // Is this, plus 4 to give spacing, less than our image?
    if ($fontw + 4 <= $width) {
        // Yay, it is.  Break out of this loop and continue with this size.
        break;
    }
}

// height: use lower left Y(1) and upper right Y(5) to calculate
$fonth = abs($box[5] - $box[1]);

// We also need to know how far below the baseline the font drops:
// Snag this from the lower left corner Y value.
$basel = $box[1];

// We want two colors for this.  We need to display a black background
// and want white text on top of that.  Declare those colors via RGB:
$black = imagecolorallocate($gfx, 0, 0, 0);
$white = imagecolorallocate($gfx, 255, 255, 255);

// Draw a rectangle in bottom left corner to be a background of the text:
imagefilledrectangle($gfx, $width - $fontw - 4, $height - $fonth - 4,
    $width,      $height, $black);

// Now, print this statement out in the bottom right corner.
imagettftext($gfx,          // The graphics object to draw on
    $fontsize,              // The font size to use.
    0,                      // The slant angle of the text
    $width - $fontw - 2,    // X value of left side of text
    $height - $basel - 2,   // Y value of the text baseline
    $white,                 // The color to do it with.
    $font,                  // The font to use.
    $statement);            // The text to print
```

Listing 18.1.2   **Continued**

```
// We are now done with our manipulations.
// Let the browser know that we are going to output this as a PNG
header('Content-type: image/png');

// And then output our new image:
imagepng($gfx);
?>
```

That's better now; the font will get smaller and smaller but always fit (it may not always be readable, though). You need to understand two main differences when dealing with TrueType fonts rather than the built-in fonts. First, no basic "height" and "width" functions are available. You need to call `imagettfbbox()`, which returns a bounding box—essentially an array containing the x/y coordinates of all four points—for a box that would contain the string. The resulting array contains following information:

- 0—X position of lower-left corner
- 1—Y position of lower-left corner
- 2—X position of lower-right corner
- 3—Y position of lower-right corner
- 4—X position of upper-right corner
- 5—Y position of upper-right corner
- 6—X position of upper-left corner
- 7—Y position of upper-left corner

Using these values, and combinations of them, allows you to know pretty much anything about the font. The second item to understand is that when specifying the position for the basic fonts, you give the top-left corner, similar to the other drawing functions. However, this is not the case for TrueType fonts. When specifying a y coordinate for them, you are giving the baseline of the font, which means the bottom of normal characters, not counting ones that drop down lower, such as 'y' and 'g'.

18.2 Drawing Tips and Tricks

The basic functions provided for drawing are easy enough to use and understand: Draw a rectangle, draw a circle, draw a line, and so on. Often you may need to do slight variations on these methods. That can be a little tricky to achieve the effect that you are going for.

Listing 18.2.1 includes examples of some of the fancier tricks you may want to use, such as making rectangles with rounded corners or adding drop shadows. After studying these techniques you should be able to extrapolate many different features that you want to create.

Listing 18.2.1   **Drop-Shadows, Outline, and Rounded-Corner Rectangles**

```php
<?php
// First of all, create a function that will automatically make a
// dropshadowed box. give it the coordinates of the primary box
// and the offset that you want the drop to be.  It assumes lower right.
function i_filledrectangledropshadow($g,
        $x1, $y1, $x2, $y2,
        $drop, $color, $shcolor) {
    // First draw the shadow box offset appropriately
    imagefilledrectangle($g, $x1 + $drop, $y1 + $drop,
        $x2 + $drop, $y2 + $drop, $shcolor);

    // Now the main box:
    imagefilledrectangle($g, $x1, $y1, $x2, $y2, $color);
}


// Create a function similar to above, but that creates an outline rectangle
//  with the drop shadow.  A more normal looking drop shadow box.
function i_rectangledropshadow($g,
        $x1, $y1, $x2, $y2,
        $drop, $color, $shcolor, $border) {
    // Time to cheat a bit.  First call our previous function:
    i_filledrectangledropshadow($g, $x1, $y1, $x2, $y2,
        $drop, $color, $shcolor);

    // Now draw a regular rectangle on top of it:
    imagerectangle($g, $x1, $y1, $x2, $y2, $border);
}


// A function to draw a filled rectangle with rounded corners:
// Just like drawing a rectangle, but also specify a radius for the corners.
function i_filledroundedrectangle($g, $x1, $y1, $x2, $y2, $color, $radius) {
    // We need to know the diameter too:
    $diam = $radius * 2;

    // Going to cheat slightly to accomplish this.  First draw four circles
    //  at the corners of this box:
    imagefilledellipse($g, $x1 + $radius, $y1 + $radius, $d, $d, $color);
    imagefilledellipse($g, $x2 - $radius, $y1 + $radius, $d, $d, $color);
    imagefilledellipse($g, $x1 + $radius, $y2 - $radius, $d, $d, $color);
    imagefilledellipse($g, $x2 - $radius, $y2 - $radius, $d, $d, $color);

    // Now fill in the middle, two well placed rectangles will do it.
    imagefilledrectangle($g, $x1+$radius, $y1, $x2-$radius, $y2, $color);
    imagefilledrectangle($g, $x1, $y1+$radius, $x2, $y2-$radius, $color);
}
```

Listing 18.2.1   **Continued**

```
// Now a version that will just draw an outline of a rounded rectangle
function i_roundedrectangle($g,
        $x1, $y1, $x2, $y2,
        $color, $border, $radius) {
    // This could be implemented by doing calls of imagearc and imageline
    //  similar to the previous function.  But since we have that function
    //  we can cheat:
    // Just call it twice with the inner color, and the border.
    i_filledroundedrectangle($g, $x1, $y1, $x2, $y2, $border, $radius);
    i_filledroundedrectangle($g, $x1 + 1, $y1 + 1, $x2 - 1, $y2 - 1,
        $color, $radius);
}


// We are going to call each of these to test them.
// Create a blank image to do this on.
$gfx = imagecreatetruecolor(200, 200);

// Declare a few colors we will use:
$black = imagecolorallocate($gfx, 0, 0, 0);
$gray = imagecolorallocate($gfx, 120, 120, 120);
$white = imagecolorallocate($gfx, 255, 255, 255);
$blue = imagecolorallocate($gfx, 0, 0, 255);

// Make almost entire background white.
imagefilledrectangle($gfx, 1, 1, 198, 198, $white);

// Turn on antialiasing so that curvy things look better.
imageantialias($gfx, true);

// Ok, try to make a blue box with a gray drop shadow:
i_filledrectangledropshadow($gfx, 5, 5, 50, 40, 5, $blue, $gray);

// How about a basic white box, with black outline, with a drop shadow
i_rectangledropshadow($gfx, 5, 60, 50, 100, 5, $white, $gray, $black);

// Insert a filled rounded rectangle, blue sounds good
i_filledroundedrectangle($gfx, 70, 5, 150, 50, $blue, 15);

// Now how about a rectangle with rounded corners, not filled in:
i_roundedrectangle($gfx, 70, 65, 160, 100, $white, $black, 15);

// Output our sample as a PNG
header('Content-type: image/png');
imagepng($gfx);
?>
```

18.3 Using Transparent Backgrounds in Images

Transparent backgrounds are useful and available in GIF and PNG graphics formats. Essentially you declare a certain color, your background, to be transparent. This means that anything beneath that area of the graphic will actually show through. This is usually used to make a graphic that will sit on most any background color (or image) without problems. It can also be used to overlay multiple images for interesting effects.

PHP provides the capability to do transparent background colors by calling the function `imagecolortransparent()` and telling it which color in your image will be transparent. Notice in Listing 18.3.1 that even though we create a solid green background, because that color is set transparent, it is not visible if you run that code and view the output.

Listing 18.3.1   **Using Transparent Backgrounds**

```php
<?php
// Create a blank image to test with.
$gfx = imagecreatetruecolor(200, 200);

// Declare just two colors, a bright green, and blue
$blue = imagecolorallocate($gfx, 0, 0, 255);
$green = imagecolorallocate($gfx, 0, 255, 0);

// Make the entire background green
imagefilledrectangle($gfx, 0, 0, 199, 199, $green);

// Draw a blue circle on the image:
imagefilledellipse($gfx, 100, 100, 30, 30, $blue);

// Set the green color as transparent:
imagecolortransparent($gfx, $green);

// Output our sample as a PNG
header('Content-type: image/png');
imagepng($gfx);
?>
```

A similar but more advanced technique involves the use of alpha transparencies. Alpha transparencies are where the color chosen can have a range of how transparent (or translucent in this case) it may be. A number from 0 to 127 specifies how see-through a color should be, with 0 meaning fully opaque and 127 meaning completely transparent.

This is actually set on the allocation of a specific color. This means that you can have any number of transparent colors, all set to different values. One common use is when antialiasing a curved line to make it appear smooth. With regular transparency, the antialiasing has to be geared toward certain background colors. But with alpha transparencies, anti-aliasing can work anywhere. Listing 18.3.2 demonstrates using multiple transparencies.

Listing 18.3.2 **Using Multiple Transparent Colors**

```php
<?php
// Create a blank image to test with.
$gfx = imagecreatetruecolor(200, 200);

// Declare a white background
$white = imagecolorallocate($gfx, 255, 255, 255);

// Make the entire background white
imagefilledrectangle($gfx, 0, 0, 199, 199, $white);

// Now make three alpha colors, each fairly transparent.
$blue = imagecolorallocatealpha($gfx, 0, 0, 255, 100);
$green = imagecolorallocatealpha($gfx, 0, 255, 0, 100);
$red = imagecolorallocatealpha($gfx, 255, 0, 0, 100);

// Draw the circles on the image overlapping:
imagefilledellipse($gfx, 133, 67, 100, 100, $blue);
imagefilledellipse($gfx, 67, 67, 100, 100, $green);
imagefilledellipse($gfx, 100, 133, 100, 100, $red);

// Output our sample as a PNG
header('Content-type: image/png');
imagepng($gfx);
?>
```

18.4 Creating a Graph/Chart Library

If any data, such as temperature versus day or stock market values, is to be presented in a meaningful fashion, it really needs to be presented visually. This usually takes the form of charts. Various forms of charts exist, such as line graphs, bar graphs, pie charts, and so on. PHP's Graphics library can of course handle the creation of charts by the building up of graphics primitives—a line placed here, a rectangle there, and some text over in the corner.

Many different aspects need to be handled, however, and to accomplish this task in a general fashion is a monumental undertaking. This is why various third-party PHP chart software exists, each trying to handle chart creation to various degrees. When you get deeply into it, so many variations exist for a generic solution: colors, grids, graph types, labels, keys, and much more.

Note

One example of these third-party libraries is the PEAR Image_Graph library (currently only in alpha at the time this book was written). It can be found at: http://pear.php.net/package/Image_Graph.

Fortunately, most basic graphs can be created with some basic algorithms. For an example of what needs to be undertaken, Listing 18.4.1 develops a class, `MultiGraph`, which creates three different forms of charts. We define a few basic types of plot: points, lines, and bar graphs. To use this class, an object is instantiated that provides the graphics object that will be drawn to. Various other parameters, such as colors, fonts, and labels, are public members that can then be set. Afterward a call to one of the methods of this class creates the chart for you. You can then change a few aspects of the configuration and generate another chart. This class should serve as an excellent starting place to develop more specialized charts for your specific needs.

Listing 18.4.1   **Chart Creations Library**

```php
<?php
// A class for drawing charts that allows its configuration to be pushed
//  into it via public properties
class MultiGraph {
    // Public class members, all of these need filled in before drawing.
    public $border_color; // Color of the border/text
    public $grid_color;    // Color of the grid lines
    public $data_color;    // Color of any data blocks
    public $g;             // Graphics object
    public $data;          // Data to turn into a graph
    public $draw_border = true;              // Should the border be drawn?
    public $horizontal_grid_segments = 5; // How many horizontal grid lines?
    public $vertical_grid_segments = 0;   // How about vertical ones?
    public $x = 0;    // X value of the upper left corner of CHART area
    public $y = 0;    // Y value
    public $w = 200;  // Width of actual chart area
    public $h = 100;  // Height of actual chart area
    public $point_size = 5;  // Size of data points when doing a Point Chart
    public $y_axis_autolabel = true;  // Generate labels for Y axis?
    public $x_axis_autolabel = true;  // Generate labels for X axis?
    public $font = 'arial';  // Font to use
    public $fontsize = 8;    // Size of font.

    // Constructor method.  Requires the graphics object
    public function __construct($graphics) {
        // Store the graphics object
        $this->g = $graphics;

        // Go ahead and turn on antialiasing
        imageantialias($this->g, true);
    }

    // Method to make it easy to set dimensions
    public function setDimensions($x, $y, $w, $h) {
```

Listing 18.4.1 **Continued**

```php
        // Just do it
        $this->x = $x;
        $this->y = $y;
        $this->h = $h;
        $this->w = $w;
    }

    // The method that will draw a line graph to the screen!
    public function drawLineGraph() {
        // We are asked to draw a line graph.  First of all draw the borders
        $this->_drawBorder();

        // Calculate the conversion factors to scale data to space given
        $yscale = $this->_calcYScale();
        $xscale = $this->_calcXScale();

        // Draw a grid if asked
        $this->_drawHorizontal();
        $this->_drawVertical();

        // Now we are ready for the data (finally)
        // We are doing a line graph, assume the key is the X value & sort.
        // Since we are sorting, make a copy to not mess up the real data
        $tmpdata = $this->data;
        ksort($tmpdata);

        // Now step through it, drawing the lines as appropriate:
        list($ldx, $ldy) = each($tmpdata);
        while (list($dx, $dy) = each($tmpdata)) {
            // Draw the line from the last x,y pair, to the current one
            // Draw the line from the last x,y pair, to the current one
            imageline($this->g,
                $this->x + $ldx * $xscale,
                $this->y + $this->h - $ldy * $yscale,
                $this->x + $dx * $xscale,
                $this->y + $this->h - $dy * $yscale,
                $this->data_color);

            // Reset data for next loop
            $ldx = $dx;
            $ldy = $dy;
        }
    }

    // The method that will draw a point plot to the screen.
    public function drawPointGraph() {
```

Listing 18.4.1   **Continued**

```
        // We are asked to draw a point graph.  First draw the borders
        $this->_drawBorder();

        // Calculate the conversion factors to scale data to space given
        $yscale = $this->_calcYScale();
        $xscale = $this->_calcXScale();

        // Draw a grid if asked
        $this->_drawHorizontal();
        $this->_drawVertical();

        // Now we are ready for the data - Now step through it
        foreach ($this->data as $dx => $dy) {
            // Draw the point for this data:
            imagefilledellipse($this->g, $this->x + $dx * $xscale,
                $this->y + $this->h - $dy * $yscale,
                $this->point_size, $this->point_size, $this->data_color);
        }
    }

    // The method that will draw a bar graph
    // NOTE:  Bar graphs assume that the keys of the array are
    //        labels, not 'x' values.
    public function drawBarGraph() {
        // We've been asked to draw a Bar graph.  First draw the borders
        $this->_drawBorder();

        // Calculate the conversion factors to scale data to space given
        $yscale = $this->_calcYScale();

        // Draw a grid if asked
        $this->_drawHorizontal();

        // Precalculate a few items to be efficient:
        //   The width of each 'section':
        $section = (float) $this->w / count($this->data);
        //   The width of a bar, we want it 70% of section:
        $bar = (int) ($section * 0.7);

        // Loop once per data item that we have - assume they are in order
        $count = 0;
        foreach ($this->data as $label => $val) {
            $count++;

            // Draw the bar to the appropriate height & width:
```

Listing 18.4.1 **Continued**

```php
                // First as a colored filled rectangle:
                imagefilledrectangle($this->g,
                    $this->x + ($section * $count) - $bar,
                    $this->y + $this->h,
                    $this->x + ($section * $count),
                    $this->y + $this->h - $val * $yscale,
                    $this->data_color);

                // Then as an outline:
                imagerectangle($this->g, $this->x + ($section * $count) - $bar,
                    $this->y + $this->h, $this->x + ($section * $count),
                    $this->y + $this->h - $val * $yscale, $this->border_color);

                // Now, since vertical grids don't really exist for bar graphs
                // We need to create the labels ourselves
                if ($this->x_axis_autolabel) {
                    // Calculate the width of the box needed by the bounding box
                    $box = imagettfbbox($this->fontsize, 270,
                        $this->font, $label);
                    $texwidth = abs($box[4] - $box[0]);

                    // Draw it going vertical
                    // Draw it going vertical
                    imagettftext($this->g,
                        $this->fontsize, 270,
                        ($this->x + ($section * $count)) -
                                ($bar / 2) - ($texwidth / 2),
                        $this->y + $this->h + 4,
                        $this->border_color,
                        $this->font,
                        $label);
                }
            }
        }

        // Support function to draw the border:
        private function _drawBorder() {
            if ($this->draw_border) {
                // Vertical one
                imageline($this->g, $this->x, $this->y, $this->x,
                    $this->h + $this->y, $this->border_color);
                // Horizontal one
                imageline($this->g, $this->x, $this->h+$this->y,
                    $this->w + $this->x, $this->h + $this->y,
                    $this->border_color);
```

Listing 18.4.1 **Continued**

```php
        }
    }

    // Support function for calculating the Y scale
    private function _calcYScale() {
        // Add a fudge for visual purposes so it doesn't ever hit the top.
        return (float) $this->h / $this->_calcYMax();
    }

    // Support function for calculating the X scale
    private function _calcXScale() {
        return (float) $this->w / $this->_calcXMax();
    }

    // Support function for calculating the maximum Y value, for scaling/etc
    private function _calcYMax() {
        // Add a fudge for visual purposes so it doesn't ever hit the top.
        // Also force round it to only 2 significant digits
        //   as this will make it look 'clean'
        $max = (float) max($this->data) * 1.05;
        // Get the 'length' of this:
        $len = strlen((int)$max);
        // Find a 2 digit ceiling, if less than 2 digits, just return it:
        if ($len < 2) {
            return $max;
        } else {
            // Keep the first two digits and pad with zeros:
            return intval(substr($max, 0, 2) . str_repeat('0', $len - 2));
        }
    }

    // Support function for calculating the maximum X value, for scaling/etc
    private function _calcXMax() {
        return max(array_keys($this->data));
    }

    // Support function for drawing the Horizontal Grid
    private function _drawHorizontal() {
        if ($this->horizontal_grid_segments) {
            // Figure out their placement
            foreach(range(1, $this->horizontal_grid_segments) as $hg) {
                // Y height for this is:
                $yheight = (int) $this->y + $this->h -
                    ($hg * ($this->h / $this->horizontal_grid_segments));
                imageline($this->g, $this->x + 1, $yheight,
                    $this->w + $this->x, $yheight, $this->grid_color);
```

Listing 18.4.1   **Continued**

```
                    // Now, IF they wanted automatic labels, give 'em
                if ($this->y_axis_autolabel) {
                    // Calculate the value for here, and display it
                    $ax_step = (int)(($this->_calcYMax() /
                        $this->horizontal_grid_segments) * $hg);

                    // Calculate the width of the box needed to display
                    //  this: Use the lower left X (0) and the upper right
                    //  X (4) to calculate width:
                    $box = imagettfbbox($this->fontsize, 0,
                        $this->font, $ax_step);
                    $texwidth = abs($box[4] - $box[0]);
                    $texheight = abs($box[5] - $box[1]);

                    // Draw it right justified:
                    imagettftext($this->g, $this->fontsize, 0,
                        $this->x - 3 - $texwidth, $yheight + $texheight / 2,
                        $this->border_color, $this->font, $ax_step);
                }
            }
        }
    }

    // Support function for drawing the Vertical Grid
    private function _drawVertical() {
        if ($this->vertical_grid_segments) {
            // Figure out their placement
            foreach(range(1, $this->vertical_grid_segments) as $vg) {
                // X location for this is:
                $xloc = (int) ($this->x +
                    ($vg * ($this->w / $this->vertical_grid_segments)));
                imageline($this->g, $xloc, $this->y,
                    $xloc, $this->y + $this->h - 1, $this->grid_color);

                // Now, IF they wanted automatic labels, give 'em
                if ($this->x_axis_autolabel) {
                    // Calculate the value for here, and display it
                    $ax_step = (int)(($this->_calcXMax() /
                        $this->vertical_grid_segments) * $vg);

                    // Calculate the width of the box needed to display
                    //  this:  Use the lower left X (0) and the upper
                    //  right X (4) to calculate width:
                    $box = imagettfbbox($this->fontsize, 270,
                        $this->font, $ax_step);
                    $texwidth = abs($box[4] - $box[0]);
```

Listing 18.4.1 **Continued**

```
                          // Draw it going vertical
                          imagettftext($this->g, $this->fontsize, 270,
                              $xloc - $texwidth / 2, $this->y + $this->h + 3,
                              $this->border_color, $this->font, $ax_step);
                      }
                  }
              }
          }
}

// Pre/setup for the date functions:
date_default_timezone_set('America/New_York');

// Create a blank image to test with.
$gfx = imagecreatetruecolor(950, 650);

// Declare a few colors
$red = imagecolorallocate($gfx, 255, 0, 0);
$manilla = imagecolorallocate($qfx, 255, 255, 245);
$black = imagecolorallocate($gfx, 0, 0, 0);
$lgray = imagecolorallocate($gfx, 200, 200, 200);

// Color our background
imagefill($gfx, 0, 0, $manilla);

// Initialize a new Multigraph
$graph = new MultiGraph($gfx);
$graph->border_color = $black;
$graph->grid_color = $lgray;
$graph->data_color = $red;
$graph->vertical_grid_segments = 10;

// Create some fake data
//  Generate up to 50 random points of data, with random values:
$chartdata = array();
for ($i = 0; $i < 50; $i++) {
    $chartdata[rand(1,200)] = rand(1,1000);
}
$graph->data = $chartdata;

// Ok, output a line graph
$graph->setDimensions(50, 50, 300, 200);
$graph->drawLineGraph();

// Now do it as a point graph with some changed grid parameters
```

Listing 18.4.1 **Continued**

```
$graph->horizontal_grid_segments = 9;
$graph->vertical_grid_segments = 15;
$graph->setDimensions(50, 350, 300, 200);
$graph->drawPointGraph();

// Finally let's create a bar graph, we need new data for that, with labels.
// Automatically generate some that is based on Month names.
$bardata = array();
foreach(range(1,12) as $mon) {
    $bardata[date('F', mktime(0, 0, 0, $mon))] = rand(1,5000);
}

// Change some options, and display the BIG bar graph:
$cyan = imagecolorallocate($gfx, 0, 255, 255);
$graph->data_color = $cyan;
$graph->fontsize = 11;
$graph->horizontal_grid_segments = 12;
$graph->setDimensions(450, 40, 400, 500);
$graph->data = $bardata;
$graph->drawBarGraph();

// Output our sample as a PNG
header('Content-type: image/png');
imagepng($gfx);
?>
```

Within this program, many decisions were made as to how to structure it. It was decided that making a class would be ideal due to the large amount of configuration needed to generate a chart. Had this been done in an functional manner, the parameter list for the "draw" functions would have been astronomically long, and/or an array of values would have needed to be used. Either way, it would not have been as convenient as just setting those values on an object as needed. Also, using on object provides the capability to draw multiple charts with small changes to configuration.

A design point was the use of many private support methods. Within these methods, small individual parts of drawing a graph can be easily handled. More importantly, common aspects to any type of graph can be done. For example, the _drawBorder() method takes care of drawing the border, which all three of the chart types may want to have. This method also includes the logic as to whether borders should even be drawn. Therefore the individual chart methods don't ever have to worry about the border drawing.

As stated, our MultiGraph class is just a starting point for a fully functional generic library. There are many issues not taken into account that you might want to. For one, the x,y values provided control only the actual chart area; all labels fall outside that. This is fine for specific uses, but someone might want to completely contain a chart, including its labels, into a certain area. Other things are left out as well, such as variations on how labels are printed, keys, multiple color schemes, and much more. Listing 18.4.1 however, serves as a good example of how to create charting software for specific purposes that you may have. Nothing can beat the flexibility of creating a solution by hand that meets your specific needs.

18.5 Automatically Creating a Photo Gallery from Digital Camera Files (Exif Data)

Digital cameras actually store a Pandora's box of additional information in any JPEG or TIFF that they create. Information about the camera itself and the specifications of the image (such as ISO speed used) will be saved. Also, most cameras actually save a small thumbnail version of the image as well—that's how they implement the preview function on the camera itself.

PHP has a library, the Exif library that can read this data. (The data is in a standard format known as the Exif specification.) This library, like many others, is actually included in the PHP distribution but is not compiled in by default. You will need to specify that you want to compile or include it into your version of PHP. For more information on this, visit the PHP documentation: http://php.net/exif.

This information can be great to use when building photo albums of your pictures. Listing 18.5.1 is a quick example that scans a provided directory for any .JPG images and, for each one, reads the thumbnail and other Exif data, displaying it to the user with a link to the full image.

This could be the basis of advanced photo gallery software.

Listing 18.5.1   **Photo Gallery Software**

```
<style>
div {
    text-align: center;
    border: 2px solid black;
    padding: 5px;
    margin: 10px;
}
ul {
    font-size: 9px;
    text-align: left;
}
</style>
<?php
// Define a path - We are assuming that this will be a relative path working
// both in the filesystem, and through the web for links:
$path = "photos/";

// Open the directory
```

Listing 18.5.1 **Continued**

```php
$do = dir($path);

// Loop through it, looking for any/all JPG files:
while (($file = $do->read()) !== false) {
    // Parse this for the extension
    $info = pathinfo($path . $file);

    // Continue only if this is a Jpeg
    if (strtolower($info['extension']) == 'jpg') {
        // We found one!  Start a DIV to display & link to this:
        echo "<div><a href=\"{$path}{$file}\">";

        // Let's try to grab the graphic, and if so, display it.
        if ($thumb = exif_thumbnail($path . $file, $width,
                $height, $type)) {
            // We got one.  Therefore first figure out the mime type of it
            $mime = image_type_to_mime_type($type);

            // Now we are going to use an HTML trick, and embed the graphic
            // directly into the webpage as base64 encoded data
            $encoded = base64_encode($thumb);
            echo "<img src=\"data:{$mime};base64,{$encoded}\" /><br />";
        }

        // In either case, place the name of the file as part of the link:
        echo $file, "</a>\n";

        // Now let's read in all the Exif data:
        if ($exif = exif_read_data($path . $file)) {
            // We got it.  So start an unordered list to display it all
            echo "<ul>\n";

            // We need to loop through each 'section' of this data
            foreach ($exif as $section => $sectiondata) {
                // If sectiondata is an array, start a new list:
                if (is_array($sectiondata)) {
                    // Output the section name, and start a new list
                    echo "<li>{$section}<ul>\n";

                    // Loop through this section now
                    foreach ($sectiondata as $name => $data) {
                        // Output this line of data
                        echo "<li>{$name} = ", htmlspecialchars($data),
                            "</li>\n";
                    }
```

Listing 18.5.1 **Continued**

```
                // Close our section off
                echo "</ul></li>\n";
            } else {
                // It's not really a section, its got data.  Echo it
                echo "<li>{$section} = ",
                    htmlspecialchars($sectiondata), "</li>\n";
            }
        }

        // Close the entire list off
        echo "</ul>\n";
    }

    // Close the div tag
    echo "</div>\n";
    }
}
?>
```

As written, this ends up generating some potentially ugly pages (as well as large). The biggest problem is that what Exif data exists depends completely on the manufacturer, and even the model of the camera. Some may only include a few fields; however, most include far more than you would expect. If you were going to truly be writing some form of photo gallery software based on this code, you would certainly need to pick a subset of the fields that you would want to display.

19

Error Reporting and Debugging

PHP COMES WITH A WELL-ROUNDED SET of functions to manage error reporting and debugging information. As you might expect, such functionality is highly valued during script development. However, you will find that, for any moderately complex web-based application, PHP's error and debugging management is crucial in providing a positive web experience, not only shielding the user from meaningless error pages but also providing site maintainers with valuable information about site usage and performance.

PHP provides two types of error management: error messages and exceptions. Error messages are the basic error mechanism of PHP; errors are created, or "triggered," most often by the PHP interpreter and core library functions, for syntax errors, bad runtime values, and invalid file system operations. As will be seen in Section 19.1, "Defining a Custom Error Handler," errors handling routines can be defined that do extra processing, depending on the error generated. A script can also explicitly generate errors as necessary.

Errors are grouped into a number of levels where each level represents a certain type and severity of error. For a complete list of errors, see http://us2.php.net/errorfunc#errorlevels. The most common error levels are as follows:

- E_ERROR—Fatal runtime errors that stop script execution.
- E_WARNING—A runtime error that is not fatal. Scripts continue to execute.
- E_NOTICE—A runtime message that indicates something that may produce unexpected results, depending on the context.
- E_STRICT—Messages that provide suggestions on improving the executing code to avoid ambiguities and other issues that may affect portability.
- E_ALL—Except for E_STRICT, this includes all errors, including errors not listed here, such as PHP startup and internal compiler messages.
- E_USER_ERROR—A user-generated error message of the same severity as E_ERROR.
- E_USER_WARNING—A user-generated error message of the same severity as E_WARNING.
- E_USER_NOTICE—A user-generated error message of the same severity as E_NOTICE.

The other method of error management, exception handling, provides a more user-controlled and localized form of error reporting. Section 19.2, "Using Exceptions to Handle Errors," introduces the concept of exceptions.

No discussion of error handling is complete without including debugging methods. PHP provides a basic set of functions for producing code trace information, all of which is explored in Section 19.5, "Generating Detailed Backtracing for Error Reporting."

Quick Hits

▶ **Set a specific level of error reporting:**

```
$old = error_reporting($new);
```

This function sets the error reporting level to $new for the duration of the script, returning the preexisting level.

Full documentation: http://php.net/error_reporting

▶ **Generate an error:**

```
$success = trigger_error($message, $type);
```

This function generates an error with the given message and type. If the type is unknown, false is returned.

Full documentation: http://php.net/trigger_error

▶ **Log a message in the error log:**

```
$success = error_log($message);
```

The specified message is written to the default error logging mechanism. If the script is run from a web server, the message appears in the server's error file; if run from the command line, the error appears in the operating system's error log. Through optional arguments, the message can be sent to an email address, debugger, or file.

Full documentation: http://php.net/error_log

▶ **Print out or retrieve a full backtrace at the current point of execution:**

```
debug_print_backtrace();
```

```
$array = debug_backtrace();
```

These functions take no arguments. The former prints out a complete backtrace of how a script got to its current point of execution. The latter returns the backtrace information in an associative array.

Full documentation: http://php.net/debug_print_backtrace

19.1 Defining a Custom Error Handler

PHP's default error handling routines simply do what is needed of them. They display a basic error message (if asked to), log it into the web server's log file, and kill off the script as needed. This is fine most of the time but lacks some extra features that might be desired. For example, you could have a script that was generating a lot of large temporary data files, and if there is an error you want to clean them up. Similarly you might want an error to automatically trigger a database rollback.

Making changes such as these is allowed through the function set_error_ handler(), which allows you to define a function that handles all errors that occur. If you do this, it completely overrides PHP's default handler until (and if) you make a call to restore_error_handler(), which restores the default error handler. Your user-defined error handler will not get any errors caused by compiling or Zend core failures.

What you want to do with the error after your function receives it, is up to you. However you do still need to call die() if it was a fatal error that should cause the script to exit. In this section, we will demonstrate a generically useful application of this. You see, as it stands with all errors written to a log file, specific errors are actually difficult to track down afterwards. Do you know what pages are generating the most errors? How many errors a day are you getting? There are so many questions that you might want to ask of your error log. Of course the best way to handle this, is to log all errors into a database. That way you can dig deeply into all the details of your errors at your leisure.

We will write errors to a MySQL database; however, it should be easy to modify to work with any database system. The specific example uses the regular MySQL extension that works with any version of MySQL. You may want to change these calls to the mysqli versions if you want to use the newer access library. In general you will need to update them to use whatever database system and access library you prefer. First we need to create a table to handle this; Listing 19.1.1 shows the SQL to accomplish.

Listing 19.1.1 **SQL to Create the Error Log Table**

```
CREATE TABLE 'error_log' (
    'id' BIGINT UNSIGNED NOT NULL AUTO_INCREMENT ,
    'errno' INT NOT NULL ,
    'errstr' VARCHAR( 512 ) NOT NULL ,
    'errfile' VARCHAR( 512 ) NOT NULL ,
    'errline' INT NOT NULL ,
    'errcontext' TEXT NOT NULL ,
    PRIMARY KEY ( 'id' )
) TYPE = MYISAM ;
```

Now that we have a table to store the data, we just need to write the custom handler and prepare to start logging all the errors to the database. Listing 19.1.2 contains the code to actually make the handler.

Listing 19.1.2 **PHP Error Handler That Writes to a MySQL Database**

```
<?php
// Define a custom error handler that will save all errors into a database.
function db_err_handler($errno, $errstr, $errfile, $errline, $errcontext) {
```

Listing 19.1.2 **Continued**

```
    // Open a fresh database connection for this, don't want to reuse
    // any that might have caused the original error.
    $db = @mysql_connect('localhost', 'my_user', 'my_password')
        or die('Error Logging DB Failure: ' . mysql_error());
    mysql_select_db('my_database');

    // Now, we need to serialize the error context to store it, since it's
    // a huge array holding all of the variables that exist.
    $ized = serialize($errcontext);

    // Ok, we should now be able to insert this error into the table.
    mysql_query("
        insert into error_log
            (errno, errstr, errfile, errline, errcontext)
        values
            ({$errno}, '{$errstr}', '{$errfile}', {$errline}, '{$ized}')
        ");

    // Go ahead and close the database connection.
    mysql_close($db);

    // Now, if this was a fatal error of some sort, just output 'ERROR'
    // and kill the process.  Otherwise, let it go on as if it didn't happen
    // The only two of these that we will see, are ERROR or USER_ERROR
    if (($errno == E_ERROR) || ($errno == E_USER_ERROR)) {
        die("ERROR");
    }
}

// Now go ahead and register this as the error handler:
set_error_handler('db_err_handler');
?>
```

With all that accomplished, if you included Listing 19.1.2 in all your programs, you would automatically start logging all errors to the database table instead of to log files. One simple way to do this would be via editing the php.ini file for your web server and changing the auto_prepend_file directive to point to this script, causing it to always load this function to every file on your system. Of course, if you are going to make this drastic change to your system, make sure that all your PHP files can handle this correctly.

19.2 Using Exceptions to Handle Errors

Defining custom error handlers can be useful as described in the preceding section. However, it also is cumbersome in that it completely takes over all error handling for you. It therefore isn't very useful to use as an error handling routine for yourself. This is where PHP 5's exceptions come into play.

PHP 5 introduced the concept of exceptions, which already existed in other languages such as Java. Exceptions, in their simplest form, are a way of causing an error to occur, breaking the current flow of the code, and dropping immediately into an error handling section of the code itself. This allows different actions to occur depending on what section of code is being executed, allowing greater control over whatever error has been encountered.

PHP implements this via the keywords `try` and `catch`. You start a `try` block and throw exceptions as needed throughout it. If an error occurs, code execution is immediately dropped into the `catch` block. There you can look at the exception that was created and decide what needs done. Listing 19.2.1 gives a basic example of this.

Listing 19.2.1 **The Use of `try` and `catch`**

```php
<?php
// Begin a try block so that we can catch any exceptions that happen:
try {
    // Let's generate a random number from 1 to 10
    $num = rand(1,10);

    // Ensure that the number is less than 3
    if ($num < 3) {
        // It's not, throw an appropriate exception
        throw new Exception('Number is too small');
    }

    // Now also don't allow the number to be greater than 7
    if ($num > 7) {
        // Another exception
        throw new Exception('Number is too big');
    }

    // Otherwise, we are happy with the number...
    echo "<p>Our new number is: {$num}</p>\n";
} catch (Exception $e) {
    // We caught the exception, so let's give the error to the user
    echo '<p>Exception: ', $e->getMessage(), "</p>\n";
}

echo "<p>Done!</p>";
?>
```

As seen, one of the great benefits of using exceptions is that you handle an error gracefully, doing whatever you need to do to correct or report the problem. So far we have just demonstrated the use of generic exceptions. The `Exception` class can be extended if you want to create your own specific exceptions. This can make it easier to handle each of them differently. Listing 19.2.2 demonstrates what Listing 19.2.1 could look like if rewritten with simple custom exception classes.

Listing 19.2.2 **Extending the `Exception` Class to Create a Custom Error Handler**

```php
<?php
// Extend the Exception class to create a 'less than' exception
class LessThanException extends Exception {
    // Create a variable to hold what the minimum number was:
    private $number;

    // Redefine the constructor to just accept the number.
    public function __construct($num) {
        // First save the number off
        $this->number = $num;

        // Now we need to call the parent constructor and pass on data
        parent::__construct("Number was less than {$num}");
    }
}


// Now also create a very similar Greater Than version:
class GreaterThanException extends Exception {
    // Create a variable to hold what the max number was:
    private $number;

    // Redefine the constructor to just accept the number.
    public function __construct($num) {
        // Save the number off
        $this->number = $num;

        // Now we need to call the parent constructor and pass on data
        parent::__construct("Number was greater than {$num}");
    }

    // Declare a function that will return what the number was:
    public function thanWhat() {
        return $this->number;
    }
}


// Now we can begin using these:

// Begin a try block so that we can catch any exceptions that happen:
try {
```

Listing 19.2.2 **Continued**

```
    // Generate a random number from 10 to 50
    $num = rand(10,50);

    // If the number is less than 25 we aren't happy:
    if ($num < 25) {
        // Ok, it was less than, so throw a less than exception:
        throw new LessThanException(25);
    }

    // Also the number shouldn't be greater than 42
    if ($num > 42) {
        // This time use the greater than exception.
        throw new GreaterThanException(42);
    }
}
// First try to catch less than errors:
catch (LessThanException $le) {
    // We caught the exception, this is really unacceptable, so error out:
    die('<p>LESS THAN ERROR: ' . $le->getMessage() . "</p>\n");
}
// Now let's try to catch the greater than errors:
catch (GreaterThanException $ge) {
    // If it was greater than, let's just invisibly reset it to what our
    // max really was:
    $num = $ge->thanWhat();
}

// We are happy with the number now so print it out.
echo "<p>Our new number is: {$num}</p>\n";
?>
```

In this case, two classes were defined that were extensions of the original Exception class. Doing this gives you the ability to define customizations to your exception, such as the $number property that was made in the thanWhat() method. Also as can be seen, you can have multiple catch clauses looking for different types of exceptions. You do need to have a catch clause for any type of exception that you plan on raising in a try block. Otherwise, you will receive an "Uncaught Exception" error, which is probably not what you want.

Note

This section has not fully delved into all the details and variations that you can accomplish with exceptions. If you want to learn more, read the PHP documentation at http://php.net/exceptions.

19.3 Timing the Execution of Your Script

When debugging your scripts, and during the maintenance phase of any project, you often need to determine how long it takes for a PHP script to run. More importantly, you often know that a certain script takes a long time to run but don't know exactly what section of code is causing the slowdown. It is useful, therefore, to have an easy way to add time tracking to a script.

Listing 19.3.1 is a small include file that defines two functions useful in tracking down execution time issues. The first is used to mark different time stamps in your script. The final one generates a report based on these for you. This primarily uses the function microtime(), which when passed a parameter of true returns a UNIX epoch like time(), except that this epoch is a float with accuracy down to microseconds.

The second function defined in Listing 19.3.1, and intended to make the listing more interesting and useful, is the debug_backtrace() function, which determines the context of where the timing call was made. Backtraces are examined in more detail in Section 19.5.

Listing 19.3.1   Script Timer Library—Filename: timer.php

```php
<?php
// Declare a global array that we will be using to store this data
$_timer_results = array();

// A function that will add a new timing result to the global
function _timer() {
    global $_timer_results;

    // Immediately grab the time in microseconds
    $curtime = microtime(true);

    // Grab a backtrace so we can see who called this:
    $trace = debug_backtrace();

    // Now, the [0] entry refers to 'right now' in the backtrace, so we will
    // use that to determine the filename and line #.  But will look
    // at the [1] entry if it exists, for the calling function name.
    $_timer_results[] = array(
        'line' => $trace[0]['line'],
        'file' => $trace[0]['file'],
        'func' => isset($trace[1]['function']) ? $trace[1]['function'] : '',
        'time' => $curtime
        );
}

// Now immediately call timer once, to always place a timer at the entry
// point of our script for us:
_timer();
```

Listing 19.3.1 **Continued**

```php
// Now create a function that will turn these results into a readable text
// string.  It will return this so that it can be dealt with as the program
// needs, either via displaying, adding as an HTML comment, or whatever.
function _timer_text() {
    global $_timer_results;
    $result = 'Timing Results';

    // Start our rolling clock at the timestamp of the first entry
    $clock = @$_timer_results[0]['time'];

    // Now, loop through all entries in the timer results to create text
    foreach ($_timer_results as $tr) {
        // Calculate how long this one took, from the rolling clock
        $thistime = $tr['time'] - $clock;

        // Reset the clock for the next loop iteration
        $clock = $tr['time'];

        // Grab just the filename of the file:
        $fn = basename($tr['file']);

        // And to make output prettier, since we don't really need
        // an extreme level of detail on the timing, let's convert
        // the time to use 5 precision points:
        $pretty = number_format($thistime, 5);

        // Now make and add the string to the results
        $result .= "\n{$pretty} secs - File: {$fn} - Line: {$tr['line']}";

        // If there was a calling function, add it:
        if ($tr['func']) {
            $result .= " - Calling Function: {$tr['func']}";
        }
    }

    // Return what we have created
    return $result;
}
?>
```

Now that we have created this script, let's use it. Listing 19.3.2 does just that by includ-ing the script, doing some various operations while showing all the different ways in which timing can be used.

Listing 19.3.2 **Using the Script Timer Library in an Application**

```php
<?php
// Let's test our timing functionality, first include the file:
require 'timer.php';

// Let's generate a hundred thousand random numbers
foreach(range(1,100000) as $r) {
    rand();
}

// Now check how long that took.
_timer();

// Generate one SHA hash, based upon the last generated number:
sha1($r);

// Did that take very long?
_timer();

// Let's create a function that will do some work for us:
function do_it() {
    // Immediately start a timer
    _timer();

    // Now just sleep for 3 seconds
    sleep(3);
}

// Now call the function:
do_it();

// Then time one last time:
_timer();

// Now generate the text results, and output them - Will be similar to:
// Timing Results
// 0.00000 secs - File: 19c03-1.php - Line: 28 - Calling Function: require
// 0.24862 secs - File: 19c03-2.php - Line: 12
// 0.00011 secs - File: 19c03-2.php - Line: 18
// 0.00005 secs - File: 19c03-2.php - Line: 23 - Calling Function: do_it
// 2.98948 secs - File: 19c03-2.php - Line: 33
$output = _timer_text();
echo "<pre>{$output}</pre>\n";
?>
```

19.4 Using Shutdown Functions to Gracefully Handle Script Failures

At times you may be faced with the task of creating a PHP script that no matter what always exits gracefully. For example, you might be writing a PHP script that is fired off by another program and ends up doing some work in the background. In this case, the PHP script may want to respond to the original script letting it know whether it completed correctly or had an error.

Using standard PHP programming, you can output an "OK" string if everything works fine; however, this doesn't handle the error conditions. Typically you will either have errors displayed to the user, which creates any number of random visible strings, or for most production servers, you have them completely hidden, which generates a blank page.

You could solve this via writing a custom error handler, as in Listing 19.1.1. This works but precludes the standard PHP error handling from still happening (logging to files, for example). Also this isn't a solution if you already have redefined the error handler for other reasons.

Another solution can present itself—in this case the use of a shutdown function. A *shutdown function* is one of your own creations that you tell PHP to run when the script exits, no matter what the reason for the script exiting. This allows you to place some code that you know will always be executed.

In this case described, you can use the shutdown function to output the appropriate value to the calling program, based on the value of a global variable. Listing 19.4.1 demonstrates how this could work.

Listing 19.4.1 **Using Shutdown Functions for Custom Error Handling**

```php
<?php
// Create a global variable that keeps the good/bad status of this script
// Preset it to 'false'. Assume the worst case unless we say otherwise.
$status = false;

// Now create a shutdown function that just outputs a simple status message
function my_shutdown() {
    // Output either OK or ERROR, depending upon the status
    echo $GLOBALS['status'] ? 'OK' : 'ERROR';
}

// Register this as a shutdown function:
register_shutdown_function('my_shutdown');

// Now that we are completely setup, also ensure no errors are displayed
ini_set('display_errors', false);

// Let's attempt to save any data sent to us to a file:
if (!(file_put_contents('saved.txt', serialize($_REQUEST)))) {
```

Listing 19.4.1 **Continued**

```
    // We had an error, just exit
    exit();
}

// If we made it here, we are done, just set the status to true, meaning we
// are exiting cleanly.
$status = true;
?>
```

Because the shutdown function will always be called, all that we have to do at the end of this script is set the status to true so that the shutdown function knows that this was a clean shutdown without error. If we call exit() at any point, it will display ERROR; it will also display ERROR if any other PHP fatal errors occur. For example, you could have a typo in the PHP script later on, and it would still just exit saying ERROR. This is a handy way to always make sure that a valid response is sent back to the browser.

Shutdown functions can of course be useful for many other cleanup tasks, such as closing database transactions or removing temporary files that have been created.

19.5 Generating Detailed Backtracing for Error Reporting

It can be useful to have detailed error messages when you are trying to debug code. This can be used to display detailed messages to the screen when in your development environment.

In Listing 19.5.1, we will define our own user error handler, as also discussed in Section 19.1. However, in this case we will tell it to only work on fatal errors, allowing the regular handler to still operate for the rest of them. Within it, we will generate a much more detailed error message than otherwise would have existed.

Listing 19.5.1 **Registering an Error Handler for Specific Classes of Errors**

```
<?php
// Define a custom error handler for more details
function detailed_err($errno, $errstr, $errfile, $errline, $errcontext) {
    // First of all, begin by noting that a fatal error occurred, and basic
    // details just like a normal error report:
    echo "<p>FATAL ERROR - {$errstr}</p>\n";

    // Now use debug_print_backtrace to give the function call list in
    // a compressed format easy for quick scanning:
    echo "<pre>\nFunction Call Tree:\n";
    debug_print_backtrace();
```

Listing 19.5.1 **Continued**

```
    // To finish off our 'extreme' debugging mode here, let's also give
    // a full backtrace dump, which will contain all variables that existed
    // and much much more.
    echo "\nFull Backtrace:\n";
    var_dump(debug_backtrace());

    // Close off that pre tag
    echo "</pre>\n";

    // That's it, time to make sure the script dies:
    die();
}

// Now go ahead and register this as the error handler:
set_error_handler('detailed_err', E_ERROR | E_USER_ERROR);
?>
```

This example makes full use of debug_bracktrace(), which gives you a full list (as an array) of all currently open function calls, variables, line numbers, and more. It also uses debug_print_backtrace(), which gives a smaller, simpler output to the backtrace to make it easier to just see the heart of the problem. Combined, this makes for as much detail as you could really care to have.

Of course, you would certainly want to make sure that this is enabled only on your development environment. You would not want this level of detail about your system to be displayed to the end user. However, you could modify this on your production server so that instead of outputting all this to the screen, it could send it as an email to you instead. That way if a fatal error happens on the website, you will be instantly notified and have all the information possible to go and debug it.

20

User Authentication and Encryption

INVARIABLY IN A WEB ENVIRONMENT, the need will arise to restrict access to an area of a website. Almost hand-in-hand, you will need to secure data either to store in a database or to transfer between different systems. In both cases, PHP provides the necessary libraries to create an environment that will safeguard user information.

Quick Hits

▶ Perform a one-way encryption of a string:

```
$secret = crypt($string, $salt);
```

This function returns a cryptographic hash of the given string using a default encryption standard, usually DES. There is no corresponding decrypt function. The optional argument, `$salt`, is used to determine the type of hashing function used.

Full documentation: http://php.net/crypt

▶ Generate a random number:

```
$result = rand($min, $max);
```

A random number is generated that lies between (and including) the specified minimum and maximum.

Full documentation: http://php.net/rand

20.1 Generating Random Passwords

Sometimes security dictates that users may not be allowed to choose their own passwords. In these cases you need some way to quickly generate them. Even if you do not have a requirement for random passwords, you will still often need to generate initial passwords for users, or use them when someone has lost his password and needs a new temporary one.

Listing 20.1.1 gives an example of a function that lets you specify an arbitrary length of characters, and it generates a random password for you containing only lowercase letters, uppercase letters, and numbers.

Listing 20.1.1 **Generating Random Passwords**

```php
<?php
// A function that accepts a parameter to specify a length, and then returns
// a random password with characters and letters
function random_password($length = 8) {
    // Declare a blank string to start from
    $pass = '';

    // Now loop for as many times as the length
    for ($i = 0; $i < $length; $i++) {
        // For this character, first give an equal chance of upper,lower,num
        switch (rand(0,2)) {
            case 0:
                // Generate a Number from 0 to 9
                $pass .= rand(0,9);
                break;
            case 1:
                // Generate a letter from A to Z via ascii values 65 to 90
                $pass .= chr(rand(65,90));
                break;
            default:
                // Instead use a letter from a to z, via ascii 97 to 122
                $pass .= chr(rand(97,122));
        }
    }

    // Return that password!
    return $pass;
}

// Test this, echo out a batch of 10 passwords, from 1 to 10 characters long
echo "<ol>\n";
foreach (range(1,10) as $l) {
    $tmp = random_password($l);
    echo "<li>{$tmp}</li>\n";
}
echo "</ol>\n";
?>
```

At the heart of this code is a switch statement that gives a random one-in-three chance of each character being lowercase, uppercase, or a number. It then randomly picks the appropriate type of character via generating ASCII values and converting them with chr(). By first randomly choosing which of the three types is used, we evenly distribute them throughout. Otherwise, because there are more letters than digits, digits would rarely appear.

20.2 Using Encryption to Protect Data

Protecting data is important in this day and age. Stories regularly appear in the news of companies having their machines broken into and having data stolen. Ensuring that any sensitive data that is kept is also encrypted is a good second layer of defense. Even if the files are compromised, someone will have to crack the encryption to access the data.

Unfortunately, the only algorithm that comes with PHP by default for data encryption is the crypt() function. This is based on the standard UNIX algorithm used for password files. This algorithm has a few drawbacks. First, it typically (specifics depend on the system) looks at only the first eight characters of the string given it. Second, it is a one-way encryption. That is, you can encrypt but not decrypt. Therefore you can never know what the original encrypted message was. What you can do, however, is encrypt something again and see whether the two encrypted strings match up. This means that this is basically useful only for passwords, where you don't ever want someone to see the password, and you only need to check against it when you have been provided a password anyway. Listing 20.2.1 gives an example of doing this.

Listing 20.2.1   **Encrypting Passwords with** crypt()

```php
<?php
// Assume that we have been given the following password:
$password = 'bob123xy';

// Now encrypt this password, we will not provide the optional second
// parameter to specify a 'salt' or 'seed' for the encryption, since the
// specifics can vary per system, easiest to leave it blank.
$enc = crypt($password);

// Now, let's assume that we've just been given a password as part of a login
// Let's try to recrypt it to match.  This time pass the encrypted version as
// the 'salt' so that it can generate it again.  The original salt is saved
// as part of the encryption process. -- This should echo GOOD.
if (crypt($password, $enc) == $enc) {
    echo 'GOOD';
} else {
    echo 'FAILED';
}
?>
```

One aspect to crypt() should be noted: the salt argument. The salt argument provides two functions. The first is a seed for the random aspect of the hashing function, similar

to the seed argument for srand(). The second function of the salt argument is to specify the type of hashing function to use to create the encryption. Although the specifics of
which encryption methods are available are system dependent, the important point is
that different methods are available. Because there are different methods and because the
goal of crypt() is to be able to compare encrypted values, crypt() needs to know
which method was used to produce a specific encryption. It does this be prepending the
result with the necessary salt information, identifying the encryption method used.
Thus, when comparing an encryption, it is necessary to pass the given encrypted value as
the salt. This can be seen in Listing 20.2.1 where the encrypted values are compared.

Although this works fine for passwords, it leaves a hole for how to handle full encryption of larger amounts of data, as well as the capability to decrypt it. PHP does provide
support for this as the mcrypt library; however, it is not compiled in by default. To get
the mcrypt functions available to you, you will have to recompile PHP as well as download and install the mcrypt libraries themselves. Full information on how to accomplish
this is available at http://php.net/mcrypt.

The mcrypt library is a powerful generic tool. Depending on the version of the
library that you have installed, you can encrypt with potentially any of 41 different
algorithms.

Given this fact and many other configuration options that exist, an entire chapter (or
book) could be written to explain them all. Listing 20.2.2 gives a basic example of how
to use mcrypt in its simplest form by encrypting a string. As written, this example uses
the Blowfish algorithm, but that can be changed to any that you want to use.

Listing 20.2.2 **Encryption Using** mcrypt

```php
<?php
// Define our text, and our 'secret password'
$text = "The market price of our stock will greatly increase next week due
to us releasing the fact that we have made 3 million dollars more than our
original $300 profit estimate that we came up with.";
$secret = "The sparrow flies at midnight";

// Before encryption we need an Initialization Vector for the algorithm
$ivsize = mcrypt_get_iv_size(MCRYPT_BLOWFISH, MCRYPT_MODE_ECB);
$iv = mcrypt_create_iv($ivsize, MCRYPT_RAND);

// Now, encrypt this data using the Blowfish algorithm:
$enc = mcrypt_encrypt(MCRYPT_BLOWFISH, $secret, $text, MCRYPT_MODE_ECB, $iv);

// Let's echo out what the encrypted version looks like:
echo "<p>Encrypted:<br />{$enc}</p>";

// Generate a new Initialization Vector to decrypt it with.
$niv = mcrypt_create_iv($ivsize, MCRYPT_RAND);
```

Listing 20.2.2 **Continued**

```
// Now decrypt it again:
$dec = mcrypt_decrypt(MCRYPT_BLOWFISH, $secret, $enc, MCRYPT_MODE_ECB, $niv);

// Now display the decrypted version
echo "<p>Readable Again:<br />{$dec}</p>";
?>
```

> **Note**
>
> To read more about the mcrypt extension and all its options, visit http://php.net/mcrypt.

20.3 Simple CAPTCHA for Real User Detection

CAPTCHA is an acronym that stands for *Completely Automated Public Turing test to tell Computers and Humans Apart*. Essentially it is a broad term that means anything that can be used as a test to ensure that a real person is sitting behind the keyboard. It is used to stop computer programs from automatically submitting forms on web pages, sending email, and other tasks.

Although the broad term can refer to any of a wide variety of methods (riddles, audio bites, and so on), the typical method employed by many applications is interpretation of a graphic. Specifically, a graphic that contains text within it that has been altered/ obscured/distorted in ways that should make it difficult for OCR programs to actually try to parse the data out of the graphic, yet, allows a human to still read it.

Many different types of distortions can be done: rotating the text; bending it; putting lines, dots, and colors on the image; and so on. Listing 20.3.1 is an example of PHP combined with the GD library discussed in Chapter 18, "Images," generating a CAPTCHA graphic.

Listing 20.3.1 **Generating a CAPTCHA Graphic—Filename: captcha.php**

```
<?php
// Generate a CAPTCHA graphic.

// Start off by defining a new image, define our dimensions
$w = 300;
$h = 50;
$gfx = imagecreatetruecolor($w, $h);

// Turn on antialiasing so that curvy things look better.
imageantialias($gfx, true);
```

Listing 20.3.1   **Continued**

```
// Declare white as our background color:
$white = imagecolorallocate($gfx, 255, 255, 255);
imagefilledrectangle($gfx, 0, 0, $w-1, $h-1, $white);

// Generate a 6-8 character string of only uppercase characters:
$str = '';
foreach (range(0, rand(5,7)) as $r) {
    $str .= chr(rand(65,90));
}

// Now, divide the width by the length to find approximate positions
// for each character to appear:
$pos = $w / strlen($str);

// Now we can loop through printing out these characters
foreach(range(0, strlen($str) - 1) as $s) {
    // Randomly generate a grayscale color, but only 'dark' ones
    $shade = rand(0, 100);

    // Declare this color:
    $tmpgray = imagecolorallocate($gfx, $shade, $shade, $shade);

    // Now, we can draw this one character, messing with it as much as
    // possible while we do so:
    imagettftext($gfx,      // The graphics object to draw on
        rand($h/3, $h/2),   // Font Size, between 1/3 and 1/2 full height
        rand(-60, 60),      // Slant angle, highly variable
        $s*$pos+($pos*.4),  // X, stabilized at equal places
        rand($h*.5,$h*.7),  // Y, Variable between half or a bit lower.
        $tmpgray,           // The color to do it with - gray
        'arial',            // The font to use.
        $str{$s});          // Just print this character
}

// Now crosshatch the entire background with various shades of gray lines
// Loop from negative height to width to ensure we draw over everything
foreach(range(-$h, $w, 5) as $x) {
    // Randomly generate a shade of gray, but not the darkest ones.
    $shade = rand(50,254);
    $tmpgray = imagecolorallocate($gfx, $shade, $shade, $shade);

    // Now draw two lines from here, One diagonally down, one diagonally up
    // at slightly random angles
    imageline($gfx, $x, 0, $x+$h+rand(0,25), $h-1, $tmpgray);
    imageline($gfx, $x, $h-1, $x+$h+rand(0,25), 0, $tmpgray);
}
```

Listing 20.3.1 **Continued**

```
// We are now done with our manipulations.  Before we output this, set
// the actual string as part of a session variable:
session_start();
$_SESSION['captcha'] = $str;

// Let the browser know that we are going to output this as a PNG
header('Content-type: image/png');

// And then output our new image:
imagepng($gfx);
?>
```

This particular version generates a mess of grayscale lines that obscure some grayscale text at various angles. Through manipulation of the variations it is readable by humans probably 99% of time and should be difficult for a computer to read without spending a lot of time on the problem.

As it currently stands, some characters might be difficult to make out. An N rotated far enough may look like a Z. This is specifically why we didn't use numbers as well because so many numbers can look like letters. There are a few options for handling this. You may want to just leave some of the letters as confusing. This will make it even more difficult for a computer to guess correctly, and if a user has to enter a CAPTCHA twice, that isn't a horrible thing. Alternatively, you may want to not include certain characters, or allow for variations when comparing. You might allow an N to count as a Z and vice versa. The safest approach of course is just to leave them in, and if a user doesn't get it from time to time, well then neither will a computer.

Now notice that this script also does something else. It sets a session variable with the string it generated. This is important. Otherwise, you won't ever be able to check this value against something that the user has typed in. To complete the example, Listing 20.3.2 builds a page that includes this CAPTCHA, asks the user to validate herself, and submits back to itself to check the value.

Listing 20.3.2 **Using CAPTCHA in a Web Page**

```
<?php
// Start the PHP session
session_start();

// If this page was submitted back to itself:
if (count($_POST)) {
    // Ensure that a session captcha was set:
    if (isset($_SESSION['captcha'])) {
        // See if this one matches the submitted value:
        if ($_SESSION['captcha'] === strtoupper($_POST['check'])) {
            // We have a valid match!  The most important thing to do now
```

Listing 20.3.2 **Continued**

```
                    // is destroy the previous captcha entry so that they can't
                    // just resubmit this same form again!
                    unset($_SESSION['captcha']);

                    // Now the script should do it's action, redirect, etc.
                    // For now, we are just going to say congratz
                    echo "<p>Congratulations, you typed it in correctly!</p>\n";
            } else {
                    // Bad attempt -- Let them know it was wrong, this page will
                    // then continue and give them a new one anyway.
                    echo "<p>Sorry, that wasn't it, try again!</p>\n";
            }
        } else {
            // The session captcha variable wasn't set, this means that someone
            // submitted successfully once, then tried to spam us with the same
            // session information.
            echo "<p>Sorry, no spamming aloud!  Go away!  Shoo!</p>\n";
        }
}
?>
<form action="<?= $_SERVER['PHP_SELF'] ?>" method="post">
Please enter the text that you see in the following graphic:<br />
<img src="captcha.php" /><br />
<input name="check" type="text"><br />
<input name="Submit" type="submit">
</form>
```

The most important part to this is making sure that after you have validated a user, destroy the session variable that held the CAPTCHA "key." If you do not do this, it is possible through a variation on session hijacking for a user to submit the same form many times, providing the same session id and the same text that matches the key. Because the key wasn't destroyed, this will work and will continue to work until that session expires. Therefore, always destroy the key as soon as possible.

20.4 Authenticating Users

Often, web areas are secured using server-based authentication methods, either with .htaccess files or through the server configuration file. Unfortunately, this type of authentication is useful only for general access control where groups of people share the same access information. Also you are limited as to the web server's built in options for how to handle maintaining username/password relations. Finally, you may simply not have access to server-based authentication. Regardless of the reasons, PHP does provide the necessary utilities to create an authentication system.

To implement a single user/single access system, or to manage usernames and passwords in another manner, authentication can be implemented in the pages themselves. You can use a web page with a form on it to do this, asking for username and password as many websites do. However, this does slightly deviate from the web standard, which has an authentication system built into it, which all web browsers know about. PHP has the capability to integrate into this and therefore you can use HTTP authentication to collect and enforce access control.

HTTP authentication is the same method used by server-controlled access. The HTTP protocol specifies a method for requesting access information through the WWW-Authenticate header request. When a browser receives a WWW-Authenticate header, it normally displays the familiar dialog box requesting username and password. PHP provides special global variables, found in the $_SERVER superglobal array, which contain the authentication information if you use this method. The relevant keys are as follows:

- PHP_AUTH_USER—Contains the value of the "USERNAME"

- PHP_AUTH_PW—Contains the value of the "PASSWORD" field

- PHP_AUTH_TYPE—Either Basic or Digest, representing the type of authorization being used

Combined with the header function, any PHP page can initiate and validate access information. Listing 20.4.1 is a single PHP script that first presents the standard username/password dialog box and then validates the given values.

Listing 20.4.1 **Using HTTP Authentication**

```php
<?php
// Check if the server has provided us with a Valid User, and password:
if (!isset($_SERVER['PHP_AUTH_USER']) ||
        $_SERVER['PHP_AUTH_USER'] != 'MyUserName' ||
        $_SERVER['PHP_AUTH_PW'] != 'MyPassWord' ) {
    // Username and Password did not match the ones we were looking for
    // Therefore send headers asking the client to authenticate.
      header('WWW-Authenticate: Basic realm="For Your Eyes Only"');
    header('HTTP/1.0 401 Unauthorized');

    // And give a generic output error message in case their client doesn't
    // understand Basic Authentication
    echo '<h1>401 Unauthorized!</h1><p>You cannot view this page</p>';
    exit;
}


// If we made it this far, we can display a welcome message!
// They successfully logged into our website.
?>
```

Listing 20.4.1   **Continued**

```
<!DOCTYPE html PUBLIC "-//W3C//DTD XHTML 1.0 Strict//EN"
              "http://www.w3.org/TR/xhtml1/DTD/xhtml1-strict.dtd">
<html xmlns="http://www.w3.org/1999/xhtml">
<head>
<meta http-equiv="Content-Type" content="text/html; charset=iso-8859-1" />
<title>Authentication Test</title>
</head>
<body>
<h2>Hello <?= $_SERVER['PHP_AUTH_USER'] ?>:</h2>
<p>You entered <?= $_SERVER['PHP_AUTH_PW'] ?> as your password!</p>
</body></html>
```

When this page is first called, the browser has no authentication information. Hence, the PHP authentication variables will not be set. The page checks for this condition and, if present, sends the HTTP authentication headers back to the browser. On seeing these headers, the browser produces the familiar access dialog box. Once filled in, the browser requests this page again as part of the standard protocol, this time sending the specified authentication information.

The script can then check to make sure it is the right information. If not, the authentication headers are re-sent, and the dialog is again produced. Authentication requests will continue to be sent until either valid information is provided or the user clicks the Cancel button on the dialog, and an "access denied" message will be given to the user.

As it stands, this script has a hard-coded username and password built into it; however, it could easily be extended to read usernames and passwords from a database. This allows for a flexible manner in which to do user authentication.

Listing 20.4.1 uses the Basic form of HTTP authentication. As of PHP 5.1, you can also use the Digest form, providing a more secure manner for authentication. For more information on PHP's HTTP authentication, see http://php.net/manual/features.http-auth.php.

III

Appendices

A

Migrating to PHP 5

PHP 4 HAS BEEN A WEB PROGRAMMING staple for such a long time, that the introduction of PHP 5 may seem like a bit of a stumbling block. Have no fear, however. Though upgrading to PHP 5 is not quite as simple as just installing the new software, the PHP developers have succeeded in making it nearly that easy. Except as noted in this appendix, all changes have been additions to the language, not modifications to existing functionality. There are a few incompatibilities between the two that can cause some issues when upgrading; luckily these issues are few and can be isolated. The rest of this appendix touches on the most common of these issues, what to look out for, and how to fix problems when they occur.

Because there are so few real issues, the best way to handle your migration is simply to go ahead and do it on a development machine that has a complete copy of your website. Then just start heading through the web pages, take note of any errors that pop up, and fix them as you do. There are plenty of small cosmetic changes and/or fixes to functionality that shouldn't have ever worked the way that they did. (As on Windows, calling `include_once()` on A.php and a.php in PHP 4 would include the same file twice. Now it doesn't.) Therefore be sure to test your code to make sure that you were not inadvertently relying on some bug in the system. A few extensions may have had some changes to their function names, such as the OCI8 Oracle extension that added underscores to all of its function names.

One final general issue to check before upgrading is whether your current PHP 4 scripts use any libraries that were marked "experimental" or third-party libraries that were not bundled with PHP. Some experimental libraries are either being replaced with new standards or simply being eliminated. One notable example is that the DOM XML extension has been replaced with the standard DOM library.

Object Model

The biggest change of course is the object model. PHP 5 has implemented a fully featured object model that includes the concept of public, private, and protected properties.

In general, however, old styles of code still work fine. If you do not specify a visibility, it is assumed to be public, which is how PHP 4 worked. Similarly the methods by which constructors are made have changed, but the old style still works.

The primary change that might affect existing PHP 4 programs is in how objects are handled when passed to a function/method. In PHP 4 a copy of the object was made. In PHP 5, objects are always passed by reference. Therefore if you expected the object to just be a copy, the code is going to have some issues in PHP 5. To learn more about the new object model and references, refer to Chapter 4, "Variables," and Chapter 7, "Classes and Objects."

Finally one small change: In PHP 4 an object with no properties was considered "empty" by functions or language constructs such as empty(). That is no longer the case.

In the end if you need to get PHP 5 working quicker and some of these object changes are causing you issues, you can disable them and tell PHP 5 to act as if it was PHP 4 by changing the configuration directive zend.ze1_compatibility_mode to true. However, this should not be seen as a final solution, only as an intermediate step to fixing all the code to work properly in PHP 4.

MySQL Module

Nothing really has happened to the MySQL module; however, it is no longer automatically included into PHP. If you want to have access to the MySQL functions, it will have to be explicitly compiled or included into the server. You may want to visit http://php.net/mysql for more details on this.

Also PHP 5 has included an entirely new library known as mysqli (MySQL Improved). This is meant to interface only with MySQL servers at version 4.1 or better and provides some additional functionality with those servers. If you want to read more about this extension visit http://php.net/mysqli.

CLI and CGI

In PHP 5 the CLI (command line) and CGI versions compile under different names/directories than they did previously. The CGI version is now called php-cgi, and the CLI version is just php. This is a change from PHP 4 where the CGI was just php, and the CLI lived under a subdirectory as cli/php.

Also now in PHP 5, when running the CLI version of PHP, the $argv and $argc arrays are always populated with the command-line information. Previously it would listen to the setting of register_argc_argv in the configuration file. Now that setting affects only CGI and server module versions of PHP.

Because of this, just be careful of configuration changes that will be needed for any servers relying on the CGI version and any command-line scripts that relied on the CLI.

Case Sensitivity of Classes, Methods, Functions

In PHP 4 the functions `get_class()`, `get_parent_class()`, and `get_class_methods()` plus the magic variables `__CLASS__`, `__METHOD__` and `__FUNCTION__`, all returned a lowercase value. So all class names, method names, and the function name were all lowercased when using these.

Now in PHP 5 they work as you would expect, returning the appropriate name exactly how it was originally defined. This means that you will need to change any code that was written that expected otherwise. A quick fix to this would be to search for any of these six keywords and to just wrap them with a call to `strtolower()`.

array_merge()

`array_merge()` in PHP 4 would allow for its arguments to be arrays or single elements. Therefore it could allow for some coding practices where you didn't need to worry about whether something happened to be an array. In PHP 5 `array_merge()` has been changed to require that all arguments passed to it are arrays, and it will generate a `E_WARNING` level error if otherwise.

Functions That Return by Reference

The one area where PHP 5 has become stricter is in the returning of references from functions. PHP 5 now requires that both the function declaration and the use of that function include the reference operand "&". This has no impact for functions already designed to return by reference. However, if your use of the reference operand was haphazard or done under the mistaken belief that execution efficiency would be increased by simply adding the operand to any function call, such scripts will now return `E_WARNING` messages.

B

SPL

SPL STANDS FOR *Standard PHP Library*. Over time its goal is to provide many standard library items that can be used by anyone in any program as part of the default PHP installation. The library is implemented as object-based classes and interfaces and are conceptually designed around *design patterns*, a set of widely accepted solutions to problems that developers face regularly.

Although that is the grand goal, currently as of PHP 5.1, SPL primarily contains a collection of objects all related to one particular design pattern: Iterators. The Iterator is a design pattern that is a generic solution to the problem of iterating over data.

You might say that this is exactly what loops are. That is true; however, the manner in which you loop over data varies greatly depending on the data itself. You have to use a different style of loop if you are reading from a data stream or directory files or even just an array in memory. Iterators attempt to define a way for you to specify a generic way to loop over any type of data.

> **Note**
>
> The rest of this appendix takes you through many examples of what Iterators can do in PHP 5; however, this brief introduction can really touch only the basics of this deep subject. For a more full understanding of the power of Iterators, read the documentation found at http://php.net/spl. Take special note of the related links and tutorials mentioned. Although SPL is a part of the official PHP distribution, the online documentation is still in development.

Basic Interface

The basic interface to using all Iterators is the same. After creating an Iterator, you can call the next() method to retrieve the next item in the series, the rewind() method to return to the beginning, and the current() method to access the current element. However, typically you don't need to use these because PHP has made it even easier by building support into the foreach loop for these. You can just surround your Iterator with the `foreach` loop, and it handles it for you. For example, Listing B.1 shows you how you would normally loop over an array of values and echo them out.

Listing B.1   **Traditional Method of Looping Through an Array**

```php
<?php
$arr = array('Guam', 'USA', 'Cuba', 'Mexico', 'Canada', 'Netherlands');

foreach($arr as $entry) {
    echo "<p>{$entry}</p>";
}
?>
```

Now instead of doing that, you can use the built-in Iterator called `ArrayIterator` that the SPL provides. Listing B.2 shows how you do this.

Listing B.2   **Using SPL and `ArrayIterator` to Access an Array**

```php
<?php
$arr = array('Guam', 'USA', 'Cuba', 'Mexico', 'Canada', 'Netherlands');

// Declare a new ArrayIterator, and pass it the array:
$arrIt = new ArrayIterator($arr);

// Now just use it inside of the foreach loop instead:
foreach($arrIt as $entry) {
    echo "<p>{$entry}</p>";
}
?>
```

Now in this simple case, it almost looks like there is no benefit to using an Iterator over the standard way of doing this. In fact, it adds one extra line of code, but that ends up missing the point. All iterative processes become as simple as a `foreach` loop after Iterators are used. So let's look at a slightly better example, that of listing the contents of a directory. Listing B.3 shows one of the normal ways of doing this.

Listing B.3   **Traditional Method of Listing a Directory**

```php
<?php
$dir = dir('.');

while(false !== ($entry = $dir->read())) {
    echo "<p>{$entry}</p>";
}

$dir->close();
?>
```

As you can see this doesn't end up involving a `foreach` loop but needs a `while` loop. On top of that you have to know about and follow a different syntax, calling `$dir->read()` to get each entry and checking for that result to be `false` to know when you have reached the end. But the SPL library has a built-in Iterator that can handle this called the `DirectoryIterator`. You use this in the same manner as the previous `ArrayIterator` but give it a directory name. You can see in Listing B.4 how similar this Iterator looks to Listing B.2.

Listing B.4   **Using `DirectoryIterator` to List a Directory**

```php
<?php
$dir = new DirectoryIterator('.');

foreach ($dir as $entry) {
    echo "<p>{$entry}</p>";
}

// Release the resource.
unset($dir);
?>
```

Now here you can really begin to see the benefits of this approach. Accessing a directory listing is accomplished in exactly the same way as an array. The object is created, used, and any resources used are released using the same exact syntax. More than that, the `DirectoryIterator` is really returning an object that can give you access to other data points of the file as well, such as the file size, creation time, file owner, and so on. Listing B.5 is the same code as Listing B.4 but adds in the file size and what type of file it is (`file`, `dir`, and so on). Doing this in the traditional manner would require separate calls to `filesize()` and `filetype()`.

Listing B.5   **Getting Extra Information Out of `DirectoryIterator`**

```php
<?php
$dir = new DirectoryIterator('.');

foreach ($dir as $entry) {
    echo "<p>{$entry} - {$entry->getSize()} - {$entry->getType()}</p>";
}

// Release the resource.
unset($dir);
?>
```

This additional information concept exists in the `ArrayIterator` as well, allowing you to access the keys if you want. This means that you don't need to do a variation on your loop if you want to access keys, such as:

```
foreach($arr as $key => $value)
```

Unfortunately the `ArrayIterator` doesn't return an object like `DirectoryIterator` does; it simply returns the current value. However, it is still possible to get the keys from it by manually stepping through the Iterator (not using the `foreach` shortcut). This is demonstrated in Listing B.6.

Listing B.6 **Accessing Keys in an `ArrayIterator`**

```php
<?php
$arr = array('Owen' => 'P', 'Steve' => 'P', 'Time' => 'D', 'Kevin' => 'B',
    'Jay' => 'B', 'Amar' => 'Q', 'Dan' => 'Q', 'Ron' => 'S', 'John' => 'F' );

$arrIt = new ArrayIterator($arr);

// Now keep looking while we have a valid entry to the array
while ($arrIt->valid()) {
    // Echo out both the key and the current value
    echo "<p>{$arrIt->key()} - {$arrIt->current()}</p>";

    // Now advance to the next one
    $arrIt->next();
}
?>
```

Creating Your Own Iterators

It's actually not that difficult to create your own Iterator because obviously that's part of the point of using objects. You can create an Iterator for any type of data that you may have. You simply need to implement the Iterator interface and then define at least the following methods: `current()`, `key()`, `next()`, `rewind()`, and `valid()`.

As an easy example, Listing B.7 creates a version of the `ArrayIterator` that works in a `foreach` loop while still giving you access to the keys.

Listing B.7 **Creation of a New Iterator for Arrays with Keys—Filename: KeyArrayIterator.php**

```php
<?php
// Declare a new class that implements Iterator, that will allow for more
// natural iteration over Arrays with key access
class KeyArrayIterator implements Iterator {
    // Declare a property to hold the actual data array
    protected $data;

    // Now make our constructor
    public function __construct($v) {
        // Just store this into our protected storage
```

```php
        $this->data = $v;
    }

    // Ok, we need to declare 'rewind' as part of the implementing Iterator
    public function rewind() {
        // Well the data is still an array, so use the array function:
        return reset($this->data);
    }

    // To implement Iterator, declare 'next' which moves the pointer forward
    public function next() {
        // Again, since an array, just use the array function
        return next($this->data);
    }

    // To implement Iterator, we need a 'valid', Whether the pointer is valid
    public function valid() {
        // Use the array 'current' function to check if we are at a valid
        // point in the array or not.
        return (current($this->data) === false) ? false : true;
    }

    // Now we also need 'key' that returns just a key for this entry.
    public function key() {
        // Just use the arrays build in 'key' function to do this
        return key($this->data);
    }

    // Finally define 'current', the real meat of this object
    public function current() {
        // Current needs to return the current entry.  However we want
        // this to really return an object that contains both value
        // and key, therefore let's do just this:
        return new KeyArrayItem(key($this->data), current($this->data));
    }
}

// Now we need to define the KeyArrayItem class that we used in the
// current function of our Iterator.
class KeyArrayItem {
    // First of all, declare properties to hold the data:
    public $key;
    public $value;

    // Now make a constructor that will accept these two data points
    public function __construct($k, $v) {
```

Listing B.7   **Continued**

```
        // Just save them
        $this->key = $k;
        $this->value = $v;
    }

    // Now as one last thing, define a __toString method that will return
    // just the value portion if the object is accessed in a direct manner
    public function __toString() {
        return (string) $this->value;
    }
}
?>
```

As shown, to make your own Iterator you only need to define a constructor and those five methods. It is straightforward. The only slightly complicated part of this example is how we made the entries be usable directly in a loop, plus have additional information. To do this we made the current() method actually return an object which has a __toString() method. __toString() is a "magic method," defined as part of PHP's object model, which is called whenever an object is simply accessed as a value. At the same time, the entry object holds the key in a publicly accessible property, so that it can also be read.

Now that we have this new Iterator, we can use it to rewrite Listing B.6 into a cleaner form using just a foreach loop as shown in Listing B.8.

Listing B.8   **Using KeyArrayIterator to Rewrite Listing B.6**

```
<?php
// Include the library for Key Iteration
require 'KeyArrayIterator.php';

// Declare our array of data
$arr = array('Owen' => 'P', 'Steve' => 'P', 'Time' => 'D', 'Kevin' => 'B',
    'Jay' => 'B', 'Amar' => 'Q', 'Dan' => 'Q', 'Ron' => 'S', 'John' => 'F' );

// Declare a new Iterator of our own devising:
$arrIt = new KeyArrayIterator($arr);

// Now loop over them all as a foreach loop and echo both key and value
foreach ($arrIt as $entry) {
    echo $entry->key, ' - ', $entry, "<br />\n";
}
?>
```

Extending Iterators and Chained Iterators

Because Iterators are classes you can of course create new Iterators that extend existing ones. In fact, we have already done so in Listing B.7. Another good example of this is the built-in `FilterIterator` class. This class is a prototype that requires that you define the `accept()` method to finalize it. The `accept` method returns true or false, whether the current entry in the inner Iterator is acceptable. This allows you to use an existing Iterator and filter out certain results from it.

At this point, we should realize the implications of the previous statement: You can in fact chain Iterators together and have them all work together. An Iterator can iterate over another Iterator.

As an example, let's extend `FilterIterator` in Listing B.9 into a regular expression-based filter. It will accept any regular expression and filter the data based on it.

Listing B.9   **Defining** `RegexFilterIterator` **and Using It**

```php
<?php
// Declare a new class that extends FilterIterator into a Regex one.
class RegexFilterIterator extends FilterIterator {
    // Declare a property to hold the filter criteria
    private $criteria;

    // Now make our constructor, it needs to take an Iterator, and the regex
    public function __construct(Iterator $i, $regex) {
        // Call the parents constructor, and store the regex
        parent::__construct($i);
        $this->criteria = $regex;
    }

    // Define accept to do the regex check
    public function accept() {
        // Just see if the regex matches the current item:
        return preg_match($this->criteria, parent::current());
    }
}


// Now to test this, first define an array of values
$arr = array('Mimi', 'Wiley', 'Tux', 'Taz', 'Iyi', 'Thundar', 'Yowler');

// Now let's create a chained Iterator.  Make a FilterIterator that wraps
// around an ArrayIterator, and only allows items with a 'y' in them.
$it = new RegexFilterIterator(new ArrayIterator($arr), '/y/i');

// Now loop and echo these all out, should include Wiley, Iyi, Yowler.
foreach ($it as $entry) { echo "{$entry}<br />\n"; }
?>
```

You can redefine `FilterIterator` as many times as you want to filter by any number of different types of criteria. The nice thing is that you can make a `FilterIterator` generic like this one is. This regex-based filter could be run against an `ArrayIterator` like it was here but could also have been wrapped around the `DirectoryIterator` to filter directory results, or any other Iterator object just as easily.

Another generically useful class exists for you to use, known as `LimitIterator`. `LimitIterator` allows you to specify two parameters, a start and stop index. This limits the data being returned to only those between those two indexes, just like the limit clause on a SQL query.

This all works because `FilterIterator` and `LimitIterator` are actually implementing an interface called `OuterIterator`. `OuterIterator` has the same five methods that must be implemented as an Iterator but also requires one additional method: `getInnerIterator()`. When creating a class that implements the `OuterIterator` interface, this method defines how the class can delve into the Iterator it is wrapping. However in practice, given the flexibility of just extending `FilterIterator` there are not many cases where you need to truly make a new `OuterIterator` from scratch.

Getting Complicated

At this point, things can start to get complicated quickly. Many variations can occur, and various classes can be predefined. For example there is a class that implements the `OuterIterator` interface called `IteratorIterator`. The purpose of this class is to turn any other class that happens to be traversable into an Iterator.

Similarly there is an `InfiniteIterator` that extends `IteratorIterator`. It automatically calls a `rewind()` when reaching the end of the Iterator within it. Therefore you can declare an `InfiniteIterator`, pass it any Iterator or just a class that implements the basic methods of an Iterator, and it will make an Iterator that never ends.

A number of other similarly varied classes already exist. Examining the documentation in detail will enlighten you to these others.

Recursive Iteration

The final topic on Iteration is recursive iteration. For example, what if you had a multi-level array and needed to output all values from it? Or wanted a full directory listing including all subfolders? Obviously a method for doing recursion needs built into the Iterator methodology.

This is accomplished via two concepts. The first concept is implemented by an interface called `RecursiveIterator`. This interface extends the regular Iterator interface by adding two additional required methods: `getChildren()` and `hasChildren()`. These methods give the programmatic knowledge of discovering whether a recursive step can begin, and if so how to access the data to recurse into.

Second, a class called `RecursiveIteratorIterator` implements `OuterIterator` and is a wrapper that will activate Iterators that implement the `RecursiveIterator` interface. It understands the difference in a `RecursiveIterator` and uses that to walk through the entire dataset.

So, in short, to recursively walk through some dataset, you need a class written that implements `RecursiveIterator` for it. An example would be similar to the Iterator implementation in Listing B.7 with the extra two methods defined.

Then to actually walk recursively through a tree structure, you need to wrap it in `RecursiveIteratorIterator` so that it actually has each part activated properly. Luckily PHP 5 has already included recursive versions of some of its SPL classes, so `RecursiveArrayIterator` and `RecursiveDirectoryIterator` already exist. For example, you can rewrite Listing B.4 to recursively echo out all files that existed from the current directory and lower; it could be written into Listing B.10.

Listing B.10   **Recursively Listing a Directory**

```php
<?php
// Declare a Recursive listing Iterator for the current directory
$rdir = new RecursiveIteratorIterator(new RecursiveDirectoryIterator('.'));

// Loop through and echo all values, WITH their path.
foreach ($rdir as $entry) { echo "{$entry}<br />\n"; }
?>
```

Wow, actually only two lines of code, and you've just printed a complete recursive directory listing.

Defining a Recursive Iteration Class

Similar to how we defined an Iterator for arrays that gave us access to its keys, you can also define a recursive Iterator for any data type that you want. In fact, to demonstrate this, Listing B.11 extends the previous `KeyArrayIterator` created back in Listing B.7 to make it able to be used recursively.

Listing B.11   **Extending `KeyArrayIterator` to Be Used Recursively**

```php
<?php
// Include the library for Key Iteration
require 'KeyArrayIterator.php';

// Declare a new class that will extend our previous one, and implement
// the ability to do recursion
class RecursiveKeyArrayIterator extends KeyArrayIterator
                                implements RecursiveIterator {
    // We need to define two methods to accomplish this.  First of all
    // define a function to check if we happen to have 'children'
    public function hasChildren() {
```

Listing B.11 **Continued**

```
            // In this case, children refers to this element being an array.
            return is_array($this->current()->value);
    }

    // Now we also need to declare a method to return the children
    public function getChildren() {
        // The way to actually access the children needs to be via an
        // Iterator, therefore just define a new Iterator here:
        return new RecursiveKeyArrayIterator($this->current()->value);
    }
}

// That was really all we had to do.  So to test this let's make an array
$arr = array(42, array(1973, 1974, 2005), 173, array('Tash', 'Livia'), 'a');

// Create the Iterator for us to use:
$it = new RecursiveIteratorIterator(new RecursiveKeyArrayIterator($arr));

// Now loop over the array. echoing it out with keys & Depth!
foreach ($it as $entry) {
    echo $it->getDepth(), ' - ', $entry->key, ' - ', $entry, "<br />\n";
}
?>
```

As a final point, it should be noted that if you are going to define an Iterator as a recursive one anyway, there is not really any compelling reason to also make a nonrecursive version of it. A recursive Iterator can be called and used as a regular Iterator as well.

Iterators can perform many more advanced services for you, hopefully cleaning up large sections of code into smaller more easily manageable parts. SPL itself is a work in progress. To find out more about the current state of the system, see http://www.php.net/~helly/php/ext/spl/, the development site for SPL. For finding out more detailed information, reference http://php.net/spl and all the other web pages that it links to.

C

Common PHP Error Messages

WHEN YOU HAVE BEEN PROGRAMMING IN PHP for a while, you start to see certain error messages regularly. Sometimes PHP can be frustrating in that the message doesn't seem to tell you much about what the actual error truly was. This appendix attempts to solve that by listing the most common errors you may encounter. For each error discussed, this appendix provides some sample code that would cause that particular error and presents a brief description of what to look for in your code.

Error Levels

The possible error levels and their meanings are as follows. For a full discussion of errors and handling of errors, see Chapter 19, "Error Reporting and Debugging."

Errors generally come in three different levels:

- Notices—Generated at runtime, these are situations where the PHP interpreter noticed an inconsistency or other oddity that, though syntactically correct, may or may not make conceptual sense. In fact these may end up being bugs in your code as PHP may interpret what you meant as something different from what the code is supposed to do. This includes `E_STRICT`, `E_USER_NOTICE`, and `E_NOTICE`.

- Warnings—Generated at runtime, these are nonfatal errors that do not cause script execution to end. This includes `E_WARNING`, `E_CORE_WARNING`, `E_COMPILE_WARNING`, and `E_USER_WARNING`.

- Errors—Often referred to as fatal errors, these are problems that cause script execution to stop. They can be generated at any stage of PHP execution, including initialization, parsing, and execution. This includes `E_ERROR`, `E_PARSE`, `E_CORE_ERROR`, `E_COMPILE_ERROR`, and `E_USER_ERROR`.

Output Result: A Blank Page

Unfortunately it is all too common for you to just receive a blank page back when you try to run a page of code. Usually this is a combination of any of the other errors described in following sections and the fact that you don't have enough error reporting turned on.

On your development web servers you should make sure that you have errors being displayed to the screen and E_ALL (or preferably E_STRICT) set as the error level to display. Also make sure that startup errors are displayed as well; otherwise, some initial parsing errors may be hidden from you. This will ensure that you will see any and all errors that will ever happen and should keep you from seeing the dreaded blank page.

The lines that you need to add to your php.ini configuration file to make sure that these are turned on are as follows:

```
display_errors = On
display_startup_errors = On
error_reporting = E_ALL | E_STRICT
```

If you do not have access to your php.ini file, you can still turn on most of the error reporting inside your code itself, via the following PHP commands:

```
ini_set('display_errors', / true);
error_reporting(E_ALL | E_STRICT);
```

Notice: Use of undefined constant asdf - assumed 'asdf'

This is a fairly common error, caused by using a raw word where PHP was expecting a string. PHP is nice in these cases and assumes that you meant to use a string instead. A line of code as simple as the following can cause this error:

```
$var = asdf;
```

Realize that although sometimes this is okay, in many situations this can cause problems. Having a computer decide for you how something should be determined isn't usually a good idea. When you see this error, look for the word in question and you will find it. Typically this will be either because you forgot to surround the word with quotes because you meant to use it as a string or it is actually a variable name and you forgot to place a $ in front of it.

Notice: Undefined variable: asdf

This error means exactly what it says. You tried to use a variable that was not yet defined. This often happens when you have a variable that you might increment at any point but never initialized to a starting value, such as zero. So the following code might be a sample culprit:

```
$asdf++;
```

The other shortcut operators such as "+=", "-=", ".=", and so on are also frequently to blame. It is true that PHP guarantees you that an uninitialized variable will be equal to NULL. However it's always a good thing to declare variables to have specific default values before you just use them. Think of the preceding example; what if some other programmer were to edit your code, not realizing it, and reuse the $asdf variable before your line of code. Now you will be incrementing from where the other programmer left off.

It is just good programming practice to make sure that all your variables are initialized before use. You can do this at the top of your page, or function, easily with a run-on assignment line such as the following, which sets four variables at once to be equal to an empty string:

```
$jen = $harry = $heather = $ron = '';
```

Notice: Undefined index: asdf

This error is similar to the previous error; however, it relates specifically to an array index instead. The array existed, but that index didn't. This can happen during loops of counting. Or it quite often happens when you are trying to access the superglobal arrays and the value you thought existed, didn't. Such as

```
if ($_GET['asdf'] > 3) { echo 'Yes'; }
```

Although you can always make sure that variables your application creates are set, there is still an issue with any variables that may appear in the superglobal arrays. A particular key may or may not be set in a superglobal due to a number of factors, such as whether a PHP script is running from a web server. Therefore you need to make sure that the value really exists before trying to access it. This is best accomplished via the isset() function. So the preceding line of code could be rewritten as

```
if (isset($_GET['asdf']) && ($_GET['asdf'] > 3)) { echo 'Yes'; }
```

Again, PHP guarantees that you will receive a NULL for your troubles if you don't check it first, but again, it is always safer to specifically test for all cases. It leads to cleaner coding practices.

Parse error: syntax error, unexpected T_STRING
Parse error: syntax error, unexpected T_VARIABLE
Parse error: syntax error, unexpected T_IF
and so on

These errors and all like them are essentially the same. They are the compiler complaining that it found one type of language construct when it didn't expect to see it. This is almost always caused by a typo in the code such as:

```
if $asdf = 2) { echo '2'; }
```

In this case the opening parenthesis for the `if` statement was forgotten, and therefore it gives the `T_VARIABLE` version of this error because it saw the "$" when it wasn't expecting one.

Any such error message that includes a word that begins with `T_`, is referring to a *token*, an internal representation of a language construct. For example, `T_VARIABLE` is the token used by PHP to indicate a variable. Similarly, `T_STRING` is the token representing a string, and so on. Many tokens are available, not all of which have obvious names. If faced with a token string that is not clear to you, you can find the list of tokens at http://php.net/tokens.

In general these can be some of the toughest errors to track down because often the line number that the error claims to be on is far away from the actual error. Also the parsing engine stops immediately when it comes on one of these errors; therefore, you may fix one to find another and another. In general the best way of fixing these errors is instead to just avoid them.

Try running your code regularly as you are coding it to find such errors early before your code gets so large that it becomes difficult to track down the issue.

Parse error: syntax error, unexpected $end

This error is related to the errors mentioned previously but worth mentioning separately. The `$end` in that statement refers to the end of the file, meaning that it hit the end of the file when it was still expecting something. Ninety-nine percent of the time this means that you are missing a "}" in your code. You will have to scan your entire file to find out where it is missing.

This error can also be generated by bad syntax related to the Heredoc construct, `<<<`. Recall that Heredoc defines a block of a PHP script to be interpreted the same way as a double-quoted string. The Heredoc syntax requires that the ending delimiter must be the first item on a line, without any other character, including whitespace, preceding it. Often, due to typos or editors that attempt to do automatic code formatting, this syntax is violated, resulting in this error.

Parse error: syntax error, unexpected '=', expecting ';'

This error also is related to the preceding errors, but sometimes PHP knows that it was specifically expecting something, such as an ";". In that case PHP adds that to the error message. How to debug it is the same; however, it is often easier because if PHP knows exactly what it is looking for, it usually is closer to the line in which it claims the error was.

Fatal error: Maximum execution time of 60 seconds exceeded

The heart of what causes this error can vary, but the overall trigger is the same. PHP has a limit built in for how long any script can run. This is to prevent a badly written page from running forever and stealing all resources from the web server. This error simply means that your page took too long to run. It's easy to simulate this, just start a loop that will never end:

```
while(true);
```

If this happens it tends to mean one of two things. First, you may have ended up with an infinite loop in your code without realizing it. Check all the loops in your code to make sure that they actually end. If so, your code is simply taking too long to run. You can either try to speed it up, or increase the amount of time PHP has to execute. You can do this from within your code by using the function set_time_limit() and passing it the number of seconds that you want to allow your script to run.

It resets the time limit at that point, meaning that you can call it multiple times, and you could even call it during each iteration of a loop, giving a certain amount of time for that specific iteration to run.

Warning: Cannot modify header information - headers already sent

This is a specific error and therefore easy to fix. Simply put, you cannot output anything to the browser before any calls to header() because all HTTP header information must be sent before content. Therefore the following code causes this error:

```
foreach(range(1,10000) as $i) { echo $i; }
header('Content-type: text/plain');
```

All that you need to do to fix this is make sure that all that calls to header() are before any output. Similarly any other functions that use HTTP header information would also have to be first, such as the setting of cookies, or starting a PHP session.

> **Note**
>
> PHP has a configuration parameter called output_buffering that tells PHP to send only so many bytes at a time. When this is enabled, it is possible to send up to one buffer's worth of data before calling header() because no data has been sent to the client yet. This is functionality that typically shouldn't be relied on because the configuration can change from server to server. If you need to check whether the headers have already been sent, you can call headers_sent().

Alternatively, if you absolutely must send a header in the middle of your page, the best solution is to use the output buffering commands ob_start() at the top of your script and ob_end_flush() at the bottom. This causes your entire page to be buffered before sending it, making it possible to set a header at any time during the page creation.

Warning: Wrong parameter count for foo()

This is a fairly simple error. In this case we didn't pass the right number of parameters to a specific function or method:

```
foo($asdf);
```

The error gives you the correct line number and you only need to determine what options you are missing, or what extra ones you used. Make sure to check that you didn't forget a comma.

Fatal error: Call to undefined function foo2()

You called a function that does not exist. Most likely this is the result of a typo such as

```
foo2(' ', $asdf);
```

However you will need to check carefully; it might happen because you forgot to include the file that has the function in it. Whatever the cause, you need to point this line of code to the correct function name, or make sure that the function really exists.

Fatal Error: Cannot redeclare foo()

This error can occur at any point during script execution and means exactly what it says: You attempted to define a function that was already defined. This often is the result of a script including a number of libraries, one of which also includes the same library script. As standard practice, you should include any code that contains function or class definitions using the `include_once` or `require_once` constructs. These constructs first check to see whether the specified file has already been referenced. If so, the file is not read in again.

Index